New American Teenagers

New American Teenagers
The Lost Generation of Youth in 1970s Film

Barbara Jane Brickman

BLOOMSBURY
NEW YORK · LONDON · NEW DELHI · SYDNEY

Bloomsbury Academic
An imprint of Bloomsbury Publishing Inc

1385 Broadway	50 Bedford Square
New York	London
NY 10018	WC1B 3DP
USA	UK

www.bloomsbury.com

Bloomsbury is a registered trade mark of Bloomsbury Publishing Plc

First published 2012 by Continuum
First published in paperback 2014

© Barbara Jane Brickman, 2012, 2014

All rights reserved. No part of this publication may be reproduced or transmitted in any form or by any means, electronic or mechanical, including photocopying, recording, or any information storage or retrieval system, without prior permission in writing from the publishers.

No responsibility for loss caused to any individual or organization acting on or refraining from action as a result of the material in this publication can be accepted by Bloomsbury or the author.

Library of Congress Cataloging-in-Publication Data
Brickman, Barbara Jane.
New American teenagers : the lost generation of youth
in 1970s film / by Barbara Jane Brickman.
p. cm.
Includes bibliographical references and index.
ISBN-13: 978-1-4411-7658-5 (hardcover : alk. paper)
ISBN-10: 1-4411-7658-6 (hardcover : alk. paper)   1. Teen films—
United States–History—20th century.   2. Teenagers in motion pictures.   I. Title.

ISBN: HB: 978-1-4411-7658-5
        PB: 978-1-6289-2278-3
        ePub: 978-1-4411-7677-6
        ePDF: 978-1-4411-4292-4

Typeset by Newgen Knowledge Works (P) Ltd., Chennai, India

For Lucy, my life's love and a model of patience

Contents

Acknowledgments	viii
Introduction	1
Chapter 1: The Rock 'n' Roll High School Picture Show: A Genre Deconstructed	25
Chapter 2: Coming of Age in the 1970s: Revision, Fantasy, and Rage in the Teen-Girl Badlands	71
Chapter 3: The Queer Kid and Women's Lib	109
Chapter 4: Bad News Jodie, or How the Disney Family Got Freaky	137
Chapter 5: Brothers, Sisters, and Chainsaws: Sibling Rivalry and Peer Centrality in the Teen Slasher Film	175
Epilogue	211
Notes	217
Bibliography	247
Index	259

Acknowledgments

The germ of this project began, predictably enough, with my dissertation, which now hangs like a ghost around the edges of this predominantly new house of ideas. Nevertheless, that germ or seed could not have grown without the generous support and nurturing of some of the best mentors a graduate student could hope for. I would particularly like to thank John Michael, Sharon Willis, and Karen Beckman for all their encouragement, wisdom, and extremely challenging questions that prepared me for the revisions to come. Most significantly for me as a feminist, it was crucial to have two monumentally influential guides like Sharon Willis and Karen Beckman to push me and insist on the best feminist scholarship I could muster. I would also like to thank the University of Rochester Graduate School whose funding through the Ball Dissertation Year Fellowship saw the initial project to fruition.

Since leaving my Ph.D. program, I have been fortunate to work in another supportive environment at the University of West Georgia where I was asked to share my work and my ongoing research not only with faculty but also with a breathtakingly bright group of students. I was encouraged to teach my specialties and create a film program I could be proud of, while also sharing my work at invited talks and more informally. However, I would like to single out one colleague, Emily Hipchen, who generously offered to read my work, my book proposals, my conference presentations, and pretty much anything else I was anxious about in my first years as a professor. Indeed, the revision of my dissertation and initial manuscript into the book I have produced here would not have been possible without Emily's skillful reading of and enthusiasm for my work. I would be remiss as well if I did not thank my students, especially those who took my upper level seminars (some many times), for questioning me and goading me into articulating my arguments about teen film, horror narratives, and so much more. The *Rocky Horror* section of Chapter 1 is dedicated to you all.

Two previously published essays of mine have provided the basis for two chapters in this book and appear here with kind permission from the publishers: "Coming of Age in the 70s: Revision, Fantasy, and Rage in the Teen-Girl Badlands," in *Camera Obscura*, Volume 66, no. x, pp. 25–58. Copyright, 2007, *Camera Obscura*. All rights reserved. Reprinted by permission of the publisher, Duke University Press; and "Brothers, Sisters, and Chainsaws: The Slasher Film as Locus for Sibling Rivalry," in *Quarterly Review of Film and Video*, Volume 28, no. 2, pp. 135–54. Copyright, 2011, *Quarterly Review of Film and Video*. All rights reserved. Reprinted by permission of the publisher, Taylor & Francis. The first of these articles was deftly guided to publication by Amelie Hastie—a kind, encouraging, and patient editorial hand, who improved both the article and my morale on more than one occasion. Perhaps most importantly, this book would never have reached the light of day without the passion and backing of my editor at Continuum Press, Katie Gallof, who championed this book from the moment we met and who was incredibly understanding when the delivery of our son Henry came right in the midst of the delivery of this manuscript.

Lastly, I have a few personal acknowledgments that will never adequately express how my family and friends' support has buoyed me through the long, long process of finishing this book. I come from a big family and as a unit they have made me as tough, quick-witted, and argumentative as I have had to be to maintain a fight for over two hundred pages. Particularly, though, I want to thank my sister Peggy, my brother-in-law Kelly, and my two nephews Nick and Charles for giving me a home, a place to read when I was supposed to be nannying, and faith in myself as an academic, even when a ten-year-old Nick was incredulous that *anyone* could teach film for a living. This book, however, is dedicated to the one person without whom no book or accolade or job matters, not one tiny little bit. Without my Lucy, there is none of the joy, strength, and contentment that enables me to go off and write a book.

Introduction

The teen film genre, so influential and some might argue detrimental to the American film industry in the latter half of the twentieth century, apparently all but disappeared for one key decade in the postwar era. During the 1970s—possibly the moment when Thomas Doherty's proposed "juvenilization" of American film truly took hold with exploitation blockbuster spectacles like *Jaws*—the teen film either could not reach its young audience when the blockbuster thrilled them and a number of homegrown American auteurs schooled them or could not compete with more timely genres like Brooksian parodies or disaster and vigilante films that better suited the disillusioned mood of the era. Or so the critical story of this genre goes. There is an overwhelming insistence in teen genre criticism that the 1970s marks a clear nadir or empty period for the production of films aimed at youth. Both Thomas Doherty and Timothy Shary, two preeminent scholars of the genre, offer this dismissive view of the period. Doherty's influential work *Teenagers and Teenpics: The Juvenilization of American Movies in the 1950s* ends its exhaustive look at the rise of the teen film in the postwar era with the "clean" teens of the 1960s, followed by an epilogue that largely bypasses the 1970s in favor of the juvenilization of all mainstream film in the 1980s and 1990s. Shary's work picks up where Doherty left off examining a wide array of teen films at the end of the millennium, from the 1980s to 2000, and dismisses the 1970s as a time when serious Vietnam-bound youth had "a different sense of their identity than that which had been provided for them in so many of the happier, hipper 60's films" and Hollywood totally "abandoned its practice of promoting teen performers."[1] Both critics, then, clearly see the 1970s as a dormant period for teens on screen: when the youthful spirit of the 1960s ended, according to Shary's teen genre textbook, "so did the output and interest in teen films," as if there were no teens or youthful rebellion in the 1970s.[2] The idea of the 1970s as a decade without youth is not restricted to film criticism, however.

In Thomas Hine's cautionary treatise *The Rise and Fall of the American Teenager*, his lengthy cultural-historical examination of the construction of the American teenager locates the titular "fall" at a predictable moment—the 1970s. According to his argument, with an end to the youth culture promise and revolutionary passions of the baby boomer generation comes an end to the American teenager as we know it. Similarly supporting this idea of the 1970s as an age almost devoid of youth, Grace Palladino's expansive study of the American teenager as a major icon of the twentieth century, *Teenagers: An American History* (published in 1996), abruptly concludes its "history" at the end of the 1960s. Both these works along with the teen film criticism clearly beg the question, how could the 1970s be a decade without youth? Where did they go? What happened in the 1970s to seemingly erase the American teenager? To begin to answer these questions, it might help to define "teenagers" more clearly as the "white, middle-class, heterosexual young people" (which could be narrowed even further to "young men") whom Hine suggests the term "was originally coined to describe."[3] Perhaps this teenager *did* have a fall in the 1970s, which is why so few commentators can locate the teen-age in the era, but the correspondence to Doherty and Shary's arguments also suggests that without the traditional American teenager, there can be no "teen film." Yet, while "the" American teenager (white, middle-class, heterosexual, male) suffers in the 1970s, his is not the only tale to tell. I am arguing that there were crucial depictions of youth on screen in America in the 1970s, but perhaps "the American teenager" of Hine's description—no longer possessing a privileged or stable identity—was rarely among them, allowing other teen narratives to come to the fore.

A film like Hal Ashby's *Harold and Maude* (1971), released at the start of the decade, begins to show the cracks in this familiar figure of "the" American teenager. While Harold is still white, male, wealthy, and presumably heterosexual, there is also something wrong with Harold, as his mother so frequently reminds us. In the opening scene, the audience is slowly introduced to a shadowy adolescent figure through glimpses of a young person moving through an opulent and darkened room. The figure's delicacy, garments, and jewelry belie easy recognition of gender and Ashby's tight framing, meant to obscure the intentions of the teenager until the shock realization of an apparent suicide attempt, joins Cat Stevens' music to mystify this strangely melancholy scene. Then, once the shock of his sudden hanging and the startlingly humorous reaction offered by Harold's mother upon seeing him in a noose—"I suppose you think that's very funny, Harold"—have sunk in, the viewer comes to comprehend that he or she has entered a very different world of cinematic adolescence, one where parents are the butt of the joke, where the young protagonist rejects all traditional futures in favor of visiting funerals and falling in love with a 79-year-old, and where a very dark humor distorts the most fundamental tropes of the maturation plot.

My book argues that one can find in the 1970s a reprieve from and revision of the "straight" (in the broadest sense of that term) developmental narrative, wherein the acculturation of the adolescent into a compliant, gendered, heterosexual, middle-class contributor to society seems the foregone conclusion or desired goal. No longer suffering the conservative ideology of the father-son drama that undergirds heteropatriarchy and fuels so many classic teen films, the screen teens of the 1970s forge new alliances and offer counter-discourses around issues of gender, generation, and sexuality that no other previous cohort of youth had raised. In an era of New American Cinema, a "crisis of confidence" for the nation, and the vocal challenges brought by the gay rights and women's rights movements, it seems only fitting that new American teenagers would emerge—not lost but found. While their parents' era defined the American teenager with the romantic male figure of James Dean, this generation of adolescents offers a dramatically altered picture of transformed gender dynamics, fluid and queered sexuality, and a chilling disregard for the authority of parent, or more specifically patriarchal, culture. A closer consideration of this decade, then, uncovers previously marginalized voices that rework the (classically male, heterosexual) American teenage story. This book challenges the neglect of the 1970s in discussions of teen film by establishing the subversive potential and critical revision possible in the narratives of these new teenage voices, particularly in regard to changing notions of gender and sexuality.

Teens on Screen: A Critical Overview and Intervention

Compared to work on other genres like horror or melodrama, critical examinations of teens on screen have been only a fairly recent phenomenon, resulting in just a handful of major works. The first significant study of mainstream American cinema's fascination with the teenager, David Considine's *The Cinema of Adolescence*, did not appear until the mid-1980s—an era when the incredible proliferation of teen films, led by John Hughes's wildly popular films, clearly demanded attention. Considine's work, however, argues for a long history of youth on screen, beginning with standout young performers from the 1930s like Mickey Rooney, Judy Garland, and Deanna Durbin. As really the first study of its kind, *The Cinema of Adolescence* begins to build a basic filmography and history of the place of teenagers in Hollywood film from the 1930s onward. Organizing hundreds of films through four emblematic topics—family, school, juvenile delinquency, and sexuality—Considine finds more variety than perhaps is expected of teen film but still laments the exaggerated and traditionalist picture of adolescence presented by a film industry that "has been spectacularly unsuccessful in realistically depicting adolescence."[4] Whether through monstrous mothers and bungling fathers or sensationalized stories of juvenile delinquency and sexual longings, the representations of youth in Hollywood film tend toward the negative and shocking for Considine so that this cinema has "not only stereotyped the young but the institutions such as family and school through which they are socialized."[5] In sum, over a 50-year span the cinema of adolescence has dramatized an unrealistic, startling tale typically centered on a white, Anglo-Saxon-Protestant, urban or suburban, male youth to the detriment of adult institutions as well as his racial, gendered, religious, and sexual others.

Only a few years later, when Thomas Doherty published *Teenagers and Teenpics* before the end of the 1980s, his focus on the 1950s and early 1960s did little to dispel Considine's conclusions about the central subject of these films and the sensational means for depicting him. In fact, by focusing on what he calls "teenpics," Doherty intensifies the sense of "exploitation" of the teenager as subject matter through the industrial practices associated with that term. Consequently, Doherty's account concentrates solely on those films sold to teens (or exploiting a teen audience) unlike Considine who takes a more catholic approach to depictions of adolescence in a wide variety of films. Centrally concerned with the teenage marketplace and the impact that Hollywood's pursuit of this audience had on the growth of a teen genre and on the broader "juvenilization" of mainstream film up to the present, Doherty follows the traditional definition of the "exploitation film" and exploitation strategies in order to examine a particular period of prolific exploitation fare at mid-century, the heyday of the teenpic. Like the exploitation films of the 1920s and 1930s, the teenpic appeals to the basest instincts in its audience with low-budget films that quickly capitalize on often sensational and "timely" subject matter targeted specifically to one demographic—in this case the teenage audience; they were "outlandish, mildly controversial, and a little licentious—and if the movie wasn't, the advertising was."[6] Dividing this multitude of mostly cheaply produced films into subgenres from "Rock 'n' Roll Teenpics" to J. D.'s, teen horror, and even "Clean Teens," Doherty illuminates a specific period and industrial practice, yet his exhaustive study easily supports Considine's thesis that the films largely present stereotypes, melodrama, and unrealistic exaggerations of parents, schools, and teens.

Yet, Doherty's argument and his emphasis on production and industrial practices emphasizes much more explicitly where this exaggeration comes from and how it might be used to persuade a teen audience. For him, these films were produced by *adults*, who exploited the teen marketplace for easy profit, and, therefore, they reflect adult sensibilities: "A product of parent culture peddled to teenage subculture, it receives its marketplace validity only from the latter but its textual values mainly from the former."[7] As cinematic narratives created by adults, teenpics unsurprisingly resolve conflict with a "generational reconciliation" that persuasively advances the values of parent culture.[8] Despite the sometimes wild rebelliousness of early teenpics, particularly those centering on juvenile delinquency, drag racing, or rock'n'roll, which validated teenagers as an independent force and flirted with alternatives to parent culture and its values, the majority of films over and over again contain or resolve these threats. Later developments such as the sublimation of the horror cycle or the domestication of the clean teenpics make this containing resolution perfectly clear, such as in the clean teenpic where an "aggressively normal, traditionally good-looking crew of fresh young faces" promote the values of the older generation by being " 'good kids' who preferred dates to drugs and crushes to crime."[9] In some ways, the clean teenpics lay bare the conservative ideology that always seemed to undergird the genre (or certainly its films' conclusions) for Doherty. As with Considine's work, this close examination of one major period of teen film reveals limiting representations and exploitation of the teenage story, which substitutes a realistic depiction of adolescence in favor of a persuasive reinforcement of dominant (adult) values.

While Jon Lewis's cultural studies-informed *The Road to Romance and Ruin: Teen Films and Youth Culture* follows shortly after Doherty's work, it is not until the turn of the new millennium with Timothy Shary's *Generation Multiplex* that Considine and Doherty's arguments are revisited and revised or renewed in a significant way. Grounded in the concepts developed by the cultural studies approach to youth and subcultures in the work of Stuart Hall and Dick Hebdige and by other postwar theorists of the psychology and sociology of adolescence and alienation such as Emile Durkheim, Lewis's work divides films about youth into conceptual categories ranging from deviancy and consumption to gender politics and nostalgia; yet, through this theoretical approach, Lewis distances himself considerably from the more typical genre study and historical analysis of the earlier two major critics of teen film.[10] Timothy Shary, on the other hand, aligns himself quite explicitly with the work of Considine in particular and shares Doherty's approach of separating films about youth into major subgenres, while also taking over at the historical moment where Considine leaves off—the early 1980s. Shary's genre study provides a comprehensive look at youth on screen in the last two decades of the twentieth century with the expressed intent of revealing an evolution of the teen film genre toward a more diverse and more positive representation of adolescence. His work is in many ways the companion piece to Considine's in that *Generation Multiplex* attempts to cover a large number of films (both mainstream and independently produced) in the period after the 50 years covered in *The Cinema of Adolescence* and seeks to show a distinct change from the unrealistic, often sensationalized, and largely negative representations of youth catalogued by the earlier critic. Nevertheless, even Shary must admit the stubborn resilience of the dominant tropes and central subjects of the genre.

Expanding on one of the most prolific periods for teen film—a kind of neoclassical era to the classical 1950s genre explosion—Shary's work considers the social, cultural, and industrial context for the new spate of films either representing adolescence or targeted at a youth audience. Specifically, he singles out the social importance of the shopping mall as an "icon of youth independence" in the United States at this time and the consequent development of the "multiplex" theater with its multiple screens and central retail location.[11] For Shary, this one development forced the hand of the film industry, which sought a way to provide products for the youth consumers populating the mall, necessitating a wider range of teen films to appeal across demographics within the youth audience. The diversification of genre would be one way to expand, drawing on "previously established genres with more dramatic impact" and revising the teen genre itself to offer a variety of characters and situations that would speak honestly to the real "social conditions" teens experience and dramatize a "complexity of moral choices and personal options" for adolescents.[12] In other words, the teen film had to evolve to offer a more diverse, realistic, and sympathetic depiction of youth where teenagers became "an increasingly self-aware and insightful group" often with a sense of "integrity or morality."[13] Whether in the subgenre of school, delinquent, horror, science, or romance and sexual awakening films, the cinematic image of youth in the 1980s and particularly the 1990s showed a complexity and depth that traditionalist and formulaic films of the 1950s and 1960s apparently lacked.

Yet even after delivering this positive news, Shary concedes that the teen film genre, while it can accommodate more "real-life experiences" and the presence of female teens and racial minorities (particularly African American teens in the early 1990s), allows a "white male dominance" to persist.[14] Forays into "progressive change" occurred, but for Shary more work needs to be done to represent girls, racial minorities outside of a delinquent context, committed social engagement by politically active or religiously devout adolescents, and serious teenage problems such as mental illness, drug use, and sexually transmitted diseases. The films of this period might exhibit more complexity and diversity in their proliferation, but the traditional image of "youth" in mainstream American cinema (as set up by David Considine in his groundbreaking study) too often dominates the landscape.

In other words, within the relatively small amount of critical work on teen film, there is a kind of consensus about which story (and whose story) dominates the films through most of the twentieth century. Recognizing that female teens remain underrepresented even in the 1980s and 1990s and racial minorities have rarely played a strong role in teen dramas, amongst other exclusions, the stereotypical "teenager" of American teen film alarmingly mirrors the figure whom Thomas Hine claims the term was coined to define: the white, middle-class, heterosexual male. His story, moreover, despite a myriad of conflicts and disappointments with parent culture, typically resolves itself with a reconciliation or maturation that brings him back into the social order to which he must belong as an adult or repairs that social order for his future. In other words, as "the American teenager," as Hine calls him, is the rightful heir of that social order, so it is *his* conflicts, disillusionment, or rebelliousness that concern these films and the dominant culture producing them. Jon Lewis views this same central conundrum or concern of the films from the other side, claiming that they typically problematize a "breakdown of traditional forms of authority" in order to repair this breakdown for that central teen.[15] Whether through patriarchy or other traditional institutions of dominant authority such as school or the church, for Lewis films representing teens centrally dramatize a restoration of the adult (paternal) authority that seems missing or has broken down. When viewed in conjunction with the typical subject of teen film—the white, middle-class, heterosexual male—this "generational reconciliation," which Doherty finds in so many of the teenpics, is easily figured in a familiar pairing: the story of father and son. If the central concern of teen films is the breakdown and ultimate continuation of social order or authority, then who better to represent this conflict in patriarchy than the father and his cultural heir.

Interestingly for my argument, Doherty claims that this longing for authority in teen film becomes most prominent after the period he examines so thoroughly in his work—in other words, in the 1970s and beyond. Rather than exhibiting the "alienation and countercultural rebellion" of leather-clad heroes who take adult authorities as the enemy (only to resolve this generational conflict in the film's final scenes), these post-1960s films reveal "well-scrubbed conformity and sexual restraint" in youth who obey and seek out paternal guidance.[16] Supposedly devoid of a rebellion against parent culture and home, these films "commemorate filial duty" in an era Doherty provocatively labels "the return of the patriarch." Yet, this apparent longing for adult discipline appears at a historical moment, the 1970s, when parent culture has struggled, stumbled, and eventually vacated the scene. In others words, the historical period under consideration in my book, when the United States witnessed not the return but the fall of the patriarch, becomes the moment for Doherty when teen film loses its nerve, its rebellious force, and its potentially subversive enactment of sexual and other tensions. However, one might argue that Doherty, in passing so quickly over the 1970s if not ignoring the decade entirely, has confused the 1970s for the 1980s, when the rise of Ronald Reagan and the conservative movement in America *could* undoubtedly be labeled the "return of the patriarch." Also, this harsh criticism of youth films after the 1960s seems a kind of willful forgetting of the "generational reconciliation" that Doherty has already established in his own period; certainly, the ending of *Rebel Without a Cause* (the urtext of Doherty's era) finally reestablishes if not commemorates "filial duty" in its conclusion. Unlike both Doherty and Shary, who states in *Teen Movies* that the adolescents of the 1970s abandoned the countercultural spirit of their immediate predecessors, leaving behind protest for just so much "polyester," I believe a closer examination of the films of the 1970s will show a resurgence of alienation and rebellion that is not so easily confined at the film's resolution, and perhaps more significantly (and unsurprisingly), this subversion of parent culture or proposal of alternatives to it comes from *other* teens, not the familiar son whose filial duty will eventually advance the patriarchy.[17]

My work, in this regard, joins a small number of feminist critics who have begun to interrogate the typical male focus of teen film genre studies *and* representations of teens in popular culture. Both Georganne Scheiner and Ilana Nash are leading figures in critical work that takes the female teen as its focus and attempts to analyze her place not only in popular representations of teenagers but also in the larger cultural and historical discourse of twentieth-century America.[18] While their work does not exactly overlap—Scheiner considers cinematic representations of female adolescence from 1920 to 1950 and in *American Sweethearts* Nash examines a broader range of popular texts from 1930 to 1965—both significantly end their discussions before the 1970s, the moment when Nash claims "the teenage girl" as she had been constructed in the century "'ended,' too."[19] Also, both critics find these young girls to be troubling figures in films and other texts about youth—at moments disturbing, subversive, problematic, and fearful (especially in terms of their burgeoning sexuality). For example, Scheiner's *Signifying Female Adolescence*, grounded in a historical approach, finds girls on screen and in popular novels and magazines to be "troubled and troubling" in every decade except the 1930s because of their ability to serve as "markers of generational, sexual, and economic change."[20] Aside from the Depression era when film censorship gave rise to a more wholesome view of "fix-it" girls like Judy Garland and especially Deanna Durbin who "were idealized as much more competent and resilient than their elders," most of the female teens examined by Scheiner disrupt and disturb.[21] While 1920s exploitation film brought audiences the flapper who was often a "sexual delinquent" pushing the "boundaries of acceptable behavior" and "challenging traditional forms of authority," the bobby-soxer of the 1940s ruled through her consumption, sexuality, and subcultural status, operating "as a destabilizing figure because she had power to subvert her father's authority" and, even as a comedic figure, following her own individual "cultural practices" and sexual interests.[22] Still, despite the disturbing potential, power, and independence suggested by girls in these films and by the active female fans documented in the final chapter of Scheiner's work, a stereotype of the female teen as emotional, self-involved, inconstant, dangerous, sexual, and "fad-" or boy-crazy had been set or reaffirmed by these popular representations.

Ilana Nash's study confirms the employment of this stereotype in the many popular texts she examines but argues less for the positive potential of female fans embracing independent girl characters and more for the recuperative or subjugating effect of these texts on young female consumers. Rather than seeing an active fan group, almost a subculture, of girls who could model themselves on the powerful, autonomous, and subversive female teens on screen, Nash fears the damaging impact of a number of texts about female teens—from Nancy Drew to Gidget—as a means of offering "their young female consumers implicit lessons in self-subordination to paternal(istic) authority."[23] While she likewise recognizes the potential for female teens to disrupt the status quo, the popular representations she scrutinizes impose a father-daughter relationship that raises the concern (and fascination) of the female teen's sexuality only to allay it with the control and wisdom of patriarchal authority. Whether in the figure of Nancy Drew, Corliss Archer, or Gidget, the female teen here may be a troubling (sexual) problem, but she is also infantilized or made incompetent and silly to guarantee her subordination and need for a father to help her and contain her. These texts, for Nash, are partly directed at and certainly calculated to honor and protect paternal authority at the expense of their young female consumers, who see their surrogates on screen emptied or diminished through stereotypical "intellectual stupidity, sexual objectification, non-human idealization, smallness of stature, or narrative displacement in favor of male characters" as a lesson for their own subjugation and submissiveness to "their domestic and institutional Fathers."[24] In other words, even in critical interventions like those by Nash and Scheiner, who offer female alternatives to the typical male story of adolescence, their conclusions nevertheless suggest comparably conservative stereotypes, resolutions, and reconciliations as those established in previous work on the cinematic teen narrative.

Despite these disheartening findings, particularly in Nash's work, my argument commends and takes up the conviction in both her and Scheiner's work to seek out alternatives and other stories that exist beside, within, or in contradistinction to the dominant and dominating figure of youth. In the historical moment between the "filial duty" that Doherty locates predominantly in films of the 1980s and the "filial subjugation" enacted by the daughters and digested by the female consumers in the pre-1965 popular texts of Nash's work,[25] I find the dangerous daughters, queer kids, and insular peer culture of the 1970s. There is a space for other versions of the adolescent narrative to appear on screen, but they can only come into being after the apparent end of the "the teenage girl" as Nash outlines her (with the entrance of second wave feminism into the national consciousness) and during a moment of destabilization for the authority that has worried over, yearned for, and supported "the American teenager" as Hine and major film criticism have defined him. What I am proposing then is a revision of the teen film genre and its stereotypical "teenager" (with all his attendant concerns, rebelliousness, and paternal reconciliation) at a historical moment in the United States when such counternarratives seem possible.

Other feminist theorists such as Linda Williams and Carol Clover have offered methods for performing such a revision of genre through interrogations of gender, and, as in the case of Clover's work, this revision has at times focused on the volatile yet rich era of 1970s American film. For feminists like Williams, certain genres offer alternatives to Classical Hollywood narrative codes and visual style that challenge truisms of film theory and criticism, both about cinematic narrative structure as well as gendered spectatorship. In "Film Bodies: Gender, Genre, and Excess" for example, she elevates three maligned genres—the "gross" and excessive "body genres" of pornography, horror, and melodrama—by highlighting the distinctiveness of their narrative (and bodily) excesses or spectacles that disrupt linear causality and then by connecting those disruptions to the effect they have on the bodies in the audience.[26] Through her investigation of the diverse pleasures available in the bodily excesses (on screen and in the audience) of these genres, Williams hopes to intervene in genre criticism from the "low" end through a reading of the unique constructions of gender and sexual fantasies in these defamed body genres as indicative of cultural change. Of course, Williams is working in the same vein as Carol Clover, whose much discussed *Men, Women and Chainsaws* contains the original article from which the term "body genres" derives. Clover's work, famously, examines the then reviled subgenre of slasher horror as a phenomenon of the era of second wave feminism when the "angry woman" can become a bona fide protagonist.[27] In an argument I will return to more directly in Chapter 5, Clover posits the slasher film's female victim-hero as a significant change in the horror genre, and her critical interest in the male viewer of horror and his identification with this Final Girl opens up an interrogation and revision of horror genre criticism's conclusions about the apparent sadistic misogyny of the films and their audience. By breaking down the constructions of gender in this subgenre of horror, Clover reveals a set of rarely recognized masochistic pleasures in the genre and transgressions of gender norms in a "one-sex model" that allows the male viewer to use the female victim-hero as his surrogate on screen.[28] Her criticism not only challenged some of the basic precepts of horror genre criticism but also provoked a considerable amount of new work on the issues of gender, sexuality, and spectatorship in horror.

My book, in turn, considers a period of a genre undervalued or derided by the dominant criticism and attempts to challenge some basic tenets of that criticism as well as major themes of the genre through the intervention of gender studies and its focus on constructions of gender, sexual difference, and sexuality. Further, I do not believe it is a coincidence that both Clover's work and my own focus on the period of the 1970s in the United States when the women's movement and the cause of lesbian and gay liberation demanded social change and altered forever the norms of both gender and sexuality. That film genres, commonly considered problem-solving operations for a culture, should wrestle with and reflect these changes seems hardly surprising. My work also is informed, like Clover and Williams', by psychoanalytic feminist film theory's interrogation of the pleasures, fantasies, and viewing positions offered by mainstream film and its genre narratives. Employing such tools to deconstruct the gendered positions, desires, fantasies, and viewing pleasures offered in teen film and constructions of adolescence, I can open a space for the screen teens of the 1970s to present a new set of pleasures from a group of new or alternative adolescent narratives. There can be a great malleability and flexibility to what Patricia White calls "generic fantasy," where the genre film both possesses the unpredictability or fluidity that characterizes the fantasmatic "mise-en-scène of desire" and uniquely exposes the unsettled relation between the engagement of the spectator and the cultural fantasy on the screen.[29] I believe it is this flexibility that makes revision possible.

Nevertheless, this revision happens at a particular historical moment that I, like other feminist critics, see working as impetus for the transformations in genre narratives,which in turn reflect the cultural change. Genre films offer a malleable fantasy, but certainly one can see how the cultural fantasy on screen would be impacted by societal change and historical events. In other words, the fantasmatic version of the teenager given through film might mirror societal change, but what is more, I am arguing that this change in culture and genre might herald the entrance of a new adolescent, or, to be more specific, the rise of new American teenagers whose stories find voice and recognition in popular culture in the 1970s. Teen film will be the primary space where I can locate these new voices, but ultimately what interests me is the figure constructed there. Who is the adolescent in our popular imagination? How have we typically constructed this fantasmatic figure, and when and why did this mythic creature, "the American teenager," change? Like

Kathryn Stockton, in her groundbreaking work on the "queer child," who probes and troubles the "problem of the child as a general idea," I would hold up the adolescent as another "ghostly, unreachable fancy" that exceeds the adult boundaries of its construction, especially in the 1970s.[30] Once a figure of nostalgia, sexual tension and titillation, primitive exoticism, and subordination and reconciliation, the new American teenagers on screen in the 1970s destabilize, unseat, and even queer the fantasy figure of the teenager as he has been figured in popular texts and genre criticism.

Finally, let me offer a note about methodologies. Since my work is focused not only on the typical narratives of teens on film but also on the construction of the teenager more generally, I do not limit myself to only those texts marketed and sold to a teenage audience. Similar to Jon Lewis in his cultural history of the teenager or Timothy Shary and David Considine in their search for a critical mass of diverse texts, this book examines "films about teenagers" as well as those explicitly sold to them in an effort to locate both a variety of alternative narratives offered in the 1970s and the broader way in which the teenager was figured in American cinema, especially at such a transformative and experimental time for that tradition.[31] Particularly, I would note that the films of New American Cinema did not target a *teenage* audience, though a youth audience is often proposed in histories of the movement, but it did certainly engage with the question of youth, oppositions to parent culture, and alternative narrative modes or new avenues of cinematic storytelling such as genre revision and parody. Yet, as I seek a variety of narratives, I do not want to suggest my book is an exhaustive genre study like Shary's work or a historical overview of a major aspect of teen film as in Scheiner's criticism on female adolescence. With its focus on one brief historical period and with a commitment to understanding the theoretical meaning and implications of the new American teenagers figured on screen, this book will read closely a number of representative texts rather than take a "pluralistic and inclusive" approach noting a multitude "pertinent perspectives," as a more traditional genre critic like Shary does.[32] I will attempt to address as many representative films of the period as I can, particularly in Chapter 1, but, again, my central concern will be interrogating the nature of a new set of narratives from other voices and the implications of these revised maturation plots for a changing conception of the teenager in late-twentieth-century America.

The 1970s: Polyester, "Me," and a Decade of Crisis

The caricature of the 1970s drawn up in popular culture and by the popular press has typically been less than flattering. As the fabled age of disco, unfortunate fashion, and unpleasant drugs, this dazed and confused epoch has long suffered in comparison with the 'revolutionary' decade that preceded it with its ambitious movements for social change, pantheon of heroes, and promises of an American Camelot—despite subsequent indications that this period of utopian promise was decidedly brief. The 1970s in these stark comparisons plays the role of the great betrayer, the killer of dreams. This decade witnessed the end of 30 years of unrivaled prosperity in the United States and, supposedly, a people's wholesale abandonment of long-held national values and beliefs. Shary's description of youth audiences fits this picture perfectly: young Americans feebly abandoned protest for the cheap façade of polyester. Here, we have the betrayal of what Tom Wolfe famously called "The Me Decade," the turning inward and narcissism of a people who have given up on their own communities and the idea of social change in favor of the "most fascinating subject on earth: *Me.*"[33] As in Wolfe's opening salvo—a professional woman who declares into the microphone at an encounter session (at an est course) her all-consuming desire to eliminate "Hemorrhoids!" from her life—the country had seemingly turned away from meaningful discourse and political commitment to find an emptiness, artificiality, and solipsistic desperation. Yet, many historians offer a decidedly more serious, worrying, and less glib view of the 1970s as a decade of debilitating crisis.

For recent historians and cultural commentators, the decade of the 1970s in the United States stands as one of the most frightening and unstable certainly in the twentieth century and possibly in the nation's history. The image that excellent studies such as Carroll's *It Seemed Like Nothing Happened: America in the 1970s* provide is one of a country apparently tearing apart at the seams due to one crisis after another—economic, political, international, and even cultural. Events ranging from the oil embargo and inflation crisis to Watergate and the collapse in Vietnam seemed to throw the country, for one historian, into "a collective, existential despair," which President Carter in a 1979 address to the nation famously identified as a "crisis of confidence" in America.[34] The country had become fragmented, disillusioned, self-consumed, and lacking any hope in the future or progress. The traumas of the past and a series of self-inflicted wounds appeared to have destroyed the American Dream, sinking the country into a nightmare from which it seemingly could not awake. The highest echelons of government had proven corrupt, opportunist, and frighteningly cynical, and the combination of recession, dependence on foreign oil, and crippling stagflation drained many Americans of the prosperity they had come to expect after the war. The indomitable American spirit suddenly seemed devoid of heroes and hope even as the country celebrated its bicentennial. On the other hand, this dark picture of the decade overlooks significant gains made by various social movements—from environmentalism to the rights movements of gays and lesbians, women, and other minorities—who saw the legal fulfillment of 1960s calls for social justice and a real cultural shift that made the 1970s "an exhilarating moment of possibility and progressive change," according to Graebner. Before turning to this other side of the 1970s story, however, I would like to outline briefly the causes for the "crisis of confidence" identified by Carter and central to many histories of the period.

The political scandals and disappointments of the 1970s are so well known I hesitate to rehearse them here. However, in an effort to contextualize the sense of "loss, limits, and failure" that Americans attributed to their view of the world and the future, one should consider the major national and international events propelling them into this mode of crisis.[35] I might add, as well, especially in regard to the political and international policy fronts, that a deep sense of distrust, disillusionment, and bitterness might be added to this list of descriptors. Perhaps no event better initiates a discussion of the political events of the 1970s than the killing of four students at Kent State University in May of 1970, where antiwar protestors in the mode of the previous decade expressed their frustration at the clear escalation of the Vietnam War through its expansion into Cambodia and were met with the indifference and force of a brutal leadership (in this case General Robert Canterbury and the National Guard). The tragic episode exposed in different ways the two major political crises of the 1970s: the shocking and humbling failure in Vietnam and the excess of executive authority that would lead to the fall of the President. In the following year, *The New York Times* would publish the Pentagon Papers, which revealed the protestors' worst fears— that Nixon had ordered secret bombings in Cambodia while publicly promising a limiting of American involvement in Vietnam (as other presidents before him had deceived the American people and even other branches of the government about the military's engagement in Indochina)—and which would presage future newspaper headlines and revelations of private documents and recordings that would bring down President Nixon.

The resignation of the President in 1974 in response to the Watergate scandal and cover-up and then the fall of Saigon in 1975 would signal a loss of a sense of American dominance and moral superiority on the international stage and deal a nearly fatal blow to any faith in government, legal authority, or dominant institutions. The White House tapes of secret recordings in the Oval Office and the revelations of political sabotage, backroom dealing, and special interests exposed in the Watergate proceedings convinced the American people, despite feeble protests from the President, that they were all just "crooks." The television broadcasts of Watergate's proceedings and constant media attention transformed the government, according to Peter Carroll, "into a raucous carnival of political corruption" and by the time Nixon resigned in August of 1974, the proof of treachery and vindictiveness at the highest levels of power in regard to the war and the political machinations at home finally broke the trust of the American people.[36] Any authority seemed suspect, overreaching its bounds and taking absolute power while committing deception after deception against basic values of democracy and freedom. The final insult would come with President Ford's pardon of Nixon shortly after taking office, when his gesture meant to heal national wounds was interpreted as just another callous protection of the privileged in office at the expense of justice and the people's will.

Yet without the economic crises that went hand in hand with the political and military trials of the decade, perhaps Americans would not have felt quite so despairing or filled with such an overwhelming sense of limitation and doom. Indeed, historian Edward Berkowitz ties these two factors together (the period's economic woes and the political and military nightmares of Watergate and Vietnam) as key in "launching the seventies as a distinctive phenomenon" culminating in an "unfamiliar sense of vulnerability in the United States" so that endless gas lines become a dominant symbol of the period much as the image of wagons of money in the streets of Weimar Germany stand as short hand for that country's crippling financial situation.[37] Like a perfect storm of economic distress, the 1970s witnessed the end of a long and prosperous industrial economy in favor of a new postindustrial one based in new technologies and service jobs, a subsequent rise in unemployment, and then the onset of inflation. In this new age of stagflation, where inflation's rising prices met with a slowing down of economic growth, Americans endured two deep recessions in the middle and end of the decade that resulted in a decrease in take-home pay as the 1970s wore on and a clear weakening of the nation's economic standing in the world.[38]

Many of these economic woes could be directly tied to those in positions of authority—first, the business leaders who closed plants or curbed their industrial output and moved work overseas and, then, the political leaders who appeared ineffectual or detrimental throughout the growing oil crisis. As a major cause of inflation, the energy crisis arose out of the country's dependence on foreign oil and in the wake of support by the United States of Israel during the Arab–Israeli conflict of 1973. Beginning in that year, led by its Arab members OPEC decided to raise prices drastically and eventually cut off oil shipments to countries not friendly to their interests, such as the United States. According to some estimates, the price of oil in the United States increased as much as 350 percent as a panic ensued, causing gas shortages, incredibly long gas lines, and an inevitable increase in prices of consumer goods.[39] In other words, the postwar prosperity of the "greatest nation on earth" had, to use Berkowitz's apt phrase, run out of gas, and the reaction by Americans was at first panic then, increasingly, despair, resignation, and hopelessness.

It should hardly be surprising, then, that Americans who felt deceived, impoverished, and abandoned by cultural institutions and national leaders would turn inward and focus on their own spiritual or individual identities. Beyond the media "cult" spectacles of the Manson Family crimes and subsequent trial in 1970 and the Jonestown massacre of members of the People's Temple in 1978, there was a sincere movement by many Americans to explore themselves and seek a personal, spiritual awakening and transformation with the help of a number of therapeutic groups and collective projects. Referred to mockingly by Tom Wolfe as "plugging in," many Americans turned earnestly to a search for self in therapeutic offerings such as encounter sessions like est, New Age religions, and Eastern practices like yoga or to a faith in separate, collective sanctuaries such as communes and "back to the land" collectives and organic farms inspired by the burgeoning environmental movement of the 1970s, which sought to construct "an alternative, do-it-yourself America."[40] As Schulman and other historians have noted, even the elderly were inspired to mobilize themselves through recreation vehicles and set up their own communities in retirement colonies and campsites, particularly in the increasingly influential Sunbelt states. Yet despite the caricatures by cultural commentators, this turn away from larger social (national) institutions or obligations in favor of personal reinvention or group and local affiliations did have political significance. When you tie the new identities of personal "plugging in" and new communities of collective living to the battles over gender or sexual identity and the cultural nationalism of different ethnic and racial minorities, you establish a pattern of Americans in the 1970s favoring "new affiliations, alternatives to the public sphere and national community," where petitions for both political and broader cultural change can benefit their group.[41] With many Americans insisting on a diversity of independent identities, the politics of *rights* for those affiliations became a central concern.

Although few would dispute the notion that the 1970s was a time of fundamental crisis for the United States government, economy, and dominant institutions, which many Americans experienced as a disastrous vulnerability, loss, and disillusionment, the consequent fragmentation was also incomparably productive for a number of marginalized groups. As David Frum argues in his conservative take on the 1970s, "disasters. . . can be liberating as well as destructive" in their opening up of a space for real social transformation.[42] The instability of what counted as the dominant American identity allowed a series of "others" to assert their own particular autonomous identity, which often resulted in political activism. For example, the cultural nationalism that emerged out of the black power and black arts movements in the 1970s would stress and celebrate a "positive, black-defined black identity" and difference from the dominant white culture, and other minority communities such as the Chicano movement, Native Americans, and Asian Americans would follow suit, embodying the notion of diversity in the nation rather than a melting pot of assimilation and integration.[43] Taking from these movements a sense of autonomy in the public sphere and of civil rights merited by a diversity of individuals within the broader United States, a number of "rights" movements—from the women's movement and gay and lesbian liberation to the rights of people with disabilities—turned their difference into a revolution.

In text after text, historians of the 1970s stress the two sides of the decade for Americans: the undeniable series of disasters, failures, and crises that so often fill accounts of the period *and* the significant, but often overlooked, moment of social change and political activism that occurred simultaneously or, in some cases, arose because of that moment of crisis. For Berkowitz, the Civil Rights movement of the 1960s, which created vital legal precedent for the liberation causes of the 1970s, focused on measurable change in legal and political arenas, but the "new civil rights movements of the seventies involved more fundamental critiques of postwar society," resulting in profound changes for the culture beyond legal amendments.[44] While, of course, the women's movement fought for an end to legal discrimination in the workplace, education (through *Title IX*), and elsewhere, as well as for reproductive rights (in the decision of *Roe v. Wade*) and the protection of women in domestic relationships, this rights revolution more significantly called for a fundamental change to gender relations and the basic norms of sex and gender. For gays and lesbians, legal rights ordinances that were granted in Miami and then quickly taken away or the end to laws allowing the firing of homosexual teachers were a central feature of their demands for rights in the 1970s, but the impact of the Stonewall riots, Gay Pride parades, and the lobbying for removal of "homosexuality" from the *Diagnostic and Statistical Manual of Mental Disorders* signified something much greater: an alteration in views of human sexuality that would call for recognition of a diversity of sexualities, not just the dominant and its deviant others. These were "fundamental critiques" of the society as a whole and demanded social and personal transformation that would change the country and its people forever.

The instability and crisis, the emphasis on differences and diversity, and the major critiques brought by the rights movements of the 1970s all suggested a changing vision of America. Who was "America" without prosperity, international dominance, trusted authorities, and a clear sense of social order and cultural norms? What national identity was possible in such a period of crisis (a question especially ironic considering the decade's fizzled bicentennial)? As Schulman suggests, one answer would be to deny the idea of one unified "American culture" in favor or "many American cultures," so that even the often-cited and incredibly powerful immigrant story might be revised to offer a "counternarrative" of unsuccessful assimilation and continued alienation or otherness.[45] Likewise, I would like to suggest that the period of crisis, instability, doubt, and questioning opened up a space both for a criticism of the master narratives or mythology of "America" and for the offering of alternative narratives or counternarratives. For example, in the troubling films of the New American Cinema, directors such as Altman, Penn, Scorsese, and Cassavetes presented major critiques of the dominant American narratives where Manifest Destiny becomes psychotic violence, "all created equal" becomes a painful catalogue of exclusions, and the American Dream becomes a wasteland of lost hopes and gender or class warfare.

Ultimately, I would add to these the idea of "youth" or youthfulness in America—its sense of itself as a young and vibrant country and its vision of its youth as a rebellious, but ultimately redeemed, white, middle-class, heterosexual male. If, in the 1970s moment, there is no longer one "American culture" but many, then perhaps "the American teenager" can become so many new American teenagers.

Conclusion: The "Lost" Generation of the 1970s

In his 1977 review of the wildly popular youth film *The Bad News Bears*, Dana Polan recognizes the film as a reflection of the youth culture coming of age in the 1970s. Contemplating this group of adolescents who were later dubbed "Generation Xers" by Douglas Coupland, wedged between the dominant populations of the baby boom before them and the boom echo after, Polan brands them a "lost generation," exactly as Coupland's moniker will eventually suggest. The North Valley Bears, for him, are victims of their historical moment, "already jaded members of a lost generation forced to be old before their time, and not really meeting that demand."[46] Incapable or unwilling to help the young Bears, the adults in the film often do more harm than good—ignoring, neglecting, and deriding their lost, prematurely aged children. Beyond these adult failings, however, Polan does not speculate as to *how* the Bad News Bears ended up this way, but his distress that they have (pre)matured into crude youth with emotional problems and little independence from the lure of consumer culture is palpable.

The "bad news" about this generation warns of an endangered adolescence, if not one vanishing entirely from American culture. Indeed, Polan's concern weighs more heavily than a dismissive view that this new generation lacks the political conviction and drive of its more famous older siblings of the 1960s. This lost generation seems entirely cut adrift from its parents and parent culture, abandoned perhaps by preoccupied adults searching for self and "plugging in" and asked to fend for itself and grow up too soon. The ghostly adolescents of the 1970s, here, seem a perfect mirror for a country that has lost its innocence and can imagine no way out from the various crises visited upon it. In a country grasping for hope and meaning and doubting a viable and prosperous future, the child or youth in some ways must become unimaginable or unrecognizable.

Other commentators, whether conservative or liberal, have troubled over and assessed this loss or neglect of youth in a decade when the

United States itself seemed to have lost its way and they often locate the root cause in the infamous "generation gap" of the decade.[47] In fact, the concern was so great that the President's White House Conference on Children in 1970 took as one of its preliminary premises that the "family in the United States is in trouble," ultimately finding that the conference reports acted as a "deeply disturbing commentary on America" where the nation could be indicted for a "vast neglect of its children" too often "forgotten" by national institutions and laws.[48] Even more disturbing in the conference's close examination of the family, the attendees discovered a frightening "isolation" of children such that they recommended programs that would bring adults and youth back into contact with each other.[49] Recent historian Peter Carroll echoes these concerns and more bluntly ties them to the era's economic crises, during which various youth cultures suffered the worst in lost employment opportunities—the "loss of a genuine future"—and, further, he claims these circumstances directly reflect "a critical breakdown in social relations across generations."[50] Due to the seeming neglect from parent culture, this history paints a picture not too dissimilar from the one offered in *The Bad News Bears*—one of missing parents, of isolated youth left to raise themselves, and of an adolescence lost without a future.

This generation gap had real implications for the financial future and emotional, physical, and psychological isolation of young people, which had allowed earlier conservative commentators like Vance Packard to caution against social change. Packard's *The Sexual Wilderness* from 1968 used what he called the unprecedented "gulf between the generations" to advise against the social change brought by the sexual revolution and changing gender roles.[51] Without parental guidance and clear social norms, the youth of the country would be lost (presumably in the wilderness) in confusion about how to act, who to be, what kinds of relationships to have, and their expectations for the future.[52] Whether a conservative jeremiad recommending a return to traditional values and sexual and gender norms or more liberal concerns for the neglect of the child in American institutions and families, a consensus was formed that the crises of the late 1960s and 1970s disproportionately affected youth and the generation gap assured that their trials would go unnoticed. They truly seemed by all accounts a lost generation.

Yet, as with the broader historical accounts of the 1970s, I must insist that there are two stories here, another side to the era and its treatment of youth. The era of crisis and uncertainty that possibly lost sight of its youth was also a time of new identities, rights revolutions, and new stories—even counternarratives—of America. The time described as "an exhilarating moment of possibility and progressive change" by Graebner could be open for youth as well. The moment when new narratives might be possible could open up the maturation plot, revealing new stories of youth just as the original seems lost. Even the much-decried generation gap could potentially serve as the kind of fissure or opening that would allow a different view of adolescence to emerge. This book hopes to give voice and representation to those new plots and different adolescents.

In each chapter, I will consider a different alternative story of adolescence—from sadistic school girls to gender-bending heartthrobs—to theorize ways that these counternarratives work to challenge and revise the traditional maturation plot as it has unfolded on film in the twentieth century. Chapter 1 will serve as an overview of the teen film genre and particularly the few traditional youth films of the 1970s such as *American Graffiti*, *Grease*, or *The Wanderers* to provide context and give a foundation for understanding the revisionary impulse that I locate in the era. This chapter will conclude with an analysis of both the parodic narratives so common to 1970s film and the genre-bending that became a hallmark of New American Cinema as a means to reconsider the state of the teen film genre in that decade when films like *The Rocky Horror Picture Show* and Corman's *Rock 'n' Roll High School* can rework and parody the basic tenets established in the previous several decades of classical films about youth. Chapter 2 moves on to one particular teenager and considers possibilities for a changed female teen audience in the 1970s, examining Holly, the young female narrator of Terrence Malick's *Badlands*, and proposing that these spectators and fans might oppose and revise the conservative ideology of the films sold to them. Unlike films such as Lucas' *American Graffiti*, which is bathed in the neon glow of nostalgia, Holly's controlling vision in the film reveals a new female authority in teen film, countering nostalgia as her own fantasies play, sometimes cruelly, with popular culture, Hollywood stars, and patriarchal order.

Chapters 3 and 4 offer perhaps the most significant revision of or alternative to the traditional cinematic maturation plot with the introduction of the "queer kid" in 1970s cinema. Through a direct engagement with second wave feminism, the career of teen heartthrob Robbie Benson reveals just how far the decade strayed from "the American teenager" of traditional accounts. Benson made a career out of defying gender norms, with his soft voice, aching blue eyes, and troubled male romantic leads who pursued strong, independent young women or, in the case of one notable film, *Ode to Billy Joe*, were seduced by older men. In other words, he gained popularity in the 1970s as what Kathryn Stockton and others call a "queer child," a gender-queer and sexually conscious young person who possesses the potential to queer traditional cinematic representations of the adolescent. Even more prominently than Benson, Jodie Foster's sexually disconcerting androgyne, which I examine in Chapter 4, dominated the 1970s as a disarmingly attractive queer kid in films such as *Alice Doesn't Live Here Anymore, Taxi Driver, The Little Girl Who Lived Down the Lane, Candleshoe, Foxes,* and Disney's *Freaky Friday*. Through her roles and star persona in these films, Foster represented the teenager as the strangely adult child, whose appearance and gravely voice signaled a gender-bending tomboy and whose engagement with sexuality disturbed and fascinated critics and audiences alike. Particularly challenging is her role in one of Disney's early attempts to address second wave feminism (*Freaky Friday*), where Foster's queer kid disrupts not only the family, which has been thrown into turmoil by mother–daughter body swapping, but also the traditional maturation plot effectively defined by the Disney oeuvre.

Finally, Chapter 5 leaves behind the relationship between parent and youth culture entirely to consider the conflicts within an abandoned peer culture in the guise of a sibling rivalry present in the infamous slasher horror films of the era. I argue that the struggle between the slasher killer and the "final girl" resembles a contest between two siblings and that the latter's victory enacts violence, not between parents and children as Clover suggests, but within the adolescent peer culture itself, often ending in an attempted (and reattempted) fratricide—a conclusion most obviously illustrated in the *Halloween* series. Ultimately, this sibling rivalry on screen suggests ambivalence in the teen subjects of the 1970s and a murderous aggression and competition within the peer group and between its male and female members in the audience. This kind of isolated or insular focus and aggression offers a counternarrative to the typical teen film wherein the relationship to parents or the patriarch and the assimilation (or not) into parent culture is the central concern.

* * *

At the end of *The Bad News Bears* (1976), the film's prematurely adult and fairly androgynous teen protagonist, played by the era's other consummate tomboy Tatum O'Neal, finds meaning and comfort in the imperfect but loving arms of the team's has-been, drunken coach and surrogate father, played by Walter Matthau. However, I would argue that the film's enactment of this classical trajectory back to the patriarch for the lost teenager in teen film is the exception rather than the rule in 1970s American cinema. So often in this decade the figures of adolescence find a different path—away from the patriarchal home or toward the mother or beyond the traditional bounds of normative gender and sexuality. They at times even abandon their ties to a neglectful parent culture in favor of their own insular conflicts and concerns. While "the" traditional American teenager might have temporarily exited the stage or failed to prove himself relevant at this moment, a new set of American teenagers, plotting a different course, filled the screens.

Chapter 1

The Rock 'n' Roll High School Picture Show: A Genre Deconstructed

Since the 1960s, the teenpic hero has more often been a Weird and Wimpy One, more liable to flash watery eyes than snarling lips. He is a hapless kid seeking direction, not a tough rebel fleeing restriction.[1]

Thomas Doherty, *Teenagers and Teenpics*

In the final chapter to the expanded edition of Doherty's groundbreaking study on teen film, the critic evaluates recent teen films from the position of a new millennium and, frankly, finds them wanting. The era his original text took as its subject, the heyday of the "teenpic" in the 1950s and early 1960s, stands for him as a watershed moment before the countercultural or New American Cinema films and then the blockbuster persuaded mainstream American film producers to take the youth market and audience as the target for most films, not just niche genre pictures. This sea change would naturally alter the form and address of those films sold to teenagers, apparently taking the teeth out of teenage rebellion and conflict. Simply, for Doherty, after the 1960s the "most fascinating trend in teenpics has been their palpable desire for parental control and authority, not their rebellion and autonomy."[2] These "postclassical" teen films for him lack a strong and adversarial parental authority in a culture supposedly without rules or a moral center so that the teen protagonist or rebel has no worthy antagonist, causing *him* to yearn for parental direction, control, and discipline. Here enters the "Weird and Wimpy" hero of the teenpic described in the introductory quote to this chapter. Without a strong or even present parent culture, post-1960s teenpics are populated by male victims, not rebels, whose longing for "parental (read: paternal) authority" leads to a preference for "stern discipline and father-son bonding" seemingly miles away from the resistance, alienation, and dangerousness of the classical (again, male) teen protagonist.[3]

As I argued in my Introduction, this sweeping claim by Doherty seems to conflate the 1970s and 1980s, neglecting the subversive potential that I find in many 1970s youth films, but it also appears to ignore the father-son focus and reconciliation with parent culture that Doherty himself insists often direct the teenpics of the 1950s. Even before the wholesome "clean teenpics" of the late 1950s and 1960s, one would have very little trouble locating a "palpable desire for parental control and authority" in monumental teen films of the 1950s—where, for example, Jim Stark desperately begs his father to "stand up" and be the paternal authority he needs. While I would certainly argue that the Weird or Wimpy teenpic hero has existed longer than Doherty would care to admit here—how else might one explain the career of Sal Mineo, for example, or the male heroes of the "weirdies" that Doherty himself catalogues—the point I would like to stress is that he has missed a key step in the evolution of the genre (the troublesome films of the 1970s) at the same time that he does a disservice to the "postclassical" period of teen films in the 1980s and 1990s that both resemble and revise their classical forerunners in enlightening ways. Although I will not be addressing the latter point until the epilogue of this book, I would like to use this opening chapter to establish the 1970s as a key moment in the evolution of the genre of teen film—its baroque or deconstructionist phase—where the weird kid is a figure to be admired and paternal authority is either rejected or lacking altogether.

However, in order to understand that baroque or deconstructionist moment in the century's films about youth, I must establish the basic parameters, formulaic features, and motifs of the genre through a brief overview of the previous decades of teen film, or a very short history of representations of youth on the American screen. Necessarily, this history will limit itself to representative films and trends for each decade or period of teen film and make use of other critical histories, such as those by Considine or Scheiner, which have already performed exhaustive studies of the periods in question. My broad strokes here are merely meant to serve as a background for the chapter's ultimate examination of the 1970s and the more traditional and then truly revisionary films to be found there. One needs to understand the basic tradition, particularly in its "classical" form, to recognize how significant films in the 1970s parody, revise, and deconstruct the values or codes of the genre and, thereby, set up a space for other narratives and counter-discourses (such as those examined in the later chapters of this book) to emerge.

A Brief History of Cinematic Representations of Youth

Although many commentators might place the birth of the teen film in the decade of the "teenager" (the 1950s), Considine compellingly argues that Hollywood has capitalized on stories of youth since its earliest days. Established for example by the Gish sisters and Mary Pickford, the sentimentalized or plucky young female heroine was a staple of early dramas and adventure serials, particularly Pickford's courageous and self-reliant tomboys, but it was not until the entrance of the flapper in the 1920s that the adolescent drama truly became a sensation. In this era of flaming youth, films such as *The Wild Party* (1923), *Our Dancing Daughters* (1928), and *The Road to Ruin* (1928) drew in eager adolescent (and adult) audiences as their exploitation material profited from what Georganne Scheiner calls "the popular image of wild adolescence and youth run amuck" and necessarily concluded with cautionary messages about troubled teens whose drinking, smoking, and sexual promiscuity ended in ruin.[4] *Our Dancing Daughters* earned countless youth fans for a young Joan Crawford, who as the unrestrained and spirited flapper Deana Medford could be the life of the party without losing her virtue unlike her careless and self-interested friends Beatrice and Ann, but it is perhaps *The Road to Ruin* that best captures the cautionary and sensationalizing spirit of these lucrative early youth exploitation films.[5]

In a quite graphic and shocking way, 1928's *The Road to Ruin* pushes the limits of acceptability with its supposed exposé of female delinquency, which was both shown to adolescents in high schools as a cautionary tale *and* banned in many cities, ending as the title promises in teenage ruin, death, and parental (specifically, maternal) culpability. The virtuous adolescent Sally Canfield (played by Helen Foster in the 1928 silent film as well as the 1934 remake) somewhat innocently starts down this road with a bit of drinking and smoking with her aptly name temptress friend Eve, but soon she is having sex not only with a high school boy but also then with an older man whom she meets at a roadhouse. Essentially, the film titillatingly exposes her descent into the debauched life of a "full-blown flapper," where unchecked pleasure and lack of parental (maternal) guidance doom her to venereal disease, pregnancy, a botched abortion, and an inevitable death.[6] Although few audience members would have needed the title card that summarizes the film's message—"Those who transgress the moral laws pay the bitter price"—the moral that was supposed to scare adolescent audiences straight as it were was muddied by the sensational scenes of pleasure, freedom, and thrilling parties, as was so often the case with exploitation films of the era. *The Road to Ruin*, then, is exemplary for its early enactment of a fundamental dichotomy in the teen film: that films meant to have a pedagogical or cautionary function for youth and adult or parental audiences often contain contradictory or disturbing sensational elements, which might leave particularly young audience members with the 'wrong' impression, ideas, or set of pleasures with which they exit the movie house.[7]

A number of films continue this focus on delinquency and ambivalent messages into the 1930s, perhaps the most notable of which are the "Dead End Kids" films. The topic of delinquency in this period begins to move away from being fodder for exploitation and more toward the form of a "social problem." While films like *The Road to Ruin* might expose serious adult problems such as venereal disease, prostitution, and drug abuse, the "social problem" film takes as its goal a kind of examination and rectification of societal issues. Whether juvenile delinquency, crime, poverty, and general misbehavior, these problems should be solved or tamed, either domesticated or brought in line though fair-mindedness, compassion, and a dose of morality. Although with an emphasis on edification, social justice, and morality, these films also owe a great deal to the crime film genre. Both the "Dead End Kids" films of the late 1930s and studio prestige features like MGM's *Boys Town* (1938) explored the possible causes for delinquency, particularly in terms of its environmental roots, but they also brought from the crime genre the familiar concluding homily that "crime doesn't pay." In fact, Considine asserts that Hollywood saw itself as capable of making a real social impact with these films, showing "no hesitation in pressing itself upon the courts, the schools, and the police force."[8] Taurog's *Boys Town* serves this purpose by holding a mirror up to society and saying through the mouthpiece of its savior-hero Father Flanagan that "there is no such thing as a bad boy," only bad social environments and corrupt institutions. Much like *Boys Town*'s criticism of the conditions of poverty in urban centers and the effects on juveniles of parental neglect, early arrest, or tough reformatories where lessons on further criminal acts might be learned, the "Dead End Kids" films, beginning with Wyler's *Dead End* in 1937 and made more notable by the fine cast and direction of Curtiz's *Angels With Dirty Faces* in 1938, focus on tenement life on New York City's East Side to expose how poverty and environment can breed a cycle of criminal behavior and gang allegiance from an early age. *Angels With Dirty Faces* particularly mirrors *Boys Town*'s moralizing social message, as its hero-priest Jerry Connolly leads the wayward kids (with 'tough guy' handles like Soapy, Bim, and Swing) away from the charismatic gangster Rocky Sullivan (played, of course, by James Cagney), who ends up getting the chair for his crimes, and towards an honest life. Yet, even so-called "social problem" films were not immune to the lure of the sensational crimes and pleasures that they decry, again attracting youth audiences thrilled by the darker criminal elements and thrilling events.[9]

However, the seriousness of a nation embroiled in the worst depression in its history also called for a different, more optimistic face of the future and so were born the clean teens and "fix-it" kids of the 1930s led by Mickey Rooney, Deanna Durbin, Judy Garland, and, though younger, Shirley Temple. These wholesome young stars brought an innocence, youthful energy and enthusiasm, and optimistic outlook to relatively light cinematic narratives, solving problems both personal and communal or social. Usually with a smile and good cheer, they were independent, strong-willed, and often more capable than their elders to provide solutions, help each other, rescue adults, and, of course, put on a show.[10] As Shirley Temple's title character in *Rebecca of Sunnybrook Farm* (1938) continually reminds the audience, kids like her are "very self-reliant," able to warm the hearts of an eager national audience (in this case as radio star "Little Miss America") by offering happiness through, as she sings it, "millions worth of golden sunbeams." Similarly, although she only saves or, to be exact, rekindles her parents marriage in her first major role in *Three Smart Girls* (1936), Deanna Durbin was every bit Temple's match in self-reliant pluck and can-do spirit, described by one critic as a "Pollyanna missionary" who might "sporadically burst into song between her incessant do-gooding."[11] Perhaps the film *That Certain Age* (1938) better captures her particular allure, as her character becomes enamored of a much older man who must let her down gently and then ultimately directs her energies into putting on a show to benefit underprivileged Boy Scouts with her more appropriately aged boyfriend.[12] Optimistic, uplifting, and wholesome roles like these were incredibly popular in the period, making major stars of these young performers and earning sizeable profits for the studios, but none was perhaps so profitable or successful as Mickey Rooney, who won fame for his role as the spirited Andy Hardy, son of upstanding and understanding Judge Hardy in a series of films that ran through the 1940s (and was even revived in 1958 with an adult Andy).[13]

The Andy Hardy series, one of the most profitable series in the history of American film, solidified both Mickey Rooney's prominence as one of the most successful male performers of his era and the image of the typical American teenager before World War II. Although the films began in 1937 with *A Family Affair*, which focused on the entire Hardy family, soon they would revolve around the character of Andy Hardy and his teenage concerns, mistakes, and romantic trials and tribulations. At the heart of the series was Andy's relationship with his moral paragon of a father, Judge Hardy, who could be stern and somewhat commanding while allowing his softer, compassionate side to show through in climactic heart-to-heart talks with his son. In *Love Finds Andy Hardy* (1938), Rooney's first Hardy film costarring Judy Garland, a typical conundrum ensues when Andy attempts to balance his finances and his romances, nearly failing miserably at both. His foolhardy decision to buy a car without all the financing lands him in a sticky dating situation where a friend's girl becomes nothing more to him than "an installment on car," but once he fails to secure the necessary funds, he must depend on the mercy, guidance, and eventual generosity of his stalwart father to excuse his debt—an act that secures Andy's unabashed love and admiration once again for Judge Hardy. According to Mark McGee, for his time period and for an audience invested in traditional values, Andy Hardy was "the perfect image of an American teenager: sometimes misguided, often confused, but basically decent, energetic, and obedient."[14] Certainly, this conclusion is supported by Rooney's special Academy Award in 1939 (along with Deanna Durbin) for their "significant contribution in bringing to the screen the spirit and personification of youth" and the special Oscar bestowed on the Andy Hardy series in 1943 for "representing the American way of life."[15] In Rooney, the period had not only a representative of American can-do spirit and fortitude—on display, for example, in the closing number "God's Country" in *Babes In Arms* (1939) performed with Garland—but also an antidote to the troubled delinquents and wayward daughters of earlier films about youth. He is, especially in the incredibly popular role of Andy Hardy, *the* American teenager that Hine describes in my Introduction: a white, middle-class, heterosexual (even Protestant) male who may not always obey his father's wishes from the outset but who eventually is reconciled with or even thankful for paternal values, rules, and discipline. However, World War II and its aftermath seriously shook the foundations for this adolescent figure such as the sanctity of the patriarchal home, and the specter of the uncontrolled juvenile delinquent haunted the screen once more.

As World War II brought in its wake uncertainty and the stirrings of significant social change for the country, so the teens on screen necessarily exhibited more turmoil and instability than "fix-it" plans and uplifting philosophies. Films like Shirley Temple's juvenile romance *The Bachelor and the Bobby Soxer* (1947) with its flirtation with Daddy-love so familiar from her earlier roles were fewer and farther between in comparison to the renewed interest in gritty depictions of juvenile delinquency. Shane's *City Across the River* (1949), developed from Irving Schulman's disturbing novel about street gangs, gives a sense of the changed climate after the war and the growing panic about the supposed 'epidemic' of juvenile delinquency, the concern over which even produced a Senate subcommittee investigation led by Senator Estes Kefauver.[16] The film resembles in many ways the social problem films of the 1930s with its cautionary prologue from a concerned expert, who warns that this "could be your city, your street, your house" and presents a problem of delinquency tied directly to "slum conditions" in the city; however, it lacks the reassuring problem *solving* of the earlier films reached through the success of a crusading savior such as Fathers Flanagan or Connolly and his reassertion of traditional American values and the 'right' patriarchal authority. Instead, the film offers a starkly realistic picture of tenement life through the conflicted teen protagonist Frankie Cusack and a truly dark, menacing view of juvenile gangs, whose members beat a "welcher" for the local thug, construct their own zip guns in shop class, and eventually murder a teacher who has punished them. Although Frankie does the 'right thing' in the end by informing on his friend, Benny, who shot the teacher, his act results in a bleak future: his own arrest and Benny's fall to his death after labeling Frank a "rat." Encapsulated in the disparaging motto of another notable movie delinquent from the same year (the ill-fated Nick in Nicholas Ray's *Knock on Any Door*), these troubled, impoverished adolescents can only hope to "live fast, die young, and have a good looking corpse." No fatherly support can remedy their dire situation or beat the odds seemingly set against them, despite both these films' impassioned pleas to address the poverty and slum conditions that appear to breed delinquency.

Furthermore, this 1940s brand of the j.d. picture revisits the fundamental dichotomy that plagued the "social problem" films about youth in a time when the divide between parent culture and youth culture seemed to be widening. Despite the excision of many of the most disturbing elements of the Shulman's novel such as rape, visiting prostitutes, drugs, and strong language by the Breen office and the filmmakers' addition of a reassuring coda to *City Across the River* where the cast was introduced to the audience as just young actors performing a role, civic groups and concerned parents still protested the film's subject matter and influence on a youth audience. A notable incident with a teacher polling his class about the message of the film only fueled the concern: when asked what the film's moral was, most students answered that Frankie should not have squealed on his friend.[17] In other words, these delinquent films walked a similar line between sensation and edification that the exploitation films of the 1920s seemed to mock and the "social problem" films of the 1930s crossed perhaps unwittingly. The adult or pedagogical message of such films was often lost on young audience members or even contradicted in their consumption of the films. Genre critic Steve Neale insists that a 1940s social problem film like *City Across the River* should be distinguished from exploitation films like *I Accuse My Parents* (1944) because "distinctions need to be made between those films which sought, at least ostensibly, to condemn juvenile delinquency, those which sought to understand it, and those which sought, either way, to use it to appeal either to a teenage or adult audience," but I wonder if such a clear distinction is possible when so many films about youth appeal to both sides, having a socially relevant message and playing to audience desires with thrilling or controversial content.[18] This question becomes more pressing as the teen film reaches its classical period in the 1950s, when the sizeable and economically powerful American youth cohort threatened to overwhelm dominant culture—even being referred to by one national magazine as a "vast, determined band of blue-jeaned storm troopers"—and expressed themselves forcefully as both viewers and consumers.[19]

While claims that the American "teenager" as we know him was invented or born in the 1950s might be a bit exaggerated—with public concern over youth increasingly prevalent in the twentieth century, from the flappers of the 1920s to the unemployed youth of the Depression and the bobby soxers of the following decade, there is no doubt that the youth cohort of the 1950s represents a remarkable historical entity, exceptional in its size and wealth, but perhaps most importantly, in its self-awareness as a unified generation. And as 1950s teens developed a generational consciousness and independence, so did the dominant culture attend to them as a unique group: "In the marketplace and the media, at home and at school, the teenager was counted a special creature requiring special handling."[20] The teenager of the 1950s was studied in the fields of psychology and sociology, investigated and worried over by national magazines and parents groups, and eagerly pursued and pandered to by advertisers, the media, and consumer culture. Yet, this generational identity and unity also seemed to breed generational conflicts and misunderstandings. As the "blue-jeaned storm troopers" comment above illustrates, such an influential and powerful youth generation necessarily elicits concern, caution, and, ultimately, fear from older generations, and perhaps no concept better demonstrates this fear than the exaggerated panic over the 'epidemic' of juvenile delinquency. Yet, one might also argue that these fears were in some ways justified in the 1950s when the obedience, parental adoration, and propriety of young people, on display for example in the Andy Hardy films, seemed so clearly a thing of the past. As McGee argues, the delinquent of the 1950s films left behind the adoration and wholesomeness of earlier teens for a realistic depiction of adolescent struggles and conflicts: "Teenagers after all did have real problems. Ideal role models were not always readily available. And sexual urges were often more than just puppy love."[21] The most notable and influential teen films of the 1950s, from *The Wild One* (1954) and *Blackboard Jungle* (1955) to *Rebel Without a Cause* (1955), certainly substantiate McGee's description, suggesting a growing divide between parents and their adolescent offspring and a worrying isolation or independence of the younger generation.

Like the gyrating, sexually threatening, and bewildering phenomenon of Elvis Presley, the most influential teen films of 1950s offered a kind of disturbing sexuality, class mixing, and menacing aggression that could not be easily resolved or reconciled by parent culture. The screen teens of the 1950s at times presented an irredeemable otherness that could not be reabsorbed into parent culture or shown the right path. To revise the motto of Father Flanagan in *Boys Town*, in the 1950s there *was* such a thing as a bad boy. Although Brando's hypermasculine biker gang leader Johnny in *The Wild One* turns out to be more tame and romantically swayed than his "Black Rebels" gang mates who ride in and wreak havoc upon the small town of Wrightsville, the film overall gives the picture of a violent youth mob in blue jeans and leather jackets ready to explode on a middle America without the adequate adult authority to stop them. The town's sheriff is ineffectual, his daughter finds herself attracted to the sullen and reticent Johnny and nearly raped by a gang of bikers, and the town's business leaders live to regret their shortsighted pandering to the heavy drinking and consuming gang. Perhaps more importantly, when the antihero Johnny responds to the question of what he is rebelling against with the bored coolness and contempt of "What have you got?" the film and its audience become his (due in no small part to Brando's performance and star allure), sympathizing with his confusion and desire for an authentic life outside of the confines of a hypocritical and conformist adult culture. The film might open with a characteristic cautionary plea, or "public challenge" not to let the "shocking story" about to unfold "happen again," yet as Jon Lewis asserts a large part of the film also provides "an irresistible and charismatic anti-hero for its young (at heart) audience" and perhaps this explains why so many critics and communities objected to the film.[22] Accused of "inspiring anarchy" and banned in the United Kingdom "out of fear that it might incite violence and inspire delinquency," *The Wild One*'s story, which was based on a real 1947 incident of a motorcycle gang rampage in the town of Hollister, California, created its own panic in adult audiences confronted with an aggressive and incomprehensible youth subculture that proved desirable to their teens.[23] A film with a much less sympathetic delinquent, *Blackboard Jungle* released the following year, would confound parents and adult commentators even further with its wild popularity for what seemed like all the wrong reasons.

Adapted from a startling novel by Evan Hunter about the New York City school system, *Blackboard Jungle* directed itself at adults who might benefit from the admonitory message of its melodrama but was embraced by a youth audience thrilled from the opening beats of Bill Haley and the Comets' "Rock Around the Clock" during the title sequence. The film follows the experiences and crusade of one teacher at an all-male vocational high school, Richard Dadier (played by Glenn Ford) or "Daddy-O" to the mocking mob of ethnically and racially diverse students in his classroom, as he rejects the cynicism of his colleagues and the defiance of his students to try to reach and educate them in the "garbage can of the educational system," as one fellow teacher calls it. Ultimately, Dadier scores a kind of victory with the students, gaining the trust and help of one of his most serious detractors Gregory Miller (played by Sidney Poitier) and seizing control of the classroom away from the bully ringleader Artie West, but he must resort to violence to do so: he comes crashing to the defense of a fellow teacher whose would be rapist is badly hurt trying to escape through a window, receives his own beating in an alley at the hands of a group of students, is nearly broken by insinuating letters sent to his wife, and finally must use force to subdue the threat of a switchblade-wielding West in the climactic scene, which ends heavy-handedly with a student named Santini using the American flag as a spear to subdue the final attacker. North Manual High School may be in the same country as the upstanding school Dadier visits with his mentor, where well-behaved (and overwhelmingly white and middle class) students sing "The Star Spangled Banner"; yet, his classroom's toughs or, as Considine calls them, "children of a concrete jungle raised in a frightening urban environment" that makes them "strangers—alien, hostile, threatening," clearly represent a different type of adolescent altogether.[24]

Through the deviant ringleader Artie West, played with a combination of menacing sneer and chilling sociopathic indifference by Vic Morrow, the film represents the adolescent as an unknowable other or "stranger" with terrifying potential for resistance—an image vehemently criticized by US commentators (and even one US ambassador) as inaccurate or exaggerated and yet congruent with the mass media's folk devil figure of the juvenile delinquent. Despite Dadier's heroic efforts, it is clear that West will never be redeemed by film's end and perhaps more frighteningly he recognizes the violent uses the state might have for him in "uniform" and prefers his own vicious law of the streets, even as jail inevitably awaits. He is as cynical and cruel as the worn out teachers at the school who see themselves as jailers or animal tamers, and, significantly, the gulf between them, for Doherty, gives "a real sense that the terms of the social contract between young and old had changed."[25] The film does not offer the usual closure provided by the moral lesson taught to delinquent youth, learned too late for example by Frankie in *City Across the River*, because West refuses the "moral superiority of the social order" to the very end, obliging his forceful removal.[26] For many commentators and educators, this conclusion was simply too much. Most famously, Claire Booth Luce, US Ambassador to Italy, pulled the film from the Venice Film Festival because of its scandalous representation of American schools, and educators across the country expressed outrage at the exaggerated depiction that was "misrepresenting and sensationalizing the situation."[27] The controversy caused by Luce's actions, of course, brought the film more attention (and the inevitable spike in attendance and profits), and no amount of sincere prologues praising the US school system as a "tribute to our communities" and championing "public awareness" as a "remedy" for juvenile delinquency could squelch the growing sense of exploitation that educators and reviewers attached to the film or the obvious enthusiasm and aggressiveness of young audience members. In fact, Doherty notes that Haley's "Rock Around the Clock" sold 2 million copies by the end of the year, fueled by thrilled teens who danced in the aisles to the title sequence playing the song and who even were charged for "minor incidents of violence" at theaters.[28] More seriously than *The Wild One*, where Johnny makes gestures toward assimilation into parent culture or at least seems to recognize the validity of adult authority and values, *Blackboard Jungle* suggests a real break between parent and youth cultures, with a dark—even deterministic—end for the true juvenile delinquent Artie West, and what's more, the new autonomous and alienating youth culture was consuming the film and raucously responding to it in large numbers.

The only worse scenario would be if these frightening and seemingly out of control teen offenders were not restricted to one biker gang in a small isolated town or a group of inner city thugs at a vocational school, but moved into that respectable, orderly high school Dadier visits or into the tree-lined, prosperous suburbs. *Rebel Without a Cause*, in other words, is the nightmare lurking underneath so much of this public concern and parental fear about juvenile delinquency in the 1950s: what if 'good kids' from 'good homes' were troubled, demanded their autonomy, or exposed that growing chasm between youth and parent culture? And perhaps worst of all, what if adult society or parents were to blame? The film famously opens with a police station scene that exposes these very fears about male *and* female adolescents. The three central teens—Jim, Judy, and Plato—do not pull up on bikes with leather jackets and blue jeans and they do not wield switchblades (yet); Jim is in a suit and tie, Plato has a sweater vest on and mixed socks above his loafers, and Judy wears a fine red wool overcoat and matching outfit. Furthermore, Jim's parents are in evening dress and Plato has an African American maid to pick him up. These teens come from affluent or solidly middle class families, so why is Judy walking the street after curfew possibly "looking for company," what has caused Jim to get "loaded" by himself, and why is Plato alone on his birthday, left to his own disturbing actions? Jim's answer—the now famous "You're tearing me apart!" scream of desperation at his parents—cannot have pleased the adult culture trying to absorb the film's and James Dean's unparalleled popularity. *Rebel's* melodrama addressed head on the social changes brought in the wake of World War II, particularly the challenges to gender norms that directly impacted the family and expected roles for father and mother. Jim may long for a father who will "stand up" and be able to tell him how to "be a man," but as Elayne Rapping contends, he is "caught up in an era in which the struggle to preserve the nuclear family was fierce, but ultimately doomed."[29] In other words, when the juvenile delinquency narrative enters the world of middle-class propriety, a domestic melodrama ensues that indicts a major foundation for dominant culture—the patriarchal family—for the troubles and confusion that lead to deviant behavior in youth, and not just marauding biker gangs or sociopathic punks from the inner city.

Ray's *Rebel Without a Cause* clearly places itself on the side of the teenager against a hypocritical and false parent culture whose methods of guidance appear as irrelevant platitudes for very real troubles.[30] Yet, the mock family that Jim, Judy, and Plato set up in the abandoned mansion, with its enactment of youth culture's ability to forge a seemingly autonomous existence, is also doomed, allowing for the Hollywood genre resolution of paternal reconciliation for the teen. Early on, Jim anxiously turns to his father for advice about the "chickie run" to which Buzz and his crew have challenged him, but all his apron-clad father can offer in the face of Jim's pressing question, "What can you do when you have to be man," is a proposal to make a list of pros and cons. Needless to say, Jim does not wait around to find out the results of his father's list making. Furthermore, when he comes home after Buzz's accidental death at the climax of the chickie run, his parents self-interestedly maintain that Jim should hide his involvement or lie to authorities, but he rails against their hypocrisy, insisting rightly that they are all "involved" and should honor their obligations. In this scene, Ray makes the most of the Cinemascope widescreen format on the stairwell to have Jim pulled between two equally failed models of adulthood, being torn apart in an off-kilter world (set off by a canted angle) where his mother attempts cruelly to dominate and his father is unable to stand up for him.

Yet, when Jim leaves to make his own home and family with mock wife Judy and son Plato, an "autonomous existence" that reveals for Doherty the 1950s teen's "instinctive allegiance to the values of peers over parents," this home is flawed as well and must be rescued by a return of patriarchal normalcy.[31] Jim and Judy's abandonment of Plato leaves him vulnerable to Buzz's gang, which causes him to flee, setting in motion the final tragic events of the film. It is as if the film can only go so far in its criticism of parent culture and its preference for the "autonomous existence" and authentic values of the new youth culture. It must resolve the disturbing presence of Plato, whose irredeemable otherness and unsettling queerness disrupt the stability and inevitability of Jim's heterosexual object choice and comforting union, as it must repress the danger represented by Judy's sexual delinquency and aggressiveness, especially considering the discomfort it causes her father. Jim's introduction of Judy to his parents after Plato's death is clearly meant to eliminate these two threats, which is only overshadowed by the fragile restoration of Jim's own family and his parent's proper roles. After Plato's death, Jim's father comes to his side and praises him for doing "everything a man could," promising to "stand up" with his son and face "whatever comes" together. In a symbolic gesture, as Jim turns away from a "cold" Plato in *his* red jacket, Mr. Stark places his own jacket over Jim's shoulders and ushers him away, with a compliant mom and Judy in tow. After so much difficulty, after disturbing fears about juvenile delinquency and a crisis in the postwar patriarchal home, and after a glimpse into the autonomy and distinct values of the new peer culture of teenagers, the film concludes with the comfort of the heterosexual middle-class couple and paternal strength and reconciliation. In other words, as Lewis contends, despite the obvious failures of the patriarch and the nuclear family (or, really, almost all of adult society) for every teen in the film, it finally "reinscribes the family ideal" as so many teen films do.[32] Indeed, *Rebel* acts as a kind of urtext for the teen film genre at the center of its classical age, wherein the narrative focuses on a white, middle-class male teen (*the* American teenager) who experiences serious difficulties accepting the norms and values of his dominant culture, leading to a dramatic rebellion, but who ultimately is reconciled with this dominant culture through the figure of his parents, or specifically his father. To fail or refuse to do so is, in the end, unacceptable and such a teen must be eliminated, as we see in Plato's tragic death.

The significance of *Rebel* and also *Blackboard Jungle* cannot be underestimated when one considers the explosion of teen films that followed their success. Examined exhaustively in Doherty's *Teenagers and Teenpics*, the wave of cheaply made imitators and followers of these two films (plus *The Wild One*) became an industry unto itself in the 1950s and 1960s, especially for independent production companies such as Nicholson and Arkoff's American International Pictures. Doherty shows a direct line from both *Blackboard Jungle* and *Rebel* to the rise of teen exploitation fare or "teenpics" in the form of rock 'n' roll pictures and j.d. or "dangerous youth" films. For example, the incredible success of Bill Haley and the Comets' "Rock Around the Clock," spurred by its placement in *Blackboard Jungle*, led to a film of the same name produced in 1956 by another low-budget film king, Sam Katzman, which grossed eight times its production costs and became, for Doherty, "the first hugely successful film marketed to teenagers *to the pointed exclusion of their elders*."[33] Known for gratifying "the adolescent glands with disheveled actresses, exotic locales (filmed in California), and freakish bipeds (apes, dwarves, and monsters)," Katzman beat his competitors to an early recognition of the rock 'n' roll craze, but they soon caught on, producing half a dozen of these rock 'n' roll films before the end of 1956.[34] *Rock Around the Clock*'s simple story of a band's discovery, the complications of their signing, and their eventual rise to fame was followed by similar films that took advantage of the rock 'n' roll controversy and generational divide over it, but this was not the only route to teenage audience pleasures and dollars, as a larger wave of films about delinquent teens would show.

Producers soon found that *Rebel Without a Cause* and James Dean's shocking premature death in his Porsche Spyder could fuel enormous fascination with not only drag racing but also troubled teens of all sorts, though typically male. From United Artists's *Hot Cars* (1956) and AA's *Hot Rod Rumble* (1957) to AIP's *Hot Rod Girl* (1956) and *Dragstrip Riot* (1958), the drag racing premise proved lucrative if short-lived compared to the juvenile delinquent cycle, which of course had many antecedents prior to *Rebel Without a Cause* (as established above).[35] Inspired by *Rebel*, *Blackboard Jungle*, and *The Wild One*, cheaply made and sensational films like *Crime in the Streets* (1956), *The Delinquents* (1957), *Juvenile Jungle* (1958), and *High School Confidential* (1958) feature a range of sometimes psychopathic or drug-dealing hoods with the obligatory switchblades in marauding adolescent gangs, who drink too much, drive too fast, and inevitably run afoul of the police. In fact, the cycle was so popular that even a few girl gang or delinquent films cropped up, from Corman's troubling *Teenage Doll* (1957) to similar pictures like *Reform School Girl* (1957), *High School Hellcats* (1958), and the Mamie Van Doren and Paul Anka vehicle *Girls Town* (1959). Although these delinquent or gang films typically conclude with a return to law and order and an elimination of the most troubling male offenders, the exhilarating freedom and unbridled aggression was not lost on the teenage audience that continued to make the films profitable, but theater owners became increasingly concerned about vandalism and violence in their theaters as the aggression and unruly behavior spilled off the screen and into the crowd.[36] As they made profits for independent producers like Nicholson and Arkoff, "teenpics"—from rock 'n' rollers to troubled teens—also amplified and exacerbated both the apparent distance between parents and their adolescent offspring and the generational identity highlighted by teen fads, lingo, and consumption of popular culture.

However, after the petering out of the last great controversial teenpic cycle of the 1950s, the horror teenpic, films about youth and marketed to youth shifted dramatically back towards more wholesome fare reminiscent of Andy Hardy or the Deanna Durbin films in a predominantly late-1950s and early-1960s phenomenon Doherty calls the "clean teenpic." The controversy, unease, and downright outrage caused by the exploitation films of the 1950s seemed to wash out to sea with the entrance of the light comic antics of the Gidgets of the teen film world.[37] Surprisingly, in an era when foreign films, auteur filmmakers, and even bold prestige productions were seriously challenging the Production Code, which would finally be replaced by the age rating system in 1968, the end of the 1950s and first half of the 1960s witnessed a return to "unabashedly wholesome entertainment that was at once teen-targeted and parent-approved," such as Sandra Dee's turn as Gidget, the "girl midget" surfer, in the 1959 film.[38] From Pat Boone's safe and courteous heartthrobs to Sandra Dee's appropriateness as a role model for young girls, the clean teen was again that decent, trustworthy, and morally centered kid next door (usually in a 'nice' middle-class neighborhood). Gidget might flirt with the bohemianism of the Big Kahuna or place herself in the liminal space of the beach and all-male surfing community where she is subject to the occasional predatory advance, but ultimately she will choose Moondoggie, who turns out to be exactly the upstanding young man (and son of a business partner) that her parents intend for her. Gidget's parents, particularly her father, might not always understand her, but they support her and in the end they know best, which amounts to her safe, middle-class, sanctioned heterosexual union with a suitable potential husband.[39]

Following in Gidget's wake, AIP again predicted the next craze of (clean) teenpics with the release of the "Beach Party" films starring Annette Funicello and Frankie Avalon. The comic romps on the beach had an element of sex appeal, but the audience could rest assured it would all end in good clean fun; like the first film in the series, *Beach Party* (1963), promises from its opening musical number, the teen film would now offer a vacation party where "nothin' is greater than the sand, surf, and salt." The central couple in the film—college-aged Dolores and Frankie—spend more time trying to make each other jealous or hitting the beach with their beach bum pals than actually sharing any intimate moments. Dolores admits in the beginning that she does not "trust" herself when she's with Frankie, and as would be appropriate to her traditional gender role, she must regulate the limits of propriety for the couple. Moreover, the film's central adult presence, an anthropologist eager to study teenagers as a "primitive" tribe, finds in the place of teenage sex or risky behavior, young women like Dolores interested in being more "than just a girl," that is, a "wife." In this beach party world of clean teens, even the biker gangs are played for laughs and pie fights replace switchblades. Simply put, as Alan Betrock describes them, these "wholesome," "perky," and attractive kids dance and play through five films in two years (*Beach Party, Muscle Beach Party, Bikini Beach, Beach Blanket Bingo,* and *How to Stuff a Wild Bikini*) in a "fantasy vision of life without serious problems."[40] Without parents around to spoil the summer party that never seemed to end (set to the music of Dick Dale and his Deltones), these clean beach teens inhabit a world where no one works, or fights about anything serious, or struggles with rapidly changing social mores (particularly in terms of gender), even as civil unrest, feminist dissension, and youth protests became more and more prevalent as the decade wore on.[41]

The last two youth-directed exploitation cycles of the 1960s finally gave a sense of the major social changes demanded by various protest movements including the Civil Rights movement, antiwar activists, and, particularly, the youth counterculture's demonstrations against institutional authorities and the status quo. However, to be sure, these films remained in the classic exploitation mode of business-savvy producers like Katzman or Arkoff, taking advantage of what they saw as timely trends that would appeal to the basest instincts of their young audience. For example, biker films, somewhat in the tradition of *The Wild One*, returned with a vengeance in 1966 with Roger Corman's AIP release of *The Wild Angels*, a fairly brutal depiction of the swastika-wearing Hell's Angels motorcycle gang that contained a startling amount of sex and violence, even rape, on its way to incredible box office receipts. According to Betrock, nearly 20 films would attempt to reproduce its success over the next three years—with titles like *Devil's Angels* (1967), *She-Devils on Wheels* (1968), and *Cycle Savages* (1969)—with each one "trying to outdo its predecessor in sheer volume of senseless violence, sex, and, of course, theater grosses."[42] Certainly more mature and graphically violent than previous teenpics, which again reveals the opening up of the film industry's subject matter in the late 1960s, the biker films nonetheless attracted a teenage audience to the drive-in once again, though perhaps not as obviously as the cycle of films Shary calls "groovy rebellion movies" that centered their plots on drug use and caricatures of the youth counterculture.[43]

While AIP's *The Trip* (1967) may represent these drug or hippie films well enough with its "groovy" aesthetic meant to reproduce the experience of taking LSD for a curious teenage audience, *Wild in the Streets* (1968) ties together many elements of the era, from youth activism to countercultural lifestyles, in a campy satire that has become a cult classic. The film's plot, which involves a young male rock idol becoming President of the United States after persuading Congress (through generous helpings of LSD) to lower the voting age to 14 and then passing a law that sends all those over 35 to LSD retirement camps, has just enough timely commentary to make it compelling and enough over-the-top farce to make it amusing. Yet, one cannot deny, as Shary argues, the film's ultimately reactionary attitude toward the youth counterculture with its "mockery of the suffrage for teens that was being sought" and its conclusion that "young people cannot be trusted with power."[44] Indeed, these exploitation films, with their adult eye focused on the bottom line, are only distantly related to contemporaneous groundbreaking films like *The Graduate* (1967), *Bonnie and Clyde* (1967), and *Easy Rider* (1969), which announced the arrival of a renaissance for American filmmaking in the 1970s that would attract a young audience with damning social commentary and formal experimentation beyond the capabilities or interests of exploitation producers. In other words, a change was coming for films directed at youth concerns, and not just for college-aged cineastes.

The Teen on Screen in the 1970s: A Lost Era?

As I detailed in my Introduction, many commentators and genre critics have found the 1970s to be a kind of "dormant" period for teen film—a time when the college-aged crowd fueled a New American Cinema and the adolescence still lingering in all audience members was tapped for blockbuster profits.[45] Yet the period, while certainly not matching the prolific teen output of the 1950s or 1980s, had its share of not only more traditional representations of youth but also a new breed of teens on screen (as I will argue for the remainder of this book). The more traditional depictions of young people, however, often marked themselves as other to the era of their release, sending the teenager (usually male) back to a time before the 1970s when *the* American teenager could incontestably dominate. In other words, for many critics the most notable mainstream teen films of the era linger nostalgically in a time before the social upheaval and antiestablishment revolts of the 1960s and before the women's or gay rights movements and national crises of the 1970s. The male teen hero of these films may not be as wholesome and full of adoration for the father as Andy Hardy is, but he enacts a reactionary longing for a time when his needs and concerns were paramount, when his struggles with parents and male rivals or with his sexual awakening eclipsed all other conflicts, when his question of "What can you do when you have to be man?" formed the emotional center of the narrative, and when his delinquency, rebellion, and final reconciliation with parent culture typically structured the cinematic story of growing up. Many of the most discussed teen films of the 1970s—from *American Graffiti* to *Animal House*—return to an earlier era when male camaraderie, rituals of hypermasculine violence, and heterosexual conquests (or at least desires) govern a narcissistic male adolescent world *before* or on the precipice of the Vietnam War, the most serious battles of the Civil Rights movement, student protests, the sexual revolution, and the beginnings of second wave feminism. It is as if these filmmakers refuse to face the historical moment of the 1970s, filling the void left by the corrupted or bankrupt master narratives with a return to a charmingly rebellious delinquency of the 1950s or a Camelot-inspired early 1960s. Indeed, they make the implicit argument for me that *the* American teenager, whose troubles and eventual assimilation dominated so many earlier films and public debate, does not exist in 1970s America—that he does not belong there, cannot be figured there, or can only appear as a ghost, a revenant from an earlier time or almost a different country.

Besides the male-centric and largely nostalgic films that I refer to above and that Shary groups under the heading of "Masculine mythologies," there were infrequent instances in the 1970s of other classical subgenres of teen film, such as the school or teacher-savior picture and the hippie lifestyle films of the previous decade, and a group of films about "unhinged" teenage girls to which I will return below.[46] The films focusing on the youth counterculture or student protest movements, such as *The Strawberry Statement* (1970), *Taking Off* (1971), and even *Getting Straight* (1970) with a slightly older Elliot Gould starring, seem more like hippie hangover films than authentic youth dramas of the 1970s. *The Strawberry Statement*, with its story of one student's coming to political consciousness based on a nonfiction source text about the Columbia University protests of 1968, belongs more to the era of Haskell Wexler's *Medium Cool* (1969) or even Penn's *Alice's Restaurant* (1969) than the post-Kent State period of 1970s youth film. Similarly, *Taking Off*, Milos Forman's first film made in the United States, feels at odds with itself and the historical moment, blending together seemingly vérité footage of an open-mic audition, which includes 1960s-esque folk and rock performances by the likes of Carly Simon and Kathy Bates, with a farcical look at parents whose teenage children have run away out into a world they no longer understand. Confronted with a ridiculous organization known as "The Society for the Parents of Fugitive Children," the parents of the film's central runaway Jeannie learn to smoke marijuana to try to better understand the lifestyle attracting their child and end up in a besotted game of strip poker with another parental couple, losing all sight of the children they were meant to be rescuing.

On the other hand, the school films of the 1970s were more like throwbacks to an even earlier period. The hero-teacher of *Halls of Anger* (1970)—this time an African American former basketball star, teacher, and school administrator—must deal with the controversial busing issue and integration of a high school with a predominantly African American student population, but for Considine the film varies little from earlier models such as *Blackboard Jungle* and *To Sir With Love* (1967) and, therefore, is "trapped in the traditional stereotypical depiction of school life."[47] Quincy Davis, the crusading teacher, must gain the trust of one key student and fight with cynical or burned out teachers and administrators, and his mixture of compassion and understanding becomes the answer for his students and the troubled school. Another example, *The Paper Chase* (1973), likewise focuses on the by-now-familiar challenging relationship between a student and his hero-teacher, although in this instance the drama takes place at Harvard Law School. Finally, the 1970s saw the adaptation of John Knowles's acclaimed 1959 novel *A Separate Peace*. The film version from 1972 belongs unquestionably to the wave of male nostalgia films I will explore further below due to its narrated recollection several years after the central events in 1943 that brought together and tested two male friends at a boarding school. Perhaps belonging less to the typical school film subgenre examined by Considine, *A Separate Peace* does document the events challenging teenage students, even if those events are recast through the central device of what Stephen Tropiano calls "private nostalgia," where the central voice of the film, an adult narrator Gene, reveals a "bittersweet memory" of his role in the tragic fall that eventually led to his friend's death immediately before their call up into to World War II.[48] Although not set in the 1950s or early 1960s like so many of the nostalgic teen films of the era, *A Separate Peace* does point to the prevalence and gendered nature of this most prominent or discussed teen subgenre of the decade, which in many ways is an evocation of a 'traditional' teenage tale that the films examined in this book work to contradict, counter, or revise.

Although I will explore the role of nostalgia and its conservative function in more depth in the next chapter with a close reading of Lucas' *American Graffiti*, I would like to provide an overview here of several films of the era that employ nostalgia predominantly in service of male teenage desires and wish-fulfillment. With varying levels of success, films such as *Summer of '42* (1971), *American Graffiti*, *The Lords of Flatbush* (1974),

Cooley High (1975), *Fraternity Row* (1977), *Grease* (1978), *Animal House* (1978), and *The Wanderers* (1979) took audiences back to an earlier era (typically the late 1950s and early 1960s) when, the films argue, life was simpler, implicitly better, and boys could be boys. As with *A Separate Peace*, for example, *Summer of '42* returns to the World War II period to sentimentalize one boy's summer of maturation and his gentle loss of virginity with an older woman. Again, utilizing voiceover narration from the protagonist's adult perspective back on his youthful loss of innocence, the film follows the memoirs of its screenwriter Herman Raucher as he looks back on a summer vacation in Nantucket during the war when he palled around with his best friend Oscy and lost his virginity at 15 years of age to a woman who had just learned of her soldier husband's death overseas. As if the plot, narration, and source material do not illustrate well enough the structuring influence of nostalgia on the film, its opening sequence signals the mood strongly from the first few shots: set to a piano score, the film opens with weathered still photos of figures in the film and then begins with the adult Hermie's voice recalling the events of that momentous summer. This voiceover predictably returns at the end of the film (set again to sentimental music) to explain how he never saw the older woman Dorothy again, but the summer changed him irrevocably, "I lost Hermie forever." At once both awkwardly amusing, as when Hermie attempts to buy condoms at the small town drugstore, and tender in its reminiscences, the film found great success with audiences in 1971, who seemed to embrace its warmhearted look back at a time, as the narrator concludes, when "we were different . . . kids were different." Undoubtedly yearning for simpler times in the past, *Summer of '42* marked the beginning of a wave of films relying on, in Shary's words, a "strategy of avoiding present realities for a sweetened memory of the past," creating nostalgia for "the early post-war era when young men still felt a sense of superiority over women."[49] Although *Summer of '42* attempts to treat its central female love object with some maturity of understanding and sensitivity, the nostalgic films that followed were less delicate in their treatment and more clearly invested in the male dominance that Shary perceives in the era's films.

While *American Graffiti* was certainly the most successful and influential of these youth nostalgia films, a number of others including *Lords of Flatbush*, *The Wanderers*, and *Cooley High* (about which I will say more later) worked to reproduce period details and a number of stereotypical characters from the 1950s and early 1960s, gesturing to films from *The Wild One* and *Rebel Without a Cause* to the numerous j.d. pictures that followed in their wake. Yet, these films of the 1970s often lacked the complexities and serious conflicts of those classical teen films, opting instead to bathe the era in the neon glow of nostalgia, a kind of convenient amnesia. As Frances Gateward describes the process of employing nostalgia in film (for him, in a series of interracial romance features from the 1990s), these examples repeat a simple formula, "deploying the expected conventions such as first person narration, evocative associations made my period music, and even more importantly, the emotive aspects of nostalgia that center on the yearning for the 'good old days.'"[50] Set in 1962, notably before the Kennedy assassination, *American Graffiti* uses the unifying voice of Wolfman Jack on the radio rather than voiceover narration to structure the events, emphasizing even more the period music that became a major, if not *the* major, emotional core of the film's nostalgia.[51] The action of the film follows the events on one night for a group of four (white, heterosexual, and mostly middle-class) male friends (Steve, Curt, Toad, and John) on the cusp of adulthood and impending college for two of them; they cruise the strip in period cars reflecting the neon of the streets, meet up at their favorite hang out (the now infamous Mel's Drive-in), revisit their high school hop, and end the night victorious at a *Rebel*-like "chickie run."

Yet, significantly, there is no tragedy at the end of this "chickie run" or really in the film itself, only Curt's wistful departure without Steve the next morning and a set of predictable futures listed for just the four male friends (not their female companions) in an influential epilogue technique repeated by many teens films since. Chasing dream girls, playing harmless pranks on the police, and revving up for the macho rivalry of drag racing on the strip consume these fondly remembered teenage selves, while the complications of the Vietnam War, student protests, assassinations, and battles over civil rights are kept at a looming distance. In this autobiographical and personal film, male conquests, surging sexual desires, and hopes and fears for the future are the central concerns for young men at the end of an era when one could expect, according to screenwriter and director Lucas, a "warm, secure, uninvolved life" (i.e. the 'good old days').[52] Gone is the menacing danger of *The Wild One* or *Blackboard Jungle* and gone are the family crises, tragic events, and psychological distress of *Rebel Without a Cause*, and in their place, Lucas powerfully constructs a fantasyland of secure masculine pleasures, even as a couple of the players (notably Curt and John) seem to recognize the end is near. Later films inspired by *American Graffiti*'s affecting brand of nostalgia, which in fact permeated much of popular culture and even fashion in the early 1970s, failed to achieve its success but nevertheless followed its chauvinist bent.[53]

Two films in particular, *The Lords of Flatbush* and *The Wanderers*, stand out as indebted to *Graffiti*'s nostalgic mode, although the latter pushes further into an uncertain future. A low-budget film best known for helping to launch the careers of Sylvester Stallone and Henry Winkler, *The Lords of Flatbush* similarly reminisces about the escapades and desires of a group of four male friends, though two—Chico (played by Perry King) and Stanley (played by Stallone)—take the film's main focus. Set in the Flatbush neighborhood of Brooklyn in 1957, the film lovingly follows the teenage friends as they chase girls, play pool, hotwire cars, and talk over egg creams at the local malt shop. Chico and Stanley, who keeps pigeons like his Brando influence in *On the Waterfront*, spend most of the film struggling with romantic entanglements, which lead predictably to a pressured marriage for Stanley to his longtime girlfriend. As the wedding scene at the end becomes a kind of neighborhood carnival and celebration of Italian–American family ties, the film lingers with the male friends who are on the cusp of a major life change. The nostalgic mood is clearly emphasized in this scene through a final series of still images from the film accompanied by the bittersweet "Wedding Song" by Jamie Carr, whose lyrics recognize that "tomorrow we may go our separate ways," so raising a toast to these friends should commemorate that bond.

The Wanderers, on the other hand, returns to Lucas' tactic of gathering popular songs from the era (as the title would suggest) to send the audience back to the male gangs and their conquests in the Bronx in 1963. Moving from "Walk Like a Man" and, of course, "The Wanderer" to "My Boyfriend's Back," "Cherry Baby," and "Stand By Me," the film wants to capture a moment in time much like *Graffiti*, but significantly this tale of male gangs and heterosexual entanglements brings the action right up to the edge of what Lucas might see as the troubles of the 1960s, confronting not only Kennedy's assassination (seen in a television store window) but also the incipient unrest and anti-establishment sentiment expressed in a performance of Bob Dylan's "The Times They Are a-Changin'" and in two of the friends' move to San Francisco in the end. Cognizant of the coming changes and even attendant to the growing racial conflict enacted in the battles between youth gangs in the neighborhood, the film still falls back on predictable set pieces like the rumble won by our group of protagonists, The Wanderers, and the lead male character Richie's forced marriage to his pregnant girlfriend. Indeed, as with both *Graffiti* and *Lords of Flatbush*, the phallocentric focus of these films can envision only two incredibly unsympathetic roles for women: the resistant, then compliant, and then manipulative girlfriend or the unattainable seductress. That a central character will end up with one of these women (usually the former) is the great tragedy of these films and clearly, then, the nostalgia is for a time before this fateful union—in other words, for a time when male companionship provided a pleasure and mastery seemingly gone forever in the 1970s.

Certainly, one of the greatest contemporary social changes that these male nostalgia films retreat from is the challenge to gender norms and patriarchal dominance brought by second wave feminism. Their endings that erase or rewrite the redemptive picture of heterosexual union offered by classical teen films like *Rebel Without a Cause* is proof enough of the fraught relations between the sexes in this period. Moreover, a handful of films that Shary categorizes under the title "girls unhinged" further work to demonize the female teen in a way not entirely unlike the films about female delinquents in the 1950s and flappers in the 1920s and 1930s.[54] In films such as De Palma's *Carrie* (1976), *The Exorcist* (1973), *I Never Promised You a Rose Garden* (1977), and *The Little Girl Who Lives Down the Lane* (1976)—and I might also add Foster's earlier role in Scorsese's *Alice Doesn't Live Here Anymore* (1974)—teenage girls appear out of control, mentally unstable, or possessed by a destructive evil power of one sort or another, suggesting for Shary a "pernicious cultural anxiety about girls' power" at the time.[55] With *The Exorcist* and *Carrie*, the period produced two enormously successful horror films offering a terrifying picture of unnatural female powers, in both instances connected to female sexuality and bodily manifestations of maturation and otherness such as Carrie's first menses.[56] *I Never Promised You a Rose Garden* follows the pattern of a number of postwar narratives about teenage mental illness—initiated most famously by Salinger's *Catcher in the Rye* and later Plath's *The Bell Jar*—some of which were adapted for film or television such as *David and Lisa* (1962), *Go Ask Alice* (1973), *Sybil* (1976), and *Equus* (1977): the troubled young person cannot be helped by parents and must find peace with the support of a gifted and compassionate psychiatrist. (*Ordinary People* [1980] will repeat this basic plot only a few years later.) Fittingly for its ties to films like *Carrie*, the troubled female protagonist of *Rose Garden*, Deborah, begins her descent away from everyday reality after a health scare with a urethral tumor that causes social awkwardness and bodily shame. On the other hand, Jodie Foster's 13-year-old murderess Rynn Jacobs in *The Little Girl Who Lives Down the Lane* does not exhibit bodily manifestations of her otherness or destructive, perhaps evil, nature, but the film does manage to tie the mystery surrounding her and her crimes to her sexual allure (e.g. attracting the town pedophile). In other words, these films make a clear connection between female power, adolescent maturation, and sexuality that they warn is uncontainable, devastating for basic social structures (like the school or family), and ultimately deadly. Delinquency in young women has typically been figured in sexual terms (whether in the flaming youth of the 1920s or female gangs of the 1950s), but in the crisis period of the 1970s the changes brought by the sexual revolution appeared to turn that delinquency and power apocalyptic. However, I will propose in chapters three and four that an attractive "queer kid" surfaces in this era to counter this maligning of young women (and gender-queer young men).

If the unheeded pleasures and mastery of young men in traditional teen film was seen as bygone in the 1970s or seized away by perverse female powers, the very end of the decade and beginning of the next—the dawning of the Reagan era—reassuringly asserted this dominance again through the return of the father, which meant no longer having to locate mastery in a bittersweet, unreachable past. Many commentators have argued for an overwhelming reactionary turn in mainstream motion pictures at this time, dubbed "Reaganite entertainment" by Andrew Britton, showing signs of emergence even before Reagan's election, as early as the mythic blockbusters *Star Wars* (1977) and *Rocky* (1976) or vigilante backlash films like the *Death Wish* series (beginning in 1974).[57] In teen examples such as *Breaking Away* (1979), *The Great Santini* (1979), and *Ordinary People*, the return of the father-son love story—in what Robin Wood calls a new era of "recuperation and reaction" through the "Restoration of the Father"—overcomes incredible obstacles including death, violence, and dysfunction to restore this central relationship from classical teen film.[58] In a year that also saw the release of Robert Benton's forceful and affecting indictment of feminist discontent and canonization of the savior-father, *Kramer vs. Kramer*, both *Breaking Away* and *The Great Santini* manage to reconcile fathers and sons who are at odds: in the former the working-class father does not initially accept his son's interests in cycling and by extension Italian culture, and in the latter the father's hypermasculine and violent Marine persona divides him from his son and family. Fitting the new era, the sons in both films find a way to create a loving bond with these, at times, dysfunctional fathers. Finally, Redford's *Ordinary People* takes this "restoration" of the father to the extreme, ultimately banishing the mother entirely from the patriarchal home. Mary Tyler Moore's Beth Jarrett stands as one of the coldest and cruelest representations of motherhood since Jim Stark's viper of a dominant mother 25 years before. Her perverse preference for her dead son is unconcealed, and the psychic damage his death and her rejection has wrought on her surviving son, Conrad (played by Timothy Hutton), proves nearly deadly. Only with the help of a challenging and paternal male therapist and the backing of his previously cowed father does Conrad make it out of suicidal despair and guilt into a future where father and son can commit to their love for each other, as the final scene finds them able to express their "love" once the mother has been expelled from the scene. In this new period of Reaganite patriarchy, the father again learns to "stand up" and be the man his son needs, and if the mother fails to comply, she becomes superfluous and unwanted.

Finally, before turning to what I consider to be a significant moment in the evolution of teen film in the 1970s through a number of nontraditional films that parody, revise, and deconstruct the values or codes of the genre, I would like to touch on one nagging point for the genre hinted at in a few traditional and certainly nostalgic films from the era. The lack of racial diversity in representations of youth in mainstream American cinema, despite exemplary films such as *Blackboard Jungle*, unfortunately persisted throughout most of the twentieth century—even into the 1970s when the advances gained by the Civil Rights movement might have produced more complex depictions of African Americans on the big screen. Yet, there are still only a handful of films depicting African American youth and maturation in the 1970s and the foremost of these, *Cooley High* and *Sounder* (1972), turn back nostalgically to the past. Aside from Ossie Davis' independently produced *Black Girl* (1972) with its current-day Cinderella story of a teenaged African American high school dropout who aspires to be a dancer, the other two notable 1970s films that address African American youth follow in the path of Gordon Parks's groundbreaking film *The Learning Tree* (1969) in their settings in the past and, in the case of *Sounder*, in a direct confrontation with racial discrimination in an earlier age (the Depression-era South). More clearly, however, *Cooley High* models itself on the traditional teen film, particularly *American Graffiti*, and updates the setting to the Civil Rights era, placing the action in Chicago in 1964. Regrettably (and possibly due to the influence of *American Graffiti*), the film lacks the political force of *The Learning Tree* and *Sounder*, opting instead for a sometimes comic and sentimental look back on high school events drawing together four male teens.

Although *Cooley High* recognizes some of the harsh realities and deadly violence differentiating the white middle-class adolescence of *American Graffiti* from the process of growing up in a poor inner city environment, for the most part the film cultivates a sentimental, nostalgic mode not unlike that of Lucas' film. Perhaps taking some of its teen film influences from its production company, Nicholson and Arkoff's teenpic factory American International Pictures, *Cooley High* also mimics *Graffiti* in its personal source material, an autobiographical script by writer Eric Monte, who attended Edwin G. Cooley Vocational High School in Chicago near the Cabrini-Green public housing projects.[59] Although produced by an exploitation giant like AIP, *Cooley High* does not even attempt the controversial and debated political force of the most popular and lucrative African American narratives of the era, Blaxploitation films. Instead, it follows the adventures and intimacies of four male high school friends (focusing closely on two) who enjoy parties, girls, pranks, and a favorite hangout, Martha's soda fountain, not unlike Mel's Drive In, and the film's popular soundtrack—featuring 1960s Motown hits from The Supremes, The Temptations, Stevie Wonder, and the Four Tops—expressively recreates the era. *Cooley High* even ends with an epilogue revealing the futures for both male and female characters in the film. Nevertheless, this evocation of the edge of adulthood for Preacher (played by Glynn Turman) and Cochise (played by Lawrence Hilton-Jacobs) does address more serious problems and realistic teenage situations than *American Graffiti*'s fantasy-like night. Through the bond between Preacher, the well-read poet who cuts class, and Cochise, the basketball star focused on fun and girls, the film follows both their exhilarating adventures partying or joyriding in stolen cars *and* their everyday lives, including realistic depictions of family life (particularly involving Preacher's working mother and his responsibilities at home) and sexual relations. Scenes involving prostitutes and sex between Preacher and a love interest, Brenda, do not shy away from mature situations that teenagers do confront.[60] Moreover, the film's ending reflects the real dangers that these working-class African American youth potentially might face: a night of joyriding in a stolen car with two other guys (Stone and Robert) ends in all four of them being arrested, but when Preacher and Cochise are bailed out by Mr. Mason, a teacher at Cooley High, the other two assume betrayal and beat Cochise to death. Preacher's drunken, graveside heart-to-heart with his dead friend combines both the film's added seriousness and the nostalgic sentiment of so many male teen films from the period; he reads a poem to his friend that commemorates their good times together and Cochise's potential to be the "the greatest" and then abruptly ends the scene with his flight from the cemetery (to a future in Hollywood as a writer) set to the bittersweet tone of the Four Tops' "Reach Out I'll Be There." While attending to a few particularities of the historical moment—the epilogue notes one character's racially motivated violent death at the Democratic National Convention—for the most part, the film ends as other male nostalgia films from the period do, with wish-fulfillment (through a career in Hollywood) and a loving remembrance of a time before the 'real' turmoil of the late 1960s and the 1970s.[61]

Parody and Deconstruction of the Teen Film

While its persistent, appalling lack of racial diversity and its commemoration of white male dominance through a nostalgic recreation of the 1950s and early 1960s might indicate a continued commitment to a traditional path for teen film, a number of films in the 1970s signaled a change in the genre—a significant moment in its evolution—even if its racial bias remained difficult to resolve.[62] In fact, before the decade began, one enormously successful film, *Easy Rider*, gave an indication of how the genre was clearly at a turning point. Peter Fonda and Dennis Hopper's youth-cult phenomenon *Easy Rider* hardly fits the typical image of a teen film, with its employment of experimental techniques from European art cinema and its place in the wave of contentious new films produced by young directors in Hollywood that would eventually be known as New American Cinema. For one, its two male protagonists Billy and Wyatt are counter-cultural dropouts on the verge of 30, not 20 (director and star Hopper was 32 during the production), and its road-film picaresque plotting and self-conscious visual style (on display, for example, in its Mardi Gras scenes) belong much more clearly to European art cinema or American avant-garde and independent film traditions. Yet, Thomas Doherty, rightly I think, recognizes the film as a "teenpic amalgam as influential in its time as *Rock Around the Clock* had been in 1956."[63] The contemporary rock soundtrack, which dominates scene after scene of road exploration and contributed greatly to the film's popularity with youth audiences, obviously harkens back to the rock 'n' roll cycle of the 1950s alluded to in Doherty's statement, but also the presence of motorcycles, drug dealing as a form of delinquency, and even a monologue about alien civilizations evoke earlier teenpic subgenres.[64] Additionally, at the time the two stars had significant teen film credentials: Fonda had previously starred in *The Wild Angels*, the influential biker film that initiated the motorcycle films of the 1960s, and Hopper was a member of Buzz's menacing gang of toughs in *Rebel Without a Cause* nearly 15 years earlier. But the question remains, is *Easy Rider* really to be considered a teen film? Is an amalgam of allusions enough to qualify it as belonging to the body of films I have been outlining in this chapter? What I would like to argue is that a film like *Easy Rider* is as much a teen film as *American Graffiti*, but rather than nostalgically reproducing a past that possibly never existed (not even in teen film), amalgams like *Easy Rider* and other parodies or self-conscious productions reproduce the basic tropes and features of the genre in a baroque or deconstructionist version of the teen film.

In sum, the remainder of this chapter will examine a growing self-consciousness in teen films or films about youth which reaches a climax in the 1970s, marking a moment of transition for the genre that suggested ways it might or should evolve. For this conception of genre evolution, my argument will proceed primarily from the work of Thomas Schatz, whose analysis and breakdown of genre film into its basic components has been profoundly influential on genre film criticism. In his pioneering text, *Hollywood Genres: Formulas, Filmmaking, and the Studio System*, Schatz not only outlines the basic conventions that make up the grammar of film genres—from narrative conventions to formulaic settings, characters, iconography, and conflicts—but also establishes a central function for those genre films produced in mainstream American cinema. Identifying each film genre as a "coherent, value-laden narrative system," he finds it to be essentially a problem-solving mechanism working to "continually re-examine some basic cultural conflict" and find a solution, or, to be more exact, a "resolution."[65] No matter which film genre we examine, the films in that genre will always present a problem, or, in Schatz's terms, "some form of threat—violent or otherwise—to the social order," and the function of the films is to deal with that threat or conflict, solve the problem, and return the social order to its comfortable status quo.[66] In a simplified overview of the Western, for example, there is often a violent threat to a small town community or isolated group in the western United States (whether that threat be Native Americans, horse rustlers, or greedy ranchers), and the action of the film and its central protagonist, the Western hero or cowboy, is to resolve this threat and return the small community to its 'normal' state. For Schatz, every central cultural conflict presented by various film genres—from civilization versus savagery in the Western to individual freedom set against domestication in the musical—is raised and resolved by the films in order to *celebrate* "our collective sensibilities" or "the most fundamental ideological precepts" we in the audience supposedly share: in other words, "they examine and affirm 'Americanism' with all its rampant conflicts, contradictions, and ambiguities. . . . As social ritual, genre films function to stop time, to portray our culture in a stable and invariable ideological position."[67] This celebration and affirmation of the status quo (or an "invariable" American ideological position) is, simply, the job of the genre film for Schatz, as well other key genre critics such as Rick Altman.[68]

So then if genre films present such a tight ideological system and process of problem and (re)solution, why would they ever change or evolve? If they repeatedly present American culture in an "invariable ideological position," how does a revision of that portrayal come about and would the new film still represent the genre? The key to answering these questions resides in Schatz's own words above: the values that these films examine and the "Americanism" they affirm are rife with "contradictions" and "ambiguities." As Shatz asserts early on in his text, the central cultural conflicts for genre films and the opposing values presented there and embodied in the hero counterpose two contradictory values, both of which the culture esteems. Therefore, genre film at its core states a cultural contradiction that cannot be resolved without loss or an excising and concealing of the excess that results from the meeting of two appealing yet competing sets of values.[69] An obvious example from classical teen film is offered in *Rebel Without a Cause* when the film's resolution through heterosexual union and social integration necessitates the elimination of Plato, who represents individual freedom or a liminal status outside of the social order (e.g. through a socially disruptive queer sexuality), which cannot be tolerated if socialization or assimilation is the ultimate goal for the teenage hero. Therefore, one can see that the repeated iteration of a cultural contradiction that cannot be resolved without loss, or what Schatz calls a "violent reduction," might result in an emphasis on the conflict rather than the resolution (or on the lengths to which the culture will go to resolve such contradictions).[70] From this knotty problem and contrary to his notion of an undeniable celebration or affirmation of the status quo through resolution, Schatz concludes that "we must consider the possibility that genres function as much to challenge and criticize as to reinforce the values that inform them," and this challenge means they often work to "*renegotiate* the tenets of American ideology," rather than reinforce their invariable truth.[71] Most importantly for the present argument, genre evolution offers a place for this renegotiation to most openly proceed. Key to Schatz's idea of genre evolution as a form of growing self-consciousness is the sense that as film genres mature, they become more aware of their contradictions and, therefore, ideologically unstable: "as genres develop their conflicts are stated ever more effectively, while their resolutions become ever more ambiguous and ironic."[72] Without a stable resolution to affirm the status quo and successfully eliminate excess, films created later in a genre's development struggle more directly with central conflicts and contradictions, articulating and emphasizing the problem it is supposedly their function to solve. By stressing the problem instead of the solution, these later genre films suggest only evolution will allow for a renegotiation of basic American tenets.

However, the models that Schatz focuses on to explicate the process of film genre evolution stress the formal innovations and self-consciousness of the later films in the genre's development rather than the ideological shake up that also occurs. Although Schatz sets up the dual evolution of a film genre's formal elements, an "internal" revision, and cultural or thematic elements, as "external" or "real world" factors force change, the majority of his discussion follows the work of Henri Focillon (in *The Life of Forms in Art*) to give a model for reworking, revising, and refining the conventional *form* of the cinematic work of art.[73] Focillon's model offers four stages in the life of a cultural form: an "experimental" stage, a "classical" stage, an age of "refinement," and finally, a "baroque" stage, also known as the "mannerist" or "self-reflexive" stage.[74] Thus, an art form like the genre film would pass from a phase when its form is established to a stage when the conventions reach "equilibrium" and then the form becomes increasingly self-conscious of itself as art, moving from a period of stylistic embellishment to the final stage where the overstated style and formal qualities become the "content" of the work.[75] For Schatz, this formal evolutionary process takes the genre film from thematic or ideological "transparency" in its classical stage to an overly stylized "opacity" as it evolves, so that the classical conventions mutually understood by both filmmakers and audience, which allowed for an unhindered transmission of "the genre's social message" or ideology, are parodied and subverted to the point that the formal conventions (and their embellishment) are all that the films transmit.[76] Simply put, later films in a genre's evolution become increasingly formalist and self-reflexive and less concerned with narrative's social function, which explains why these later films are often considered more artistic and complex (ambiguous, ironic, stylized) and attractive prospects for so-called auteurs. While this model might prove useful for understanding some of the parodic elements in 1970s teen film, it does not address the thematic and ideological critique equally central to this evolutionary moment for the genre.

Cognizant as well of external or "real world" factors that might influence the narrative world of a film genre and the audience's acceptance of it (e.g. the changing views of Native Americans as the twentieth century progressed), Schatz briefly examines another model focused particularly on the Western by semiotician and psychoanalytic film theorist Christian Metz. Metz argues in *Language and Cinema* that genre films, while often possessing elements of parody even in their earliest iterations, become more of a self-critique as the genre evolves. For example, although a "classic" Western like *My Darling Clementine* (1946) might have elements of self-parody, as the genre progressed through the 1950s, it began a period of "contestation" when the hero faltered and "looked forward to retirement," destabilizing the basic conflict of the genre and contesting the certainty of its outcome.[77] By the time the Italian Westerns by Sergio Leone came along, the genre had moved for Metz from "contestation" to a mode of "deconstruction," where the "entire film is an explication of the code and of its relation to history" resulting in "critique" rather than simple parody.[78] It is the "relation to history" that differentiates Metz from formalist analyses such as Focillon's because it stresses cultural history rather than just formal progression. As Schatz concludes in his summary of Metz's argument, the "classic-parody-contestation-critique progression" asserts a growing self-consciousness in the audience and genre filmmakers concerning *both* the formal qualities of the genre and its "social function."[79] In other words, as a genre evolves, the films and their audience become more aware of the conflict being waged between competing values and the ideology seemingly reinforced by the film's resolutions, and the films themselves, therefore, begin to deconstruct or critique that conflict, its central combatants and solutions, and its "relation to history." The renegotiation of the ideological work of classical films in the genre has begun and a challenging or subversion of these basic codes becomes possible, enabling the genre to evolve both formally and thematically.

What I am arguing, then, following Metz's model is that the 1970s offered a moment of critique for teen film that went beyond parody in a number of films which deconstructed the genre's codes and their "relation to history" or American master narratives. First, however, this section will address the strong presence of parody in films of the period and a critical self-consciousness. Elements of parody had been present in the teen film genre since its classical period when exploitation films of the late 1950s multiplied teenpic elements to a ridiculous point of excess, but it was not until the Beach Party films of the 1960s that one might argue the genre entered a phase of parody and possible contestation. As I mentioned above, the Beach Party films reproduced elements from the earlier subgenres of teenpics, such as the juvenile delinquent on a motorcycle, only to use them as points of humor. In the original *Beach Party* the beatniks who read poems at "Big Daddy's" and the bikers led by a ridiculously unthreatening Erik Von Zipper (played by 40-year-old television comic veteran Harvey Lembeck) parody some of the most menacing or disturbing youth subcultures from the 1950s with a comic exaggeration that was all part of the 'good clean fun' of the films. One might even argue that the casting of Disney's most famous Mouseketeer from the 1950s, Annette Funicello, and the bestselling teen crooner at the end of that decade, Frankie Avalon, had a self-aware quality to it. Nevertheless, the aspects of parody present in these 1960s films would themselves be referenced and expanded upon in one of the biggest hits of the 1970s, the musical phenomenon *Grease* (1978).

Adapted from the incredibly successful Broadway musical created by Jim Jacobs and Warren Casey, *Grease* follows the trials for a teenage couple and their friends at the end of the 1950s, and although it incorporates the signs and, particularly, the sounds of 1950s youth culture, it is not exactly from the same nostalgic point of view as *American Graffiti* and others. While I agree with Shary that the film's ending for Sandy and Danny reinforces a "masculine ideal" by returning to the earlier era's sexual double standard for young men and women, I am not so sure that the film is only "paying homage to the older films," such as the beach movies of the 1960s and juvenile delinquency films of the 1950s.[80] Rather, I would argue that the film's self-conscious references to (and casting of) icons of 1950s and early-1960s popular culture reads at times like a challenging parody of teen film, as opposed to sincere reverence or nostalgic longing. Holding back from the term parody, Stephen Tropiano's examination of the film as "self-conscious nostalgia" gives an idea of the bewildering number of references or uses of 1950s and 1960s popular culture in the musical: Rizzo famously references Sandra Dee (the original Gidget) in "Look at Me, I'm Sandra Dee," teen idol and beach partier Frankie Avalon emerges as Frenchy's angel in "Beauty School Drop Out," and most of the adults in the film are played by film, television, and stage icons of the earlier period—from Joan Blondell and Eve Arden to Sid Caesar and Dody Goodman.[81] Particularly, though, I would like to consider the "Sandra Dee" number, along with Rizzo's solo complaint "There Are Worse Things I Could Do," and the Frankie Avalon song

"Beauty School Dropout," all of which were part of the original stage production. Although the male greaser number "Greased Lightning" surely provides evidence of the film's parody of masculine (and latently homoerotic) hot rod teenpics and drag racing subplots with lines like "With new pistons, plugs, and shocks, I can get off my rocks/You know that I ain't braggin', she's a real pussy wagon – Greased Lightnin'," the self-conscious parody by and sincere concerns of female teens perhaps best highlights the film's moments of contestation.

Through the female teens in the film, *Grease* does more than play to masculine fantasies or reinforce sexual double standards. Instead, certain musical numbers critique these double standards and parody the teen films from earlier eras that reinforce them. Most obviously, "Look At Me, I'm Sandra Dee" allows Stockard Channing's Rizzo to perform a biting mockery of the rules of sexual conduct or gender norms and the ways that popular culture, from *Gidget* to Elvis Presley, fuels them. Her blonde-wigged exaggerated performance of the coy "virginity" of the likes of Sandra Dee, Annette Funicello, and Doris Day points out the unreality of these female models and the ridiculousness of their purity—never drinking, swearing, smoking, or "rat"-ing their hair—which the scene reinforces with her eye rolls and the laughter of the other Pink Ladies. Towards the end of the song, she presents perhaps a more realistic picture of female desires underneath the lyrics' false protests, flirting with the photo of Troy Donohue, opening her legs at the line "I'm no object of lust," and perfectly mimicking the gyrating pelvis of Elvis Presley while simultaneously squealing the line, "Keep that pelvis far from me!" In fact, her performance of hyperfemininity transforms queerly in the end to its opposite, as she seems to be imitating the Italian–American machismo of her costar John Travolta with her intonation and body movements at the vulgar lyric, "Hey fongool, I'm Sandra Dee!" Her performance, therefore, underscores the artificial nature of both feminine and masculine performances in popular culture and subverts them through an accurate and self-conscious comic imitation.

In her solo "There Are Worse Things I Could Do," Rizzo then answers this system of gender norming and sexual double standards with the very real anguish experienced by a female teen on the wrong end of that social order—a delinquent as only a girl can be in teen film. She might be "trashy" and "no good" according to dominant culture for acting on her desires with "a boy or two," but to her a "worse" thing to do would be to tease, to flirt or "press against them when we dance" and then "refuse to see it through," as 'good girls' are taught to do as part of the hypocrisy of the double standard. Finally, with perhaps the most strength and conviction she has exhibited so far in the song's performance, Rizzo questions the greatest myth of all, saving oneself for "Mr. Right" by taking cold showers, when this dream just "won't come true" for many women. This verse is perhaps the closest the film will come to recognizing both the harsh realities of the sexual inequities that insist on *female* purity before marriage and the major tenet of second wave feminism and the sexual revolution that contested women's subordination of their desires to the single "dream" of finding self-worth in marriage and "Mr. Right," which could amount to throwing a "life away" as Rizzo fears. Although the scene ends with a return to her jealousy and vulnerability in the turmoil of intimacy with Kenickie, Rizzo's combined impact in these two songs not only mocks the conventions of teen popular culture in beach movies and Elvis performances but also contests the treatment of female teens in that popular culture and the dominant culture of the time. She provides a self-conscious rebuttal to decades of teen film where the female sexual delinquent appeared as tragic or a monster; Rizzo is no monster and, even more provocatively, she is not punished for her deviant sexual behavior or her outspoken criticism, as the end finds her *not* pregnant and happily paired off with her favorite sexual partner.

"Beauty School Dropout," on the other hand, focuses its parody on both the fantasy of the male teen idol and the class biases of many teen films. In another sympathetic portrayal of a working-class female teenager (until the very end, Rizzo certainly plays the working-class, dark other to Sandy's middle-class, blonde suburban virgin), the loveable airhead Frenchy sees little use for high school when her dream is to be a beautician, but sadly she fails at this dream as well, struggling in her classes at beauty school and dyeing her hair bright pink in the process. Yet, interestingly, the film continues to follow her plight, even if as a subplot, which perhaps reveals the original musical roots for the film: a stage production named after the infamous "greasers" of the 1950s whose working-class masculinity defined a youth subculture formed around greased-back hair, gang violence, and hot rods. Frenchy's experiences documented in the song, being placed between the options of beauty school or finishing high school and joining the "steno pool," mark a rare instance of addressing working-class female adolescence beyond girl gangs and sexual delinquency. Her teen idol angel, Frankie Avalon, might mock her difficulties, having "flunked shampoo" and dyed her hair a color that perhaps only "a hooker" could appreciate, but the song does focus on her concerns and her future. Moreover, the cruelty of her teen angel's honest evaluation serves to puncture the romance inherent to the male teen idol-crooner figure. Frankie Avalon might be dressed in all white and have a burst of sun rays like a halo around his head, but these devices work to accentuate the parody of the number, lampooning the dreamlike visions of teen idols in popular culture with his cruel straight talk. Looking like an angel but talking like a devil, Avalon's lyrics mention her nose job, ask why she keeps her "feeble hopes alive" when she does not have "the drive" to complete beauty school, and likens her to a "hooker." In his seemingly worthwhile attempt to convince her to "go back to high school," he insults her and berates her, "Who wants their hair done by a slob?" In the end, despite his being the teen idol of beach parties of the 1960s, Frenchy must surely welcome his return to "that malt shop in the sky." She does go back to Rydell High, but the film has managed to voice concerns and aspirations that rarely appear in teen film and has done so at the expense of the fantasy of the romantic male teen crooner.

I would argue that these moments of parody and self-consciousness can disrupt the conventional resolutions that work to conclude the film with the "masculine ideal" that Shary proposes. As the final scene finds everyone "together" and all problems and differences settled, the musical number again foregrounds excess and spectacle with Danny and Sandy lifting off into the sky in the mythic Greased Lightning above the celebrating carnival of teenagers. The cartoonish unreality of this moment serves to underscore the falseness or fantasy wish-fulfillment of the many happy endings, especially in terms of heterosexual romance, that resolve the disturbing conflicts of teen film (*Rebel Without a Cause* being only the most obvious example). Through these examples, the film evokes Metz's model of genre evolution at the point of using parody for the purpose of contestation. *Grease* may not work as a complete deconstruction of the genre, but its parody has elements of criticism. It is important to be clear about my use of the term "parody" here, since Metz does not define the term in his analysis of genre. In their overview of comic forms in popular film and television, Steve Neale and Frank Krutnik differentiate parodies from genre hybrids in that film genre parodies create humor through "gags and funny lines which specifically use as their raw material the conventions of the genres involved."[82] In simplest terms, parodies imitate and reproduce familiar features, conventions, or even icons of a genre to make us laugh.

Nonetheless, there is some debate about the potential critical or social impact of genre parody. Neale and Krutnik, following the prominent work by Linda Hutcheon, insist that one must distinguish between parody, which merely cites and highlights "aesthetic conventions" of another artwork, and satire, which "draws on – and highlights – social ones."[83] On the other hand, despite finding film parody to be "a comic, yet generally *affectionate*, and distorted imitation of a given genre, auteur, or specific work," Wes Gehring allows for the possibility of an "undercutting" of the codes of the genre in what he calls the "creative criticism" of film parodies, wherein they take a "critical approach" to conventions of the genre and possibly "provide a historical tenor of the times."[84] It stands to reason that the humor created in parodies often will come from an undercutting or critical exaggeration of features of the genre and not always in an "affectionate" way. Moreover, if one considers the breakdown of genre provided by Schatz, it is difficult to imagine separating the formal conventions of the genre and the values and social order offered there. How can one distinguish between the conventional conflict or hero of a genre and the values or social norms inherent in or expressed by them? Schatz argues, for example, that the hero or central protagonist of genre films often contains within him or her both sides of the cultural conflict at the center of the genre's problem-solving mechanism; therefore, if a film genre parody undercuts or lampoons the basic features and beliefs of that hero, then certainly the values of the social order and its central concerns fall under criticism. This critical potential of genre parody, which seems closer to Metz's sense of parody and contestation, is better reflected in Simon Dentith's more recent definition of "parody" as "any cultural practice which provides a relatively polemical allusive imitation of another cultural product or practice" because he specifically adds the word "polemical" to address the "evaluative aspect of parody" and its more "contentious or 'attacking' mode."[85] While he does not insist that all parodies employ a ferocious attack—and in fact some parodies serve a conservative function by "policing the boundaries" of expression—he does strongly argue for a "subversive" tradition of parody that "attacks the official word, mocks the pretensions of authoritative discourse, and undermines the seriousness with which subordinates should approach the justifications of their betters."[86] It is this definition of parody that perhaps best captures Metz's notion of parody and contestation in the life cycle of a genre: a genre reaches a point where a series of films employ parody to critique, attack, and mock the authoritative discourse that is the codes and values of the genre. Parody becomes the tool then for subordinates to undermine the authority of the status quo being reinforced or affirmed in the genre film's classic resolution.

Focused more on literary parody than the many recent popular uses of it, Dentith does recognize a proliferation of the mode in postmodern works of art and the popular texts influenced by them, which I would argue must include the wave of popular film parodies in the 1970s. The works of Mel Brooks are perhaps the principal examples of this development in 1970s American cinema, but numerous comic films during the era employed parody directed at various genres, including of course *Grease*, which David Cook labels as a "spoof" or "parody of 1950s rock 'n' roll programmers and 1960s beach-party movies."[87] Indeed, Cook recognizes parody as "the quintessential comic film form of the seventies" thanks in large part to the success and influence of films such as Brooks' *Blazing Saddles* (1974).[88] However, he relies on Gehring's definition of parody, focusing on formal and aesthetic qualities and the notion of "affection" found there, which encourages him to suggest that works by filmmakers like Brooks act as both "tribute" and "send up" so that the allusions in the film parodies "incarnate the decade's dual (and somewhat schizoid) impulse toward cynical nose thumbing and reverent nostalgia."[89] Raising that other major trend in 1970s cinema (nostalgia) interestingly establishes the undeniable self-consciousness and allusions central to so many teen films in the 1970s, which would indicate a moment of genre evolution, but again I would argue that the works employing parody like *Grease* do more than pay homage or "cynically" thumb their nose at earlier genre films.

Significantly, the concept of "attacking" parody offered by Dentith and echoed in Metz's notion of contestation and critique more closely resembles another major trend in 1970s cinema outlined by Cook: genre *revision*. Announced by the mixing of serious and comic genres in *Bonnie and Clyde* (1967), a film largely considered the inaugural work of New American Cinema, the period saw a series of attacks and reconsiderations of classical Hollywood genres by the young filmmakers of the New Wave. For Cook, the "splintering and dislocation of classical genres" begun by *Bonnie and Clyde* was taken up then by Hopper's *Easy Rider*; both films were inspired by the challenging of Hollywood narrative and genre conventions in the "particular brand of modernism" of the French New Wave, which utilized both "exaggeration and parody" in addition to visual experimentation.[90] Thereafter, a host of filmmakers from Penn and Kubrick to Altman and Bogdanovich experimented with the form of classical film genres and even went so far as "revising, 'correcting,' and/or deconstructing them."[91] For the purposes of this chapter, I would like to move from some of these more renowned, auteurist examples of genre revision to consider the impact on the teen film genre (already hinted at in the reference to *Easy Rider*) of the experimentation with genre in the period. Although Cook labels it both a parody and a genre hybrid, *The Rocky Horror Picture Show*, like *Grease*, contains moments of revision or, one might argue, deconstruction of a number of genres, one of which is the teen film.[92]

While many critics note the mixing of genres that makes *The Rocky Horror Picture Show* such a carnival of filmmaking and film viewing, noting in particular the blending of science fiction, horror, and the musical, few recognize the film's attention to a number of cycles within the teen film genre, particularly those favored in the exploitation fare of the 1950s and 1960s.[93] Although Hoberman and Rosenbaum's history of *Midnight Movies* establishes that Richard O'Brien, the show's creator and one of its stars, originally started writing a rock musical entitled *They Came From Denton High* and wrote from his passion for B-grade science fiction films *and* the 1950s rock music made into a phenomenon by the teenagers of that era, Weinstock's recent work only locates a few studies that mention the allusions to teen film in *Rocky Horror*'s multitude of genre allusions.[94] He cites Kincade and Katovich's study, which recognizes the film as partly a parody of the "genres that dominated the 1950s and early 1960s 'teenage' movies," and he seems to agree with Twitchell's assessment that the entire film could be read as an adolescent sexual rite of passage where the young person learns "it's okay to be a wild and untamed thing for a little while, but ultimately one must grow up."[95] Just on its surface and in a different way from *Easy Rider*, the film seems an amalgam of teenpic subgenres or cycles. Obviously, the early romantic musical numbers between Brad and Janet hearken back to the clean teenpics and Beach Party films of the late 1950s and 1960s, and Eddie's presence and intrusive burst of "Hot Patootie, bless my soul, I really love that rock 'n' roll" allude to both the motorcycle and delinquency teen films of the 1950s as well as the rock 'n' roll cycle of films initiated by *Rock Around the Clock*. Eddie even has his own female fan, Columbia, who at one point dons the iconic beanie and ears of members of the Mickey Mouse Club. Also, one cannot forget that one of the most prolific and popular cycles of teenpics in the 1950s was the subgenre of horror. Particularly, *Rocky Horror* appears to be referencing that group of teenpics known as "weirdies," which incorporated any number of fantastic elements—science fiction, gothic horror, freaks and monsters (even zombies), or an array of shocking plot points—as long as the film could be made quickly and the outrageous plot and sensational title would attract the teenage audience.[96] Particularly, two films—*I Was a Teenage Frankenstein* (1957) and *How to Make a Monster* (1958)—stand out at antecedents for Frank-N-Furter's antics and creation of Rocky; these teenage monster movies, according to Harry Benshoff, are exemplary for a trend in the teenpics of the era in which adult scientists, psychologists, or teachers "prey upon same-sex teenagers and attempt to turn them into monsters," often with Charles Atlas-like physiques.[97] However, it is in the figures of Brad and Janet, who decide to visit their high school science teacher, Dr Everett Scott, on that fateful night, where the film engages most directly with that tradition of youth on screen.

After the introductory song "Science Fiction/Double Feature," which establishes quite well the film's play with a classical genre and the icons and stars central to it, the film soon focuses on a young couple whose confusion, fear, and reeducation will make up one of the key subversions and genre revisions in *Rocky Horror*. At the wedding of their friends Ralph and Betty, Brad Majors and Janet Weiss appear to be two wholesome young people from the Eisenhower era or even the early days of Kennedy's "Camelot"; Janet has caught the bouquet in her lavender wedding suit and dreams of becoming someone's wife. Yet, as the two walk past the billboard that reads "Denton: Home of Happiness," the sound of crows and thunder in the background strikes a disquieting note. Even as Janet gets her wish and Brad's cliché-saturated love song "Dammit, Janet" produces the ring she so clearly desires, the film makes a mockery of their courtship through Riff Raff and Magenta dressed as the figures in Grant Wood's "American Gothic"; the two serve as backup singers, punctuating inane lines like "The river was deep, so I swam it" with a nasally chorus of "Janet." Brad may think the ring proves he is "no joker," but he is certainly the butt of the scene's joke in his high waters and plaid tie and cummerbund so that the audience suspects of the three options ("good, bad, or mediocre"), their love will go the way of the third. Janet's concern for the size of the ring compared to Betty's confirms their shallowness and Brad's dress and demeanor expose him as, for lack of a better word, a square. In another era, perhaps of clean teens and young love, this declaration of love would have provided the climax of a film's plot, bringing Frankie and Annette back together again at the end of another Beach Party for example, but here the scene ends with them standing in front of a small coffin, a child's size, and loomed over by the dour faces of Riff Raff, Magenta, and Columbia in mocking puritanical black. The innocence and assurance of their heterosexual union would appear to be dead on arrival. They are as the Criminologist describes them in the next scene—"young, ordinary, healthy kids" on a night out—but the playing of Nixon's resignation speech in this same scene reinforces the message of the opening: these "normal kids" may have fit in an earlier era, but in the post-Watergate, post-Vietnam 1970s, their sincerity and innocent, virginal romance become a joke. Their marriage is empty before it began or headed to a soulless American Gothic. We have a mockery and a clear critique of teenybopper romance in this version of teen film, and the expected heteronormativity and resolution of integration and domestication for the young couple is certainly not assured.

Unsurprisingly, then, once they enter the mad world of the Frankenstein place with its unruly mixture of genres and pop or youth culture allusions, they are corrupted by its strange world and its 1970s brand of sexual delinquency. Confronted by a different sort of party than the beach kind, in which one takes a "Time Warp" with a freakish group of Transylvanians and is the guest of an imposing new delinquent, the "Sweet Tranvestite" from Transsexual Transylvania, Brad and Janet initially attempt to maintain their composure and their purity. Though Janet does have the sense that "This isn't the Junior Chamber of Commerce," she still holds on to her traditional values, asking if Frank is Columbia's husband despite ample evidence from the "Sweet Transvestite" that such conventionality is not likely. Yet, when they are stripped of their clothes and invited up to Frank's lab to meet his newest creation, Rocky, their old values lose hold. Janet defends Brad at first by insisting she prefers men without "too many muscles," but soon she finds herself in bed with Frank after he has already shared his "bridal suite" with Rocky. She resists at first, arguing for her virginity, but soon she is taking Frank up on his offer of pleasure and moving quickly from the notion that she was "saving" herself for marriage to a flirting assurance of Brad's deception, "Promise you won't tell Brad." Then, more disturbingly for the traditional values of the teen film, Brad also betrays Janet with Frank in an identical fashion. Brad wants to blame Frank for their liaison, but he also agrees all too quickly with Frank's logic that "there's no crime in giving yourself over to pleasure." The young heterosexual couple has been divided and opened up by the pleasures that the androgynous and ambisexual Frank offers, bringing them gladly from the 1950s and 1960s right up to the new queer pleasures of the 1970s.

Beginning with a subversive parody of young romance on the verge of holy matrimony, the film moves to a critique of compulsory heterosexuality and a deconstruction of gender, two aspects of the traditional teen film rarely challenged before the 1970s. What one critic calls the film's "unrelenting deconstruction of Americana" extends to the young couple of teen film, whose traditional values and stock codes unravel in the face of the gender-queer and sexually open delinquent, Frank.[98] Janet, the "normal" young woman with a Peter Pan collar and excellent manners, not only has sex with Frank but also implores Rocky to "Toucha-Toucha-Toucha-Touch" her, experiencing a kind of sexual revolution appropriate for the era, and Frank's sexual conquest of Brad queers the upstanding young male hero of the genre, just as Frank has already queered the motorcycle delinquent Eddie. In this one instance of genre revision or deconstruction, *Rocky Horror* lays bare the homoeroticism of biker or male gang films and allows for the sexual tension in *Rebel*'s famous triangle of Jim, Judy, and Plato to be released, or come out of the closet. Frank's play with an overly stylized or campy performance of gender detaches it from sexuality, and the pleasure that he gains from this play convinces the young heteronormative couple to join in. As I will explore in Chapters 3 and 4, this queering of teen film and its characters and plot is not isolated to one film. However, as Jeffrey Wienstock notes, many critics view the ending of the film as a disciplining of these subversive desires and gender play since Frank's death and the aftermath suggest a rejection of his devotion to "absolute pleasure" and a return to the status quo, that is, "one must grow up."[99] Yet, I agree with Weinstock's contention that the film's dark ending ultimately struggles to contain "the subversive force of the rest of the film and especially of Curry's *tour-de-force* performance" so that the audience mourns the return of the social order, feeling a "painful absence and a sense of missed opportunities" that make them "resent" or reject the status quo rather than embrace it.[100] It is this subversive power and critiquing ability that I would also stress in *Rocky Horror*'s play with genre, gender, and sexuality in the realm of the teen film.

Figure 1.1 P. J. Soles and The Ramones demolish the 1950s teen film and Rock 'n' Roll High School *Credit: New World Pictures/Photofest*

While one might note a similar vein of parodic or campy excess in other films of the era, such as Walter Hill's 1979 cult classic *The Warriors*, which at times takes the juvenile gang or delinquent film to farcical extremes, I would like to conclude with a film produced by Roger Corman at his New World Pictures studio, the last of the low-budget studios in the ilk of teenpic giant American International Pictures. *Rock 'n' Roll High School* (1979) seems in many ways to be the last gasp of the teenpic exploitation films and yet its self-awareness and critique also herald an evolution for teen films insisted upon in the 1970s. Recognized by Doherty for its recycling of "predecessor narratives" from the teenpic heydays and for "revamp[ing] old genres," *Rock 'n' Roll High School* reads in the critic's description like an exemplar of a deconstructionist moment in genre evolution: the film is "a slick catalog of teenpic influences, cheerfully appropriating and demolishing the conventions of the 1950s prototypes."[101] The film's basic plotline, of a teenage student fighting an oppressive school administration for her right to love and play rock 'n' roll music (specifically, The Ramones), could be taken from any number of the rock 'n' roll teenpics from the 1950s that were initiated by *Rock Around the Clock*, and the allusions to these films begin early. In a moment playing on two of the most famous scenes in one of the most influential teen films of the 1950s, *Blackboard Jungle*, a boring lesson on Beethoven is cut short not when the teacher's records are smashed but when his turntable is commandeered by Riff Randell, the central female protagonist played by P. J. Soles. She announces "This is Rock 'n' Roll High School!" to a cheering group of students in the courtyard lunchroom who begin to dance to The Ramones' "Sheena Is a Punk Rocker" as the credits roll. Taking the opening credits of *Blackboard Jungle* to the extreme, the music spreads through the school on the public address system, spurring students to throw away their work and dance in the halls and eventually crashing the glass doors of the Board of Education where a new tough principal is being introduced to Vince Lombardi High School. The film sets up a common generic battle between Riff and the iron hand of Principal Togar, but the choice of a female protagonist as the central delinquent or trouble maker locates the film firmly in the second wave feminism of the late-1970s. Yet, the real change comes with the film's secondary focus on Tom, the blonde-haired blue-eyed varsity athlete (played by Vince Van Patten), who becomes the target for much of the film's ridicule and revision.

Tom, the captain of the football team who epitomizes *the* American teenager as he has been constructed in twentieth-century popular and dominant culture, has become an outcast or misfit in the 1970s rock 'n' roll high school. He is, in short, a loser, who bores girls out of dates and is hopelessly behind the times. In the opening credit sequence, he is singled out in his white letterman's sweater and school tie reading a book entitled *Dancing Madness* and following guide feet on the cement to try to keep up with the music of The Ramones, which is so naturally enjoyed by all the other students. To add insult to injury, a major subplot of the film then becomes Tom's quest for a date with Riff Randell, who is only interested in the unconventional punk otherness of The Ramones. He is forced visit the school's odd scam artist hustler Eaglebauer (played by Clint Howard) to ask for help, having to admit his virginity and "sexual" emergency in a stall of the boy's bathroom and pay with a credit card for a promised date. In other words, the film has taken the white, middle-class, heterosexual male teen who has predominantly represented adolescence on screen and made him the butt of the film's jokes (much like Brad Majors), as the new central teenager Riff declares him "not half as hot as Joey Ramone." Tom must embarrassingly take lessons on how to woo a girl from Howard's sleazy Eaglebauer, who teaches the football star with a blow up doll that punches Tom in the face when he tries to caress her breasts. When Tom finally finds a real girl who is willing to practice with him, he fails to find her breasts even as she seems eager for his contact. Ultimately, Tom wins and then loses a date with Riff, who stands him up for The Ramones' concert, and somewhat predictably Tom learns how to assimilate into the new teenage crowd by joining in at the concert and helping Riff connect with her favorite band; he wins the interest of Kate (the girl who was eager to "practice" with him) and the two of them end up with a punk rock makeover. In this 1970s version of the teenpic, it is the traditional American teenager who must revise himself to fit in the peer culture that has so clearly changed. The freaks, it would seem, are running the show and the teen film must change accordingly through a self-conscious recognition of the outdated codes and values of the classical films of the genre.

Ultimately, the ironic self-reflexivity and deconstructive humor of The Ramones' punk rock is mirrored by the film itself. At the concert, the band plays songs like "Blitzkrieg Bop" and "Teenage Lobotomy" and the lyrics to the latter appear on screen, with words like "LOBOTOMY" and lines such as "I got no mind to lose" in bold block letters. The knowing punk irony of these songs makes the band a perfect contrast to a group like Sha Na Na, whose nostalgic recycling of 1950s rock punctuated the *Grease* soundtrack. The Ramones self-consciously play on the rock music and iconography of the 1950s but from a critical, confrontational, and humorous position that insists, for instance, that "I'm a Teenage Lobotomy!" The film then takes its cue from this postmodern punk position and announces its own self-consciousness about the genre and tradition it uses and revises. As the final confrontation between Principal Togar and Riff Randell comes to a climax, the film has a disc jockey (ala Wolfman Jack) comment on the action. Riff, The Ramones, and their mob of crazed teens, plus the music teacher, descend on the school and react to the principal's action of burning rock records by taking a chainsaw to the student's "permanent records" and tearing apart the school. Then, in what seems like a direct reference to *American Graffiti* and other rock 'n' roll films, the d.j. breaks on screen and with an exaggerated and self-aware performance assesses the moment: "Miss Togar has given the students of Rock 'n' Roll High an ultimatum, a classic confrontation between mindless authority and the rebellious nature of youth. The moment of truth is at hand. What will these kids do next?" Just as Doherty describes it, this is clearly a film that playfully and amusingly takes on the tropes of the genre and enjoys disrupting and reversing them. Rather than bend to mindless authority or join in a fantasy carnival of good will (as in *Grease*) or reconcile with parent culture, these teenagers choose instead to blow up the school. The school burns down as The Ramones perform Riff's song "Rock 'n' Roll High School" and no reconciliation with parent culture is sought or desired. There is no disclaimer as in *Blackboard Jungle* that this does not happen at good American schools; instead, the d.j. ends the film by informing the audience that if they have a principal who gives them trouble and they "want this to happen" at their school, then they can give Screamin' Steven a call. Authority has been removed and these "peculiar" (or one might even say, queer) and "ugly ugly people" like The Ramones have taken over.

In Metz's description of genre evolution, the films that move past contestation to deconstruction transform the entire film into an exposition or breaking down of the genres codes and their "relation to history." By considering 1970s films like *Rock 'n' Roll High School* or *The Rocky Horror Picture Show*, one can propose a moment when the teen film genre is so self-conscious that these amalgam films can break down the codes and formulae of the genre and revise them in terms of their relation to history. These are not merely formalist projects that work in a baroque mode of mannerist self-consciousness in terms of form. These films do understand and play with the basic form and style of teen films of the past, but they also challenge the ideology and competing values of the genre's classical films. It is not enough merely to parody the conventions of the genre; these films work to contest and review the basic protagonists, iconography, and conflicts as well. The gender conformity and bias of so many classical teen films come under attack in *Rock 'n' Roll High School* and *Rocky Horror* (and even in *Grease*, as I have discussed) as female protagonists voice their desires and concerns and, in the latter case, gender becomes denatured and disconnected from the body and sexuality. The compulsory heterosexuality and heteronormative resolutions of the tradition are challenged by *Rocky Horror* and even by the queer moments in *Rock 'n' Roll High School*—for example, in Eaglebauer's blow up doll and in the nonconformity and otherness of The Ramones fans, one of whom can be seen in a t-shirt that reads "queer" while waiting in line for tickets to the concert. Perhaps most importantly, the genre's typical resolutions of reconciliation with parent culture or specifically paternal authority and of assimilation or integration of the rebel through heterosexual union are rejected by these films. They conclude by destroying the school and defying authority or by mourning the elimination or loss of the nontraditional hero rather than accepting the adult world and its values. These are not always the most revolutionary or hopeful endings, as one might propose the subversiveness of Frank or even of Wyatt and Billy the Kid in *Easy Rider* has been contained in their deaths, yet these films do suggest that the traditional values of the genre are no longer acceptable and elimination or destruction is preferable to assimilation or reconciliation. This marks, for me, the possibility of a major turning point in the genre—an opening up of the genre that the teens in the following chapters exploit to great effect.

Chapter 2

Coming of Age in the 1970s: Revision, Fantasy, and Rage in the Teen-Girl Badlands

Partway through Terrence Malick's *Badlands* (1973), the teenage narrator of the film, Holly, enters into a kind of daydream, triggered by images in her father's stereopticon and advanced by her voice-over. From within her forest 'idyll' with outlaw murderer Kit, who has dispatched with her father and driven her from her burning home, Holly imagines an alternate narrative for herself, as Kit goes about daily chores. With her eyes in the viewfinder, Holly asserts that she is really "just a little girl" with "just so many years to live," and, then, the scene shifts to her point of view—the screen is masked-off to mimic the viewfinder and then a picture slides toward the camera (and presumably Holly's eyes), bringing us in alignment with her view through the stereopticon. Holly's voice-over, possibly inspired by the first image, asks a question that indicates her desire to begin rewriting her story: "Where would I be this very moment if Kit had never met me, or killed anybody?" Then, the images proceed from one location to another, as the voice-over contemplating her life continues—images of the Sphinx, a mother and child, two women by a piano, and lovers in a field. Immersed in Holly's point of view, the scene offers a montage of possibilities: for instance, what might have happened if her mother had never died or, in the future, whom she might marry. In this one small interlude, we see the female teen simultaneously as spectator *and* storyteller. The last shot in the series zooms in on a man and a woman in a field; the male soldier's face is turned toward the ear of the woman, who is looking out of the frame. Holly's voice-over ponders what her future husband is doing (clearly indicating it will not be Kit), but the image shows a woman lost in thought or in her own faraway vision, much like Holly here and in the final scene of the film. The voice-over may be describing a male partner, but the scene is expressing a female viewpoint and a female consciousness, one that seems to have revisionary powers.

Unfortunately, the critical assessment of Holly has not recognized this revisionary potential, consistently deeming her a vapid, passive conduit for the messages of consumer culture in the United States of the 1950s, and particularly for those sold in fan literature. Loosely based on Caril Fugate, the female half of a real-life criminal pair (with Charles Starkweather) from the late-1950s who went on a killing spree that began with Caril's family, Holly narrates nearly the entire film, while Kit (the Starkweather figure, played by Martin Sheen) behaves more like a character of *her* invention. As a very young Sissy Spacek plays her, Holly's demeanor and narration are ethereal, the words tumbling out in a dreamlike, languorous monotone. Early on, critics picked up on the strangeness of Holly's narration as a major defining feature of the film, although their assessment of it was never too flattering. Vincent Canby praised the film as one of the great "intelligent" surprises of the New York Film Festival of 1973, but his patronizing view of Holly, a view not to be undone despite protestations from the filmmaker,[1] reveals itself in the very first paragraph of his review: she is "on the verge of being pretty though she still looks something like a cookie that hasn't yet been baked," passing the time by reading "aloud from a movie magazine" (149).[2] This image of Holly as a naïve, unfinished, uncritical teenybopper whose vocabulary and imagination seem entirely absorbed from popular culture, remains relatively unchanged in the critical discourse on the film.[3] Like Canby, most critics ignore the significance of a very young, female character being given charge of an authoritative voiceover and relatively omniscient narration (she discusses events in Kit's life that happen in her absence, and her narration frames the film from some time after the events of the plot), although he does recognize that it is her voice we repeatedly hear on the soundtrack, employing "the flat, expressionless tone that an uninterested schoolgirl might use when reciting Joyce Kilmer's 'Trees.'" Further, the world of the film, according to Canby, "could be an extension of either a television series or one of the stories Holly reads in *True Romances*," though he qualifies this possible nod to Holly's creative powers with a reminder of the true talent behind the masterpiece, Malick, who remains "clear-eyed and mostly without any romantic notions," in contrast, of course, to his addled, sentimental female narrator.

While many critics, such as Brian Henderson, continue to highlight an ironic distance between the filmmaker and a narrator who remains unreliable "by virtue of her youth and naiveté, by her inability to grasp the nature and meaning of what she describes" and who, therefore, becomes "the victim or butt of the implied author's irony" (41), the rare feminist attempt to recoup Holly and the dominance of her narrative voice does exist.[4] Joan McGettigan commends the two female narrators from Malick's first two films, *Badlands* and *Days of Heaven* (1978), as exceptional in their briefly empowered positions as governing voice-over storytellers. However, McGettigan ultimately agrees that Holly's voice-over is limited by the clichés of pulp-fed romance. On the one hand, Malick's female adolescent narrators contradict the traditional use of male, authoritative voice-over in Hollywood film and speak from both diegetic and extra-diegetic positions, resulting in voice-overs that "serve more to destabilize the discourse than to provide the traditional interiority of character narration."[5] Holly, for instance, stands above the viewer in the hierarchy of knowledge, since she is clearly privy to more information and doles it out as she sees fit, sometimes even assessing the feelings and interior motivations of other characters and self-consciously establishing the main themes and structure of the film. On the other hand, though, the themes and patterns Holly provides for the film come to her, according to McGettigan, "via the rhetoric of the romance novel and home economics class" and this rhetoric confines her: "Holly's voice-over relentlessly interprets events we witness in terms of romance; no matter how we may react to her and to Kit, the voice-over reminds us that she considers this the story of her first love."[6] Accordingly, she narrates with the clichés she has learned about such a "first love" plot.

In the end, McGettigan cannot ignore the 'reality' of Holly's life as a female adolescent in the 1950s. She is a character who "has little opportunity or ability to control her own life," since the "film presents the two men [father and gun-crazy lover] as her entire range of life choices."[7] In sum, this reading identifies the tone of Holly's narration as empty, bored, or, at times, disillusioned by her dream lover and celebrates her control of the narrative as disruptive of classical Hollywood modes, but, nevertheless, the critic ultimately places Holly back in a familiar story. She has "no alternatives" to the path from father to husband, and she appears "willing to accept her role."[8] For all the power she has wielded as narrator, Holly still remains a "helpless and disadvantaged" character, and it is the *male* characters who "take action."[9] Their acts of violence set the story in motion, and the female commentary afterward merely follows the pattern provided for it by popular romance.

Rather than acquiesce to this sort of convenient resolution of Holly's disturbing voice, I would like to remain with that female adolescent narrator and the disruptions she creates, even working within clichéd language and the generic conventions of the lovers-on-the-run plot. What, I ask, would it mean to think of the entire film as Holly's creation? What kind of new perspectives might be gained by imagining the entire film as her fantasy? How would one then theorize her evocation of a James Dean stand-in as her father's killer, only to tear him down in the end, having him arrested and sentenced to death? What kind of fantasy or wish-fulfillment might we be witnessing? And what would such exploration offer in terms of conceiving an adolescent spectator and film fan, particularly a female one, in the 1970s? Through the narrator of *Badlands*, this chapter examines the revisionary possibilities for that 1970s female audience and proposes that these spectators might be more critical and active readers of the conservative ideology of the films than previous work on the genre has suggested. Critics who dismiss or disparage the female spectator of teen film, casting her as the "little sister," duped by narratives that reinforce the bond between father and son and through that bond reassert patriarchal order, have simply not considered the likes of Holly.

From the perspective of the early 1970s, *Badlands* revisits what might be called the "primal scene" of teen film, paying tribute to its most legendary icon, James Dean. However, through the frame of spectatorial fantasy, the film may also rewrite that scene from a female perspective. Laplanche and Pontalis describe the primal fantasies as representations of the "major enigmas that confront the child" in the guise of origin myths, such that "the primal scene pictures the origin of the individual; fantasies of seduction, the origin and upsurge of sexuality; fantasies of castration, the origin of the difference between the sexes."[10] According to this definition and proposing the film as *Holly's* fantasy produced sometime in the future, I envision both a return to the origin of teen film, and, moreover, the origin of the female spectator for those films, whose idiosyncratic and challenging perspective provides a way to understand or even problematize the teen viewing subject. While not strictly a "teenpic," the film marks Holly as a fan and, with her return to the 1950s and use of James Dean, suggests the resistance and re-visions possible for female (teen) audiences from the perspective of the 1970s. Holly's retrospective point of view reveals an ironic, at times cruel, distance from the male teen idol, and perhaps more importantly, her fantasy also *involves* her in a violent refusal of the patriarchal home, emphasizing the capacity of female adolescent fantasy to rewrite the conservative resolutions of Hollywood films in the 1970s. In *Badlands*, Holly, the 'simple' teenage girl, proves to be an active, even aggressively destructive, fan who has an agenda and fantasy all her own.

Not-So-*Giant*: Holly's Vision of "Young Love"

In order to establish the possibility of an overarching fantasy structuring the film, one might begin with the ethereal and strange, even affectless, qualities in Holly's voice-over, as well as her framing of the plot from a position some time and some place in the future. Furthermore, privileging Holly with a kind of authorial control does not constitute a huge leap in critical understanding of the film, since critics like Henderson have already hinted that this world is, in a way, her domain, contending that her framing voice-overs "enclose the narrative" and give her "dominion over it."[11] More provocatively, Adrian Danks finds that Holly's "chilling but homely voice-over" rationalizes or familiarizes the film's "otherworldly imagery," making her "relation to the events off the film . . . equally multifarious and strange."[12] But while Danks does not pursue an examination of this strange relation and then, without further explanation, attributes Kit's resemblance to Dean to his status as an "emanation and reflection of the image culture he emerges from," I would argue that these two points are intimately connected. The fantasy hypothesis would explain Holly's "strange" relation to events both outside of and within the film and would posit her as the source from which this James Dean-type emanates. Rather than just being the translator of the film's "deeply troubling and inexplicable events into a simplistic, conventional, 'negative' narrative of self," as Danks suggests, Holly creates these deeply troubling events, composing a narrative of self that is far from simplistic, and that is, indeed, radically *un*conventional.[13]

This fantasy reading also provides a reason for her unreliability as a narrator: caught up in the dreamlike world of *Holly's* fantasy, the viewer might feel unmoored at times and dependent on the unpredictable and yet oddly familiar work of the unconscious. Even the one possible obstacle to recognizing the entire film as Holly's fantasy—Kit's one brief voice-over towards the end of the film—might be attributable to the radical flexibility of her fantasy. During the Nat King Cole dance scene, Kit's voice overtakes the music on the soundtrack, pleading, "If I could sing a song like that." However, Holly's voice quickly reasserts itself: "Kit knew the end was coming." A simple explanation from psychoanalytic work on fantasy may suffice to account for this nearly ghostlike entrance of Kit's voice. Several theorists, since Freud, have noted the flexibility of positions for the subject to occupy in her or his own fantasy. Such movement and flexibility is one of the central features that makes fantasy so attractive for feminist critics. It allows for oscillation between gender roles, sexual orientations, passive and active positions, and masochistic and sadistic desires.[14] All work together in the same subject throughout all different points of the fantasy, including the very structure of the fantasy itself, which Laplanche and Pontalis explain as "a scenario with multiple entries" such that in the phrase "'A father seduces a daughter'" nothing clearly affirms "whether the subject will be immediately located as *daughter*; it can as well be fixed as *father*, or even in the term *seduces*."[15] In other words, Holly, as the subject producing the fantasy, can be located in all the figures in the fantasy, as well as in the very actions of the scenarios.

In addition to the recognition that the particular structuring work of fantasy can create the plot of the film as idiosyncratic to Holly's desires and flexible to change and detours according to her whims or needs, I would emphasize the point that her fantasy is reliant upon the popular culture, including films, that she has consumed. In defining Freud's term "phantasmatic," Laplanche and Pontalis note that this central structuring principle for the subject and the subject's fantasies has "its own dynamic" and the phantasy structures are "constantly drawing in new material."[16] Therefore, contrary to the view favored by critics that Holly is "*limited* by her pulp-magazine perspective," one might look to Freud's patients who helped to develop the psychoanalytic understanding of fantasy in order to discover how those examples of popular culture might function in Holly's narration.[17] The young women who admitted to beating fantasies, in "A Child is Being Beaten," rely upon other narratives to fuel their fantasies, particularly melodramatic adolescent fiction like the "*Bibliothèque rose*" or *Uncle Tom's Cabin*, in fact "competing with these works of fiction" by producing "a wealth" of fantasies and imagined (brutal) situations.[18] Likewise, *Badlands* seems to exhibit just such a competitive spirit: as Holly and Kit wander through the open, western fantasyscape, and she becomes increasingly disappointed or dissatisfied with the plots she develops as well as with her James Dean-like leading man, her fantasies become more violent. As her frustration with the imperfections of her imaginary world grows (or as her competitive spirit grows), it seems as if she metes out even more punishment and exhibits less patience with the progression of her plots.

Most importantly, though, Holly's imaginings illustrate the revisionary potential of fantasy, providing an example of the rewritings of patriarchal law brought to light by feminist rereadings of the beating fantasies. Defining fantasy as a restaging of Oedipal scenarios or, in David Rodowick's terms, as "a contingent event, the possibility for renewing terms of meaning, identity, and desire," feminist theorists propose the possibility of subverting or revising those familiar scenarios in fantasy.[19] Indeed, Holly's vision—humiliation of the male outlaw-hero, vengeful murder of the father, and denial of patriarchy—presented as what Patricia White terms "female-authorized popular culture," defies the resolution Freud constructs for his female beating patients and replaces his male authorial voice with hers (208). In *unInvited: Classical Hollywood Cinema and Lesbian Representability*, White recognizes a subversive rewriting of the beating scenario in Todd Haynes's short film, *Dottie Gets Spanked*. Working from Deleuze's rereading of Freud's male masochistic fantasies in which the father might be hidden in the role of the person being beaten, White contends that Haynes's film "illustrates the homoeroticism of Freud's version and the subversiveness of Deleuze's and suggests that the father is hidden in the spanked and the spanking Dottie."[20] This example provides White with a filmic representation of her notion of "retrospectatorship," in which Haynes can "rewrite patriarchal law enunciated from the (gay) male point of view, a wish that grants power to the female acculturating agent." Essentially, I offer Holly's fantasy here as another example of such a rewriting, although from the female (sadistic) point of view. *Badlands* stages the possibility of a female-authored fantasy of the 1950s from the place of the 1970s, a "retrospectatorship" that "revises cultural authority" (in the guise of Kit-James Dean and Holly's father) in a mocking, violent, and destructive way.[21]

The film opens, innocently enough, with a young teen in her bedroom with her dog, the private sanctuary where, stereotypically, much daydreaming and fantasy-play occurs for young girls.[22] But quickly, *Badlands* differentiates itself from the innocence and dreamy young love one typically expects from early teen fantasy through an abrupt shift in scene to the back alleyways of Ft. Dupree, South Dakota, and to the decidedly unromantic work of our male lead: garbage collecting. Instead of depicting the naïve, moony-eyed gushing of a young girl in the midst of her "first love," as critics like McGettigan suggest, the first major section of the film uses irony and simple rejection to mock and thwart the fantasy lover. This 15-minute montage of vignettes outlining the progression of their relationship, which is almost completely dominated by Holly's voice-over narration, identifies Kit as a James Dean look-alike and attributes to him an overabundance of romantic qualities, but it also hints at the underside of this fantasy—the cruelty, aggression, and destruction later to appear more prominently as its driving force.[23] While Holly approvingly admits in voice-over before their second meeting that Kit is "handsomer than anybody" she has ever met—"He looked just like James Dean"—the image track both supports and lampoons the likeness. From the first, Kit appears a rebel without a cause indeed: we see him, dressed in a white T-shirt, jeans and boots, failing to succeed as a garbage collector or to convince his coworkers to agree to dares or bargains, and he is almost run over by the garbage truck driver when he asks for a cigarette. Furthermore, at the whim of his 15-year-old creator, who says at their first meeting, "I shouldn't be seen with anybody who collects garbage," he changes from Dean-as-teen-rebel to Dean-as-upstart-cowboy (as in *Giant* [1956]),[24] moving from one fantasy role to the next faster than Holly can say, "I gotta run."

Holly's story proves, at least initially, to be an ambivalent fantasy—one that conjures up a dream lover, who seems possible only in a 15-year-old girl's imagination, just to refuse him and abuse him. When Kit first walks up to Holly twirling a baton in her front yard and asks her to take a walk, she responds by saying, "What for?" At their second meeting, directly following her voice-over wherein she appreciates his Dean-like handsomeness, Kit greets her on her porch and she quips sarcastically out loud from within the diegesis, "Well, stop the world." At this moment, she begins to reveal how tough an audience she can be: she takes a line directly from Dean's costar in *Rebel Without a Cause* (1955)—"Well, stop the world" is the greeting Judy [Natalie Wood] offers to Jim when performing her bad-girl role on the first day of school—and seems to use it mockingly. In other words, Kit may look just like James Dean, but Holly does not always give him the star treatment. He asks her to take another walk and she demurs, pleading homework. Still, he persists, and on their walk he wonders if he can call her "Red." She refuses his intimate request for a pet name and then complains of a headache, cutting their date short. Furthermore, throughout these brief, early encounters, Spacek's face occasionally registers mild curiosity, but more often than not her expression is one of discomfort and annoyance. In the first two encounters Holly walks ahead of or away from Kit, leaving him alone in the frame, and she is always the one abruptly to end the meeting.

In the face of this indifference, Kit still relentlessly performs the romantic lead. While Holly describes his new job as "work at the feed lot," he refers to himself as a "cowboy." He platonically courts her— taking her for walks and drives without initiating physical contact— while Holly voices how he is not "interested in [her] for sex." Despite their fairly significant age difference (10 years), he thinks she is "mature for her age," and he appears to enjoy her conversation and company, even pursuing her over her father's objections. Holly reveals in voice-over that she is "not popular" in school, but Kit chooses her anyway, even though he "could have had any other girl in town." In sum, his adoration of and obedience to her seem nothing short of unbelievable: "He didn't care what anybody else thought. I looked good to him and whatever I did was okay. And if I didn't have a lot to say, well, that was okay too." This last remark highlights a notable feature for these characterizations of their romance—they come from *Holly's* voice-over, even when describing Kit's thoughts and feelings. Through a kind of free indirect discourse, Holly provides access to Kit's mind, or, in other words, his interiority is only available to us through her agency. In this way, Holly's fantasy can rewrite Kit's speech and his involvement in their relationship retrospectively. She offers her details of their budding romance and, I would add, stages their rendezvous. Holly has created the most understanding, romantic, and acquiescent leading man possible, yet she does not reciprocate in kind.

Instead, Holly rewards his romantic efforts with more indifference or even mockery in her act of storytelling.[25] While the *voice-over* tells of his appreciation and approval of Holly, as cited above, the screen (or visual projection of her fantasy) shows him going about his unromantic work at the feedlot. She announces, "Little by little we fell in love," but on the screen we see Kit running a machine to restrain cows at medication time, then feeding cows, kicking them in the head to separate them, and ignoring a sick animal. This ironic division between voice-over and visual track has been commented on by several critics as a central element of the film, but most, like Brian Henderson, view the narrator, Holly, as the "butt" of the filmmaker's irony, while I would offer Kit as the object of *her* irony. In a sense, what the film might be dramatizing is a female spectator's revision and humiliation of James Dean. Shot in soft afternoon sun, this sequence shows him dressed the part, in a denim jacket, jeans, cowboy boots and hat, and her voice-over tells of his romantic nobility, but the virtual tour through his day at the feed lot undercuts both Kit's posturing and the ethereal quality one might expect of a young girl's romantic daydream.

As the initial sequence continues, her derision of the Dean-like romantic lead turns darker, escalating to the point that she humiliates and belittles him after what should be the climactic moment of this young love plot: blissful heterosexual union. The next scene in the feedlot accentuates again the cruelly ironic juxtaposition of image and voice-over suggested above. A medium close-up of Kit staring through barbed wire is recontextualized by Holly's voice-over, "In the stench and slime of the feedlot, he'd remember how I looked the night before," followed by a long shot of cows in the mud. Moreover, the dire fate of the cows at the feedlot haunts these moments, as they struggle or appear sick or trapped, and a foreboding sense of danger creeps in. In fact, briefly after the second scene at the feedlot and after Holly reveals that "he wanted to die" with her, the sequence is disrupted by an interlude about her fish, whose untimely death Holly orchestrated, though she now regrets it. One cannot ignore the disjunction between the images of lovers cuddled together with her voice-over attesting to his undying love (or death wish, as the case may be) and the sudden cut to her pet fish in its bowl, soon being carried into the backyard to die. Perhaps taking the foreshadowing too far, the scene ends with a close-up on the fish, gasping for life in the seemingly innocuous garden behind her house, and the fish appears, gasping, again on Kit's nightstand during Holly's vision of him at night in bed.

Shortly after the fish's demise, the two young lovers consummate their union, but with little fanfare. Kit expresses his desire to commemorate their first lovemaking by smashing their hands with a rock, but Holly's reaction indicates the aggression of her growing indifference and boredom with her male lead. While his wish for commemorative mutilation points to an underlying masochism, her refusal to attribute significance to the event or represent it romantically indicates quite the opposite desire—pleasure in cruelty. She verbally assaults his male prowess and deflates her own rite of passage. Appearing absolutely unimpressed by her 'first time' (a familiar trope from teen films), Holly asks, "Is that all there is to it?" and then adds a vicious final jab: "Gosh, what was everybody talkin' about?" As in the earlier scenes, she walks away from him, while he pursues her out of the frame, pathetically still inventing ways to memorialize the occasion—first, smashing their hands, then taking the rock with him, and then choosing a smaller, more portable, commemorative rock. Such an indifferent and cruel response to her 'momentous' sexual initiation, coupled with the harsh treatment of her fish, possibly forewarns that it will not be too long before Kit finds himself in the dirt gasping for air.

In short, the voice controlling and structuring this narrative does a good bit more than tell "the story of her first love." There is a fantasy here that incorporates the fictional icons of a first love plot, but that ultimately proves bent on aggressive violence, first aimed derisively at the Dean-like romantic lead of heteronormative fictions and then more viciously at institutions of power, such as the patriarchal home or law enforcement. Because the fantasy abuses and humiliates a young man, it evokes the model mentioned above of Freud's female cases from "A Child Is Being Beaten." In this essay, the female patients have fantasies that Freud separates into three phases, but two of the phases involve the beating of another child, not the fantasizer, by an adult. The first phase can be represented by the phrase, "a child is being beaten," which Freud transforms later into "My father is beating the child," but the third phase increases the number of (male) victims and excludes the father, selecting a surrogate for him.[26] Furthermore, this last phase of the female beating fantasies has received significant attention from film theorists for its model of spectatorship: the girl pictures a boy, or usually, a group of boys, being beaten by an authority figure (fatherlike) while she "looks on." Obviously, since the female patients describing their beating fantasies to Freud never appear to be the child being beaten, they may be considered sadistic and violent. Freud does his best to reintroduce masochism into the picture, since these are after all *female* patients, by introducing a middle phase to the string of fantasies, an unconscious phase only discovered during *his* analysis wherein the beating is turned back on the female patient's self as punishment for her incestuous wish for the father ("I am being beaten by my father"). Several feminist critics have questioned Freud's logic on this point and reasserted the idea that the fantasies establish a very clear example of fluctuation between sadism and masochism, or in Rhona Berenstein's words, "cross-sexed and non-specified identifications and desires" that include even "cross-sex identification with sadistic adults."[27] What I am suggesting here is that Holly's fantasy offers something more than simply a return to female masochism and the incestuous wish for the father.

For this reading of *Badlands*, the beating fantasies do suggest at least one precedent for female fantasy wherein a primary pleasure derives from someone else's pain and humiliation, particularly a boy of similar age. Holly's sarcastic quips that ridicule Kit's James-Dean-pose make sense if she is allowed the pleasures of sadism.[28] Moreover, I find in Holly's retelling a position suggested by, but foreclosed in, Freud's analysis of the beating fantasies, where he finds only "the form" of the third phase to be sadistic, not her "satisfaction" from it.[29] In Holly's case, she has placed *herself* in the fantasy and becomes the active creator of the humiliation (beating), further emphasizing the intense sadism of this particular fantasy. She does not merely "look on," but assumes the abusive, controlling role of the father or father-surrogate in the beating fantasy—a position denied by Freud's analysis but valid within the framework of the phantasmatic, where, as noted above, she can be located in position of "daughter," "father" or "seduces." Holly verbally assaults Kit, wishes for his death ("at times I wished he'd fall in the river and drown so I could watch"), and eventually betrays him, which results in his capture and death sentence.

Furthermore, this fantasy is not satisfied with abusing and humiliating Kit. It turns to more serious prey and attacks Holly's father, bounty hunters, and even Kit's friends. In other words, Freud's version of the beating fantasies does not go far enough to explain (or restrain) what is played out in *Badlands*. Unsurprisingly, not once in Freud's female cases is the beating fantasy directed at the father or authority figures, but considering the contortions he goes through to place the girls in the masochistic position, other "complications," to use Freud's term, seem just as valid. If the girls, having turned away "from their incestuous love for their father," can somehow "abandon their feminine role" and spur their "masculinity complex" into activity, which allows them, "from that time forward," to want to be boys, but, specifically, masochistic "whipping boys," might not this same process spur their masculinity complex into another role entirely, that of the sadistic "other person in authority" performing the beating?[30] In fact, might this not be yet another example of the contingency of fantasy—that its pleasure is fluid and revisionary, locating the subject in the role of the spectator, or in the role of the masochistic male "whipping boy" (adolescent girls finding their masochism in the Freudian male homosexual role?), or in the role of the abusive authority figure? Fantasy makes all of these "complications" possible.

The example proves even more fruitful when we consider, as I mentioned above, that the impetus for the third phase of the beating fantasy is the adolescent literature the fantasizer has consumed and against which she competes in the productive act of fantasizing.[31] According to the critical assessment, Holly's narration suffers from her "corrupted-by-pop," clichéd, "pulp magazine" perspective, which is supposedly mocked by the true controlling voice, Malick's. But the beating fantasies introduce another possibility: Holly may be consuming that popular culture and using it to formulate a competing fantasy in which she can control the action, as well as the male lead, and use the terms of popular culture to disrupt its messages. In other words, through her fantastic creation, Holly gains authorial control and uses this voice for a pleasurable dismantling of the male lead *and* the popular culture that invented him. As White's term "retrospectatorship" proposes, classical Hollywood film "belongs to the past" but can be "experienced in a present that affords us new ways of seeing" and chances for revision, or even, in this case a kind of revenge.³² Accordingly, one might consider this fantasy, which Holly retells after some time has passed, as originating in adolescence and being reworked and revised many times over, incorporating memories, experiences, and popular culture, such as characters and even dialogue from that archetypal teen film, *Rebel Without a Cause*. While it is unclear exactly when Holly's fantasy takes place—since she wonders at one point about the identity of her future husband but in the end recounts Kit's execution and claims that she married the son of the lawyer who got her off "with probation and a lot of nasty looks"—it must be considered significant that the "present" of *Badlands*' release that would offer "new ways of seeing" is the early 1970s, a period of great progress for second wave feminism in the United States (in fact, Roe vs. Wade was decided in January of the same year the film was released). One might even say that this female-authored adolescent fantasy, while always possible, found the historical moment for its enunciation in the 1970s—a point I will explore more fully below.

Patricide and Counter-Nostalgia in the Badlands

The radical potential for Holly's authority becomes pronounced as the initial love plot ends. Possibly dissatisfied with, or bored by, the "first love" story (and its male lead), Holly shifts her narrative focus and, once again, rewrites Kit's role, dramatically transforming the fantasy from humiliation and play to violent revenge. After Kit commits his final act of sentimental commemoration, letting a balloon drift off with their keepsakes attached, and Holly's voice-over again undercuts him ("Something must have told him that we'd never live these days of happiness again"), the action turns to another field where Holly and her father are having a disagreement. She calmly reveals in voice-over that her father has discovered her "running around behind his back" with Kit and plans to kill her dog as punishment, but the emotional impact of the scene is revealed by the change in the soundtrack to a frantic chiming piece from Carl Orff's "Musica Poetica," which is paired with Holly's silently screaming face on the image track. Here, the contrast between Holly's calm, inexpressive voice-over and her screaming face is striking—almost as if we are trapped in a nightmare with a dispassionate unconscious, one that cannot hear us scream. The fantasy has suddenly turned terrifying and Holly's extraordinary show of emotion threatens future retribution. The next cut presents the recipient of her undeniable, but muted, rage: a long shot of her father in the upper right of the frame, coolly pointing his gun, first at the camera and then lower at the dog, who is out of focus at the bottom of the frame and motionless, with his back to the viewer. The loud, traumatic gunshot, which causes a quick movement in the dog, marks the first sound in the scene from within the diegesis and is significant for its return in the parallel scene of Holly's father's slaying.

For the crime of killing her dog, her father is shot only a few scenes later in a strikingly similar way, and the fantasy lover—who attaches sentiment to keepsakes, but then quite literally does not prove much of a lover—performs much better as an instrument of *Holly's* revenge and anger. Even in an exchange of glances between the two men in the scene, Holly seems the source of the action, at one point illuminated and in focus (looking on) at the center of a three-shot at the top of the stairs, as if highlighting her awareness of the triangulation of desire supposedly serving patriarchy wherein the power and energy flows "between men." In the act of shooting, Kit appears in the same stance as Holly's father in the field: he stands in the left side of the frame, at medium distance, with his left hand at his side and his right hand holding the gun pointed low, while the father is out of focus in the bottom of the frame, though further to the right than the dog. Additionally, the soundtrack emphasizes the connection. As the thunderous crack of Kit's gunfire fades—an echo of the earlier traumatic intrusion of diegetic sound at the dog's death, only Holly's voice and a dog barking in the distance can be heard. Simply, Holly has had her revenge. More or less abandoning the romance plot, Holly's fantasy, instead, releases the aggression only hinted at previously and plays out desires for adventure, criminality, and sadistic violence—ultimately, murderous wish-fulfillment whose target is the father, or his surrogates, even if one of those surrogates turns out to be Kit.

In the end, what makes *Badlands* such an exceptional film is its consistent and aggressive denial of traditional values, social structures, and authority, particularly paternal, up to the final frame—exactly contrary to the male nostalgic films of the 1970s, such as *American Graffiti*, discussed in the previous chapter. Moreover, as Kit becomes enamored of the law and more like her father, Holly becomes less enamored of him, until she eventually abandons him completely. In other words, as that bond between father and son completes its Oedipal cycle and the son ascends, Holly kills off that new father as well. Several critics have noted Kit's growing appreciation of the law and his likeness to Holly's father. Malick himself puts into perfect relief Kit's particular brand of conventionalism: "He thinks of himself as a successor to James Dean—a Rebel without a Cause—when in reality he's more like an Eisenhower conservative."[33] No 1950s rebel, Kit aspires to be "like" the rich man he chooses *not* to kill toward the end of the film, reciting conservative homilies into his Dictaphone: "Listen to your parents and teachers. They got a line on most things, so don't treat them like enemies," or "Consider the minority opinion, but try to get along with the majority of opinion, once it's accepted." He even takes the rich man's panama hat, which makes him physically resemble Holly's father. One critic, Neil Campbell, contends that this ascension to the father's role drives Kit's actions in the film. The young killer's "search" turns out, regrettably, to be about "*becoming* a father to Holly and about finding a level of acceptability within the community in which he lives."[34] That this search becomes the central joke of the film, and, I would add, a reason for Holly's aggression towards Kit, nonetheless appears to Campbell as more of a tragedy than a triumph.

Holly's narrative vision has little patience for Kit's quests, especially not for his authoritative longings, and, in her repeated ridicule of him, she undermines the 'authority' and cultural myths he mimics. For Campbell, in Kit's "quest for conformity and responsibility," he adopts the "voice of reason and lawfulness, in imitation of 'adult' acceptability his violent actions undermine," but his imitations all sound "humorous." However, his ties to "classic, mythic American traits" such as rugged individualism and his likeness to "the frontiersman his gunplay suggests" somehow turn his imitations of authority from comic to tragic.[35] Campbell concludes, in the end, that both Holly and Kit are "contained by home and the law, and all their potential energy and imagination turned to waste," leaving only "a chilling circularity reflecting a pessimism about society's motivating values."[36] On the contrary, I find that Holly's "imagination," rather than going to waste, proves to be a source for this damning criticism so typical of the 1970s and understandable pessimism about any number of "society's motivating values." While Campbell reads Holly's narration as a "romantic fantasy of love and honour," in other words a nostalgic look back at her first love,[37] I reiterate that Holly's fantasy acts, instead, as the major source for the ferocious criticisms and dark humor of the film.

The backbone for Campbell's "classic, mythic American traits," namely paternal authority or dominant masculinity, receives the brunt of her fantasy's criticism, ridicule, and violent rejection, which resonates with other films in the era in which *Badlands* appears, though with a difference. Robin Wood, without focusing on *Badlands* in his work on 1970s film, contends that the era is notable for producing a number of new American works with "incoherent" structures and plotting that served to disrupt and criticize conventional order: "The questioning of authority spread logically to a questioning of the entire social structure that validated it, and ultimately patriarchy itself: social institutions, the family, the symbolic figure of the Father in all its manifestations, the Father interiorized as superego."[38] The reading of *Badlands* offered in this chapter and in the other alternative maturation plots throughout this book would certainly support both Wood's notion of the disruption caused by feminist protest and his contention that, in the 1970s, the "possibility suddenly opened up that the whole world might have to be recreated" (here, in fantasy), but Holly's particular, female-centered version of criticism and rejection is neglected in Wood's work, as well as in other accounts of the era. Indeed, *Badlands* fails to fit the mode of a New American Cinema characterized by "raging bulls" or discontent, fragmented *male* heroes— for example, Travis Bickle of *Taxi Driver* (1976) representing the "critique of the patriarchal hero" in 1970s film.[39] Malick's film has been likened to *Bonnie and Clyde* (1967) and has obvious parallels to the earlier film, even an acknowledgement in the credits, but through Holly's narration, it presents a much darker, more critical tone and perspective on the "outlaw" couple.[40] It is as if, instead of relegating this strange and deeply disturbing young voice to the margins, as Scorsese does in *Alice Doesn't Live Here Anymore* (1974), *Badlands* places her front and center, giving over the narrative to her increasingly derisive point of view. Unlike in the films just mentioned, Holly's narration or female authority evokes an active, even aggressive, feminism that traditional teen films and other popular films of the era, even films by the "new" auteurs of American cinema, worked to silence or assuage with the resolution of heteronormative romance.

More significantly for this chapter and in the context of 1970s, film critics wrongly confine *Badlands* within the model of the "nostalgia film," a label which Campbell's assessment of Holly's voice-over suggests. Marsha Kinder compares *Badlands* with two other films of the period, Spielberg's *The Sugarland Express* (1974) and Altman's *Thieves Like Us* (1974), which are "set in rural America sometime in the past" and depict sudden violence "juxtaposed with humor or nostalgia."[41] As a reaction to male buddy narratives dominating 1970s cinema, these three films, for Kinder, "revive the heterosexual couple" but place them outside the law and in a "powerless" past where they can reflect back on a "sick society" in the present—Kit as "the banality of evil, personified by Nixon" and Holly as his pathological, passive, and emotionless accomplice.[42] In a more derogatory way, many critics liken the film to Lucas's *American Graffiti* (released in the same year) or, to a lesser extent, Bogdanovich's *The Last Picture Show* (1971). For example, in his work on teen film, Jon Lewis couples Malick's film with other "hopelessly romantic" and "nostalgic works" such as *Graffiti*, the television series *Happy Days*, and other examples of male nostalgia in 1970s teen film that I have detailed in the previous chapter, describing Holly's voice-over as "clouded" by the "teen magazines she reads incessantly" so that her voice "underscores the banality of nostalgia."[43] Eager to fit the film into a genre he feels is dominated by "nostalgia for authority," Lewis neglects the terrible violence and darkness central to *Badlands* and, I would contend, fails to see how Holly's narration itself vividly defies nostalgia and its regressive, filial longings.

If one understands *Badlands* as the retelling of a young woman's "first love," a clouded fantasy drenched with adult sentiment, then the comparison to *American Graffiti* makes sense. However, even those critics who compare the two films struggle with the association. Lewis defines Malick's film as "[q]uite a different nostalgia," while Kinder locates an "exaggerated" nostalgia, an "*American Graffiti* turned gothic";[44] the last phrase begs the question, if it is "gothic," can we still call it "nostalgia"? Rather than searching for an appropriate term, why not see the film as a reaction to or against a nostalgic evasion of the present? Why not recognize the strong current in Malick's film that counters nostalgia as one finds it in *American Graffiti* and a number of other male teen films of the 1970s? Holly's female-authored fantasy and revision surfaces at a historical moment in which feminists launched an impassioned resistance to the regressive and conservative desire for 'simpler' times indicative of nostalgia and so central to Lucas's film, and her active subversion of any romantic notion of the 1950s seems to echo that resistance. While Holly's narrative does offer a return to the past and, I would argue, one woman's perspective on the past, her retrospection appears quite different indeed from nostalgia, as a close comparison to *American Graffiti* will show.

Contrary to Jameson's definitive reading of *American Graffiti* as the prototypical "nostalgia film" composed of a fashionable pastiche of retro styles and popular culture, I would recognize the element of strong sentiment and a conservative position vis-à-vis the present, that is, the longing for a past with more traditional values. For Jameson, the "nostalgia film" projects a pastiche, which considers the "'past' through stylistic connotation conveying 'pastness' by the glossy qualities of the image, and '1930s-ness' and '1950s-ness' by the attributes of fashion."[45] These films do not attempt to represent a 'real' past or contend with the less savory events in that past, but, instead, the intertextual references and self-reflexivity of mass-produced images turn back in on themselves, only able to represent the past of popular culture.[46] However, this spectacle or pastiche of glossy 1950s-ness can serve to mask a reactionary attitude toward the present.[47] In this reading, the neon lights and exquisitely slick cars in Lucas's *American Graffiti* might be nearly spectacular enough to efface the gender inequalities of the 1950s and early 1960s US culture, inequalities written into the drama of the film itself up to the last moment— the epilogue that offers a future for the four male leads but not for the females. Still, some feminist readings contend that nostalgia films often do not even depend on so much smoke and mirrors, laying bare a desire to return to a time when women 'knew their place.' For example, Doane and Hedges locate in several texts by contemporary male writers a desire to return to the past, which surfaces in diatribes against "the degeneracy of American culture," a degeneracy tied, not coincidentally, to "the rise of feminist authority."[48] Within calls "to restore American values and the American family," certain writers "construct visions of a golden past to authenticate woman's traditional place and to challenge the outspoken feminist criticisms of it."[49] In the very act of erasing the future of its female leads in the final epilogue, *American Graffiti* reveals its opposition to the changes surfacing in the late 1960s and early 1970s.

Despite Lucas's possible intention to make, in Jon Lewis's words, "some sort of comment on American youth on the edge of the Vietnam war," the film is saturated with the young director's nostalgic, semiautobiographical moments.[50] Unlike *Badlands*, Lucas's film prefers the soft glow of neon to any harsh edge, "far too lovingly Kennedyan to provide a broader, darker, angrier picture of what was shortly to come."[51] Indeed, while Lewis finds the film "narratologically bittersweet," I would emphasize the sweet over the bitter.[52] Whether in narrative, dialogue, camerawork, or soundtrack, the film admits an end must come but prefers to bathe itself in those prelapsarian moments. Rather than only succeeding in depicting the "attributes of fashion" or a "1950s-ness," the film clearly captures (at least one man's) longing for a very particular moment.[53] Admittedly, by opening with Bill Haley and the Comets' "Rock Around the Clock," Lucas exposes the film to the argument that it is merely a pastiche of past popular culture representations of the 1950s, *Rock Around the Clock* (1956) being the first successful attempt to wed rock 'n' roll and exploitation film in a synergistic union of record and ticket sales. Also, as I mentioned in Chapter 1, the song is notorious for its earlier appearance in *Blackboard Jungle* (1955), which was accused of inciting violence in teens.

Moving beyond the genre clichés demanded by the last-hurrah-before-college narrative and beyond the allusions to popular culture, one can see individual care given to certain moments and certain locations that, added together, offer the audience an intense feeling of longing and regret. Three settings, to which the film repeatedly returns, despite their possibly hackneyed symbolism today, gain emotional weight with each pass of the camera. Mel's drive-in, the location for the first establishing shot of the film, which was almost certainly made cartoonish by the television series *Happy Days*, provides the central gathering place of the film and is the first location wherein Lucas reveals his dependence on lighting, usually neon, to evoke both a glamorous beauty and otherworldly quality to these moments. Similarly, the strip, populated with perpetually rowdy cruisers, the second of the film's preferred settings, provides ample opportunity to establish tone with reflected light, usually colored, from stoplights, shop windows, and, again, neon signs. The third setting, the "hop," uses lighting effectively, but also relies on narrative elements to solidify the director's more-sweet-than-bitter vision.

The return to the "hop" presents an example of one of several scenes of nostalgic longing by the characters within the nostalgic film itself. That these moments seem to raise the specter of irony and ridicule only to overwhelm it with sincere sentiment and tenderness might be the most determining factor in labeling the film overtly nostalgic. Curt jokingly confesses in the parking lot of Mel's drive-in that he is going to the hop in order "to remember all the good times," attempting to cover over the clearly sentimental and clichéd action with sarcasm and light laughter. However, once at the hop, his behavior on this "last night in town" before heading east to college follows the rulebook for strolls down memory lane, literally. He walks down the halls of his old high school, touching surfaces, and, finding his old locker, he opens it and smiles whimsically. Not satisfied, Curt seeks out his favorite teacher, Mr. Wolf, who only stayed one semester at Middlebury before returning home, and asks his advice about whether or not he should leave for the uncertain offerings of college. Naturally, the teacher responds by chastising Curt and advising that he "experience life," and the message is that one has to move on or waste away in corrupted, arrested development. But even on this point the film offers conflicting messages, since the central figure representing the refusal to grow up, John Milner, the 20-something drag race king, receives the undeniable sympathy of the film.

When Susan Douglas describes the emancipatory power of music and dancing for teenage girls in the beginning of the 1960s, perhaps she is thinking of a different hop than the one depicted by Lucas in *Graffiti*. This hop promotes, or comes close to worshiping, all-male groups and a male-dominated "romance" where the slow dance can wash away all sins, rather than Douglas' revolutionary dancing where "boys and girls didn't have to hold hands anymore, boys didn't have to lead and girls didn't have to follow" and where "girls had a lot more autonomy and control as they danced."[54] When Steve, Laurie, and Curt arrive at the hop, the camera never documents their entrance, instead preempting them with an extended dance sequence set to, of course, "At the Hop."[55] The scene is one of those loving vignettes that Jameson might dub as a piece of the pastiche, with cuts between energetic dancers dressed in appropriate late-1950s apparel and perfectly period all-male group with matching cherry-red jackets and ducktails. Beginning with a crane shot of the bleachers which moves left and forward into the dancing crowd, much of the scene switches between a handheld view of the dancers themselves, in their sock-feet and poodle skirts, and a series of views of the performers.

The kinetic energy of the dancing, intimate as it might be, is overshadowed by the long takes of the band members and their instruments. The camera returns again and again to these six men with their red jackets and thin black ties illuminated by more light than we have yet seen in the film, since the scenes before this are shot outside at night (at Mel's and on the strip). We view them from extreme long, medium and close distance, at one point getting an extreme close-up of the electric guitar obviously meant to remind us of the reign of rock 'n' roll. Lucas underscores the significance of his adoration for this type of group with one fairly long take at the end of the scene: the medium shot shows in profile several teenage girls whose upturned faces are illuminated by the spotlights reflected off the performers. The overall effect of the dancers and the close-ups on the band is to express a particular energy and a reverence for something as important to the filmmaker as it appears to be to those teenage girls. In the end, the feeling extends to the heterosexual couple, Steve and Laurie, who conclude the hop sequences with the well-worn king and queen of the school spotlight dance. Although they have been arguing (because Steve wants to "see other people") and Laurie has nearly emasculated Steve with her recounting of his failure to "make the first move," the magic of this scene seems to bring them back together. The hop, as we see it, concludes with a close-up on the couple, embracing in a slow dance with the spotlight behind them creating a yellow halo around Laurie's head as she clasps on tighter.[56] The power of this moment, of this band, of this place is sincerely offered as supernatural, as restorative, as ideal.

To fully understand the ideal created by the nostalgia of *Graffiti*, one must address the character of John Milner, who seems both its embodiment and its end point. He is first introduced through his reputation in the opening scene, as he pulls his infamous hot rod into Mel's drive-in. Steve is attempting to convince Curt to leave for college, begging him not to end up like John: "You can't stay seventeen forever!" However, Lucas's film does ensure that John stays seventeen forever by concluding the narrative with another one of his roadway triumphs and shutting down his future in the epilogue by announcing his death in a car crash, the same fate met by one of his rebel models, James Dean (though in physique and character he much more resembles Marlon Brando). The romance and mythology generated by Dean's untimely death need not be rehearsed here, but, needless to say, having John Milner live on and grow old as the town's local mechanic would not have fit the parallel mythology Lucas is offering. Despite Steve's disapproval in the beginning, the remainder of the film bestows magnanimous honor, psychological depth (when most of the other lead characters lack it), and a tender sympathy on this king of the strip, and the nostalgia for his passing, which he himself senses is near, perhaps most the clearly represents the film's nostalgia for the era now gone.

Like the performers at the hop, what could easily turn into cliché or a generic joke (as he does in Linklater's *Dazed and Confused* [1993]), the aging hot-rodder ridiculously past his prime, is treated with loving attention and respect. He could potentially lose heroic status when he is tricked into taking a girl's kid sister into his canary-yellow dream machine, but instead he strikes up a friendship with the wisecracking 15-year-old, forming possibly the film's only honest connection. As the young girl Carol learns to like and trust him more, the audience has more opportunity to appreciate and trust him. John also performs the role of hero-savior well enough, and the penultimate scene of the film resolidifies both his mythical status and his doomed state, two factors essential for nostalgia. He unselfconsciously plays the part by saving Carol from a carload of menacing young men and fighting off Toad's attackers who also stole his car. Toad, the film's stereotypical comic relief 'geek,' says of John after his rescue, without a hint of irony, "you're just like the Lone Ranger," and the film offers nothing to suggest the contrary. He defends his friends and looks after Carol, and, although the police appear to be harassing him, he refuses to go through a red light while drag racing Bob Falfa, his new competition. In two scenes in which he faces his own mortality and vulnerability, he even proves humble: in the junkyard with Carol, he reveals a knowledge of every crash that put the cars there and recognizes his own luck avoiding the same fate, and before his race with Bob Falfa, he seems to admit that his time as "number one" might be up.

    The final drag race, held on the unbelievably named "Paradise Road," of course puts off that eventuality one more time, as he beats Bob Falfa, whose car flips into a ditch. Remaining the great champion for lesser beings like Toad, John himself knows better: "I was losin', man. He was pulling away from me just before he crashed. He had me." But Toad will not hear of it (and presumably neither should the audience): "You've got the bitchinest car in the valley. You'll always be number one, John. You're the greatest."[57] And within the narrative of the film, this pronouncement remains true, despite John's obvious exhaustion in his reply, "Okay, Toad ... we'll take 'em all." Finally, the camerawork once again provides direction in how to understand both Toad's adoration and John's nostalgia for his own now-lost youth. As in the scene at the hop, the viewer is encouraged to adore the object of desire by the audience within the film. Lit by the sunrise, we see Toad in partial profile, his mouth slightly agape and his head angled up, as he praises John, who is also in the frame, walking a few feet away. When they have nearly reached the victorious car, the camera that has been tracking alongside them pauses and allows Toad to pass, and we see John, much as Toad does, at the driver's side of the car, silhouetted by the morning sun. Although John sighs right after he says, "Okay, Toad," he takes his responsibility one more time, proving a figure worthy of nostalgic longing. Furthermore, just as with the hop scene, the appreciation of a great figure from the past extends to the heterosexual couple, Steve and Laurie, who conclude the scene embracing

FIGURE 2.1 The sunrise glow of male nostalgia at a drag race on "*Paradise Road*"
Credit: MCA/Universal Pictures/Photofest

and walking toward the camera set at a low angle. The rising sun behind them creates another halo that is joined on the soundtrack with a final punctuation, the sound of The Platters' "Only You."

George Lucas's *American Graffiti* unabashedly portrays the essence of nostalgia, not just a patchwork of fashionable objects and cultural references. Svetlana Boym insists that nostalgia must always be at odds with itself, both full of loving and loss. It always consists of a longing for the past and an understanding that the past has passed: "Nostalgic love can only survive in a long-distance relationship. A cinematic image of nostalgia is a double exposure, or a superimposition of two images—of home and abroad, past and present, dream and everyday life."[58] John Milner can only be the king of the past if he stays in the past. Lucas's film cannot help but admit that the "better life" is somewhere outside of this "turkey town" (as Steve calls it in the opening scene), but the emotional pull of the entire film is back to that town and to that time. The camera slows to take in certain moments and the filmmaker bathes certain people and objects in a glowing light. Since the epilogue indicates that Curt was the only one of the (male) characters to get out and survive (Toad has been listed as missing in action in Vietnam), then one might propose that this story is *his* nostalgic trip back, as a possible stand-in for Lucas himself. Furthermore, the final scene of the film supports such a reading.

After wavering all night about whether to stay or go, Curt decides to take that plane east, and Steve, who has been trying to convince him to go, decides to stay, presumably to be with Laurie. "Goodnight Sweetheart Goodnight," by The Spaniels, can be heard in the background, as Curt climbs the staircase up to the plane with his transistor radio prominently part of his carry-on luggage. Once in the plane, we see Curt at close distance and from a low angle taking in what he has just done. Rubbing his eyes slightly, showing exhaustion, he opens them to gaze down out the window, and at this moment "Goodnight Sweetheart Goodnight" ends. The next shot presumably reveals what Curt has been watching on the ground, an aerial view of a road, fields surrounding it, and a white car traveling in the same direction as the plane. It is not quite possible to determine if the car is Steven's white Chevy, but one might propose that the lives of his friends and Curt's life are now about to diverge just as the plane and the car will separate. When we return to Curt in the cabin, he is still looking down, but then sets his eyes on the horizon, and this last view of Curt dissolves into blue, which turns out to be the sky he is in and a final shot of the plane. The only sound on the soundtrack is the plane's engine from afar as the images of the four male leads (made to resemble high school yearbook pictures) are superimposed on the blue with their appended epilogue text. It does not seem too much of a stretch to imagine the film we have just seen as already being played in Curt's mind, the nostalgia for what he has left already solidifying those images and moments. In Boym's terms, he has already begun his "long distance relationship."

In light of the film's conclusion, one could stress an aspect of nostalgia, according to Boym, that might seem self-evident: its life in fantasy. At its simplest, nostalgia rises up as a feeling, "a sentiment of loss and displacement," but importantly it is a longing "for a home that no longer exists or has *ever* existed."[59] Infused with a utopian inclination, nostalgia takes on both meanings of that term, no place and the ideal place, and for this reason, it must exist, at least partly, as fantasy. Boym contends that nostalgia is both feelings of loss and "a romance with one's fantasy" of what was lost.[60] Moreover, as Andrew Higson and others suggest, this romance and imaginative practice often contain reactionary or regressive wishes for a 'simpler' time, usually spurred by a mourning "for the loss of an enchanted world with clear borders and values."[61] In these terms, then, we have the fantasy of *American Graffiti* that lovingly celebrates an enchanted past, but within itself is simultaneously mourning its passing. The expression on Curt's face as he stares out that plane window tells well enough the regret but resignation about the end. Curt, now writing in Canada, presumably to avoid the Vietnam War, can only visit this "enchanted world" in fantasy—a fantasy in which the good guy finishes first, the head cheerleader remains devoted to her guy, and the smart *guy* gets a scholarship to go east. In other words, the wish is for a world without Vietnam, Watergate, women's lib, civil rights, gay rights, et cetera, which in this fantasy turns into an enchanted, idyllic early 1960s.

Returning now to Holly and her trials with Kit, one is immediately struck by the contrast—by the way *Badlands* works as a relentless, ferocious rejection of the fantasy just outlined above. When Kit and Holly board *their* plane at the end of their 1973 film, he is being sent to his death and she is taking in the horizon knowing that she denied him help before his capture. Rather than feeling guilty, she appears distant from Kit, comfortable with her "probation," which was almost certainly dependent on her testifying against him. The hallmarks of the fantasy above have been turned upside down or completely destroyed in Holly's story. While the secondary players have changed, the action of boarding the plane is strikingly similar. Kit and Holly are led by police officers and soldiers to their plane, not their parents (who, in Holly's case, are dead), but the farewell ritual remains. Kit has become incredibly friendly with his arresting officers, particularly the young officer Tom who immediately recognized his resemblance to James Dean—"You know who that son of a bitch looks like? You know, don't you? I'll kiss your ass if he don't look like James Dean"—and his goodbye seems heartfelt (as does Tom's). When Tom says, "Good luck to you," he feels a need to reiterate the sentiment, "I mean it," and Kit appears to appreciate his emotion: "I know you do. Good luck to you too." One might even say the two together act like a inverted version of Toad and John Milner. But, of course, this farewell is not bittersweet or regretful; such sentiment is made strange and comical by the irony of Kit's situation. He is a multiple murderer who is signing his extradition papers on the back of an arresting officer and flying off to his certain imprisonment and death. As he moves to board the plane, the camera pans to follow his swaggering progress, the ridiculousness of his bravado punctuated by the shackles attaching him to an escorting police officer. "Goodnight, Sweetheart, Goodnight" might have overstated the black comedy, so Malick instead returns to a less buoyant section of Orff's "Musica Poetica" as the plane prepares to take off. Nevertheless, the artificiality and absurdity of Kit's posturing has been communicated.

In the very last moments, though, the film does accentuate one more time the irony of its treatment of this 1950s icon (a homicidal John Milner, if you will) and does so, importantly, through its female narrator's viewpoint. We find, in the final shots, that it is Holly, not Kit, who serves as Curt's counterpart, gazing out the plane window and, thereby, framing the narrative with her perspective (and her voice). The tenor of that perspective, as I have tried to show, has been skeptical and nearly unforgiving since the opening of the film. Kit's posturing has never been well received and his dire fate not mourned but anticipated: shortly after they create their forest hideout or idyll, Holly admits, "at times I wished he'd fall in the river and drown so I could watch." Her view of him in the end appears exhausted and unamused, as she narrates in voice-over a kind of epilogue to match *Graffiti*'s. Over views of the plane taking off, Holly tells of their trip back to South Dakota, of Kit's confinement in solitary and his ability to sleep through his confession read aloud in the courtroom, of his sentence "to die in the electric chair," and of her timely marriage to the son of her lawyer, who got her "off with probation and a lot of nasty looks." Her voice-over concludes shortly after the point of view shifts from outside the plane to in, ending with the information that Kit died "on a warm spring night" six months after his sentencing, which is spoken over a medium shot, from her perspective, of Kit and his escort seated together. Kit looks out the window, but the viewer never shares his view. Instead, we watch from Holly's seat as Kit performs his act one more time.

Glancing down after staring out the window, one might expect him to express regret or anxiousness, but instead he asks the officer where he got his hat. The ridiculousness of the question in his present situation is, at first, ignored by the officer and then treated with slight amusement. He somewhat sarcastically replies, "You're quite an individual, Kit," but Kit seems pleased. With a quick cut to Holly in close-up, we are reminded of whose perspective we have been sharing. Once again, the film differentiates between Kit and Holly through camera distance. He and the officer are viewed at medium distance, while Holly, whose point of view has directed the plot and whose perspective will create the final shot of clouds, stares back at Kit in close-up. Kit, naturally, has missed the officer's meaning and wonders if "they'd take that into consideration." The exchange of looks between the officer and Holly and Kit and Holly conveys well enough the attitude toward Kit. The officer responds by looking directly at Holly, sighing, and then staring out the window. In turn, Kit also seeks a response from Holly, trying to catch her eye and appearing a bit proud of himself despite the officer's clear annoyance.

The response comes in the form of an even tighter close-up on Holly's face as she tries to smile but can only manage a partial response. It is not exactly the appreciative reaction or approval Kit desires (and has been receiving from police officers since his capture), and it is made worse by *her* dismissive stare out the window, just like his escort's. She does not turn her head, but rather breathes out, maybe a sigh of relief, and shifts her eyes away from him. The final shot, again similar to Lucas's film, is presumably the sky from Holly's point of view. With a sunset and clouds steaming past the airplane, Malick achieves the same idea that *Graffiti* hints at—that the tale we have just witnessed originated in the mind of the person gazing out the window, as ethereal and changing, one might propose, as those clouds. We have the epilogue for the two main characters coupled with an individual perspective, but an entirely different tone. No longing, no regret, and certainly no world "with clear borders and values" offered here. Instead, Holly seems slightly exhausted and possibly relieved to see that world pass away, and Kit proves to be the antithesis of John Milner, oblivious to his fate and absurdly proud of his fame and "accomplishments."

While the emotional pull of *American Graffiti* brings the characters and possibly the viewers back, longing for and loving that past paradise, *Badlands* pushes relentlessly forward, though clearly on a road to nowhere. Sadness, longing, and emotional attachment simply do not exist, or they ring false, as pretense. The film and Holly's voice-over are clear on this score. She might have a fleeting thought of being "taken off to some magical land," but it is immediately and definitively quashed: "but this never happened." Although Kinder's review of the 1970s "outlaw couple" films continually returns to the idea of nostalgia, she aptly identifies this tone and the origin for it: "the dominant mode of *Badlands* is satire; hence, it is pointless to attack the film for a lack of warmth."[62] She notes how, in the scene where Kit and Holly burn her childhood home, with her father in it, elements of "the nostalgia and ritual are slightly overdone, almost reaching an exaggerated expressionism," but I believe she is closer to the point when she claims a few sentences before that these elements are "mocked" in the film.[63] Indeed, *Badlands* is an *American Graffiti* turned upside down and made comic, or at least tragicomic. However, this designation also does not quite fit. The violent refusal of and, more importantly, destruction of those elements that *American Graffiti* so lovingly enshrines makes it a dark satire indeed. After all, those "dolls that look almost human, and the antique furnishings and memorabilia" pictured in Holly's house are being engulfed in enormous flames, and the romantic hero, according to Kinder, "represents the banality of evil personified by Nixon."[64] Is it any wonder that Holly wishes him drowned?

In fact, Vera Dika's argument in *Recycled Culture in Contemporary Art and Film: The Uses of Nostalgia* identifies more clearly the reaction to such "banality of evil," suggesting an "emotional tone" which, for her, is "better described as rage or despair."[65] I would argue that *Badlands* sides in favor of rage rather than despair, a rage pointed directly at the era or fantasy of an era Lucas creates in *American Graffiti*, a kind of anti-nostalgia. While Dika maintains that Malick's film both damages "the tone of nostalgia" in Lucas's film and, more generally, "accosts the vacuity of these supposed 'happy days,'" our arguments diverge over the focus of that attack. She finds that Malick uses popular culture of the 1950s and work from certain fine arts movements to set up "an American ideal" in order "to cast doubt on the 1970s," setting up "the post-Vietnam War, post-Watergate America, as a 'bad' land of guilt, disappointment, and tarnished dreams." This era, for her, receives the force of the film's attack, even though it is set in the late-1950s. Instead, the images and popular culture from that earlier era, not the historical details, create a strange surface where an innocent, idyllic America appears completely out of reach. The simulacra of past popular culture—textual references such as Holly's voice-over in the form of "a journal entry lifted from 1950s popular culture sources such as modern romance magazines and novels" or plots from crime films of the 1940s and 1950s—combine with traumatic events to criticize the present.[66] With these extratextual references, *Badlands* can at one and the same time "give rise to feelings of nostalgia for a lost idyllic past," and then it can undercut those feelings by opposing the images and soundtrack to traumatic events that point to the historical present, with an allusion to Vietnam in the forest idyll sequence or to Kennedy's assassination in Kit's rendezvous date.[67] The "historical trauma of loss" and disappointment joins overused images of Americana in the 1950s to indict the contemporary era.[68]

In other words, Dika cannot quite escape in her analysis the presence of loss and the wish for an idyllic somewhere that comprise nostalgia. Yet, she does insist that wherever those sentiments exist in the film, they are quickly undercut in order to make a statement about the historical present. Her argument requires a better time and place in order to indict the present, but does Malick's film locate this idyll in the 1950s or allow it to exist at all? *American Graffiti* certainly returns to and clings to an idyllic time before the trauma caused by the loss of President Kennedy and of brothers in Vietnam, but, while *Badlands* might exhibit a "traumatized response," as Dika claims, it is not clear this response is directed toward the present. Moreover, Dika's argument appears at odds on the film's treatment of the 1950s, asserting that it assaults those "'happy days'" but also that its representation of James Dean definitely "is not meant to ridicule the original star."[69] Dika reveals *her* reluctance to accost the 1950s in her reading James Dean's imago in the film, admitting that the film "evokes a marginalized James Dean, one whose profession is that of a garbage man" without somehow indicating ridicule or attack; instead, her "Dean replica" is simply "set in a new historical context" meant to show that the "1960s had irrevocably damaged the American innocence and vigor James Dean once signified."[70] Surely, the suggestion that James Dean represented "innocence and vigor" indicates a skewed or nostalgic view of the time and of Dean's iconic status, which often has stood for recklessness, neuroses, and the contradictions of the middle-class nuclear family. One must wonder at the refusal to investigate *Badlands*' unmistakable indictment of the 1950s, while simultaneously viewing the 1960s solely as an era of trauma and lost innocence, not as a dramatic moment in US history when minorities and women fought for civil rights and a young generation challenged an increasingly corrupt and belligerent government. The film *is* critical of the 1950s, locating trauma in that 'cold' decade before Vietnam and Kennedy.

Remaining in the 1950s offered by *Badlands*, I would emphasize the trauma there and the film's indictment of that decade. Perhaps, it might be useful here to return to a term I mentioned earlier in this chapter: the "primal scene." James Hay has adapted that term to describe the kind of nostalgic fantasy offered in *American Graffiti*—a "mythos about the golden age of youth culture."[71] However, *Badlands*' return to the origin of youth culture in the US, and of teen film, more clearly reveals the disturbing elements and effects of that primal fantasy. Returning to the primal scene should not evoke pathos or golden-hued longing, but rather an unsettling trauma (to be exact, the trauma of witnessing or fantasizing about witnessing parental intercourse, which is interpreted as violence on the part of the father).[72] This traumatic experience, representing the origin of a particular American teen subject, rightly should be set in the 1950s, but a return to that original scene might remind some, particularly women, of a less-than-idyllic time. Without exactly the drama of the Kennedy assassination or the Vietnam War, the decade does have its traumas: Communist witch-hunts, lonely crowds, crises of masculinity in the organization man, sexual double standards for adolescent girls, viper mothers, and feminine mystiques. Malick's film touches upon several of these traumas, for example posing Kit as the Eisenhower conservative and Holly as a future wife looking back at the era, and, unlike *American Graffiti*, it acts as a *criticism* of postwar conventionality that serves a patriarchal status quo and of double standards meant to dominate the female teen, revisiting the moment in order to tear it apart, burn it down, or shoot it in the back. Furthermore, alluding to James Dean and the popular culture of the time, at least partly, serves to confront the media and the traditional teen film for its role in propagating exactly the fantasies central to Lucas's film—those golden-hued fantasies of the prom king and queen, the good father, and the brave outlaw son.

Moreover, I must stress again that these attacks and criticisms come from the voice and vision of a young woman's experience. While Holly does pepper her narration with some phrases and plotlines from popular romances and other media, they sit uneasily next to the cruelty and violence that permeate this fantasy world of hers. Any attempt to find nostalgic traces in her sometimes clichéd recounting of her "first love" runs right into a wall of blank expression, dismissal of the romantic lead, and murderous wishes, some carried out to fruition. *Badlands* depicts a woman returning to the 1950s where, as a motherless 15-year-old girl, she runs off with a young man who inspires no passion in her, who kills her father before murdering several others, and whom she eventually abandons to the authorities and his certain death. Surely, this vision of the 1950s is more bitter than sweet. Rather than return to a time when traditional values and borders held sway, this fantasy returns to murder the father, lampoon the male "hero" as an absurdly conservative, fame-seeking product of his age, and reveal the law to be corrupted by this mock-hero. To understand the effect, imagine that *Graffiti*'s Carol runs off with John Milner after he has killed her family, Curt, and the police officers who foolishly stop him for speeding, and then she turns him in on the very strip of road where he has been, not "king" of the drag racers, but a garbage collector.

A Blossom Fell: Re-Envisioning Teen Girl Spectatorship

Appropriately for such a fraught political moment, this dangerous, dark, and humorous vision, delivered in a young girl's deadpan, poses a serious threat to both Kit *and* her father.[73] Not satisfied with just humiliating and controlling Kit, although he proves useful in meting out her punishment, she has her father murdered and solidifies her control. In the two parallel murder scenes, she reveals how she can manipulate Kit, remove the obstacle to her desires, and punish him as the guilty party. Her father is literally shot down like a dog, and she remains blameless: she suggests far too late that they might call a doctor or the authorities, but excuses her own involvement, "Listen, I'll say how it happened . . . the part I saw." Nevertheless, the overwhelming visual splendor of the sequence comes with her father's destruction and the burning of her childhood home, indicating again our access to Holly's vision—its joyous destruction, devoid of nostalgia and thrilled by engulfing so many symbolic objects. The addition of a choir to the children's music sets up a mock ritual, while the enormous flames consume the patriarchal home, with the patriarch in it. Other significant objects engulfed by flames include a painting of the baby Jesus, Holly's bed (shot from several angles), her dollhouse, her father's work, and even the family piano. Holly leaves the house uneventfully, as if she were setting off for a vacation, and her voice-over, which notably returns as Kit is lighting the flames, seems to take an ironic view of Kit's actions: "He was gambling for time." But the visual star of the scene is surely the fire, majestically elevated by the choir's voices and emphasized by the camera's lingering over its devastation. Much as the point of view in *American Graffiti* lingers on the beloved objects and moments of the time, the cars, the band at the hop, the drag race, so here the action slows to take in and emphasize the devastating flames, possibly communicating as much pleasure (though of a different kind) as the sight of neon reflecting off John Milner's car. Rather than grieve, the film seems to celebrate the father's annihilation.

Once her instinct for cruelty and violence is let loose against patriarchal order, the desire for more seems insatiable and transfers itself to Kit as he increasingly indicates his authoritative aspirations. With the patriarchal home in flames, Holly's plotting turns to a familiar next step—lovers on the run. The two lovers, deemed "James" and "Priscilla" at Kit's request, hit the road like "spies" with some of Holly's schoolbooks and movie magazines. But this plot really only has one conclusion: one of them has to die (and it is not going to be the fantasizer). While the lovers are hiding out in a forest à la *Swiss Family Robinson*, their mock honeymoon initially appears amusing, but then one of their chickens dies, like the cows and fish before it, announcing that their new idyll is as shaky and doomed as the young love plot. Unfortunately, Holly's treatment or representation of Kit has not become kinder due to his service as an instrument of revenge, and his success in creating a home in the forest only betrays him as a father-figure and, therefore, dooms him. Shortly thereafter, he fails at catching fish for their dinner, resulting in Holly's wish that he would drown so she can watch. It is as this point that she begins to imagine a life without Kit via the stereopticon. Consequently, when three potential captors (bounty hunters) come into their forest fairy tale and Kit murders all of them, the fantasy might be coldly working out *his* eventual capture and death. Any pretense to a romance story has been abandoned in favor of violent action, and the aggression again takes representatives of male authority as victims, presaging Kit's downfall by tying him to both the father and the most recent victims. What might have begun as a beating fantasy with the romantic lead as its whipping boy has suddenly entered an entirely new phase, as a staging and replaying of patricide in whatever form that symbolic figure takes.

Significantly, for theories of spectatorship, it is at this moment that the film most clearly marks Holly as a film fan. Although her acknowledgment of Kit's resemblance to Dean and her witnessing of the murders have already exposed her identity as a spectator, her evident boredom and growing disregard for Kit place her pleasures as an audience member at the forefront. Needless to say, she proves to be a disenchanted, aggressive, and tough crowd of one. For the remainder of the film, failing to interest Holly becomes a capital offense. The anxiety about pleasing her is palpable when they find a new hideout with Kit's old coworker, Cato. This new mock-ideal community resembles more than any of the others Penn's *Bonnie and Clyde* hideout, but Kit and Holly have long since lost their ability to be in a "gang." While eating lunch at his house, Holly herself tries to break the boredom and anxiety by telling a joke, and Cato responds with a fantastic tale, desperate to keep her interest or at least to distract the pair of killers. As if cued by knowledge of popular culture, he attempts to appease her by inventing a buried treasure scenario (old Spanish coins found in the neighboring field), but once the story proves a ruse, Kit shoots Cato in the gut as he tries to slip away. Back in the house, with Cato slowly dying on his bed, Holly still appears bored, looking through catalogues and playing with Cato's pet spider. Even the young couple who shortly thereafter drive up to the house fail to interest her and, therefore, cannot stop the inevitable progression of the violence. She speaks to the other girl, as if she were a confidant, about sticking by Kit, but after he shoots at the couple, she loses interest in him as well. Judging from the last few scenes, the worst trait for a character in *Badlands* has become not their moral reprehensibility, but their monotony. Losing Holly as a fan, Kit finds, brings severe consequences, expressed as isolating indifference: "At this moment, I didn't feel shame or fear, just kind of blah . . . like when you're sitting there and all the water's run out of the bathtub."

The sepia-toned manhunt fantasy immediately following this remark indicates that the search targets Kit alone, and, from this point, he can expect exactly such an outcome. They remain together on the run, but Holly is no longer emotionally present. In the rich man's house, she questions whether there might be "something wrong with [Kit's] bean" and separates herself from *his* actions, removing herself from blame again, insisting that she never told Kit to shoot anyone. Therefore, when she says in voice-over, "We couldn't go on livin' this way," and Kit answers from within the diegesis, "Why not?" one begins to suspect that his days are numbered. The exchange, here, between Holly's voice-over and action within the diegesis, even dialogue by Kit, offers more proof that the entire story is one of Holly's inventing. She composes the voice-over and invents the male lover who will be her companion. She can even invent dialogue for him and dress him like James Dean, going as far as giving him James Dean's mannerisms. However, unlike Dean who died tragically young as his career was taking off, Holly's leading man outlives his welcome and must be killed off.

Figure 2.2 Holly betrays her James Dean, barely looking at him at the film's end
Credit: Warner Bros./Photofest

The true confirmation comes ironically when the film most clearly designates her as a film fan and consumer of fan literature. At one moment, she reads with enthusiasm from "Star Hollywood" about Pat Boone (an issue whose cover pictures Elizabeth Taylor and headlines promise the inside scoop on Tony Perkins and James Dean) and, shortly thereafter, declares Kit's fading, for her, as a star: "He needed me now more than ever, but something had come between us. I'd stopped even payin' attention to him." Like a fan who stops writing letters to and about her favorite star, Holly goes quiet, spelling out entire sentences on the roof of her mouth "where nobody could read them" (least of all her previous creation who is beginning to have an inkling of his fate). Their dance to Nat King Cole's song of betrayal in love, "A Blossom Fell," repeats her feelings and foretells of her coming unfaithfulness: "I thought you loved me./ You said you loved me./ We planned together/ To dream forever./ The dream has ended, / For true loved died." It is a perfect inversion of the final, golden dance between Steve and Laurie in *American Graffiti*, with its disjunction between the heterosexual couple and its foretelling of violence and betrayal.

Moreover, her voice-over highlights the inversion and points out that Kit realizes the end is near as well: he "dreaded being shot alone, without a girl by his side." True to his premonition, Holly refuses to accompany him in his final flight from the police and remains separated from him until they board the plane, on his ride to prison and then death. her confession that she "got off with probation and a lot of nasty looks" implies that she made a deal and testified against Kit. Holly's fantasy then has one last jibe at Kit. He is not captured by the police, nor does he outwit them. Kit stops his Cadillac on a dirt road (one he might even had drag raced on) and shoots his own tire. This act, juxtaposed with Holly's voice-over that sarcastically notes how he "claimed to have a flat tire," directly undermines the deputy's appreciation of his James Dean looks and reinforces the film's cruel play with 1950s culture. While the police officers prove an eager new audience, Holly, as noted above, can barely look at him in the final moments of the film.

A particular grouping of desires and pleasures—humiliation, revenge, punishment, and annihilation—are thus articulated in Holly's narration and at play in her pulp-fed mind. At times, they work as the main impetus for her fantasy creations, her plotting, and her treatment of her male star. A teenage consumer of popular culture, particularly as a spectator and fan of film culture, she fills her imaginary with stars and genre conventions, even stealing dialogue. That active sadism, an instinct for cruelty and mastery, fuels her narration should not be an unfamiliar idea for film theory. As Laura Mulvey famously wrote, "sadism demands a story, depends on making something happen, forcing a change in another person, a battle of will and strength, victory/defeat, all occurring in linear time with a beginning and an end."[74] But, also famously, Mulvey was speaking of a male sadism that takes the female as its guilty and passive object. Perhaps, it is here that we find the main obstacle for critics of *Badlands*—that an instinct for cruelty and mastery lies behind a raw (unbaked cookie), passive, blank, *female* face. A young teenage girl with her mind filled by film images and gossip from the latest movie magazines cannot possibly have fantasies like these, can she? Well, yes. For example, the girls who fantasize about boys being beaten while they look on in "A Child Is Being Beaten" are not only adolescent but also influenced by popular literature, although Freud does his best to diminish or disavow their sadism. Moreover, it might just be this teenage girl's film spectatorship and movie fandom that encourages both an active, sadistic relation to the screen and a fantasy-work that can rewrite all sorts of plots, even patriarchal ones. Holly's fantasy, on this score, may even rewrite the beating fantasies, finding the boys and the father interchangeable.

The beating fantasies and their representation of female spectatorship have received much attention from film theorists who find in them the seeds for a new understanding of the cultural and personal fantasies confronting one another at the moment a viewer sits down to watch a film. Particularly important for this reading of Holly's narration, Patricia White's return to the fantasies makes a case for their centrality in developing a theory of fantasy that "helps us to understand how representation is subjectively engaged, how it transforms consciousness and the unconscious and shapes the way our desire is structured and lived."[75] "Retrospectatorship," then, underscores the subjective fantasy of viewing and re-viewing films, wherein the personal interacts with the cultural, including the "memories and experiences of other movies" enjoyed by fans. As White stresses the importance of fandom and fan communities in encouraging both fantasy and revision of the codes of Hollywood films, so Holly's reading of fan magazines, therefore, becomes central for understanding the way in which she revises the stories offered to her, rather than passively accepting them and regurgitating them as a "first love" popular romance.[76] However, unlike White's representative example of retrospectatorship in the film *All About Eve* (1950), *Badlands* contains a sadistic fantasy which re-views the experience of teen female spectatorship as characterized by disturbing interactions between *male* stardom and (ostensibly heterosexual) female fandom.[77]

Holly's omniscient voice-over and controlling vision not only show that female authority and authorship are possible, but they also expose a female spectator's mind at play, sometimes cruelly, with popular culture, male Hollywood stars, and patriarchal order. At 15, she may have been in love, but by the 1970s she can also retrospectively use her imagination to recast the lead roles in that romance and revise it according to her desires. While masochism may exist in her fantasy, Holly also very clearly exhibits a desire to master, especially with regard to her male lead. Telling the story from some distant future, in which she may be married to the son of her lawyer, Holly is, for some critics, recuperated under male dominance and conventional order—first obeying her father, then Kit, and now her husband. But why not see this fantasy as her escape from or refusal of the resolution that marriage represents, a feminist refusal particularly resonant in the 1970s? More importantly, the basic mode of that escape is figured as a retrospectatorship that can only be set in motion through avid film spectatorship and fandom. Holly's narrative establishes the possibility of a different teen spectator: a girl who consumes film and popular culture only to subvert it, rewrite it, and bend it to her desires—a marginal subject of the 1970s re-envisioning Hollywood's conventions as female-authored adventure, violence, and punishment of patriarchal order.

In conclusion, I would like to return to the particular object of popular culture so prominently featured in Holly's fantasy—James Dean. One might consider Holly's marginality intimately connected to her membership in possibly the least valued film audiences in cinematic history—teenage girls, so her evocation of James Dean and even *Rebel Without a Cause* might be an exact revenge.[78] As with *Uncle Tom's Cabin* for Freud's patients, the melodrama to which she returns in formulating her fantasy is a kind of originary moment. Often considered the archetypal teen film, *Rebel* represents a major origin of *the* American teenager, which Holly views from a decidedly disenchanted future moment. The 1950s and this defining film for the decade represent a desperate attempt to reassert a normalized, Oedipal family drama. The passionate male hero, Jim Stark (James Dean), aches to know the 'right' role for him in society, with his peers, and in his family. Despite his gloriously tragic alienation (and method acting), Jim simply seeks a return to normative gender roles and Oedipal order, to a place where a father can confidently tell his son what to do "when you have to be man." Jim is even willing to attack his own father—throttling him while his mother screeches in psychoanalytically-informed horror, "you'll kill him!"—in order to learn how to "stand up" as a man. As I discussed in the previous chapter in another troubled 1950s Hollywood resolution of melodramatic eruptions, Jim does "stand up" in the end, reasserting heterosexual union with Judy and winning the approval and firm support of his father, but only through the violent erasure of an alternative teen plot, represented by Plato's desires. For Judy, who begins the film in the police station, having been picked up for walking the streets, the narrative serves to beat her into submission, just as her father slaps her at the dinner table for expressing her incestuous wish (a request for a kiss). She finally finds "love" with the very boy she sarcastically greeted with "Well, stop the world" and acquiescently smiles in Jim's arms in the end.

For critics of the genre, Judy's fate signifies the place for any girl in the genre and, moreover, for any girl watching. Jon Lewis briefly considers the female teen only to conclude that the pairing of *father and son* acts as the representative model for the destabilization of authority in postwar teen films and the resulting quest to resecure it on the part of the wayward son. Lewis encapsulates Jim's angst neatly: "What Jim wants most is hardly the stuff of a rebel. He just wants his father to tell him what to do."[79] When, in the end, Jim does solve that conundrum, the film "like so many other teen films, reinscribes the family ideal."[80] This genre narrative of wayward sons, so often repeated in traditional teen films, performs a love story in which the female part merely serves as a pathway "between men," to use Sedgewick's well-known phrase. Within this framework, the female star and female viewer are resolved, neglected, or used within the loop of filial desires. Vicki Lebeau characterizes this situation in terms of a different family contest, wherein the female viewer becomes the pathetic sister duped by her brother's pretenses to patriarchal legacy; she is complicit in her brother's rightful ascension to his father's place, and ultimately becomes "the daughter of a seductive paternity working within and beyond cinema."[81] From these critical perspectives, films like *Rebel Without a Cause* enact a male teen fantasy of rebellion from and eventual rescue by the good father who has temporarily failed his duties. When the father does not appear, the films act as a paean to his absence, at their heart nostalgic. For the female viewer, though, they encourage complicit agreement with, if not active support of, this other romance.

If only for this reason, I have explored Holly's story, her wonderfully funny and terribly dark refusal and humiliation of James Dean. Like an avenging Natalie Wood/Judy (who has no last name in the film, presumably because she will take her husband's soon enough), Holly interrupts that traditional father-son love story, destroying one and then the other as he takes his place. From a later time, in which a 'romantic' view of the 1950s can be contradicted by the damage done by adjustment therapy, the suffocation of the nuclear family, and "the problem that has no name," she revises the story she has presumably witnessed many times through subjective fantasy and writes her own adolescent tale; the family ideal is burned to the ground and James Dean does *her* bidding, follows her plotting, and exits the stage before her final close-up. *Badlands* refigures the (teenage) female viewer and fan, projecting *her* fantasy—a fantasy full of rage at and criticism of the popular culture and the patriarchal order that keeps trying to silence her.

Chapter 3

The Queer Kid and Women's Lib

As I established in the Introduction, critics have often considered the 1970s as a kind of nadir in Hollywood's popular representations of adolescence that dominated screens in the 1950s and were reborn in the Reagan era. However, what Shary calls this "dormant" period for teens in film produced some of the most compelling and complex depictions of an adolescent's relationship with his or her mother.[1] Whether through the pairing of mother and son or mother and daughter, acclaimed films like *Alice Doesn't Live Here Anymore* (1974) or *An Unmarried Woman* (1978) focus on a central and emotionally significant bond between a mother and her preternaturally mature child. As I will explore in the next chapter, Jodie Foster's turn in *Freaky Friday* obviously continues in this vein. Even two of the most successful horror films of the era, Friedkin's *The Exorcist* (1973) and DePalma's *Carrie* (1976), wrestle with the adolescent's antagonism with and dependence upon the mother. Furthermore, two of the teen stars singled out by Shary in *Generation Multiplex* as "prominent exceptions" to Hollywood's abandonment of "promoting teenage performers" in the 1970s—Jodie Foster and Robby Benson—acted in several of these filial dramas or confronted women's lib in other ways, for example in Benson's roles as sensitive suitor of independent and sexually aware teen girls.[2]

I will return to the female "prominent exceptions," Jodie Foster and Tatum O'Neal, in the next chapter, but Benson, the central teen star for this discussion, presents an intriguing exception indeed during this "dormant" period for teens on screen. In this era, Robbie Benson made a career out of defying gender norms, with his soft voice, aching blue eyes, and troubled male romantic leads who pursued strong, independent young women or, in the case of one notable film, were seduced by older men. From his early teen love story *Jeremy* through the daring *Ode to Billy Joe*, in which he plays one of the few gay teens on screen before the revolution of New Queer Cinema in the 1990s, to the popular skating romance *Ice Castles*, Benson cultivated a star persona centered on emotional vulnerability and other feminine features that were matched with a lean, muscular physique on display particularly in *Ode* and in teen fan magazines of the period such as *Tiger Beat*. While many male teen stars of the 1970s exhibited in such publications—for example, Leif Garrett, Scott Baio, and Shaun Cassidy—typically displayed this same androgynous combination with its roots in the front men of glam rock, Benson coupled this striking androgyny with roles opposite strong female leads, seeming to champion female empowerment, and with an openness to the changing definitions and boundaries of sexuality (e.g. to include teenage homosexuality). In short, like the more prominent Foster, teen star Benson gained popularity in the 1970s as what Kathryn Stockton and others call a "queer child," a gender-queer and sexually-conscious young person who possesses the potential to queer traditional cinematic representations of the adolescent.

The Queer Kid in the 1970s

This period in the United States, as many recent historical accounts have emphasized, is marked by what President Carter famously called a "crisis in confidence," in that a majority of Americans had lost faith in the effectiveness and honesty of dominant institutions. The scandalous failure of key American master narratives—from the integrity of the president and the power of the armed forces to the seemingly unending postwar affluence—opened up space for a number of counter-narratives not the least of which were produced by the women's and gay rights movements.[3] Indeed, as Andreas Killen argues particularly in regard to the year 1973, the concomitant failure of dominant, patriarchal institutions and the rise of feminism cannot be considered just a well-timed coincidence. Viewing the Watergate scandal as a "symbolic killing of the father," Killen suggests that "in a nation coping with, or celebrating, the symbolic death of the father, women emerged as central voices and symbols of the new cultural configuration."[4] This new "cultural configuration" had lasting impact on the nuclear family, which many warned was in "crisis" due to increasing divorce rates and the supposed "generation gap," and included an increasingly vocal and politically powerful gay rights movement.[5] However, while cultural commentators at the time might have lamented the crisis in the nuclear family brought by the sexual revolution and identity politics, recent scholarly work on the 1970s celebrates the potential for change brought by the rights movements. In his introduction to his edited collection on the popular culture of the 1970s, Shelton Waldrep's defense of the "disruptive nature of the seventies" focuses on the era's "ambiguity," which is often manifested in changes in gender and sexuality, and he cites this ambiguity as productive of the period's "generative and disruptive influences."[6] The "crisis of confidence" for the dominant culture is, therefore, held up as an opportunity for those on the margins or the previously disempowered to find a voice amidst the disruption and instability. The 1970s then is beginning to represent, for recent cultural critics and historians, a period of possibility for those reveling in the fissures opened up by crisis.

Killen's work *1973 Nervous Breakdown* similarly emphasizes this disruptive pairing of gender and sexuality through popular culture in its examination of the crisis of the family as broadcast on national television in PBS's groundbreaking documentary *An American Family*. Producer Craig Gilbert's observational documentary program that followed the Loud family through their everyday lives and into marital dissolution has been considered one of the major precursors to current reality television but was most significant at the time for its engagement with debates around the "crisis" in the American family, which seemed to reflect the dire state of American culture itself. According to Jeffrey Ruoff, Gilbert's understanding of the concerns raised by cultural commentaries such as Roszak's *The Making of the Counterculture* and Reich's *The Greening of America* led him to address directly the family as locus for the "anxiety over the divorce rate, the women's movement, new sexual mores, gay liberation, and the generation gap."[7] He chose his family, the Louds, well: the opening episode reveals in its framing device from last day of filming that Pat and Bill Loud have separated during the eight months of the PBS observational experiment. The debates that Gilbert hoped to provoke about the changing American family and the end of the American frontier came almost immediately and vociferously from critics whose overwhelmingly reactionary conclusion was "that the program chronicled the breakdown of American culture."[8] For recent commentators like Killen, *An American Family*'s exposure of the "meltdown of the nuclear family" and the unraveling of traditional "myths and promises" of the nation might be understood in terms of the productive postmodern moment reflected in the series itself, as well as in son Lance Loud's connections to Warhol, and in terms of the alternative narratives possible in a world of "a symbolic abdication of authority" by the father.[9] Two central figures, for Killen, drive the series and bring "the traditional family most sharply into question" (58); having recently come out of the closet to his family, the oldest son Lance lives in the Chelsea Hotel in New York and rubs elbows with Warhol's Superstars, and his mother, who visits him in New York during the second episode, becomes the other "central character" of the series through her growing discontent with her marriage.[10]

The first two episodes of the series, originally aired on January 11 and 18, 1973, set up this central pairing of the mother encouraged by women's rights and her queer kid who escapes suburbia. After a voice-over introduction from producer Gilbert that sets up the family and the location of Santa Barbara, the first episode opens on the family home on New Year's Eve, 1971 (the last day of filming), and Gilbert announces the unusual circumstances of the evening—that the family will not all be together due to Pat and Bill Loud's separation. We see a great deal of Pat Loud on this New Year's Eve by herself, as a spectator to her children's festive antics, and the use of the marital revelation from the beginning haunts her presence for the rest of the episode, the majority of which takes place on the *first* day of filming in the late spring of 1971, and, indeed, colors the entire series. As Ruoff suggests, the effect of this opening disclosure is that "viewers look for signs of a troubled marriage" for the rest of the series, and the failure of the marriage or the Loud's "broken home," as Lance mockingly later calls it, becomes the central drama of the program.[11] The only other location revealed in the opening episode is Lance's room in the Chelsea Hotel, where the cameras find him in the spring of 1971 having happily left the 'normalcy' of Santa Barbara behind. Significantly, as we see him tidying his room, Lance is given a voice-over in which he embodies the authority of this sound element by introducing his siblings to the audience. Through his details about them and editorial comments, we come to know the younger members of the family—his preference for his youngest sister Michele and his antagonism with his "arrogant" 17-year-old brother Grant, for example. The device allows him to control our future perceptions of the siblings, for in the simplest terms, as Ruoff comments, the entire scene "endorses Lance's point of view" on the family—a privilege not granted to other Louds.[12] The program's focus on the points of view of the two central characters is solidified by the second episode, which follows Pat to New York to visit her oldest son.

In the second episode, as in the climax of *An American Family*, the series unites the concerns of and changes in the mother with the self-conscious counter-discourse offered by the queer son. When she goes to visit Lance in New York City, Pat comes face to face with his new life, including rubbing elbows with Warhol Superstars like Holly Woodlawn at the Chelsea and going to see the "transvestite variety show" Vain Victory. While his mother appears uncomfortable, she also clearly has a close bond with Lance and listens as he confides in her, telling her how he "stood apart from everybody" at home. She admits to finding it "strange" to be on her own without "dad" but clearly enjoys their day out and the prospect of even seeing Jackie O's apartment. In another kitschy moment, Lance takes his mother to a Tarot card reading where the viewer is reminded once again of the ominous future announced at the opening of the series. The Tarot reader declares it a "Year of Change" and informs Pat that "something is ending," which leaves the audience to find further significance in the noted absence of "dad." By episode seven, when the parents take separate vacations and Pat appears to be 'finding herself' in Taos, New Mexico, the program has offered many such clues to the growing discord and the apparently inevitable failure of the marriage.

Always, in the background of this instability is Lance, laughing off his father's platitudes about becoming "a man" able to take care of himself or referring to the "great devious things" he and Pat got up to in New York City. It is as if his mother's decision to change her life has been validated or at least encouraged by Lance's repeated subversions of authority. In the episode before Pat's announcement that she would like Bill to move out, the scene cuts from the obvious tension between husband and wife to Lance in Paris where he announces to friends that he is writing a play "on women's liberation" about a prostitute "who becomes a bird." Symbolically, by his own recognition, Lance only returns to Santa Barbara once Bill has moved out of the house. He refers to this period in the family history as a mock allegory—the "return of Lance versus the fall of the father"—and repeatedly ridicules the seriousness of the situation; when his brother Grant notes that "Dad is being a real pal nowadays," Lance responds mockingly that Bill "has to compensate for the family tragedy—sigh." His one meeting with his father gives him the opportunity for passive aggressive teasing about Bill "taking the business of being a father too lightly" and then noting in an offhanded way how "together mom is." To be sure, the series is unambiguous in its presentation of the children's reaction to the separation that clearly favors their mother. Pat is shown spending a great deal of time at home with her children, again watching them at play, while Bill works at his hotel alone. The separation episode even ends with Grant serenading his mother with the Beatles' "Mother Nature's Son," half-seriously announcing that "this one's for mom."

Yet, Lance's relationship with Pat is the most meaningful, as Bill even comments at dinner before their separation, and one might argue that his flight to New York City immediately preceding the filming acts a proto-liberation narrative for the mother's own coming to consciousness—an interpretation further supported by her following flight to New York in the second episode. While this pairing of queer kid and the mother of women's lib works to subvert the traditional family and its central authority figure, I would argue that it does not entirely destroy the family but instead rewrites its dominant narrative. Pat's relationship with her children remains strong all the way through the final day of filming, even though her behavior at the New Year's Eve party hints at her own loneliness and loss. The series reveals an emotional cost for the breakdown of the traditional family, but it also establishes, in a typically 1970s kind of way, that the dominant family narrative can be and, in fact, has been rewritten due to the impact of the women's and gay rights movements.

While an enormous amount has been written about the influence of second wave feminism on the traditional family and on American culture in general, less work has focused on the other central figure in the drama outlined above: the queer kid. Indeed, Harry Benshoff writes off the idea of a nonproblematic queer kid in mainstream cinema where "when queers and families do appear in Hollywood films, their stories have generally been scripted from the perspective of the presumably straight family."[13] However, more recently, following Michel Foucault's analysis of a history of sexuality that emphasizes a multiplicity of discourses ostensibly about and productive of sexualities (especially those most repressive and controlling of sex), new scholarship has turned to the fraught discourses surrounding the sexuality of children. In *A History of Sexuality: Volume I,* Foucault includes "the sexuality of children, mad men and women, and criminals" as the focus of special scrutiny during the "explosion" of discourses in the eighteenth and nineteenth centuries when the proliferation of knowledge, regulation, and confessions of sexual others reified and legitimated the heteronormative adult couple.[14] More recent work—from James Kincaid's *Child-Loving: The Erotic Child and Victorian Culture* and Eve Kosofsky Sedgwick's essay "How to Bring Your Kids Up Gay: The War on Effeminate Boys" to Kathryn Stockton's full-length study *The Queer Child*—focuses particularly on the figure of the child and dominant Western narratives that construct and deny the sexuality of children.[15] As the editors of the 2004 collection of essays *Curiouser: On the Queerness of Children* describe it in their introduction, the normative narrative about children insists that "children are (and should stay) innocent of sexual desires" *and* that they are "also officially, tacitly, assumed to be heterosexual."[16] The queer child, for them and for the other writers in the collection, upsets both of these "comfortable stories" about Western childhood. They argue for a broad understanding of the term "queer," defined as outside the "normal," but, specifically, the queer *child* becomes "that which doesn't quite conform to the wished for way that children are supposed to be in terms of gender and sexual roles" or the one "who displays interest in sex generally, in same-sex erotic attachments, or in cross-generational attachments."[17] The queer child disturbs and subverts the typical constructions of childhood in narratives that are fueled by both utopianism, in the child's representation of the future, and nostalgia, which necessitates the innocence of the normative child in a "preferred past."[18] Sedgwick's proto-gay child, for example, by definition cannot be innocent since sexuality is raised in the very term and suggests an alternative to the compulsory heterosexuality of the normative narrative of maturation, resulting in "open season on gay kids."[19] The queer child, or "queer kid" as I have called Lance Loud, Robby Benson and Jodie Foster, exposes the convenient fiction of an innocence that allows the child to become a screen for adult desires and bends or queers the "straight narrative line" to inevitable heteronormativity and gender role compliance, offering instead a polymorphously perverse narrative path.[20]

Kathryn Stockton, the theorist whose work most fully examines the bent narratives associated with the queer child, proposes a far-reaching effect for this figure. The queer child, for her, must be understood in terms of a particular temporality involving retrospection and narrative deferral that produces what she calls a "sideways" growth. She argues that throughout the twentieth century, the proto-gay or queer child has rarely been allowed to appear, since sexual categories are "culturally deemed too adult," or surfaces only "through an act of retrospection and after a death."[21] The "death" to which she refers here is both the death of childhood and the death of a straight life. For the child who feels "different," the naming of that queerness can "arrive only after [the child] exits its childhood, after it is shown not to be straight." Once the possibility of a straight self has died, in adolescence or just after, the queer child can be "now born—albeit retrospectively."[22] The "asynchronous self-relation" caused by this (queer) time out of joint, and the "ghostly 'gay' child" that results, offers Stockton a way to rewrite the teleological narrative of hetero-maturation. She can "pierce (deflate, or just delay) the vertical, forward-motion metaphor of 'growing up'" by reading the "sideways growth" of the "publicly impossible child whose identity *is* a deferral (sometimes powerfully and happily so)." In fact, these stories of sideways growth are more common than one would think, as she finds the tropes of deferral, misdirection, and delay in texts ranging from Freud's case studies to Gus Van Sant's *Elephant* (2003). Yet, Stockton is willing to go further by proposing deferral as characteristic of "childhood" itself; the category of childhood becomes queer for her by virtue of being "either homosexual . . . or, despite our culture's assuming every child's straightness, not yet straight, merely approaching while crucially delaying (in its own asynchronous fix) the official destination of straight sexuality and therefore showing itself as estranged from what it would approach."[23] While her sophisticated and incredibly persuasive argument might exceed the narrow bounds of the present chapter, I would propose that Stockton's notion of a "sideways" narrative trajectory initiated by the "ghostly" queer kid offers a way of understanding the 1970s' representations of teens on screen as a misdirection or swerve from the dominant, normative cinematic story of youth and maturation. Indeed, Shary's descriptor of the 1970s as a "dormant" period for teen films and stars evokes Stockton's notion of the delay or deferral of sideways growth.

As the historians and cultural critics cited above suggest, the 1970s as a decade has been painted in similar terms, as a swerve from the great American master narrative—the Me Decade awash in self-involvement, crises of confidence and disco where, to borrow the title of Peter Carroll's groundbreaking study, "it seemed like nothing happened." Yet this detour on the road to Reagan's "Morning in America" should not be discounted for the same reasons Stockton pursues her "ghostly" queer child. Like the alternative family narrative on display in the Loud's Santa Barbara home, the 1970s disrupts the "comfortable stories" of American mythology, particularly those of paternal authority and tough, rugged, aggressive masculinity. Of course, Ronald Reagan brings these back with a vengeance, but this only serves as further proof of anxieties caused by their collapse. The example of Lance Loud and his mother, Pat, demonstrates the potential in the detour by establishing a counter-discourse and revision of the family narrative (the queer kid bending the straight line to heteronormativity), yet this one example is not isolated. The pairing of the queer kid and the women's movement drives a number of mainstream films of the era, offering a series of illustrations of "sideways growth" for the adolescent and the woman tied to him or her. For teen actors of the period only slightly younger than Lance Loud, the queer kid (and the alternative narratives produced in his or her wake) turns into a starring role. Robby Benson, the first star I will focus on here, cultivated a persona through film choices, interviews, and fan magazines that did not conform to traditional gender norms but instead embodied a desirable androgyny. Further, his roles engaged openly with adolescent sexuality, including the queer sexuality of a homosexual experience. Most importantly, and appropriately for the era, this queering of male adolescence through challenges to normative masculinity and sexuality earned him great popularity and success as a teen idol.

Robby Benson: Queering the Male Teen Idol

Years before his name became synonymous with the young male "sentimental softie" of romantic melodramas like *Ice Castles*, Benson emerged as a star due to his talent as an actor and longevity in the business (rivaling even Jodie Foster's) and due to his particular version of sensitive and vulnerable masculinity.[24] He began his career at age 5 on the musical stage in New York City, the child of show-business parents. By the time he had his breakout role in *Jeremy* at the age of 16, he had already acted on television, stage, and screen. He proved to be a versatile and independent performer, singing the theme song, "The Hourglass Song," for the film *Jeremy* and co-writing his first feature film, the basketball romance *One on One* (1977), at the age of 21 with his father Jerry Segal. Accordingly, interviewers and reviewers often comment on his intelligence, sensitivity, and mature professionalism. Even fan magazines reiterate this poised and capable, but gentle, male star image. Introducing Benson to its devoted readership as the "talented young man" in *Jeremy*, the fan magazine famous for its pin-ups of male teen stars, *Tiger Beat*, entices readers to "Meet Robby Benson!!!" with two photos of the star framing the page: in one he is the casual, wholesome every-teen dressed in jeans and sneakers, smiling through his shaggy, Beatles-like hairdo, and in the other he stares more daringly out at the viewer in a medium close-up that serves to accentuate his soft lips and blue-grey eyes, while he is toughened up a bit by the addition of a jean jacket. The text itself presents exactly the kind of complex and gender-queer star persona that becomes Benson's trademark. The initial description softens him, highlighting his "soft brown hair" and his "expressive blue-green eyes" sometimes hidden by glasses that keep sliding down his nose, but he is always the talented professional, who may be "soft-spoken" but is also "independent" and known for his "politeness, intelligence and concern about his fellow man."[25] In short, he is painted as capable and successful but also as the "shy, but not at all awkward," romantic young man who "spends hours strumming on his guitar" and is "in love with being in love" and would never be aggressively or sexually threatening to the young readership.[26] The poorly disguised attempt to retain some normative masculinity in his great enthusiasm for sports (although contact sports are absent from the list of favorites) is slightly undermined by the previous paragraph, which describes his ideal girl. Teen idol Benson prefers "[q]uiet, reserved and independent girls, who have a good sense of humor, intelligence, and enjoy sports," or, something like the readership of *Tiger Beat*; in other words, he desires an equal, someone who can match his intelligence, strength, and interests. Later interviews with Benson and his choice of roles certainly support this early fan magazine picture of a sensitive and conscientious young man who is not afraid to find his equal in the liberated young women of his era.

In one of his earliest successes, *Jeremy*, Benson creates the foundations for the star image detailed above. Through the story of a young cellist who falls in love with a talented dancer at a prestigious arts school in New York City, *Jeremy* teams Benson up with capable first-time costar Glynnis O'Connor, who rejoins him three years later in *Ode to Billy Joe* and who supposedly became a love interest for Benson off the set as well. The film begins by establishing the likable but awkward central character of Jeremy Jones (Benson), a slight young man with thick glasses and a "crazy kid" habit of picking winners in horse races on which he never bets. His music teacher warns him that he will "never be concert quality," that his "energies are too divided," but Jeremy has a passion for playing the cello. As he starts to pursue Susan Rollins, the dancer he falls for after accidentally stumbling upon her ballet practice, Jeremy distinguishes himself in her eyes through the "emotion" he displays while playing the cello. The viewer is brought into a similar recognition through long close-ups on his impassioned face as he plays. He may never be "concert quality" (since his energies quickly become divided between the cello, Susan, the horse track, and even the basketball court), but his devotion to music and the arts in general is strong. He admits to Susan, "I really feel things when I play music," and carries poetry with him to read at the park. Furthermore, the film explicitly roots the romantic, artistic passions of the protagonist in its breakout star Benson by opening *Jeremy* with his performance of the ballad "The Hourglass Song," which pleads for a love on borrowed time or not to "just throw your love about." Noting Benson's musical contribution in promotional press and in the closing credits, the film encourages the audience's identification of Jeremy with the young star (even placing the title over his bare-chested figure in the opening), thereby engaging fans in the kind of intimate knowledge and consumption of a romantic lead and star that magazines like *Tiger Beat* depend on for their circulation. *Jeremy* owes its success in large part to the suggestion that the story's passionate but inexperienced young lover *is* Robby Benson.

Benson's offscreen relationship with Glynnis O'Connor and the stirring, natural connection between the two characters on screen only strengthen this elision of star and role and also establish the version of masculinity embodied by the star. Introduced by a string of signifiers in the opening credit sequence including his cello, books of literature, a chessboard, and racing posters, Jeremy is marked by feminine vulnerability from the beginning. A point of view shot during the opening exposes his blurred vision without his glasses and once he puts them on, his appearance shifts from one of a lithe male physique awakening to the bookish and nerdy awkwardness of the young schoolboy. The character we come to know over the long early sequence before he spots Susan avoids simple classification—he moves quickly from philosophical discussions on a beach stroll with his music teacher to playing basketball with his considerably more mature best friend Ralph—but predominantly reveals intelligence, artistic and emotional sensitivity, and charming eccentricity. His anguished attempt to call Susan for the first time gives the film a painful honesty but also fits this decidedly unmacho youth; his voice even breaks as he tries to make conversation with her over the phone. One gets the sense that without the advice and encouragement of the more experienced and aggressive Ralph, Jeremy might not have called her at all. In turn, Susan's independence and self-assured nature complement Jeremy's shy pursuit. She seems a fitting companion, appreciating his passion for music *and* having ambitions of her own. As one critic puts it, she is "more than his equal in sincerity, talent, and need."[27] At the climax of the film, when they spontaneously and mutually decide to have sex, the scene at one point shifts away from their faces to a close-up on Jeremy's hands fumbling with the clasp on her bra. With control and calm, Susan sits up, stares lovingly down at him, and unclasps her own bra—an example of the "bittersweet discomfort" that makes the film "true and moving" for another reviewer.[28] Susan responds to Jeremy's vulnerable and inexpert masculinity with a sure hand and sincere feeling. In fact, they both seem to admire in each other those very qualities that fall outside gender norms.

A large part of Benson's star persona then lies not only in his gifted and vulnerable roles but also in his respect for strong female counterparts. In a 1977 interview with Randi Bourscheidt of *Interview* magazine, Benson shared details about his close relationship with his *Jeremy* costar Glynnis O'Connor that remarkably resemble their on-screen roles. Set up by the interviewer to appear conscientious and hardworking with a knack for playing "very naïve, soft-spoken, pretty" male roles, Benson himself reconfirms that image offered by *Teen Beat* several years before; the valedictorian of his high school class who remains enthusiastic about reading and writing poetry, he confesses to wanting "to write about the way I feel" and express himself in "very personal" music.[29] The recipient and subject of his songs and poems is none other than Glynnis O'Connor, whom he calls a "great lady." He claims to have written every poem, story, and note about her for three and a half years while he worked to be with her as much as possible. Yet, he also appreciates her drive and independence that led her out to the west coast where she is starring in a series: "She's fantastic, I wish she were here right now." Like the conclusion of *Jeremy* where the title character loses his fantastic girl when her father returns to his job in Detroit, the young romantic Benson has no choice but to let his love go where her ambitions take her. The same tragic, romantic plot plays itself out again only a year later in one of Benson's most successful films, *Ice Castles*, in which his character chooses to sacrifice his own ambitions to help his beloved regain her previous stature in the figure skating world.

Both *Ice Castles* and the film he co-wrote with his father the previous year, *One on One* (Johnson, 1977), present Benson as equally admiring of and dependent upon accomplished, successful women who resemble his description of Glynnis O'Connor. While the figure skating romance begins with a focus on the return of the prodigal son Nick (Benson), who has left college for uncertain dreams of a professional hockey career, the narrative quickly shifts to the drama of his aspiring girlfriend, Lexie. Played by Lynn-Holly Johnson, herself a successful amateur skater who joined the professional Ice Capades circuit in 1977, Lexie gains confidence from her small town Iowa coach (played by a curiously butch Colleen Dewhurst) and discovers a "power in mind" and desire for the sound of the crowd at a regional competition. Inspired by her newfound ambition, she wins her father's permission to train with a top coach at a premier training facility and discovers serious expectations for her strength and ability there: her coach warns, "If you're not tough enough, you're never gonna make it." As Lexie excels in the "tough" environment and gains confidence in her own abilities and desires, the film cuts back to scenes of Nick struggling on his hockey farm team and becoming increasingly more envious of her accomplishments and growing fame. He chooses to miss her most important performance in a specially arranged television special, preferring to wallow in his own self-pity after having just quit the hockey team in resignation and confusion, admitting, "I don't know what I want." As Lexie's success reaches a crescendo, she foolishly falls at a party and nearly blinds herself, but afterwards when she needs him, Nick appears at her side to goad her back into skating again. He plays to her pride and ambition by provoking her to empower herself, imploring, "don't act helpless with me" and "don't let me control you!" With his encouragement and belief in her abilities, Lexie does make it back to Olympic trial form and nearly fools the entire crowd at sectionals, finding Nick at her side again when she falters on tributary flowers. Of course, the conclusion offers the idea that she cannot succeed without his help and confidence in her, yet the film also suggests that he should sacrifice his own needs for her accomplishments and accept her talent and skills as equal to, if not greater, than his. A similar humbling experience occurs for another Benson character, the basketball star Henry Steele in *One on One*, who is not only abused by a dictatorial head coach on his new college team but also increasingly dependent upon the strength and talent of his academic tutor, Janet Hays (played by Annette O'Toole). The film reverses the possession of athletic ability (Robby seems to have it this time) but does not change his gravitation toward independent, successful women. He needs the older female graduate student to help with his history class and his substandard basic academic skills, forming in the end another partnership that highlights the strengths of both of them.

All of these examples, from *Teen Beat* introductions to more mature romantic roles, suggest that Benson carefully formulated the kind of teen star he wanted to become. He favored a focus on his own intelligence, talent, and artistic sensibility—even at times his own vulnerability—and preferred a partner who was his equal in drive and ability. In other words, to use the parlance of the time, he played the part of a "liberated" young man. Looking beyond the few sensitive or "liberated" men of 1970s American film like Alan Bates in *An Unmarried Woman* or Kris Kristofferson in *Alice Doesn't Live Here Anymore*, many critics offer a vastly different picture of masculinity on screen in the era than that presented by Benson. Joan Mellen's study of masculinity in American film takes Clint Eastwood's Dirty Harry as her model for the "violent, equally ferocious male hero" of the decade's cinema, contending that "[m]ale sexual survival itself becomes dependent upon a man's becoming a violent vigilante" like Harry Callahan or Travis Bickle.[30] One might also think here of the "easy riders" and "raging bulls" of Biskind's work or the violent patriarchs of *The Godfather* series. Although not to the excess of Hollywood film in the 1980s that, according to Jeffords, "highlighted masculinity . . . as a violent spectacle that insisted on the external sufficiency of the male body/territory," the era's films did largely underscore the place of violent and aggressive masculinity in the American character.[31] However, it is important to note that these critics are predominantly focusing on *adult* male roles on screen in the 1970s.

For adolescents, normative masculinity appears much more elusive. Timothy Shary argues in an article on "bad boys" in Hollywood film that the young male leads of the 1970s like Benson or John Travolta acted out "conflicted" male roles, as did performers in films like *The Warriors* (1979) or *Breaking Away* (1979).[32] In contrast to the teen films that would follow in the 1980s where boys expressed "a new sense of aggression that renewed their ideals of masculine potency," which was often illustrated by "the lecherous longings of sex-starved lotharios," the conflicted young men of the 1970s appeared "confused, intimidated, and insecure, with the implicit fallout of Vietnam and Watergate weighing on them heavily."[33] Citing as an example the "repressed homosexuality" of *Ode to Billy Joe*, Shary establishes Benson as one of the troubled male teens who reflect the instability and ambiguity of the gender expectations in the era. Jeffrey Dennis goes one step further to suggest that the teen magazines and films of the era both promoted androgyny and hinted at the sexual ambiguity of male stars. He singles out stars like Shaun Cassidy, Robby Benson, Leif Garrett, and Jimmy McNichol for their "soft, pretty features, feathered hair, and swiveling hips," representing an "intensification of the androgyny visible in teen idols' stage presence since the days of Frankie and Fabian."[34] However, these 1970s stars offer something new: visual narratives and star discourses about "best buddies" of theirs "resulted in an openness to same-sex romance unprecedented in the history of the teen idol." For Dennis, films like *American Graffiti* or *Grease* and television shows like *Happy Days* belittle heterosexual desire "while the love of comrades can redeem the world."[35] When one combines the homosocial or homoerotic bonding of the narratives with the teen idols who "made their careers out of hints, innuendos, and 'is he gay' posturing," the decade's youth-oriented texts and male leads begin to look queer indeed, especially in comparison to the violent aggression of their adult counterparts.

FIGURE 3.1 Leif Garrett and Tatum O'Neal pose together as the teen idol becomes a queer kid *(Credit: Photofest)*.

Furthermore, a brief consideration of the construction of the male teen idol in the 1970s points to a queer ambiguity in addition to the era's fashionable androgyny for young performers. When one looks at the way the teen idol must be constructed in order to appeal to a wide variety of fans, supposedly female, a queer undecidability or availability becomes apparent. The teen idol transforms into a kind of queer kid due to his blankness or refusal to be defined or settled by one romance or stated relationship. It is not quite that he is not-yet-straight, but he is also not yet defined by a heterosexual union or commitment because fans are supposed to fantasize he is available to them or might be attracted to them. In an overview of the decades of teen idol creation and promotion in *16 Magazine*, the editors and magazine staff are clear that their teen idols were not supposed to have partners or girlfriends no matter how many times fan letters asked them about their romances. In an interview with David Cassidy, fan favorite from 1969 to 1973, the editor states clearly that "the point was to make it seem as if you were available to any one of the fans" and Cassidy agrees that it was "to fulfill a fantasy" for the young fan dreaming of being chosen by him.[36] Now, the editors of *16 Magazine* assume that this fantasy is shared by only female fans, but there is no reason to exclude a male readership also fantasizing about the young, shirtless, and vaguely committed male idols. Indeed, in his expansive work *Gay Fandom and Crossover Stardom* Michael De Angelis argues that this ambiguity or vagueness is key for gay fans and spectators of male idols or film stars and that some stars like Keanu Reeves play up this ambiguity to appeal to queer fans as well: "the audience's continued emotional investment in the star figure, and the star's continued accessibility to the desires of spectators across the lines of sexual orientation, depend on maintaining the star's ambiguity by perpetually deferring the disclosure of an emerging 'truth' that ultimately centers on the star's sexuality."[37] The star or idol then becomes sexually alluring but not to a clear audience or subject; like the queer child, he is the deferred promise of a sexual availability but to any one of the readers of the fan magazine who can fantasize over the pullout poster in the middle. Jeffery Dennis, moreover, argues that during the 1970s these teen idol or teenybopper magazines had to open themselves up to a male readership due to declining sales and increasing print costs; the magazines like *Tiger Beat* and *16* featured more general interest articles and started to focus on both male and female performers.[38] *Who's Your Fave Rave* reveals this expanded market in a feature article on Kristy McNichol, at her height of popularity from 1977 to 1980, where the popular tomboy is described as an "outdoorsy, active, sports-loving, girl-next-door type" and a male fan has written in to question whether she is dating Scott Baio or Jeb Adams.[39] Therefore, I would ask, as Dennis does, might it not be possible that boy fans were interested in male stars and writing them letters in addition to pursuing the undeniably butch McNichol, which is not even to mention the queer desire or attraction expressed for her in female letters by very ardent fans.

One interesting case in the overview of *16 Magazine* further reinforces the queerness of the idol business in the 1970s. In the middle of the decade, sandwiched between the popularity of David Cassidy and that of the much more effeminate Shaun Cassidy was the brief hey day of Elton John (from 1975 to 1977). Although John did not court the teen idol attention or often comply with the requests of teen fan magazines for photographs and interviews, he was, according to *Who's Your Fave Rave?* "the #1 requested star" by their readers at the time and he received the "most fan mail," despite being for them "one of those unlikely teen idols whose oddness helps define the category" due to his being "unlovely, asexual (so it was thought), flamboyant."[40] It seems as though John's "oddness" was confirmed by the editors when he announced his bisexuality in *Rolling Stone* magazine, which in turn supposedly lost him his teenage fans, but the initial statement of an "oddness" that helps to define the category of teen idol and the subsequent mention of Liberace's popularity decades before suggests to me that there has always been something queer about the teen idol, by definition. His availability as a passive object of desire and spectatorial consumption and his vagueness about his intimate life (no matter if he is closeted or not) defy normative masculinity and again make sex an open secret of ambiguous word play and guessing games, much like the working of the closet.

There is also no denying that female fans of Elton John are expressing a kind of queer desire for nonnormative masculinity and gay innuendo. In one photo in *16 Magazine* a balding Elton John is clad in a feather and sequined outfit and headdress and as he smiles gently into the camera, the magazine confidently declares, "The Girl He Chooses – She Could Be You!"[41] Interestingly, the editors take this moment to reinforce the notion of magazine-mandated availability where the standard meant "the assumption that every guy we wrote about was available to you: even when the editors knew otherwise."[42] Obviously, this comment assumes the "you" is female, but it also reinforces my sense that the availability of the teen idol has a definite queer potential, in this case masking a closeted star who in real life was available not only to any "*girl* he chooses." For other readers, queer consumers and fans, the magazine also offered tantalizing hints when Elton promises to "tell all" in another issue of the magazine. With knowledge of homosexual coding, a reader could easily guess at John's queer sexuality, as underneath his "glittery façade," John is a "small town boy" who admits to being an "antiques freak" and "clothes addict" and who has publicly professed love for only one woman, Billie Jean King (obviously a few years before her coming out as a lesbian).[43] In other words, Elton John not only reinforces a queerness in the 1970s teen idol but also suggests a range of pleasures for various readers and fans triggered both by ambiguous descriptions and apparent availability, as well as not-too-subtle coding.

The one teen star, though, who defines the nature of young male idols and fan objects of the decade for me and who closely mirrors Robby Benson's teen magazine discourse is Leif Garrett. Garrett was not nearly as successful an actor as Benson, but he made an incredible career out of simply being a teen idol—moving from television series to three films and then six rock albums followed by world concert tours. His career in some ways hinged centrally on him being a "sex symbol" with wildly popular posters and album covers rather than a talented star of one particular medium.[44] Dennis calls him a "mega teen idol" and perhaps is thinking of Leif when he describes the male stars of the period as "soft" or "pretty" with feathered hair but also with "only the lead pipe invariably shoved down one leg of their red-fringed jumpsuits offering any hints that they were to be taken as boys."[45] One poster sold to promote his first album is typical: Garrett faces the camera confidently with feathered long hair, a slight knowing smile on his face, and a white suit and burgundy shirt signaling the height of 1970s fashion; his shirt is open down to his navel and even though his hands are in his pockets, there is also a noticeable bulge in his trousers. The excerpts from *16 Magazine* in *Who's Your Fave Rave?* share this come-on aesthetic of an "androgynously pretty face" and immature body, even for a fairly young star.[46] Leif often appears shirtless in the magazine with his signature long, blonde feathered hair and early pubescent chest exposed. Even visiting "Leif At Home!" means several views of him shirtless in his bedroom, in the dining room, on the terrace, drinking Perrier, answering the phone, et cetera.[47]

In an interview with the magazine's editors, Garrett admits to being not as innocent as the magazine made him out to be or as available to fan fantasies, but he does recognize the suggestiveness of his star discourse. An older and wiser Garrett, whose struggles with drugs and alcohol and legal issues are well documented, shares with the magazine's editors the early roots of his troubles, in the "mischief" he would get into as a young star offered drugs, alcohol, and sex, and his chagrin at being asked to make a record and tour without any vocal training just due to his incredible success as a teen idol in magazines like *16*. In other words, one of the most notable of the androgynous male teen idols of the period was manufactured by the objectification and innuendo of teen fan magazines, yet an older Garrett recognizes the potential of this flirtation and ambiguity for various audiences. In a clumsy and offensive way, he identifies the queer possibility in his stardom and the magazine's construction of him as a shirtless sex symbol: "It's so weird, this sort of semi-developed young man. Plus it makes me think how weird it might have been for those pedophiles out there!" In what is a worst-case scenario for Garrett, he *does* point to different spectators and consumers of these images, not just the young girls that the magazine continually insists are the only fantasizers in front of the multitude of shirtless pubescent and prepubescent pinups in their publication. The imagery of teenage "hunks" like Garrett or Scott Baio, who's described as "sweet" and "sensitive" and appears shirtless in one of the magazine's spreads with his jeans pulled down by his hands so that his underwear band shows, clearly is open to both male and female, young and older readers, and Garrett has intuited this despite the magazine's mandated heteronormativity.[48] These sensitive, longhaired, and slight-chested young men offer up an androgyny and undefined sexual allure that establishes another example of the era's queerness and lucrative promotion of what I have been calling the queer kid.

Although Benson did at one point admit to dating his costar O'Connor, he was constructed by teen magazines like *Tiger Beat* as available and suggestively posed with his soft blue eyes and bare chest just like Leif Garrett, Scott Baio, and the other androgynous male idols of the era. Benson certainly epitomizes the nonnormative masculinity or androgyny of the "soft" and "conflicted" male teen idols of the period— even complexifying the image above with an unashamed appreciation of or admiration for the "liberated," independent young women of his day—but his role in 1976's *Ode to Billy Joe* ties him directly to the sexual ambiguity of the era and to the other rights movement—gay rights— that had begun a campaign for more positive depictions on screen. A film ostensibly fleshing out the lyrics of Bobbie Gentry's 1967 hit song of the same name, *Ode to Billy Joe* follows the difficulties of two young teens in Chickasaw County, Mississippi who fall in love despite her parents' disapproval and whose affair ends tragically when the young man, Billy Joe, jumps off the Tallahatchie Bridge to his death. The film's promotional materials promised to give up the "secret" of the tragedy at the core of Gentry's ballad and the revelation of Billy's sexual experience with his sawmill boss, Mr. Barksdale, brings the film to a melodramatic end. Yet, the queer element did not hurt the film's success or Benson's career. On the contrary, the film was enormously successful at the box office and a boon for Benson himself. *Box Office* magazine reported in 1977 that the fan mail resulting from *Ode to Billy Joe* gave Benson "the clout to be high on the priority list at Warner Bros., and that particular popularity was one of the reasons the studio accepted his script for 'One on One' and assigned him to star in it."[49] The young actor also shrugged off any possible controversy with the role in his talk with *Interview* magazine in the same year, finding "nothing wrong with it" because Billy Joe had been drinking and "was seduced" and being surprised by taunts in the schoolyard after the film's release: "I never ever thought, I never had the feeling when I read it, even in the back of my mind, that said, 'You better be careful because this could hurt your career.'"[50] As *Box Office* magazine proves, he had no reason for such worries since the film dramatically improved his standing in Hollywood and with fans. The queer kid, it seems, was proving quite popular in the 1970s.

The film begins, though, perfectly in line with the other Benson romances of the era, even pairing him once again with his costar from *Jeremy* and real-life love interest Glynnis O'Connor. The first half of the film develops their budding romance strained by her traditional family and the repressive and contradictory expectations for a girl of 15 in 1953. Predictably, Benson's Billy Joe encourages Bobbie Lee's independence and growing discontent with the norms that dictate proper behavior and sexual innocence for a girl her age. For the teenage girl caught between her impassioned rereading of her two worn out copies of *Torrid Romance* and the pastor's edicts to "respect" her body as "God's temple," the pressures and confusion of adolescence eventually boil over into a direct confrontation with her father, at the center of which is Billy Joe. With Billy Joe determined to call on her at her home, Bobbie Lee must confront her father about his rule forbidding her to "receive gentleman callers" at her age, and though she struggles through several excuses for what might be "bothering" her, including their home's lack of modern plumbing and electricity and her father's "attitude," she eventually comes to a forceful declaration that she *is* old enough to receive callers. When her father disagrees, she goes out and meets Billy Joe on the road to her house anyway, and the two end up acting out her father's greatest fears in an impassioned embrace right out of *Torrid Romance*. This meeting, furthermore, offers another example of a Benson character choosing an assertive and independent-minded female partner. When they meet on the road to her house, Bobbie Lee is angrily talking to herself and criticizing her father and the family situation as "dictated by the 1925 Sears and Roebuck catalogue." Bobby is amused by her angry defiance and responds jokingly to her rude assessment that he is "about as welcome as a drought" at her house, asking himself as much as her, "How can I like you? You are very unlikeable." The two seem equally matched as she evaluates herself as either "adopted or depraved" and he confronts her with the retort that he is simply "deprived," at which point they kiss. While their mutual enjoyment is abruptly cut short by a fall in the pond, they have established in this early scene their shared strength and rebelliousness.

The film is certainly remarkable for its enlightened depiction of the conflicting messages offered to young women of the 1950s and the consequent pain and frustration experienced by them. According to David Considine, this representation of a "young girl trapped between biological imperatives and societal demands" provides proof of Hollywood's "more sophisticated response to adolescent sexuality" in the period, although for him its treatment of homosexuality does not prove as progressive.[51] In particular, Bobbie Lee's sincere complaint to her mother about these competing demands on her (soon after her moonlit swim) aptly summarizes the central conflict of the first half of the narrative. Her mother can only agree with her daughter when confronted with the obvious contradictions: "When we go to town, you dress me up real pretty and you like for me to be attractive . . . and then Brother Taylor says 'don't' and papa says 'can't' and there I am all primed up to be a woman, only I'm not allowed to be anything but a child." Her plea for understanding, moreover, is reinforced by the camerawork, which holds on Bobbie Lee in a medium close-up for long periods as she offers amusing analogies to her predicament such as "givin' somebody a brand new high-powered car and sayin', 'here, it's all yours, but don't drive it.'" She clearly has captured the film's sympathy as well as her mother's and earns an ally in this scene when her mother agrees to argue on her behalf. Like the depiction of Holly in Terrence Malick's *Badlands*, *Ode*'s recognition of the conflicting forces and needs in this young girl's life foregrounds the female teen in a way rarely seen before the 1970s and works to revise the common popular conception of the 1950s teenager. Bobbie Lee is even granted an authoritative voice-over at the end of the film evocative of Holly's, and one might argue, since its source material is Bobbie Gentry's song set in her own hometown, that *Ode* similarly privileges a retrospective and critical female point of view of a 1950s adolescence—a claim further reinforced by Gentry's voice (and hit song) opening and closing the film. Released during the era engaged with the debates of second wave feminism, the film highlights the "double standard" that feminist writers such as Barbara Ehrenreich and Wini Breines have since associated with the conformist 1950s.[52] Yet with *Ode*, joining in the passion of these criticisms is once again Robby Benson, whose Billy Joe feeds into and yet recognizes the girl's conflicts (as his characters in *Jeremy* and *Ice Castles* do) but also ends up having serious concerns of his own.

Unlike Malick's *Badlands*, which is certainly a philosophically and visually more sophisticated film, *Ode to Billy Joe* uses Robby Benson and the character of Billy Joe to define its revision of the 1950s, at least in part, as queer. Beginning shortly after Bobbie Lee's articulate complaints of the double standard tormenting her, the second half of the film deconstructs the engaging romance between Benson's character and his proto-feminist equal through an isolated homosexual encounter Billy Joe has with his boss, Mr. Barksdale. This one homosexual experience solves the mystery of Gentry's song, providing the reason for Billy Joe's suicide off the Tallahatchie Bridge, but it also quite abruptly swerves the narrative off its expected (normative) course, much to the displeasure of some critics. Particularly, Richard Eder of the *New York Times* found the film's revelation and final moments irreconcilable with the charming opening romance (so much so that he wrote two articles decrying it). Eder's initial review praises the first half of the "Southern country romance" for the moving depiction of the couple's "timid and then more demanding courtship, the families, the rural background," but he recoils at the second half where the filmmakers invent an explanation for the song's mystery "that is grotesquely out of keeping with the life" established in the opening.[53] He favors the young lovers together, finding Billy Joe to be "an eager, grandiloquent, charming youth" and O'Connor's Bobbie Lee to be "rebellious, thoughtful, and fun," but paints the climactic revelation, which he never names or describes, as "totally arbitrary and without logical or emotional relation to what has gone before," ending the film in "ridiculous melodrama."[54] As if the charged language of this review (bordering on the vitriolic) were not enough, Eder contends in a following article that the film is "sabotaged by forcing the two characters into an incredible plot line."[55] In other words, the small—and in the end tragic—act of straying from the "straight narrative line" of the heteronormative maturation plot becomes grotesque, incredible, arbitrary, and ridiculous sabotage.[56] However, it is clear from his response that the supposed target of this sabotage (heterosexual romance) and the weapon used to derail it (homosexual experience) have anything but an arbitrary relationship.

Viewed more closely, the film's editing betrays a close relationship between the normative romance and the forces that threaten to subvert it long before the queer events at the jamboree midway through the film. The chaotic happenings at the jamboree, which include excessive drinking, fighting, sex with prostitutes, and an offscreen sexual encounter between Billy Joe and Mr. Barksdale, all have antecedents in earlier scenes. After we are initially introduced to the young couple and learn more about Bobbie Lee's conservative home life, the film cuts from her playing the piano for her pastor to her brother and Billy Joe watching a stripper called "The Choctaw Princess." Bobbie Lee's brother James, his best friend Tom, and Billy Joe (who all work together at the Barksdale sawmill) drink beers and watch the performance until the women get off work, at which point James leaves with Belinda Wiggs, the Chocktaw Princess, Tom leaves with one of her coworkers, and Billy Joe is left alone outside the bar. When he is propositioned by another older woman who is leaving the bar, he looks embarrassed and walks away. This scene obviously foreshadows his rejection of the prostitutes at the jamboree, whom he abandons for the affair with his boss. Billy Joe fails to follow the model of aggressive masculinity performed by the older boys and looks genuinely disturbed by the prospect of what the woman is offering. He literally chooses a different path from heterosexual initiation in walking away.

This possible alternative path—the rejection of heterosexuality for another narrative—is alluded to again in the scene immediately following Bobbie Lee and Billy Joe's moonlit walk and falling embrace into the pond. The film cuts from Billy Joe's plea, "I am deprived, Bobbie Lee," to a distinctly homoerotic scene at the sawmill. With a topless and glistening Billy Joe lifting boards in the background, James and Tom shirk their work to practice their musical act for the jamboree, until Mr. Barksdale interrupts them to insist that they get back to work like the admirable Billy Joe, who falls under the older man's gaze. In fact, James and Tom are caught in the middle of an exchange of looks (and shots) between Mr. Barksdale and Billy Joe, who continues his shirtless labor, lifting boards as they talk. After Mr. Barksdale leaves, the charged atmosphere translates into a flirtatious discussion about stardom and the insult Billy Joe feels at being called a "tadpole" by James. Tom escalates the offense by taking hold of the strapping young tadpole and asking, "If I kisses ya, will I turn into a frog or a prince?" It is difficult to tell in this altercation, where Tom supposedly feigns an interest in kissing Billy Joe, who is the frog prince and who is the princess. To kiss the frog is to be the princess, but Tom claims he will turn into a prince; therefore, the homophobic baiting has the effect of offering an alternative possibility for a very old fable—that there could be a prince who kisses the frog prince.

The meaning of this counter-narrative is further reinforced by Tom's suggestion of which musical stars they might model themselves on: Bing Crosby and Doris Day. At the mention of Doris Day, the camera holds for a brief moment on Billy Joe's interested reaction and then cuts back to James's continued teasing (of Tom this time): "You keep it up and you might turn out to be another Doris Day." Tom's mincing response, with his effeminate "You really think so?" is clearly meant to evoke laughter, but the presence of Benson's well-toned physique and their repeated physical contact suggest sincere currents of sexual curiosity and play, particularly between a feminized Tom and the pinup Billy Joe. In this strangely provocative scene, the film hints at the iconography of gay male culture more appropriate to the increasing visibility and "pride" of the 1970s than the oppressive and disciplinary atmosphere of 1953, offering perhaps a subtext for contemporary audience members who understand the code. Doris Day's series of films with Rock Hudson that largely contributed to her iconic status in the gay community began with *Pillow Talk* in 1959, so the reference is conspicuously anachronistic in this setting. Day did have enormous success with her gender-bending title role in *Calamity Jane* in 1953, but Tom's performance certainly indicates that the film is alluding to her connection to "sissies" rather than butch lesbians.[57] This scene, which has a direct parallel in the jamboree sequence, recognizes immediately after his (hetero)romancing of Bobbie Lee that Billy Joe has another possible course of sexual awakening open to him—a counter-narrative where two princes meet and find common interest in the songs of Doris Day.

At the jamboree, which initiates the second half of the narrative, the contradictory currents that are meeting at the queer figure of Billy Joe come to a climax that irreparably warps the heteronormative romance plot. All of the elements previously edited in juxtaposition to the young couple's romance are gathered in one place and create a frenzied atmosphere that is ultimately expressed in the rapid cutting of the final moments of the jamboree sequence. Tom continues his awkward flirtation with Billy Joe, repeatedly interrupting the excited meetings between the two lovebirds and dragging Billy Joe away to drink with him. The prostitutes brought to the outbuildings as additional "entertainment" for the local men recall the older woman who propositions Billy Joe outside of strip club. His reaction to the prostitute's offer at the jamboree reveals a much more serious rejection and initiates the chaos in the crescendo of rapid cutting and accelerated music that concludes the sequence, which one might read as a cinematic equivalent of the inner conflict that results in his sexual encounter with Dewey Barksdale offscreen. The film seems to argue in the content of brief shots edited together in a staccato style that Billy Joe has been struggling in a storm of violent, aggressive (even perverse) hypermasculinity and drunken heterosexual debauchery that repulses him so much that he either chooses homosexuality as a peaceful alternative or falls into another man's arms in disgust.

The scene where he first enters the makeshift whorehouse certainly emphasizes confusion and repulsion. Once Billy Joe and a cajoling and laughing Tom come through the sliding door, the film shifts to a subjective point of view shot, signaling Billy Joe's perspective through handheld camerawork and repeated reactions shots of his shocked and increasingly dismayed face. Tom's laughter and baiting ("Go ahead, Billy Joe. Go on, get you some!") can always be heard in the background, but the scene focuses on Billy Joe's awakening: as he inches closer to the available prostitute, the camera tracks in toward her and the image begins to blur. Registering his sadness, confusion, and then revulsion in increasingly closer reaction shots, the film also brings the audience into his experience by creating an echo on the soundtrack. By the end of the scene, we have entered a kind of tunnel with Billy Joe, as what appears to be his first contact with heterosexual intercourse frightens and confuses him into a state of semiconsciousness. Finally, through an abrupt cut to James and a girl taking advantage of the bed of an empty truck in the parking lot, the scene ends without any resolution to Billy Joe's predicament other than a final blurred shot moving toward the beckoning prostitute. It is at this point that the entire sequence descends into chaos.

One might assume from the progression of shots above that Billy Joe has moved in to take the prostitute up on her offer, but the series of rapidly cut shots that conclude the sequence reveal only the dissolution of the jamboree into a testosterone-fueled mayhem where Billy Joe is nowhere to be found. Cued by a new, faster piece music driven by the banjo, the pace of the editing picks up at the same time that James starts a fight with a group of Alabama boys who have previously driven his father off the road in a drunken game of chicken. The scene quickly cuts from the fight to the sliding door closing off the prostitute's building to the madame beckoning new customers and back to the fight. That these shots are cut to the pace of the music is emphasized by a cut back to the banjo playing and then the audience clapping before repeating the earlier cycle of shots. Reminiscent of what some critics have called the "MTV-style" of editing, as the tempo of the music becomes faster, the editing follows suit, relying on shorter and shorter takes and creating a more disorienting perspective. The cycle of similar shots repeats three times, but each time with a difference: in the second cycle the madame is replaced by a view of the sheriff in bed with a prostitute and the third time through we see Mr. Barksdale yelling at offending partygoers then another sex scene and then back to the fight, which has descended into a confused pile of bodies on the ground. Not in one of these snatches of imagery do we see Billy Joe and the sequence ends with another abrupt cut from the door slamming to boards on a conveyor belt at the sawmill. The eruption of the sound of the saw on the soundtrack (and the sudden end of the music) is the only indication to the audience that the chaos is over. In this next scene, we discover that Billy Joe's father has not seen his son since the night of the jamboree and it will take nearly the remainder of the film to discover what might have happened so that "he's afraid to go home," as James conjectures. What this frenetic series of shots has established, however, is the violent, masculine world Billy Joe seems to have rejected. Normative masculinity, the film suggests, articulates itself through violence—as the scene where Bobbie Lee and her father being driven off the road has already established—and destabilizes the community through drunken excess and exploitation of women. Not surprisingly, along with the film's disruption of heterosexual romance through a homosexual counterplot comes a critique of a destructive normative masculinity that ultimately takes Billy Joe as its victim.

Billy Joe, as the antithesis of this ruinous masculinity, wins our sympathy even before his refusal costs him his life. When he confesses his "sin against nature, a sin against God" that he has "been with a man," the audience, like Bobbie Lee, has every reason to side with him. He has contrasted himself to the destructive masculinity at the jamboree by tearfully seeking out Bobbie Lee and making an impassioned plea for her love, while also articulating how the social forces disciplining teenage sexuality have hurt them both. Moreover, his attempt to be with Bobbie Lee again (and consummate their relationship) is touching in its failure. He stands up and must unequivocally accept his own agency in the homosexual act, refusing to blame it on alcohol, his imagination, or the other man. Yet, at this point, the film seems to come up against the boundaries of traditional Hollywood representations of gay youth, conforming to the "old formula when it came to homosexuality" of an inevitable suicide.[58] Billy Joe feels the pressure of acting truly as "a man" and cannot recognize that he has already faced "up to things," as he says. His subsequent suicide comes as little surprise to close observers of Hollywood cinema, but I disagree with Vito Russo's assessment that the film is merely a "reflection of 1950s masculine mythology" and ultimately endorses Bobbie Lee's keeping of his secret because "legends cannot be queer."[59] While Bobbie Lee seems to erase Billy's Joes courageous confession in the end by allowing the community to think that he has impregnated her and committed suicide out of this shame, the entirety of the film performs a much more convincing critique not only of normative masculinity but also of the social forces that lead her to this silencing of his queer voice.

Even in its final scene, when Bobbie (as she leaves town) admits her complicity in keeping Billy Joe's secret so that he can be the heteromythic "legend" who "made a desirable girl pregnant and then just flew away," the presence of Dewey Barksdale continues the critique of heteronormative culture. His poignant and honorable intention of admitting his own role in the young man's difficulties reminds the viewer again of the film's sympathetic portrayal of Billy Joe—the young man whose counter-discourse was contrasted with a destructive and exploitative masculine heterosexuality. Through the moving performance of James Best as Mr. Barksdale, the film concludes not with an endorsement of Bobbie

Lee's repressive scheme but with a lament for the young man who has been effectively erased by it. The other man, like an older, closeted vision of Billy Joe's silent future, must stand there painfully listening to this young girl say, "we can't have people believing that Billy Joe McAllister jumped off a bridge because of a man, can we?" and he has no recourse. While the dialogue performs a detestable erasure of Billy Joe's alternative narrative, the scene itself, like the jamboree sequence, indicates the human cost of normalizing forces and the perversity inherent in the functioning of dominant culture. We are reminded, in the miserable figure of the married and wealthy Mr. Barksdale, of the queer kid grown up and forced into a seemingly inevitable heterosexual maturity that masks its own spuriousness. The film ends then, I would argue, on the side of the queer child, who can only appear, of course, as a ghost.

In its demand for the audience's sympathy, the title role in *Ode to Billy Joe* sets Robby Benson apart as a crucial representative for the queer kid in the 1970s. Having already distinguished himself in his refusal to comply with normative gender roles (in his film choices and star discourse), Benson here swerves away from the narrative line of "normal" maturation as achieved through heterosexual romance and brings a responsive audience along with him. As I have already mentioned, the financial success and fan reception of *Ode to Billie Joe* allowed Benson the kind of clout he would need to create his own projects with Warner Brothers. In other words, in this period a teen idol like Benson could queer male adolescence and stories of maturation and stand to gain even more fans. Although his character Billy Joe's suicide provides another tragic example of Hollywood's inability or refusal to envision a healthy or happy gay character, the film does have the effect of exposing the way in which the "queer child" is constructed. Because the film uses Bobbie Gentry's 1967 song as a framing device, it is established from the beginning that we can only ever learn Billy Joe's "secret" in retrospect, long after he has taken his own life. Moreover, and again fitting with Kathryn Stockton's formulation, the queer child comes into view as a ghost, after the death of the possibility of a straight life and the death of childhood. Unfortunately, in the case of *Ode to Billy Joe*, the queer adult Billy Joe is also an impossibility from the beginning, or only seen through a glass darkly in the figure of closeted and pitiable Dewey Barksdale.

Yet, even in its dismal conclusion, the film articulates and ties together the concerns of the women's rights and gay rights movements. By leaving town, Bobbie Lee illustrates the ultimate consequence of the double standard for a young woman who gives in to her biological urges and thereby becomes a social pariah, while her male counterpart becomes a "legend." Yet in her silence that fuels the pregnancy rumors, she suppresses the more profound transgression that calls into question the inevitability of the heteronormative path, which works to discipline and control both women and queer kids. Our new sensitivity to both silences, however, has been achieved by the end of the film in mourning for Billy Joe. Both queer kid and artificially-created legend (or star), teen idol Robby Benson stands at the center of these concerns without flinching. In *Ode to Billy Joe*, he reiterates his challenge to aggressive and exploitative dominant masculinity and again supports the concerns of an articulate and passionate young woman who appears his equal, but this time he goes one step further, expressing those oppositions to cultural norms in sexual terms as well. His performance in *Ode to Billy Joe* earns the audience's alliance with a confused and conflicted queer teen, and, in the 1970s, this work is the stuff of legends.

Despite the predictable tragic ending for Billy Joe, this film and others starring Robby Benson mark a moment of change in the 1970s when the teen star could challenge normative masculinity and sexuality and ally himself with the strong, independent women of second wave feminism. While it is true that the film, as Considine argues, "conformed to the old formula when it came to homosexuality" by ending in a queer teen's suicide, it also belongs to a larger group of films and teen performances that foreground the queer kid as central to understanding adolescent sexuality and gender in the 1970s, not to mention family dynamics and new alliances as I will explore further with Jodie Foster in the next chapter.[60] Films such as *Harold and Maude* and *Alice Doesn't Live Here Anymore* pair a preternaturally mature teen with an older woman or mother in close relationships that one might call odd or, in the case of Harold and his elderly paramour, even queer. These films veer away from the typical or 'normal' tale of teenage maturation by failing or refusing to resolve their conflicts with normative heterosexual union with the appropriate teen love object or reconciliation with the paternal. The queer kid and the maternal or strong female lead of women's lib find a new path together in the 1970s, revising teen film as it has been constructed in the twentieth century, and as the next chapter reveals, this new powerful relationship is not only between a son and his mother or a male suitor and his lover but includes the daughters of the 1970s as well.

Chapter 4

Bad News Jodie, or How the Disney Family Got Freaky

In a documentary bonus feature on the 2004 DVD rerelease of *Freak Friday* (1976), entitled "A Look Back with Jodie Foster," the actress, director, and producer considered to be one of the most powerful women in Hollywood looks back at the making of this popular family film and, further, at her own career at Disney and the political, industrial, and personal environment surrounding the mid-1970s production. In fact, the bicentennial moment of 1976 was a very good year for the young Foster; she cemented her place as one of the most prominent teen stars and American female actresses of the 1970s in this year that saw the release of five films in which she starred and critical acclaim not only for her work as teen prostitute Iris in Scorsese's *Taxi Driver*, which would earn her an Oscar nomination, but also for other roles in *Bugsy Malone*, *The Little Girl Who Lives Down the Lane*, and even *Freaky Friday*. A self-proclaimed "Disney kid," Foster describes this successful, prolific period in surprisingly personal terms in "A Look Back." Contemplating the productive stage of her career in her early teens—Foster would go on to make 15 feature films by the age of 18—she admits it was the "beginning of a real self-consciousness" for her. The film conjures up for her a "strange time" and a "painful time," and the Oscar-winning star pointedly represents her teen self as a body-conscious and uncomfortably self-aware young girl "going through the same things" that Annabel, the teen protagonist of *Freaky Friday*, is experiencing on-screen. Yet, as the featurette continues, the depth or poignancy of the pain for the teenaged Foster only grows in her further reminiscences about the film. She reaffirms that "it was just a very difficult time" on a film where she was trying to find her "way," characterizing the entire period in terms common to definitions of troubled adolescence in the twentieth century; she laments that she had "all the passions of an older person but none of the freedoms." Annabel might not have said it better.

Foster's recollections, while they echo typical views of the 'storm and stress' of adolescence, also raise the sense of something else—a difference or strangeness associated not only with the teenaged Jodie but also with the film *Freaky Friday* itself. This "strange time" for the young actress takes place on the set of a film frequently remarked upon for its "oddness" by reviewers.[1] As a Disney film with a quasi-Oedipal conflict at the heart of its body swapping narrative between a teen girl and her mother, there is, in Foster's own words, "something kind of weird about the whole thing." With characteristic intelligence in "A Look Back," Foster recognizes the Oedipal inflections of a film in which a wife calls her husband "Daddy" and a daughter behaves like a jealous wife, all of which combine to create "a kind of strange, perverse world." Yet, Foster is also astute enough to recognize what may be the root of much of the film's strangeness and perversity, "Disney's attempt at talking about feminism." Working as a contract player allowed her to get to know the studio well, and her insider's assessment reveals a studio accustomed to employing willful neglect of social movements or social change not considered part of "Disney's mandate." Therefore, she finds *Freaky Friday* to be a strange gesture towards second wave feminism for the studio, which concludes unsatisfactorily for the tomboy Annabel, whose conflict is resolved with "conventional aspirations for women at the time," such as to "have a boyfriend and wear lipstick." Yet, for her, Annabel's mother, Ellen, does achieve a kind of comfort with her own body and sexuality that results directly from the subject matter.

I would argue, however, that Foster should not be so quick to discount her own role in the "strange, perverse" effect of the film or the significance of Annabel's female masculinity for Disney's "weird" approach to feminism. Annabel's conflicts around gender and sexuality, consistently echoed in Foster's own star discourse at the time, do not rest easily in the film's hasty attempt to contain them at its conclusion. The strange world of *Freaky Friday* resonates, both for its illustration of the historical moment and for its place in a group of mid-1970s films that redefine adolescence on-screen and possibly the cinematic family through the disturbing pairing of the queer kid and women's lib. As a major teen star of the period, Foster came to define the era's teenager as the strangely adult child, whose appearance and gravely voice signaled gender-bending tomboy and whose engagement with sexuality disturbed and fascinated critics and audiences alike. In other words, Foster symbolizes her cultural moment because of her enactment of the era's ambiguity, instability, and various sexual revolutions. Her sexually disconcerting androgyne, who

FIGURE 4.1 Jodie Foster "looks like a boy and talks like a man" as the principal queer kid of the 1970s *Credit: Warner Bros./Photofest*

according to one reviewer of *Alice Doesn't* "looks like a boy and talks like a man," seems the mirror image of Benson's femme suitor of women's lib.[2] In *Freaky Friday* Foster's queer kid disrupts not only the family, which has been thrown into turmoil by mother-daughter body swapping, but also the traditional maturation plot effectively defined by the Disney oeuvre. The mother-daughter relationship at the center of this film offers a volatile combination of the queer kid and women's lib in 1970s cinema. Foster's queer persona and the studio's gesture toward feminism combine to create a contradictory tale of negative Oedipus, wherein the girl's masculinity and the mother's centrality as a love object challenge the heteronormative representation of the patriarchal family and the straight (Disney) story of growing up.

Jodie Foster as Feminist Poster Child

In a review of Adrian Lyne's film *Foxes* in 1980—a mere eight years and 13 films after Jodie Foster began her feature film career—Andrew Sarris perhaps best captures the impact of Foster's queer kid. He tries to put words to his appreciation of the young star who carries this 'alienated youth' saga on her petite shoulders. *Foxes*, with its "amalgam of youth-rock-culture clichés set against the Los Angeles landscape," might disappoint in places, but Jodie Foster, the film's "heavy-lidded, hoarse-voiced authority," never does.³ In a statement suggestive of the obsessive nightmare that will soon make Foster the most famous stalked celebrity in the world, Sarris admits to being a serious fan: "From that first moment in *Alice Doesn't Live Here Anymore* when I mistook her for a boy instead of a girl, my attachment to her has gone beyond enchantment to enchainment."⁴ What are we to make of such a strange and fascinating confession? Andrew Sarris, renowned film critic and central proponent of auteur theory in the United States, admits his *enslavement* to the star power of the gender-queer darling of 1970s cinema, falling in love at first sight with her tomboy ambiguity and deep-throated female authority. One hears, perhaps not surprisingly, the echoes of fan adorations of gender-bending idols Rudolph Valentino or James Dean here. Foster, also like a mirror image of Robby Benson, commands the screen with her contradictions and her androgyny, projecting for Sarris both "hidden reserves of psychic, moral, and physical strength" and the "vulnerability of the young." Yet, if her performances in this period betrayed a current of vulnerability, they rarely located it in a youthful innocence.

On the contrary, Foster became one of the primary examples of the strangely, even perversely, adult children of 1970s cinema. From Tatum O'Neal and Jodie Foster to Alfred Lutter in *Alice Doesn't Live Here Anymore* or the entire team of *Bad News Bears*, the wise child was often the calm, sardonic center of a tumultuous adult world in 1970s cinema or reflected what Michelle Abate has recognized as the shift in the 1970s "to present children as sexually aware and socially savvy rather than naïvely angelic."⁵ Beginning with her role as the impudent Audrey in Scorsese's *Alice Doesn't Live Here Anymore*, who is considered by Burstyn's Alice as "a little mature" even for her "very weird" and "very spooky kid" Tommy (himself a precocious young teen with an adultlike rapport with his mother), Foster spent the mid-1970s perfecting the queer effect of the preternaturally mature child, both on-screen and off. As one critic at the time put it, "[i]ronically, it is the role of an ordinary child that has eluded even the busy Miss Foster."⁶ In the space of one year, she played both the eerily composed young prostitute Iris in *Taxi Driver*—who invokes "women's lib" and calls her would-be knight Travis a "square" for suggesting that "a girl should live at home"—*and* the seductively witty gangster's moll in a cast full of children in *Bugsy Malone*, not to mention a teenage murderer in *The Little Girl Who Lives Down the Lane* and a 30-something mother trapped in a teenager's body in *Freaky Friday*. Moreover, as with Robby Benson, her maturity was both rooted in undaunted expressions of sexuality and indicative of changes brought by second wave feminism.

Indeed, as her manager-mother once contended in an interview with *American Film*, Jodie Foster came to embody that social movement: "It was just at the beginning of the women's liberation and she kind of personified that in a child. She has a strength and uncoquettishness. Maybe it comes from being raised without a father to say, 'Turn around and show Daddy how pretty you look.'"[7] If in Foster the era had a model liberated child of the feminist moment, then it would stand to reason that her star discourse would emphasize characteristics reflecting her strength and skill, such as intelligence, toughness, and professionalism, as well as her sexual freedom.

From very early on in her career, Foster's interviews, reviews, and feature articles established the figure of a gifted child with intelligence and stamina beyond her years, whose decorum and work ethic put most adults to shame, not to mention other young stars like Tatum O'Neal or Robby Benson.[8] The lore that soon developed around Foster as she became an Oscar-nominated young star in the mid-1970s exploited key anecdotes to construct her as a prodigy and the ultimate professional: that she learned to read at a very young age and could memorize scripts in a couple of passes, that she was attacked by a lion costar in her first feature for Disney (*Napoleon and Samantha*) and soldiered on to finish the film, or that when she was not dutifully working with her on-set tutor, she was top of her class at the *Lycèe Français* in Los Angeles. Like some kind of dream vision for the women's movement, she excelled in her workplace, supporting her family through superior intelligence, talent, and toughness—driven by her confidence and will. There seemed to be no limit to her ambitions, as a 1977 article in *Films Illustrated* warned: "Jodie at seventeen is a formidable prospect. Three years ago she wanted to be a lawyer. Two years ago she wanted to be President of the United States. One year ago she wanted to be a film director. Now she seems content to follow her winning streak as an actress. Tomorrow . . .?"[9] Seemingly hovering at the edge of world domination (tomorrow . . . the world?), Foster came to represent a simple but significant concept for women of the era: she was consistently defined by her power, or, perhaps more specifically, her power and skill. Formidable, strong, and ambitious, she was no Shirley Temple, the other major child star with whom she is often compared. According to her star discourse, she did not need charm, cute pluck, and an adult male foil (or tap shoes) to succeed. She had her wits, talent, and potency, and a seemingly insatiable drive toward accomplishment. Also, unlike Temple, she openly confronted the seemingly innocent sexual allure that has always hovered around child stars, particularly female ones. Contrary to Temple's innocence, which for Ilana Nash is key to her "visually pleasurable sexual spectacle," as this emptiness or innocence "invites a symbolic penetration" by adult (male) desire, Foster's roles defiantly assert her recognition of sexuality, confronting the desire that would take her as its vulnerable object.[10]

Her role as the young prostitute Iris in Scorsese's *Taxi Driver* stands out as the obvious example of this disarmingly detached knowledge of and confrontation with sexuality. As a 13-year-old actress playing a prostitute of roughly the same age, her "terrifying self-assurance," in Vincent Canby's words, not only signals the impact of the sexual revolution but also sets Foster apart as the preeminent (perversely) adult child of 1970s cinema.[11] While one might argue, as B. Ruby Rich does in "Nobody's Handmaid," that this adulthood is forced onto Iris and sits uneasily on her like a mask, there is no denying the self-assurance and strength in Foster's performance, as well as her willingness to confront the economy of desire that works through adult male control and abuse of young female sexuality. Her performance in *Taxi Driver* runs counter to what Vicky Lebeau has called a "fundamental" belief in the modern period that children must be distinct from adults—a difference primarily reaffirmed through the "regulation of sexuality."[12] Therefore, for Lebeau, narratives like *Lolita* (or one might think, *Taxi Driver*) become key in constructing and reinforcing this distinction by representing the "child who 'knows' sex" as the "very symbol of a childhood lost," in other words no longer a child at all. One of the most stunning achievements of Foster's performance in *Taxi Driver*, then, is her ability to challenge this fundamental distinction, seeming *both* child and adult rather than one or the other, while clearly possessing and expressing that knowledge of sex.

Foster's character Iris undoubtedly 'knows' about sex. Despite her young age and diminutive stature, she matter-of-factly performs her duties and in one scene draws Travis in to her hotel room with a tough, seasoned routine. Clearly a performance, Iris's bored come-on to Travis—"You looking for some action?"—brings him into her space where she takes command of him briefly, even having to coax him into the room where she appears both cynical and assertive in directing their sexual contact. She laughs, rolls her eyes, and propositions Travis with remarkable candor, confidently urging him to decide how he wants to "make it" and appearing merely bored and frustrated with her attempts at fellatio and his repeated refusals. Although Travis believes he can somehow be the savior of her childhood or innocence, Iris's behavior counters this fantasy with an alarmingly clear-eyed acceptance of her unredeemable experience. If, as Nash proposes, the "key to successfully representing a girl's erotic appeal is to render her *un*conscious of it, or not in control of it—to 'hollow out' her subjectivity, her will, or her competence," then *Taxi Driver* upends this logic, undoing the terms of the girl's "erotic appeal" and, thereby, challenging the male control of it (if only briefly).[13] Iris has, at times, the overly mature, even jaded, attitude toward sex that is the antithesis of Travis' confusion, naïvete, and strange romanticism in sexual matters, exactly reversing the dynamic Nash exposes in traditional representations of young girls that reinforces patriarchal dominance, privilege, and authority over women.

At the same time, however, the film also clearly stresses the immaturity, impracticality, and vulnerability that she possesses right alongside her sexual candor and bravado with Travis. Her intimate scene dancing with Sport (often referred to as the "Scar scene") reveals her subjection to the adult male predators who barter with her body and keep her tethered to an exploitative system through emotional and physical manipulation and abuse. Scorsese shows the complexity of her situation and her motivations, as she undeniably reveals herself as a vulnerable figure in Sport's much larger arms (ironically reinforced by his references to her as his "woman") and yet also expresses her need and desire for him, closing her eyes as they embrace and dance. Perhaps more interestingly, in the scene immediately preceding this one where she meets Travis for breakfast, she swings wildly back and forth between a kind of helpless immaturity and confident assertiveness. She confronts Travis with her own opinions about returning to her parents or about her adultlike relationship with Sport and uses humor and insults to disturb him. Yet, at the same time, we see her childishly focused on her jelly and sugar sandwich or we listen to her express faith in astrology to prove Sport innocent and blithely share her dream of escaping to a commune in Vermont. There is something so guileless in her smiling assurance that Travis is a "Scorpion" and yet she has the strength and assurance to shrug, lean forward in her chair and confront Travis with her final ironic rebuttal, "What do you want me to do? Call the cops?" In other words, the film illustrates beautifully the concept of the strangely adult child favored in 1970s cinema: Iris has an undeniable knowledge and acceptance of adult sexuality and mature relationships, while simultaneously possessing a childish vulnerability or naïvete in other areas. For Foster this defining role showcases her self-assurance, mature intelligence, and tough-guy bravado without sacrificing a kind of youthful openness and authenticity even in sexual matters.[14]

While certainly a significant part of her power came from an asserted confidence in or comfort with sexual situations—such as in her roles in *Taxi Driver*, in *Alice Doesn't Live Here Anymore* where she played the daughter of a prostitute, or in *The Little Girl Who Lives Down the Lane* where she has the first beginnings of a sex scene while being stalked by an older man—Foster's liberated woman-child defies easy categorization, particularly due to her blurring of gender and sexual boundaries. Befitting critical conceptions of the "queer child" discussed in the previous chapter, her chosen roles and star discourse repeatedly swerve from traditional or normative narratives about the child, about young girls, or even about child actors. Foster asserts a knowing, dispassionate attitude toward sexuality when children (especially young girls) are to remain innocent of such things. She disturbs commentator after commentator with an intellectual maturity and composure that no child should possess. Finally, and not least of all, she fails magnificently at conforming to the strictures of normative gender. In nearly every role during the decade of the 1970s, Foster plays the butch to Shirley Temple's femme. As film critic Elizabeth Pincus argues in Pratibha Parma's 1996 reverential documentary, *Jodie: An Icon*, Foster's work has become "iconically queer" for a devoted audience of lesbian fans because of her young butch persona during the 1970s that defied normative gender for girls: "she was a tough, scrappy, street urchin type; she was tomboyish; she was kind of butch; she wasn't playing by the rules." Fan after fan in the documentary reminisces about Foster's films of the 1970s, relying on the same descriptors: "tough," "spunky," "cocky," and, of course, "tomboy." It would appear that Andrew Sarris was not the only viewer enchanted by Foster for queering the line between little boy and little girl, disrupting the strictures of gender.

Without naming it as queer, writers have often hinted at the particular appeal of Foster's gender-bending since early in her career, yet as with the male teen idols in the previous chapter some have also linked it with the sexual ambiguity central to her star persona. One particularly revealing meeting with Andy Warhol for *Interview* magazine in 1977 flirts repeatedly with the various queer boundaries of her persona, both in terms of gender and sexuality. From the introductory description of her wearing "blue jeans tucked into knee-high leather boots, a brown tweed jacket over a beige blouse, and a newsboy cap" and with a "voice as low as her mother's is high," the interview shifts from banal details and movie promotion to Warhol's baiting questions like, "when are you going to get married?"[15] Foster's matter-of-fact response, "Never, I hope," does not deter Warhol (or his co-interviewer Catherine Guinness) from returning to the topic. His questions about her sense of style seem to confuse the 14-year-old star, who admits to preferring jeans and T-shirts, and repeated queries about going on dates and kissing are immediately rebuffed: "I don't have time [for dates] with my movies, and that's what's important to me."[16] At key points, her role as the sexually ambiguous tomboy directs the article, though typically through the interviewer's innuendo.

Foster presents a butch persona but refuses the forays into her intimate life. Possibly encouraged by Warhol's admission that he felt it "actually made it better" in her "strange" part in *Alice Doesn't Live Here Anymore* when one could not tell whether she was "a boy or a girl," Foster confesses that she is not interested in clothes, shopping, or putting on makeup and "can't understand" when people call her beautiful. In one particularly telling moment, she admits a preference for the casual atmosphere of California because "if you go into a restaurant, there's no way they'll say, 'You have to have a tie,'" which suggests her concern for or identification with a male dress code (an identification certainly reflected in her sartorial choices for the interview).[17] One comes away from this interview wondering how much of a kinship the queer icon Warhol felt with this young butch star with so little to say about her sexual life. When Foster rejects the idea of marriage, guilelessly proposing but in gender-neutral terms that "it's got to be boring—having to share a bathroom with *someone*" (my emphasis), Warhol gushes, "Gee, we believe the same things."[18] Her attraction for him, as for other observers and commentators, seems to reside in her ingenuous queerness and intriguingly closeted sexuality.

Although during the 1970s at least (in other words, before her eighteenth birthday) her queerness largely formed her allure, there certainly comes a point in Foster's career where her approaching adulthood and continued sexual ambiguity or silence about her private life is less charmingly tolerated or flirted with. For example, two films released in 1980 starring a nearly 18-year-old Foster, *Foxes* and *Carny*, gave reviewers ample opportunity to hint at the actress' possible homosexuality. Janet Maslin's review of *Foxes*, which ostensibly is praising Foster in contrast with her costars (particularly Sally Kellerman), cannot help but lean toward innuendo: "Mother and daughter have two scenes together. One is a fight that serves mostly to highlight the incompatibility of their acting styles: Miss Foster is stunningly direct, Miss Kellerman hopelessly stagey. The other scene is harder to describe. But it ends, after considerable rambling, with the two of them in bed, reading Plato."[19] As I will show below, this queerly sexualized pairing with the mother has its roots in the "tomboy" charm of Foster's earlier roles. In comparison to reviewers like Maslin, however, the nature and function of her youthful queerness has been directly and more fully addressed by film scholars.

Spurred not only by the heated debate resulting from the release of *Silence of the Lambs* in 1991 but also by the advance of queer theory in the academy, several writers have attempted to explain the workings of Foster's queer persona in sexual terms. Christina Lane relies more on the idea of "sexual liminality" in her 1995 article on Foster's star discourse than the term "queer," but her examination of that way that her "persona *encompasses* such oppositions as masculine/feminine, public/private, gay/straight, in/out rather than submitting to their binary structure" clearly is engaging with the central ambiguity of queerness.[20] Recognizing Foster's ability to offer both "markers of 'butch' lesbianism, such as denim, leather, or men's clothing" and "a persona that is quite feminine," Lane claims that the actress' strategic androgyny has the possible effect of "redefin[ing] sexuality as a fluid category," which surely echoes the definitions of queer as that which is opposed to normative limits or the restrictive binary of sexuality (into a simple opposition of hetero and homo).[21] However, it is Terry Brown's article engaging with the "lesbian postmodern" that most closely resembles my own interest in Foster's persona as a queer child. Although more concerned with Jodie Foster as a representative example of the indefinable identity of the "postmodern (lesbian) subject," about whom "we cannot say anything for sure" and who collapses "such categories as gay/straight, public/private, queer/normal, inside/outside, secrecy/revelation, butch/femme, fantasy/reality," Brown's article does document the queer effect of Foster's early tomboy roles on critics and fans alike, citing interviews, reviews, and Foster's own choices as an actor and director to establish a coded discourse on her butch persona.[22]

Writers like Brown and Lane, however, convincingly argue for a diminishment of Foster's "tomboyish excess" as her career transitions into adult roles, yet this argument persuades me to examine even more closely the working of that excess and the threat posed by her queer child. Brown attributes this "tomboyish excess" to all the performances by the young Foster but contends that such excess is only safe "as long as she's a child."[23] The tomboy, as Judith Halberstam's work on "female masculinity" consistently argues, is only tolerated as a transitory figure—a ghostly phase abandoned on the path to heteronormative womanhood. As she contends in her essay "Oh Bondage Up Yours! Female Masculinity and the Tomboy" (in the edited collection on the queer child cited above), the tomboy can receive approval for behavior that shows signs of "independence and self-motivation," but once puberty begins, "the full force of gender conformity descends on the girl."[24] According to these norming forces, Terry Brown suggests that Jodie Foster had to grow up into the "smiling femme that the mainstream media has gone to lengths to construct," abandoning her "tomboy excess" to maintain her star status or transforming it into "something that could be comprehended within the heterosexual economy of mainstream cinema."[25] While Brown moves forward in Foster's career to insist that a kind of "cinematic desexualization" is the way that Foster can retain her butch toughness without threatening Hollywood's heteronormative system, I would like to stay with that queer excess of the young star and consider its historical significance and disturbing potential, especially for the Disney family.[26]

Gender Chaos in the Disney Family

Of all the films in one of the most prolific periods in Foster's career, *Freaky Friday*, with its light comic jaunt through a mother and daughter's mind-body swap, might seem like an odd choice for close examination. *Taxi Driver* offered Foster the early role of a lifetime, earned her an Oscar nomination, and, by her own admission, encouraged her to take the craft of acting seriously for perhaps the first time. *Bugsy Malone*, Alan Parker's feature film directorial debut, was nominated for the Golden Palm at the Cannes Film Festival. *Alice Doesn't Live Here Anymore* created a critical firestorm about the film's engagement with women's issues (a special section of *Jump Cut* in the summer of 1975 was devoted to debates about Scorsese's version of the woman's picture). Yet, *Freaky Friday* is not only one of the few of Foster's films in this period directed at a youth audience (despite Parker's ostensible intentions with *Bugsy Malone*) but also one of her very rare interactions with an intact nuclear family, which, I will argue, turns quite freaky indeed with the introduction of the queer kid.

In this rare instance of a Foster character's family life—and perhaps illustrating why it is so rare—she turns the patriarchal family upside down. B. Ruby Rich establishes a disturbing pattern for Foster's familial roles throughout her career (in her article for the Walker Arts Center's 1991 retrospective on Foster's films, "Jodie Foster: Growing Up On-Screen"). She points out that beyond *rarely* being "given a nuclear family like so many other celluloid girls," Foster's characters could even be in grave danger within the family unit, as "she is terminally ill all the way through *Echoes of Summer*," or, conversely, prove to be a "menace to the nuclear family."[27] Certainly, Foster can be considered a "menace" to the traditional family in *Freaky Friday*, but not exactly for the reasons that Rich offers in her revision of the Walker Arts Center material for *The Village Voice*, "Nobody's Handmaid"; she claims that "the sexuality that inflects the Foster persona" collides with the nuclear family in the film, which results in an "Oedipal perversity" that causes the audience "to hold its breath while the movie tiptoes around Daddy's game responses to the wife who now calls him 'daddy' and the daughter who now calls him 'Bill'."[28] Yet, in order for this "Oedipal perversity" focused on Daddy to work, the sexuality to which Rich refers becomes necessarily *hetero*sexual and Foster's menace, therefore, decidedly less queer—or disruptive.

Freaky Friday, though, as Foster asserts in her on-screen interview for the DVD, is centrally a "story of mother and daughter" and plays to the audience's "primal fascination with this symbiotic relationship" between the two.[29] Through its focus on the mother-daughter relationship, the film offers an Oedipal conflict but not exactly (or not only) the positive Oedipus scenario that Rich suggests above. While this Disney vehicle for Foster attempts a kind of positive Oedipus narrative for the girl, who takes her mother as her rival for the attention and love of the father (and his surrogate, the neighbor-boy Boris), feebly resolving her conflict by suggesting Boris as the appropriate object of her desires, the actress at the center of the conflict—the daughter of this odd family romance—tells another tale. Foster's queer persona and the studio's gesture toward "women's lib" combine to create a parallel and contradictory tale of negative Oedipus, wherein the girl's masculinity and the mother's centrality as a love object fundamentally challenge the heteronormative representation of the patriarchal family and the straight story of growing up.

The opening credit sequence sets up exactly the kind of perverse experience I am suggesting that the film offers despite its conventional Disney resolution for Foster's character Annabel, which attempts to contain the queerness she unleashes. With its animated illustration of the mind-body swap that sets the "freaky" narrative in motion, the opening sequence offers a simplified version of the tension and then growing intimacy between mother and daughter, which is centrally expressed in the Golden Globe nominated original theme song, "I'd Like to Be You For a Day." This duet reflects the dissatisfaction exposed in the film narrative when mother and daughter cannot communicate or find common ground, but it also recognizes the desire for intimacy between the two.

The lyrics begin with their need to understand and identify with each other closely enough to appreciate each other's situation and difficulties. If one was the other "for a day," mysteries and emotions could be explored: "To stare through your eyes/ Would start revealing/ All the things you're feeling." Yet, it is not enough just to read the other as a book "and learn it," as a mother might with her child's diary, but the experience should create intimacy, "Lovin' every page as I turn it." However, the song makes clear that the extent of this intimacy is not merely emotional or mental. With an image of the animated Mrs. Andrews (Barbara Harris) and Annabel (Foster) holding hands and whispering to each other, the song insists on a physical connection: "There's so much more I need to understand/ It's not enough to simply hold your hand/ And hear the words you say/ I want to touch you/ I want to reach you/ In every single way." As the song concludes, it returns to its foreshadowing of the film's plot and conclusion—that the body swap can be used by the mother to "put you back on the track when you go astray" and share in the daughter's life—but the preceding verse has exposed the film's strange and perverse world of mother-daughter union.

This verse suggests that the exchange of bodies is just that—bodily contact—and leads to an intimacy between the two that exceeds "simply" holding hands. Clearly, the word "touch" might be used figuratively here, but the sense of a literal touching is also a possible reading. In fact, shortly after the body swap the filmmakers flirt with a moment of physical exploration by the daughter, of the (m)other's body. One gets a sense, even in the brief introductory instance of the "touch" of this song, that the narrative engages with an excess or a set of meanings beyond its control, as if investigating the relationship between mother and daughter becomes too much ("every single way"), expressing desires that are frustrated by "not enough." Yet, despite this troubled beginning, the film proceeds with its manifest agenda of the domestication of Annabel, ostensibly through her mother's guiding hand to put her "back on the track" of normative femininity and heterosexuality.

From Annabel's introductory voice-over onward the project of normalizing the masculine teen girl (and by extension Jodie Foster) is set against Disney's odd foray into the concerns of second wave feminism, as daughter and mother divide the focus of the film between them. It is almost as if Disney's solution to the threat posed by feminism is to domesticate and feminize the younger generation of women who are muddying the waters. With the film's ending, Disney can reinstate what one critic calls the studio's "worldview"—that the "model of a woman to emulate . . . is one who lives to get her man"; the heroine of a Disney animated film, for example, "may adopt some of the contemporary feminist attitudes, including being more vocal, being physically strong, and being self-sufficient, but she only finds fulfillment in romantic love"—specifically, I would add, heterosexual romance.[30] Yet in *Freaky Friday*, by concentrating on the relationship between mother and daughter and encouraging their intimacy, the film exposes the possibility of another plot and another outcome in which the daughter chooses the mother as her love object and the mother is infected by the daughter's strength and activity. First, though, I would like to examine the film's apparent project for Annabel. As her opening voice-over shows, she is *supposed* to be on the "track" of positive Oedipus wherein she learns to identify with her mother's castration and embrace her own passive position, femininity, and even masochism on route to her eventual transferral of her love for her father to his male surrogate. This project, particularly the effort to feminize the tomboy, proves harder than perhaps the film's producers anticipated.

Annabel's opening voice-over works to establish that this young adolescent girl sits on the cusp of 'normal' womanhood and, thereby, sets up an obvious maturation plot for the film. When she introduces herself and her room, the camera pulls back to reveal the chaotic existence of a teenaged girl, with a monopoly board spread out in front of a dollhouse, soccer gear, and mountains of clothes. Annabel describes herself as "female, blonde—natural, of course" and as a young girl watching her weight and conscious of the changes in her body; she stares predictably at her modest bust. After a brief digression into her rivalrous relationship with her younger brother Ben, she returns to her own everyday concerns of school, friends, and field hockey practice before landing on one of her favorite subjects: dear old dad. It is at this point that the Disney predilection for a particular brand of family values and normalizing first emerges. Annabel introduces her parents by immediately zeroing in on her father, William Waring Andrews, whom she describes as both a "fantastically cool person" and the "most beautiful person in the world." Clearly, these comments are meant to foreshadow the Oedipal disarray set in motion when mother and daughter switch bodies and a wife begins referring to her husband as "daddy," but they also serve to lead effortlessly into the film's heteronormative molding of Jodie Foster and her character Annabel. The voice-over explains that her father is "almost" the most beautiful person in the world in comparison to the neighbor-boy Boris (played by Marc McClure). Boris is the "fox" upon whom Annabel has her crush even when he will not reciprocate due to a "little incident" in their past that Annabel fails to explain.

In this move from the "fantastically cool" father to the "fox" Boris, the film suggests that Annabel has transferred her affections appropriately from her father to Boris and, therefore, it sets up a typical maturation plot for the young female teen: get through the events of this freaky Friday and proper heterosexual union will be your reward. As if on cue, having established her male love object and investment in her father's validation, the film turns immediately to her rivalry with her mother. Noting that they "haven't been hitting it off too well" lately, the opening voice-over sets up her Oedipal antagonism with her mother. The touchy subject of the mother concludes her opening voice-over, and their relationship and, presumably, the lessons her mother can teach about becoming a woman become the major focus of the remainder of the film. In just this opening scene, the film seems to set up the positive Oedipal trajectory for Annabel, who should turn her rivalry with her mother in an accepting identification with her castrated state and eventually transfer her love for her father to an appropriate substitute—that is, Boris.[31]

And in some respects the film *does* continue dutifully along this trajectory or straight narrative path toward heteromaturation and 'normal' progression of the Oedipus complex for girls. Annabel learns to recognize her mother's domestic situation and adult demands, and she even keeps some of the more feminine touches her mother adds to her appearance after a furtive afternoon of shopping and beauty treatments in Annabel's body. The newly coiffed Annabel goes on a date with Boris in the final scene after he admits that she "look[s] great," and their union is sanctioned by her father, who finds Annabel to be "just like" her mother at the end of it all. When both Annabel and her mother respond with a "thanks" to Mr. Andrews' comparison, we are supposed to believe that Disney's domestication of the unruly female adolescent has been a success. After her freaky Friday in her mother's high-heeled shoes, she has learned humility (passivity), to care for others (heterosexual object choice and motherhood), and the feminizing magic of a set of curlers (masochism?). Yet, her day spent with her mother or in her mother's place has also raised the concept of women's rights, which begins to contradict the easy resolution offered by her relationship with her father and her teenage romance with Boris.

Although the film works to convince the young female adolescent to appreciate her mother's challenging duties as wife and caretaker—her difficult daily chores, her myriad of responsibilities, the emotional demands of marriage and motherhood—her more "liberated" attitude and resistance as a result of the women's movement too often successfully criticize the burden placed on women in the home. These criticisms, often directed at the patriarch, pass from daughter to mother during the "freaky" events of the day and suggest an infection of the mother with the daughter's independence. Initially the second "most beautiful person in the world," the father appears more like a chauvinist pig to Annabel once she has swapped bodies with her mother. After being given a list of chores before he drives off for work, Annabel bristles at his attitude toward her (in her mother's body), "Oink oink, daddy!" At this point in the film, we have the criticism coming through Jodie Foster's voice-over and not Barbara Harris' voice, as Annabel has just begun to inhabit her mother's body, so the film does not quite argue yet that the wife or adult woman is ready to be liberated. The daughter's contact with her mother's condition, however, has begun chipping away at her Oedipal adoration for the father—"Iron this, polish that, go here, go there. As a dad, you're super. As a husband, you're more like a traffic cop"—and turned her off the traditional roles for women; she swears there will be no "personal maiding" in her future. By the end of the film, in fact, it is not entirely clear what Annabel has learned after her day in her mother's shoes other than the difficulty of her mother's position and her own ignorance of her mother's strengths.

Furthermore, toward the end of the film, her rejection of a subordinate female situation seems to spread to the mother's body, as Barbara Harris' voice begins to shout the label "male chauvinist pig" toward Mr. Andrews. The housewife, still possessed by her daughter but finding her own voice, explains to her young son the unequal terms of the marital relationship that allow her "chauvinist" husband to expect her to create a formal buffet dinner in an afternoon: "A male chauvinist pig is a husband who spends three months taking bows for a big shindig he's gonna throw and when he blows it, he gives his wife three hours to save his skin." Gone is the adoration for a "super" dad and in its place comes the resentment and anger resulting from an inferior position and the lack of value placed on domestic work. Then, as final proof that the contagion has passed from daughter to mother, the daughter's shouts of "chauvinist pig" in her mother's voice become refusal by the wife once Ellen Andrews has returned to her own body, "Don't honey me!" Disney's foray into feminism, through the voice and figure of Jodie Foster, seems intended to show the adolescent girl how "dumb" she has been in her lack of understanding the woman's role, but her out of body connection to her mother has had the opposite effect on the adult woman, giving her the independent voice that her daughter possessed at the beginning of the film.

In its attempt to approach the subject of feminism, the film finds itself at cross purposes, allowing the voicing of feminist concerns but then wanting to put the genie back in the bottle of wholesome Disney family entertainment (i.e. serving the patriarchal order and reinforcing the status quo of Main Street). The result is chaotic and ideologically uncertain. Even the film's tagline betrays this central ambivalence, asking "How Freaky Would It Be If You Turned Into Your Mother?" Following the argument of the positive Oedipus scenario for the girl, the figurative meaning of this question appears ridiculous. It is not "freaky" at all for the young girl to turn into or become like her mother as an adult; rather, it is *the* path to normalcy. The perversity resides in the question itself, suggesting that the adolescent girl has no interest in becoming her mother and accepting her secondary status and heteronormative life plan. Disney ultimately does not want to argue as such in its conclusion of Annabel's story, yet much of the film returns to the inherent criticism of the question. Despite her new look and concluding date with Boris, Annabel's body swap with her mother has repeatedly shown her that turning into a wife and mother is the freaky, insulting, and maddening situation she should avoid at all costs. Who would want to be a personal maid, unpaid chef, or servant when you could be an independent figure and the "star of the show" (as Mr. Andrews calls Annabel)? Not even the "fox" Boris appears worth that sacrifice.

Perhaps more importantly, the casting of Jodie Foster and her performance in the film strains this conflict to its breaking point. It may not be strange for any girl to become just like her mother, but turning the "iconically queer" young Foster into an obedient hetero-domestic goddess moves beyond freaky and into the realm of the unimaginable. This strong young actress, who according to her own mother served as a powerful symbol of the women's movement, could hardly be expected to fit easily into a domestication narrative. In her interview for the DVD release, Foster makes her distance from Disney's intention with Annabel quite clear. She describes the film as promoting a supposed "little girl fantasy" of being the "ugly duckling who in some ways is underappreciated" and insecure about her own looks but who, through some "magic spell," turns into Cinderella and receives all the appreciation she desires as the "most beautiful and sought-after person on earth." Yet, her response to this "little girl fantasy" comes as a blunt rejection: "I can't say that I shared that fantasy as a young person." Besides prompting the unasked question—what was your girlhood fantasy, then?—this statement suggests that the young person asked to act out this "ugly duckling" narrative harbored a fundamental resistance to her role. I would argue that this resistance not only comes through in Foster's performance but also, strangely, in Disney's casting of her in the first place. By the mid-1970s it must have been clear that Foster was shaping up to be the exact antithesis of a feminine and wholesome Shirley Temple-like child star, yet the company still cast her in this odd Oedipal family drama where apparently all she needed was to shed her braces and get a new hairstyle in order to transform her into a compliant young woman. In other words, this piece of casting reveals yet again an ambivalence towards the project by its producers. Disney wants to engage with the issue of feminism, so it casts one of its contract players perfect for such a role but then asks her to enact a fantasy that she does not share or, literally, embody. The figure of the queer kid might work for the premise of this "Freaky Friday" bedlam, but safely resolving her bodily presence proves quite difficult indeed, even for Disney.

Interestingly, the resistance posed by the era's defining child star and iconic queer kid begins in the same opening scene in which she offers her adoration for the patriarch and his surrogate. As I have described above, the scene introduces the audience to the teenage protagonist Annabel, whose voice-over describes her physical appearance, her fights with her little brother and mother, and of course her love for her "cool" father and the "fox" next door. Yet her actual appearance on-screen, dressed in a sports jersey nightgown and with tussled shoulder-length hair, immediately signals the gender-queer image that Foster had projected since her infamous small role in *Alice Doesn't Live Here Anymore*. As Foster stomps across the messy bedroom to face a closet mirror in her sports jersey, she affects the tough-guy tomboy stance adored and emulated by the queer fans interviewed in *Jodie: An Icon*, which contains a clip of this very opening scene. Once at closer distance, we share a privileged view of her female masculinity with her almost shoulder-length blonde hair cut short enough and with feathering on one side to resemble the androgynous locks of the era's male rock stars and pin ups. In fact, when she comes face to face with 1970s heartthrob Vince Van Patten in the next scene, their hairstyles are remarkably similar, although his is partially hidden under a soda jerk cap.

As she stares at herself in the mirror, her glare and pouting mouth resemble nothing so much as a young tough trying to pump himself up. Accordingly, when she sticks her chest out to mime the voice-over's discussion of her bust size, it looks as if she is showing off her potential muscles, not her girlish figure. This sort of aggressive masculinity, exemplified in her many tomboy roles of the 1970s, carries throughout the scene, not only in the shots of her physical prowess on the hockey field but also, most simply, in the voice on the soundtrack.[32] When Annabel quips from her voice-over in response to her untidy room, "Don't knock it. I like it this way," the mock-gangster bravado is carried off by Foster's distinctive voice. Often remarked upon as low and gravely, her trademark 'adult' voice helped define her gender-bending image for critics and supposedly won her the nickname "froggy." Here, her froggy voice serves to reinforce the female masculinity visible on screen—Annabel dressed in an oxford shirt, sweater, and jeans accessorized with a white shell necklace that completes the surfer-boy look—and creates an ironic distance from the words of the screenplay.

Although the audience is supposed to be meeting the typical young female teen who dislikes her braces and disagrees with her mother, the look, sound, and demeanor of Foster's tough-guy routine disrupts any easy reading of this scene, especially at the moment when she moons over her neighbor Boris. Having introduced a charmingly butch Annabel, the filmmakers have no choice but to play this moment for laughs, allowing Foster to press her face comically against a window pane, distorting her nose and squashed lips as her deep voice labels him a "fox" and purrs "Mmm mmm" at the sight of him. Our reverse angle view of Boris completes the joke when a very frail-looking, disheveled Marc McClure shuffles out of his house for the paper and then dramatically inhales his nose spray under Annabel's (and our) gaze. It is no wonder that due to some unnamed incident in the past he has taken to avoiding her. This slender, vulnerable boy seems no match for "tough, hard-nosed, rock 'em sock 'em super jock Annabel," as her field hockey coach calls her, either on the playground or anywhere else.[33] The script may suggest him as the appropriate object for her affections (after her father, of course), but Foster's performance and undeniably masculine presence, both on-screen and on the soundtrack, create a disjoin here that the filmmakers have no choice but to play for laughs.

One might argue that a major aim of the film is to feminize, normalize, and discipline such an assertive and aggressive tomboy, but this becomes difficult when so much of the film extols the strengths of Annabel as the "star of the show." As her mother struggles through the teenage girl's day at school, we see that Annabel excels at a number of activities that simply overwhelm Mrs. Andrews. Moving from photography and typing classes to field hockey play offs and the final aquacade show, the body swap both emphasizes the tomboy daughter's leadership and dominance in a competitive sphere like athletics and denigrates the mother's responsibilities as difficult but demeaning. While the field hockey coach and other players acclaim Annabel as the lynchpin of the team's success and Mr. Andrews boasts that the aquacade will be a hit because of his "star" daughter, the teenager's difficulties with her mother's duties like laundry and cooking once she has entered her mother's body seem more an indictment of the domestic situation than of her lack of aptitude for it. Despite its apparent plot to get Annabel "back on track," the film privileges her masculine qualities, following a trope typical of "tomboy" films wherein the young female protagonist is valued for her independence and self-motivation (as long as it remains contained in childhood or adolescence).[34]

The film articulates the unequal value placed on the two gender expressions particularly during the field hockey game sequence. In this scene, Mrs. Andrews (in her daughter's body) loses the game by scoring on the wrong goal, even though the team is counting on her to score her "usual zillion goals" for them. Then, the mother's failure in this competitive arena is contrasted through cross cutting with Annabel's success in her mother's body when she joins her brother Ben in a pickup baseball game at the park. Her display of physical skill and aggressive desire to win (even fighting with a young umpire) earns her brother's/son's respect and leads to a genuine connection between the siblings, although Annabel's recognition of her love for him can only be expressed in internalized voice-over. These two intercut scenes suggest that Annabel's masculine strengths are to be valued, even as the result softens her behavior slightly, but the mother's feminine role in the home suffers in comparison. As Sean Griffin argues in *Tinker Belles and Evil Queens*, this validation of Annabel's female masculinity is "unusual for the conservative Disney," even going so far as to conclude that Mrs. Andrews in the end "realizes that Annabel is fine the way she is."[35] However, "conservative Disney" is caught in a bind here: by affirming what Griffin calls "non-feminine roles for women" and, I would argue, by devaluing the mother's traditional femininity, this studio product diverges from the Disney practice of defining young women as passive damsels in a manner that cannot be rectified or erased through a set of curlers and a last-minute (and blatantly arranged) date with Boris.

Perhaps not surprisingly, one of the consequences of this ambivalent approach to changing gender norms is that gender quickly exposes itself as masquerade. The body swap literally unhinges gender from the body, of course, as the feminine housewife must maneuver in her daughter's athletic milieu and the masculine daughter must inhabit the role of domestic helpmate. Yet, the film seems to go out of its way to highlight the strange humor of the performance of gender, for example by having Foster as Annabel imitate the voice and mannerisms of Barbara Harris, which transforms her notorious "froggy" voice into a higher pitched motherly tone. In fact, the mother-daughter body swap appears to have thrown all stable gender identity into disarray. As soon as Mr. Andrews leaves the house for work, Annabel takes the first opportunity to play with the femininity typically displayed by her mother, putting tremendous amounts of makeup on her mother's face and then labeling the ridiculous result "Sadie the painted lady" from within her voice-over. Meant to resemble a little girl playing dress up with her mother's belongings, the scene contradicts such seeming innocence through Foster's sarcastic tone in the voice-over. It accentuates the humor of Barbara Harris' excessively made up face and her struggles to place her fake eyelashes with the constant harangue from the voice-over that mockingly refers to the clownish visage as "lovely, my dear, simply lovely" and "just gorgeous!" The combination of exaggerated makeup, fake eyelashes, and Foster's deep voice undoubtedly suggests a teasing drag performance under way here, which seems to have lasting impact of the remainder of the film. One might even see the entire body swap as a lesson in drag where the mother and daughter play with each other's gender expression.

Perhaps most interestingly, this overt performance of gender resurfaces when Annabel uses her mother's body to forge a relationship with Boris. The entrance into heterosexual romance frustrates and confuses the teenage tomboy, so the opportunity presented by her mother's body and voice inspires an intriguing play with identity. After giving up on her mother's chores or "personal maiding," Annabel decides that her mother's body might be useful for something after all (winning over the "fox"), yet her forays into the performance of "gorgeous" femininity prove both comic and predictably queer. Her appearance is that of a slightly less made up (not quite "Sadie the painted lady") version of her mother with tousled hair and in her bathrobe, but the voice speaking the lines remains Foster's froggy voice-over. In a classic trope from teen films, Annabel's bewilderment about what to say when she calls Boris forces her to rehearse her greeting with a couple of overtly gendered versions. First, she lowers her voice-over even more and approaches him like a male buddy, "What's happening, man?" and then she switches to a campy deep whisper as a performance of female seduction, "Hiya, loverboy." Although ultimately her mother's regular voice works as the simplest solution, Annabel's initial attempts not only expose her difficulties with the basic parameters of heterosexual romance but, more importantly, tie those difficulties to a fundamental misunderstanding or confusion of gender norms. Her performance suggests that she might choose to act as the laid-back masculine pal or the husky, desirous femme fatale, although she may prefer to be both or neither. While she decides on the opportune resolution offered by her mother's body, this does not make her use of her mother's voice any less of a performance. Once again, the combination of Foster's voice-over with the image of Barbara Harris has driven a wedge between the body and gender expression, here exaggerated by the masquerade of voice as it freely jumps across a range of gendered alternatives, not appearing to privilege any one.

Annabel's play with identity here and in her earlier feminine masquerade with makeup seem to open up a veritable Pandora's box of gender mayhem touching every member of her family. Annabel's continued misreading of the norms that make gender performance necessary (attaching the correct voice, or behavior, or appearance to the correct body) spreads like a virus. For example, her failure to understand that a pantsuit and tennis shoes might not be the "sexy, slinky" feminine outfit at the heart of Boris' schoolboy fantasy is followed shortly thereafter by more gender confusion for *him*, the basis of which becomes a running joke for the remainder of the film. Stumbling upon Annabel's slovenly room, he is astonished to hear from a defensive Mrs. Andrews (Annabel) that it belongs to the younger brother, Ben; he cannot believe that Ben would have a "canopy bed" and dollhouse. In a phrase typical of this oddly conflicted film, she responds to his apparent disapproval with two divergent explanations: "He's a very peculiar boy. He's liberated." Typically, failure to follow gender norms is considered perverse *or* liberating, but in *Freaky Friday* it becomes both.

What's more, this liberating perversity keeps spreading. Gender has become so unhinged at the end that Mr. Andrews cannot judge even his own wife's gender as she parasails past him at the water show. Referring to her as a "young man" daredevil in the sky, Mr. Andrews must be corrected by his coworker, "I believe you've got your sexes mixed up, Andrews. It's not a he." Andrews sheepishly confesses his own mistake and hints at the serious gender trouble for the entire family caused by the mother-daughter body swap: "It's not a he; it's a she. My wife!" It would appear from these several instances that the presence of a gender-queer child, especially one who is in such close contact with her mother's body, has the effect of throwing everyone else's identities into doubt. In other words, the presence of a butch tomboy in a woman's body is just too much for the 'normal' Disney family or community to bear.

In short, Disney's foray into feminism has opened up questions the film seems unprepared to answer. What happens to the other members and traditional relationships when the queer child becomes the center for a Disney family? What are the consequences of focusing on the mother? Where does authority reside in this new family home, or is stable, knowable identity possible there? Unable to definitively answer any of these questions, the film can, however, locate the source of the trouble without much difficulty. As Boris indicates to the woman he believes to be her mother, Annabel presents a seemingly irredeemable problem: "Mrs. Andrews, you shouldn't blame yourself. I mean, it's not your fault that Annabel's the way she is. She's probably what they call . . . a . . . bad seed." Leaving aside for the moment the innuendo or open question in Boris' inability to voice exactly what one might "call" Annabel or what word one would use to define "the way she is," the attribution of the label "bad seed" clearly directs blame at her for the chaos of the day, but more importantly, it defines her abnormality as internal and innate. Although she does not resemble the saccharine sweetness or blonde precociousness of Rhoda Penmark in LeRoy's 1956 film version of *The Bad Seed*, Annabel performs a light comic version of her competitiveness, aggression, and disquieting closeness to the mother, although of course without the three murders. She may not ask "for a basket of kisses," but Annabel's intimacy with her mother becomes a problem that the film cannot solve. What I would like to suggest is that the combination of her disruption of stable gender identity and her growing attachment for her mother offers an unintended counter-narrative to the positive Oedipus scenario preferred by the film. Or to put it another way, masculinity in a young girl does not become too serious of a "complex" until her choice of object (the mother) becomes perverse or abnormal, and this perversity is exactly the excess that the film's ultimate feminized resolution for Annabel fails to contain.

"I Want to Touch You": (Mother) Love at the Aquacade

It would seem on the surface that the privileging of Annabel's masculinity does not pose a serious challenge to patriarchal authority because, in the first place, the dominance and superiority of masculine power is reinforced by this aggrandizement of the tomboy and, second, the film offers a reassuring conclusion with its supposed domestication and feminization of Annabel. Yet, this situation stretches the narrative logic to its breaking point. As a maturation plot, the film falters at its most basic premises: it becomes plainly obvious from early on that Annabel's pursuits and skills are already valued highly above her adult mother's and so the obvious question arises, why should she grow up? Femininity and traditional roles for women are devalued, so in some respects Annabel was already on the right track and must now abandon it for reasons that remain murky at best. To complete this maturation tale, she must give up the prized masculinity, lose her tomboy independence, and embrace demeaning femininity for the reward of . . . Boris? And yet the film does offer another reward and one that does not necessarily involve abandoning assertiveness, activity, or independence. This more direct narrative line leads her into her mother's arms and in this scenario her masculinity becomes a thornier issue.

The masculinity to which I am referring above, which is termed by Freud the "masculinity complex," is certainly not a revolutionary solution for the liberation of the female subject, but it does disrupt Freud's usually unassailable Oedipal logic, just as it wreaks havoc on this Disney family. As Freud outlines it in his essay on "Female Sexuality," the girl exhibiting a "masculinity complex" rejects the idea of her own castration, holding on with "defiant self-assertiveness to her threatened masculinity," and takes the role of the aggressive, competitive male, despite her recognition of female castration.[36] In other words, to place it in the *Freaky Friday* scenario, she recognizes her mother's subordinate position and yet refuses to abandon her own independence. Not only refusing that passive position, she goes further, according to his introductory lecture on "Femininity": she "even exaggerates her previous masculinity, clings to her clitoridal activity and takes refuge in an identification with her phallic mother or her father."[37] All of this activity and identification with the phallus would not be so much of a concern if the girl eventually abandoned this "defiantly rebellious" stance and embraced her passive aims (as the ending of *Freaky Friday* asks her to do), but Freud repeatedly projects the same future for this masculine girl that ends not surprisingly in homosexual object choice or what he calls the "extreme achievement of such a masculinity complex."[38] Penis envy aside, his picture of this female patient's masculinity complex resembles Annabel Andrews quite a bit: she was a "spirited girl, always ready for romping and fighting" and not "prepared to be second to her slightly older brother," and Freud cannot help but notice that she "was in fact a feminist," who felt it was "unjust that girls should not enjoy the same freedoms as boys, and rebelled against the lot of women in general."[39] However, his patient manifests not only these active and principled passions but also a "strong mother fixation," which acted with already present homosexual currents in the libido to create female object choice. With this particular "fixation" comes the idea of the negative Oedipus complex, which was developed in the work of female analysts such as Jeanne Lampl-de Groot and Helene Deutsch.

Simply put, the negative Oedipus complex recognizes the place of an erotic attachment to the mother in the development of the female subject. Toward the end of his essay on "Female Sexuality," Freud attempts to address the "complications" that occur when the child "returns to the attachment to her mother which she had abandoned," but he defers to other literature in the field at this point, particularly the work of female analysts.[40] He, for the most part, agrees with Lampl-de Groot's findings that before the Oedipus phase there exists the "girl's sexual (phallic) activity towards the mother," which she gives up as a result of her recognition of castration, causing a "turning-away" from this earlier sexual object.[41] The girl must go through this earlier phase, the "'negative' Oedipus complex," before she can pass into the "positive" phase. However, both Freud and Lampl-de Groot are concerned about a possible "return" to the mother after entrance into the positive Oedipus situation. Teresa de Lauretis perhaps best summarizes the complications created by this return via Lampl-de Groot's theory of the negative Oedipus complex: "If the repression of the girl's negative Oedipus attitude is not successful, or if it is, but her love for the father is also subsequently disappointed, then she will either not give up her 'masculine attitude' or resume it after the failed attempt to love the father passively."[42] Of course, in Laml-de Groot's "extreme" cases, the reluctance to give up this "masculine attitude" or the resumption of it after disappointment with the father results in female homosexuality, which de Lauretis laments as neither a "new or better understanding of female homosexuality" than Freud's.[43] Nevertheless, the presence of the negative Oedipus complex offers at least a more complicated understanding of Oedipal affairs for the female subject and puts forward another narrative underlying or competing with the normative path. Emphasizing the mother obviously shifts the focus of the conventional maturation tale for the daughter, and the "complicated process of returning" to the mother as love object, as Deutsch refers to it, not only defies the inevitability of positive Oedipus but also makes for a queer disruption in Disney family values.[44]

Let me be clear. I am not suggesting that the "masculinity complex" and negative Oedipus represent a progressive or liberatory flight from patriarchal structures and dominance or that they are an acceptable 'explanation' for homosexuality in women.[45] Rather, I am arguing that the film's employment of a particular female masculinity disturbs its manifest attempt to assert a 'normal' positive Oedipus maturation for the girl and disorders the nuclear Disney family by aligning the mother and the daughter in a love relationship (with repeated expressions of an erotic attachment), which results in a deflating or devaluing of patriarchy and a queering of gender and sexuality in general. While I am certainly not interested in heedlessly equating her assertiveness, aggression, and competitive drive with an inexorable lesbian future, I would propose that the film emphasizes her masculinity and then raises the possibility of female-mother object choice alongside its unsatisfying and contradictory heteronormative plotting, thereby placing the inevitability of the latter resolution in doubt.

Interestingly, the entrance of negative Oedipus into Freud's accounts of "Femininity" and "Female Sexuality" produces just such a queer undecidability in the plotting of female maturation. His mention of Lampl–de Groot and Deutsch in the first—his introductory lecture on the "enigma of women" and femininity—prompts the concession that "the development of femininity remains exposed to disturbance by the residual phenomena of the early masculine period," sending the woman regressing back to the "fixations of the pre-Oedipus phases."[46] This frequent occurrence means that throughout women's lives there exists the possibility of a "repeated alternation between periods in which masculinity or femininity gains the upper hand," which "we men" interpret as enigmatic but is merely "this expression of bisexuality in women's lives."[47] Interestingly, in the earlier essay on sexuality this "alternation" is not figured in terms of gender but rather object choice. After his consideration of the convolutions that take the little girl from "intense *active* wishful impulses directed towards the mother" to her turning away from her mother and the rise of "passive" aims for her libido, Freud again admits to the "complications" of negative Oedipus where she "returns" to her attachment to her mother after a "disappointment" from her father.[48] These complications raise a distressing idea indeed—that a woman might "in the course of her life" change back and forth "from one position to the other," at once taking the passive position vis-a-vis her father or his surrogate and then reversing course to return to her "sexual (phallic) activity" towards her mother, and so on.[49] In other words, negative Oedipus has broader consequences than its supposed connection to female homosexuality. It clearly challenges the primacy or inevitability of the "normal" Oedipal scenario for women, offering instead the idea of fluidity or "alternation" in the course of their extended sexual, erotic, or gendered lives. In short, this account of negative Oedipus introduces queer possibilities for many more women than his case history of one lesbian patient would indicate and suggests "complications" for Annabel's maturation plot that extend beyond the facile ending of a pizza date with Boris.

Contrary to other films of the era such as Friedkin's *The Exorcist* where the active pursuit of the mother takes on monstrous proportions, *Freaky Friday* almost charmingly flirts with erotic attachment to the mother (and mother surrogates). Yet, it is unquestionable that the body swap works to bring the daughter in close contact with the mother's body, betraying perhaps a dream of union with that body and not necessarily one of pre-Oedipal, pre-phallic bliss. Indeed, at the exact moment of this otherworldly swap the erotics of the bodily confrontation are unmistakable,

FIGURE 4.2 The body swap puts butch Annabel into tantalizingly close contact with the mother's body *Credit: Walt Disney Pictures/Photofest*

though briefly glimpsed. Even as it introduces an electronic score reminiscent of the period's horror films, the split screen swap itself maintains some distance between mother and daughter until the overlay of matted primary colors and the eventual superimposition, but the aftermath is less controlled. Initially alerted by (what else?) the sounds of their new voices, the two women register shock and confusion, which Annabel (now in her mother's body) remedies with a bit of exploration. Cued by Annabel's voice-over as it narrates the action, the pace of the scene slows from its rapid crosscutting to a slow deliberate camera movement—the tilt—up the mother's body.

The slow tilt up Mrs. Andrew's body begins with her right hand on her right leg, caressing up the stocking as Annabel's voice-over directs it up "mom's legs." The camera continues to follow as both hands run up the thighs, gliding over the crotch, and meeting to together at "her stomach" before a brief pause. At this point the hands come apart with splayed fingers pointing inward toward each other as they come up and over the place of Mrs. Andrew's breasts. Annabel's voice-over at this point seems overwhelmed by the thought of describing what the hands nearly touch, stammering "and her . . . a . . . her . . . a" before looking up from her gaze at the body in shocked recognition. After this stunning encounter with the contours of the mother's body, she is only able to cover her mouth in distress (and perhaps some excitement) and conclude, "wow." Moreover, the soundtrack seems to reflect her excitement or wonder at this moment, as it shifts from the more ominous electronic tones during the swap to a more romantic trill of string instruments during the slow tilt up. Even upon her definitive recognition of the swap as she looks at her mother's reflection—"Mom's body has got my mind in it. I'm mom"—she is still appreciating the adult female body, caressing her mother's lips before perversely and comically announcing, "I love your teeth." The scene remains one of the rare moments when the premise for the freaky events of this one Friday, the body swap, is cause for unconcealed pleasure in the contact between daughter and mother.

In a film that playfully toys with Freudian concepts (the Oedipal perversity of a wife calling her husband "daddy" and the knowing winks of school counselors), the filmmakers apparently have failed to read their Freud closely. Introducing a masculine girl and reveling in her active successes and then spending an hour and a half bringing her closer to her mother is a recipe for (positive) Oedipal disaster. The film, consequently, offers two competing and contradictory scenarios: in one Annabel accepts her mother's passive position and feminine lot and acknowledges the proper love object no matter how weak and wheezing he might be; in the other, Annabel refuses the passive position, teaches her mother how to be active, and then aggressively pursues her mother's love, body, and attention. The introduction of the second surely puts the certainty of the first into question. Or, to borrow de Lauretis' phrasing in her description of Freud's imposing of the positive Oedipus complex on his female patients, the introduction of the second thread exposes the first as a nothing more than a "passionate fiction" structuring the narrative for the filmmakers.[50] Like Freud's fiction, it is the "fantasy that a girl must desire the father and wish to bear a child in his image" that leads to the heteronormative resolution with Boris, but this passionate fiction is directly contradicted by another fantasy, a competing fiction that not only would like to *be* mother for a day but so much more. As the Golden Globe nominated original theme song "I'd Like to Be You For a Day" makes clear, the duet between mother and daughter reveals another wish, as they sing to each other: "I want to touch you/ I want to reach you/ In every single way."

The plot for much of the remainder of the film revolves around this relationship, bringing together the mother and daughter and emphasizing the resultant understanding between them. They learn how hard each other's day and responsibilities might be and the trite wisdom of walking in the other's shoes. Therefore, the film necessarily highlights a growing closeness between mother and daughter, which the daughter announces as "love" in the climactic scene. However, there are indications throughout the film that the body swap, as the daughter's exploring hands above would indicate, has opened up a complicated mass of emotions and desires both for women and *between* women. For example, in the scene following Boris' declaration that Annabel is probably a "bad seed," we see Mrs. Andrews, in Annabel's body, struggle with the horseplay and violent intimacy between girls on the field hockey pitch. After rousing speeches during which the two predictably butch female coaches rally their teams around the prowess and threat of Annabel's athletic skill, the person who might win the game single handedly ("tough, hard-nosed, rock-em-sock-em super jock Annabel") fears she has joined the marines when she has only entered into the latently erotic world of team sports. As if in answer to the opposing coach's suggestive command to "get Annabel Andrews and get her good," Annabel's best friend Virginia encourages her with a rousing "go get 'em" and a slap on the rear. Yet this cliché of homoerotic bonding in organized men's sports, particularly football, carries some weight here for the filmmakers who emphasize the butt slap by following Virginia's hand with the camera, panning down and to the right slightly, to frame the touch more clearly.

Then, as the game itself begins, the opposing team takes its coach's advice quite seriously and begins its own sadistic play with Annabel's body. The other female teens hit her legs, disarm her of her field hockey stick, and eventually shove her over onto the field by slamming into her backside. As the game continues, we see a series of close shots of Annabel's body taking the abuse of knocks to her midsection, hits on the buttocks from opposing sticks, and even an elbow to the face as the other team taunts her, "can't you take it?" Her coach has little sympathy, insisting that she not "just lie there" and take it. Poor Mrs. Andrews seems wholly unprepared for the rough play and kinky discipline of all-female athletics, even in a supposedly noncontact sport. Similar to the scene of bodily discovery, the film argues once again that the body swap has opened up a world of contact between women, or at least allowed it to come into focus more clearly. These moments of flirtation with homoerotic play stand out as odd intrusions into the film's heteronormative plot, raising the idea, yet again, of a different set of pleasures in the body swap.

Interestingly, like Annabel's liberated ideas about what constitutes the behavior of a "male chauvinist pig," this opening up of desires between women spreads to Mrs. Andrews as well (possibly it was beaten into her?). After her rough experience on the hockey field where she concludes by scoring on her own team—itself an unintended evocation of slang phrase for homosexuality as 'batting for the other team'—Mrs. Andrews resolves to refashion Annabel's body while she has control over it, so she visits her husband's office to secure the credit card she will need. Once at her husband's office, she (in Annabel's body) takes notice of his new secretary, Ms. Gibbons, whose auburn-haired, lip-glossed beauty is emphasized immediately by a rapid zoom on her face. The recognition of her beauty does not stop there, however, as her hourglass figure becomes an area of focus when she leads Annabel/Mrs. Andrews to her boss's office door. Again, as in the two previous instances, camera movement follows the avid interest in the female body, looking down and following her rear end as it sashays across the office. Provocatively, this close up on Ms. Gibbons' backside as she walks away is followed by a reaction shot of Annabel/Mrs. Andrews (Jodie Foster), who seems stunned but whose eyes noticeably look downward toward Ms. Gibbons' rear, which is again shown in the next shot as confirmation of Annabel's gaze, the eyeline match confirming the object of her interest. The scene is meant to reveal Mrs. Andrews' petty jealousy and insecurity through her voice-over, which exasperatedly laments, "You've got to be kidding" at the sight of Ms. Gibbons. Yet, her use of the Annabel disguise (and Foster's expression) to warn the secretary away from her husband, even threatening her with a hockey stick, opens the film up to a second set of meanings in the exchange of looks between women, or to be more specific in the gaze of the teenage tomboy taking in the attractive adult woman again.

Even though Ms. Gibbons takes the hint of the jealous threat and changes into her trench coat (and eventually dons thick glasses and puts up her hair to mask her beauty), she does not avoid the attention and prying eyes of the other woman/girl. Mrs. Andrews shrewdly might have "already seen [her] action," so to speak (in voice-over), but Annabel cannot seem to keep her eyes off of it. When Ms. Gibbons stands next to her by her father's desk, Annabel/Mrs. Andrews stares down at the other woman's outfit, repeatedly looking, in fact, toward her breasts now covered by the trench coat. Even as Ms. Gibbons shifts away and uncomfortably pulls her coat tighter, Annabel continues to stare up and down her body, pausing at her chest. If this is jealousy, it has certainly taken the form of interest long hinted by psychoanalysts—that jealously reveals an intense connection between the jealous person and the rival rather than confirming the original relationship that supposedly spurred it. In short, Annabel/Mrs. Andrews appears much more interested in Ms. Gibbons in this scene than anyone else, especially Mr. Andrews who resurfaces like an afterthought after Ms. Gibbons has left the room. The intense connection and desire (and threats of violence) flow here, again, between women, and on the image track the clearest direction of desire follows the gaze of the masculine teenage girl (and the eyes of Jodie Foster), just as the body swap scene traced the girl's exploratory thrills though Foster's voice. Furthermore, one might contrast this moment with the opening scene in which Annabel spots the "fox" Boris. Both scenes have a comic element—in one we are supposed to chuckle at the housewife's middle-aged jealousy and in the other we experience the goofiness of young love—but the object of the humor and its significance differ dramatically. In the opening scene, Foster's performance creates a distorted caricature of young heterosexual romance, which the filmmakers undercut further with the introduction of the sniffling "fox," but the office scene has Foster playing it straight, as it were, as she takes the other woman under her serious and aggressive gaze, which has the opposite effect of validating that desire rather than lampooning it.

Ultimately, though, the central explosive relationship that set these freaky events in motion must reach its own climax by the end of the film—mother and daughter must sort out their feelings for each other after this contact with each other's bodies and lives. Even after Mrs. Andrews has femmed up Annabel's appearance at the beauty parlor and Annabel has ruined the dinner meant for her father's big event (with the ineffective assistance of Boris and her brother), the two find a way into each other's arms. Annabel confesses that she wants her "mommy" and drives off in the car with Boris and Ben (even though she does not know how to drive) in order to save her mother, who faces certain disaster on water skis. The slapstick chase that follows instigates the swap back of minds into bodies but leaves mother and daughter, now in the right body but in the wrong place, still in precarious positions; one flounders on skis she cannot handle and the other careens through traffic aware that "mom needs us." This comic chase straight out of Mack Sennett's oeuvre—complete with prat falls into pools, undercranked camerawork, physics-defying leaps, and violence without serious consequence—serves to defer the climax of mother-daughter union. Similar to dreamwork, the film postpones their reunion for over ten minutes of screen time through a series of unbelievable twists and obstacles, thereby creating a sense of the union's significance for the viewer by delaying our gratification as well as that of the two women. The last-minute rescue format should create suspense, but it also has the effect of implying a nervous anticipation for Annabel who seems to drive through most of Los Angeles county before reaching her destination, where she is only stopped by crashing the VW bug into the water. When Mrs. Andrews lands safely next to the VW after being confused for a "young man" by her husband and puncturing the float holding the dignitaries, including Mr. Andrews, Annabel reaches across the divide and expresses passionate concern for her mother, to which her mother responds with validation of their new bond: "It's nice to know you care, my darling." Her recognition of her daughter's love, stressed in a medium close up of Annabel's face, the sides of which Mrs. Andrews holds gently as the two stare into each other's eyes, produces a smile from Annabel.

After extending the chase scene, the film allows the mother and daughter to linger in their reunion. In a shot-reverse series, the scene is divided between over the shoulder shots of the two declaring their love and mutual appreciation, alternating back and forth so that the viewer experiences the full effect of their locked eyes and sincere expression. Annabel stresses her feelings as she assures her mother that she *does* care and "really" loves her, while Mrs. Andrews responds in kind ("I love you too, darling") and hugs her close. This long day and even longer chase sequence ends in the embrace of the happy, wiser couple who are brought together by their new understanding of each other and new knowledge of themselves, "so much smarter" and "so much dumber" than they ever thought before. The film seems to argue at this point that Annabel has learned some humility and is not as concerned about her looks, but what I would emphasize is the feeling of conclusion at the coming together of these two women. Although her mother appears confused at first when Annabel wants to discuss "the way I am," she hugs away the awkwardness of the moment, again referring to her daughter as "my darling" and clasping the back of her head to bring her in for their second embrace. As Annabel closes her eyes tightly and enjoys the physical contact she has been longing for since the initial body swap, it feels as if we have reached the blissful culmination of this maturation plot. The film has been heading toward *this* marriage of mind and body all along.

Yet, I would add that the significance of this union and its potential to rewrite both the patriarchal family narrative and the conventional adolescent story does not go unrecognized by the film. As I mentioned above, Mrs. Andrews' ill-fated role in the aquacade show, which finds her destroying every composed aspect of the group performance, is best symbolized by her accidental puncturing of the dignitaries raft out in the center of the lake. The film returns to shots of her ski having punctured the pontoons of the raft lest the audience forget and does so again immediately after her final embrace with Annabel. Then, as Mr. Andrews' important client praises him for the excellent show and declares that his family is "a bunch of comedians" who put on one of the "funniest, cleverest" shows he has ever seen, the penetrating ski finally does its work and the raft swiftly sinks to the canned laughter of all on board. In this penultimate scene, the patriarch, his male boss (played by heart throb Vince Van Patton's father, Dick), and his VIP client and their wives are all scuppered by the freaky events of the mother–daughter body swap and the final shot of their embrace. Through this editing, the film suggests for a moment, that the communion of mother and daughter has the potential to sink the father and his system of hierarchical privilege—an act that perversely and nervously produces laughter on the soundtrack.

Conclusion

Meant finally to feminize, domesticate, and normalize the queer female kid, the concluding scene with Boris and the introduction of their upcoming date appears in comparison as a mere afterthought to the grand climax at the aquacade—a tacked on ending to diffuse the obvious pleasure of the union of mother and daughter. In this brief final scene, which reveals a newly coiffed Annabel and supposedly directs her onto that traditional path of heteromaturation, one wonders how successful the resolution really is, especially in conjunction with the dramatic closure of the preceding passionate female embrace. Boris approves of Annabel as a "completely different person" now and she seems to acquiesce to this disciplining of her "bad seed" past, to being the "level-headed woman" that Boris needs. Yet, when they head off for their pizza date, Annabel hangs back and then invites her brother Ben to go along. In a moment reminiscent of the now infamous ending of *Now Voyager*, Annabel, ever the queer kid, delays the seemingly inevitable romance or indefinitely defers it by inserting her brother between them (placing the stars in the picture rather than asking for the moon), refusing the coupling with the third wheel of Ben. Boris is disappointed and, pointedly, it is Ben and Annabel who walk off together hand in hand. One can note, as well, in this view of Annabel with her brother that the hair might have changed in the mother's makeover of her butch daughter, but this represents a merely cosmetic alteration. Annabel, dressed in a man's shirt and jeans, walks away from the camera with her now-familiar relaxed, athletic gait that can only be called boyish. The supposed transformation, again thanks to the presence and mannerisms of Jodie Foster, does not quite take. Instead, it is exposed as another failed performance of normative gender and sexuality, despite the presence of one manly Boris.

The traditional maturation plot for a teenage girl, encapsulated in the opening and closing scenes of this film, is a familiar one indeed. A troubled female subject at the beginning of the film—unsure how to manage the transition from the child and daughter of the beloved patriarch to the mature, passive recipient of his male surrogate's advances—the girl should be humbled by the experiences of her freaky day and make her way towards adult femininity and heterosexual commitment. Like the many mid-century stories about teenage girls such as *Gidget* that are analyzed by Ilana Nash in *American Sweethearts*, this plot employs the girl's story to reinforce a particularly American myth that composes domestic space as an ideal of the "father-centered family unit."[51] Disney's films, one could certainly argue, stand as one of the most powerful purveyors of this myth in twentieth-century popular culture. While this narrative form often exposes the anxieties about the teenager's potential to "disrupt the patriarchal status quo," the ultimate goal of the girl-centered texts examined by Nash is to instill in their "young female consumer implicit lessons in self-subordination to paternal(istic) authority—for that authority is ultimately what these entertainments were designed to celebrate and protect."⁵² But let me emphasize, as Nash does, that the girl-centered texts she considers are largely a mid-century phenomenon, ending with the *Gidget* television series in 1965—the "last moment in which the original tropes of adolescent girlhood consistently cohered."⁵³ In other words, *Freaky Friday* might attempt to invoke those original tropes and that conservative maturation plot for adolescent girlhood, but such an anachronistic project is doomed to failure, as Disney's own troubled, self-conscious engagement with second wave feminism in the film and the casting of Jodie Foster clearly show.

In this period, not surprisingly one of the most difficult in Disney's corporate history, the classical Disney ethos of innocence, heteronormativity, and father-centered 'family values' breaks down. The family—that symbol, for Giroux, of "ideological unification through which Disney defines its view of capitalism, gender, and national identity"—is undone by a different maturation plot, one that centers on mother and daughter and leaves the patriarch comically sinking in the middle of a lagoon.⁵⁴ The more typical "repressive pedagogy" that Giroux locates in Disney products, which functions to naturalize one mythic America by excluding the "subversive elements of memory," has strayed dangerously from its lesson plan.⁵⁵ While we are still focusing on the white, middle-class, suburban family (Disney can't stay *that* far), the pedagogy of gender and sexual norming has clearly been disrupted by the mother–child reunion. Unfortunately for Disney, the subversive element that should be marginalized out of its discourse has been brought in by one of its own contract players: Jodie Foster. As many commentators have noted, at the heart of the Disney ethos is a construction and reification of innocence that masks any number of unpleasant social and historical realities—from American imperialism to the sexuality of children. For example, Elizabeth Bell and her coeditors write in their introduction to *From Mouse to Mermaid: The Politics of Film, Gender, and Culture* that Disney's "trademarked innocence operates on a systematic sanitization of violence, sexuality, and political struggle concomitant with an erasure or repression of difference."⁵⁶ Foster's star discourse and other film roles ranging from *Bugsy Malone* and *Taxi Driver* to *Alice Doesn't Live Here Anymore* certainly fail to "sanitize" violence and sexuality, while *Freaky Friday* itself chooses to engage with the political struggle for women's equality even as its resolution attempts a kind of willful forgetting or repression. Consequently, when Foster's strangely adult child is let loose on the patriarchal Disney family, she queers both the company's naturalization of a traditional version of the American myth and its construction of a childhood innocence that erases difference and nonnormative sexuality.[57] It must have been a strange viewing experience indeed for the audience member shocked and disturbed by Foster's performance as world-weary teen prostitute Iris in *Taxi Driver* to witness later that year her role in *Freaky Friday*, where Disney's "trademarked innocence" fails to sanitize the upturned family, the butch female teenager, and the excited sound of Foster's voice exploring the contours of her screen mother's body.

Freaky Friday replaces the supposedly wholesome father-centered family ideal of classical Disney texts with an at times passionate love affair between daughter and mother, signifying a nonnormative (and counter-Oedipal) trajectory for the young female subject rarely offered by either Disney or other teen narratives. Typically, the world of Disney family values might present obstacles to the preferred outcome of heterosexual union, family togetherness, and happily ever after, but the certainty of the final resolution is rarely in doubt. Men and women, animals and humans, Americans and 'exotic' others will ultimately know their place. In what Chris Holmlund has called the "sexual politics of the Disney universe," traditional gender roles are typically reinforced despite a begrudging recognition of female empowerment, and "all sexuality must be expressed in service to the family, that is, all sexuality must by definition be heterosexuality."[58] In other words, the only nascent sexuality that *Freaky Friday* should validate is the final joining of Annabel and Boris, who has already been established as the inheritor of the beloved father's rights in the opening scene and whose heterosexual union with Annabel should reproduce the patriarchal family. However, this last-minute endorsement and celebration of heterosexuality—what should be the fundamental tool in the Disney universe for "naturalizing the heterosexual patriarchal family structure"—struggles to compete with the centrality and intensity of the mother-daughter relationship.[59] As with their screwball ride through Los Angeles, Boris and heterosexual romance are relegated to the passenger seat, while Annabel and her queer desire drive frantically towards the mother. Without the primacy of heterosexual union, the Disney family and the "politics of the Disney universe" come into question, while the inverse must also be true. As the film disturbs the patriarchal family with a freaky investment in the mother, so it dislodges the primacy of heterosexual union and the straight story of growing up.

One way to understand the significance of this subversion of Disney family values and the straight story of American girlhood is to contrast it with another of the era's narratives of perversely adult children, *The*

Bad News Bears. As I mentioned in the Introduction, this top-grossing tale of misfit youth introduces the tomboy, played by one of the few teen stars of the period and yet another of the prematurely aged children of 1970s cinema, Tatum O'Neal, but her path, like that of her damaged and crude fellow Bears, is unambiguously back toward the father. The drunk, washed-up manager of the North Valley Bears, Buttermaker (played by the lovable grouch Walter Matthau), sees the athletic potential in O'Neal's Amanda, but he repeatedly expresses his desire to have nothing to do with her mother. In fact the film itself contains very few mothers besides marginal figures literally on the sidelines, despite the film's open recognition of women's movement's legal battles for the right of girls like Amanda to play Little League baseball. With a cast full of strangely adult and queer children, who self-identify as a collection of outcast 'others'—from "Jews" and "Spics" to "pansies" and delinquents, the film has the potential to offer an alternative maturation plot. Yet the focus of the film remains resolutely on the father-figure, who learns how to parent properly in this age of loveable losers, allowing the team to lose the championship game but loving them in spite of their failures and oddness.

Moreover, our central female lead—the tomboy who has given up her butch ways at the beginning of the film but returns to the field and her boyish appearance (complete with shell necklace) soon enough—has one simple goal: to win the love of the perverse and failing father. Despite her tough talk and mature bravado (insisting that 11-year-old girls do go on dates to Rolling Stones concerts), what she longs for at the end of the film is quality time with Buttermaker. The climactic scene at the championship game concludes with a tender moment of intimacy between the dysfunctional father-figure and his adoring tomboy daughter—a touching closeness that perfectly mirrors Annabel's embrace with her mother. Jodie Foster and Tatum O'Neal may have both perfected the role of the unsettling adult child who confronts the adult world with her brash female masculinity and worldly experience, but O'Neal contrastingly put this queer child in service of the father—both in *Bad News Bears* and, perhaps more notably, in her Oscar award-winning performance in *Paper Moon* (opposite her own father). O'Neal's skill at reforming, supporting, and embracing the fallen father won her acclaim, but it also placed her in a long line of female teen stars who sustained this father-centered version of American girlhood throughout the twentieth century, as Nash's work establishes. Jodie Foster, on the other hand, consistently presented an alternative to this conservative tale—a new version of American girlhood.

As Foster herself reminds us in her "Look Back" interview for the DVD release of *Freaky Friday*, she plainly did not share the "little girl fantasy" that resolves the "ugly duckling," misfit female teen by returning her to a traditional female role vis-à-vis heteropatriarchy. Instead, she embodied an entirely different fantasy, despite the attempt to contain her at the end of this film—a fantasy that embraced the mother, shook the Disney family, and thrilled an audience of misfit teen girls who were seeing themselves on-screen for perhaps the first time. Foster's queer kid shone in the 1970s as a reflection of the undeniable force of the call for women's equality in the United States and as a sign of the crisis not only for national mythologies but also for the traditional maturation plot put in service of these myths. There may have been few teen film stars in this decade, but Foster, like Robbie Benson, shows them to be capable of challenging the foundations of the straight, white male story of growing up that will return with a vengeance in the 1980s. Yet, in this brief but significant reprieve, the queer kid ruled.

Chapter 5

Brothers, Sisters, and Chainsaws: Sibling Rivalry and Peer Centrality in the Teen Slasher Film

To miss out on the importance of the sibling is to miss out on the place of death. Even without a sibling death, the wish to kill siblings or the sense of being annihilated as a unique subject by their presence is a crucial aspect of the human condition.

—*Juliet Mitchell,* Mad Men and Medusas: Reclaiming Hysteria

In her effort to place the "importance of the sibling" and, consequently, death at the center of recent psychoanalytic theory, Juliet Mitchell turns to the story of Antigone. What new insights might come, she asks in the follow-up to *Mad Men and Medusas, Siblings: Sex and Violence,* by shifting the focus from Oedipus to Antigone—from a narrative of "sexuality and reproduction" to one of death?[1] Recounting Antigone's tale of mourning and murder, wherein her brothers, who are Oedipus's sons as well as his brothers (as she is both his daughter and his sister), kill each other eventually resulting in Antigone's suicide after she attempts to mourn both brothers equally, Mitchell finds a representative narrative or mythic model for the sibling's relationship to death. This archetypal sister understands "the meaning of death" as "both inevitable and absolute," which is the lesson the sibling or sibling surrogate teaches the subject. Through the sibling's presence, the subject learns about death "because the very existence of that brother in the first place has been experienced as a *death* of the subject's self."[2] Based in the concept of an absent self, Mitchell argues in favor of a new model for the development of the subject, one that provides an alternative to the hierarchical parent–child dynamic. In turn, she proposes the primary importance of death as a foundational absence for the subject before the entrance of sexuality, the phallus, and sexual difference.[3] Perhaps more simply, though, in terms of the generic forms of popular culture, Antigone's tale also very much resembles a modern horror story—murder, rotting corpses, familial betrayal, live burial, and more death. Sibling deaths and sibling murderers, in fact, abound in modern horror, particularly beginning in postwar American horror films and reaching a generic peak in the slasher films of the 1980s, although they have received little critical attention.

The specific connection between siblings and death also appears mystifying for the horror films themselves. At the end of the pre-credit opening for *Halloween II* (1981), the sequel to John Carpenter's monument of slasher horror *Halloween* (1978), Dr Loomis responds to an exasperated neighbor who complains of being "trick-or-treated to death" with self-righteous invective: "*you* don't know what death is." As the film progresses through its often-imitated slasher formula plot, it seems that neither Loomis nor the film itself knows exactly what or who "death is"— why death has come to Haddonfield in the particular form of escaped mental patient and teen slasher Michael Myers. For a film consumed with death, *Halloween II* does little to clarify Michael's drive to death. The filmmakers erase any specificity or even humanity from the figure of the slashing monster, in fact cutting the shot of Michael's revealed face that is in the conclusion of the first film but not in the replaying of that scene at the opening of the sequel. While this second film in the series occasionally allows a glimpse through Michael's eyes, more often it works to demonize and dehumanize the killer as an empty, evil bogeyman—the monster rising up from the Id or the embodiment of "Samhain," the Lord of the Dead.

From the second shot of the film (of Laurie and the kids), however, *Halloween II* reveals the obvious obstacle it will continue to come up against in attempting to dehumanize or make symbolic the figure of Michael Myers: he is focusing his assault on an intimate, on family, on his own sister—Laurie Strode. To borrow the advertising phrase from another 1980s horror sequel (*Jaws: The Revenge*), this time, as with last time, "it's personal." The revelation of Laurie Strode's identity as Michael's younger sister is in many ways the great surprise twist that made this film notable for the growing slasher film audience, yet the film seems conflicted about or reluctant to pursue the significance of this newly defining disclosure. Initially, the film indicates the importance of sibling rivalry and the place of sibling aggression for its own series through a direct citation of one of its influences. The place of sibling aggression surfaces early in *Halloween II* through the insertion of the opening to George Romero's *Night of the Living Dead* (1968) in a frame-within-a-frame, replaying on a TV the gothic-influenced graveyard scene, with its own allusions to Universal's horror classics, in which the brother, Johnny, taunts his sister: "They're coming to get you, Barbara!" Yet, despite this early foreshadowing allusion, the film, through Dr Loomis's obsession with the "Samhain" or unconscious reading of Michael, veers away from the significance of this sibling rivalry until the final act's revelation.

When the filmmakers finally offer the surprise of Laurie's sibling tie, through the unveiling of Michael's hidden file by Marion Chambers, Dr Loomis is still wrestling with several other official readings of Michael's actions such as the meaning of the name "Samhain." Even though his earlier claims that Michael Myers "isn't a man," that there was "nothing in him . . . that was even remotely human," point toward a supernatural explanation for the killer as inhuman evil, his confrontation with Samhain returns him to his own psychiatric expertise of the unconscious mind and its dark recesses, as Michael becomes a kind of Id run amok. However, at this moment, the film offers, yet again, an alternative reading, and the same alternative as before: Michael is coming for his sister. Interestingly, as Chambers introduces this new, contradictory explanation for Michael's behavior, Dr Loomis seems to abandon entirely his reading of the killer as a walking, stalking representation of the darkness inside ourselves and orders them to hurry to save Laurie with simple reasoning that Michael "killed one sister 15 years ago and now he's trying to kill the other!" Now that Dr Loomis has finally seen the sister, the other readings of Michael—as Samhain, supernatural Lord of Death and essentialized evil or as the monster of dark human desires—fall away. Still, Dr Loomis never asks the most obvious question. He recognizes the centrality of Michael's aggression toward his sisters, but he goes no further to understand *why* Michael might desire this terrible sororicide.

In fact, this is a question that many critics have posed to the film—what in the unconscious desires of these films makes Michael kill these particular teenagers in the violent and possibly sexual way that he does—but these same critics, like Dr Loomis, fail to examine the teenage victim truly as a *sister* or the killer as a brother. For example, Tony Williams succinctly summarizes the common critical position on the film, that Michael represents "the return of a patriarchy violently punishing the younger generation."[4] Despite Michael's status as a "child in an adult's body," Williams finds that he both embodies "rage from the patriarchal unconscious" and is an "apocalyptic figure removed from family roots, recreated according to the desires of a community in crisis"; he is the scapegoat that "crisis-ridden America" needs to fulfill its violent unconscious desires to return to traditional mores.[5] In all of these guises, he is somehow "removed from family roots" but also acts as a surrogate for the Father or the dominant culture. He is never just a *brother*. Yet, the films' focus on Michael and Laurie as siblings offers a startlingly new direction for the teen film narrative wherein the parental relationship is secondary, if present at all, to the peer or sibling connection.

I would argue that the killer's role in *Halloween II* as Samhain, Lord of Death, and as Michael Myers, murdering brother, are not two separate readings but together illuminate both the killer's motivation and the audience's pleasure in viewing such horrors. Returning to the epigraph above as a theoretical starting point, this chapter seeks to refocus critical attention on the importance of that sibling not only for horror genre criticism but also for its revision of teen film's traditional focus on parent–child conflict. For Juliet Mitchell, to understand the formation of any human subject, one must recognize the importance of sibling, peer, or "lateral" relationships and their connection to foundational fears of self-annihilation and lack of unique identity. Moreover, these fears can again become particularly acute during adolescence, which is the emblematic developmental period for experimentation with and final formation of identity, and can renew those wishes to kill the sibling (or, often in adolescence, one's peers) in order to stave off annihilation.[6] This combination—the fear of the lateral other (sibling) who can replace you and then the murderous wishes that seek to preempt or prevent the symbolic murder of one's self—helps to define the particular struggles of adolescence *and* elucidates the desires, horrors, and pleasures exhibited in the slasher film and in its audience. Simply put, Michael Myers is both the Lord of Death and the homicidal sibling, just as Laurie is both for him, and these frightening tales of sibling rivalry in the 1970s show that this relationship proves more powerful than the parent–child conflict of traditional teen films.

The Importance of the Sibling

Once one takes it as a project not to "miss the importance of the sibling," an alarming number of them come into view. Indeed, if one merely examines the three horror films since *Psycho* that have received enormous critical attention and seemed, at times, to define "American horror" in the last half of the twentieth century—*Night of the Living Dead*,

The Texas Chain Saw Massacre (1974), and *Halloween*—it would be hard to overlook them. Johnny and Barbara give way to Sally and Franklin (and Leatherface and the hitchhiker), who are followed by Michael and Laurie. *Psycho* trades one blonde sister for the next, while *Poltergeist* (1984) spares a brother as his sister is exiled to purgatory (or the television). *Carrie*'s (1976) adolescent monster has no biological siblings, but she certainly suffers at the hands of and takes her revenge upon a brutal peer culture. Moreover, for slasher films of the 1980s, the brother and sister battle becomes a kind of leitmotif within the subgenre, or, as Vera Dika contends of the "contemporary stalker films," the brothers and sisters of *Halloween*, *Prom Night* (1980), and *Terror Train* (1980) reveal an "overvaluation of family ties" in the guise of siblings.[7] After the initial film in the series, *Friday the 13th Part 2* (1981) develops the lateral relationship between a grown Jason Voorhees as the killer and the young counselors at the summer camp as his victims and peers, including his "final girl" combatant Ginny. One might even argue that in *A Nightmare on Elm Street* (1984), Nancy and Glen, who never consummate their relationship despite plenty of opportunity, can be understood better as brother and sister than as boyfriend and girlfriend, which, of course, would not preclude sexual desire. Indeed, as the prototypical sibling horror story, Poe's "The Fall of the House of Usher," shows, guilt-ridden aggression and murderous competition between siblings cannot easily be divorced from lateral incestuous wishes.

Nevertheless, within the critical discourse on the horror film, these pairings, most often set up as antagonists, are not examined as siblings but come to represent other dynamics—often parent–child. This is not to say that the family is neglected in the criticism. Quite the contrary is the case, with the parent–child relation figuring prominently in some of the most influential readings by Robin Wood, Tony Williams, Vera Dika, and, of course, Carol Clover. Yet, in all of those just listed, a focus on the hierarchal relationships in the family predominates and the lateral relationships are subsumed within a dominant Oedipal model. By making the "child" one his primary "Others" whom "bourgeois ideology cannot recognize or accept but must deal with" though oppression and who resurface in horror film as the return of the repressed or, simply, the monster, Robin Wood suggests the family as a central locus for horror's dramas.[8] Centrally, his work focuses on the "child-monster" as a product of the family.[9] Even with Carpenter's *Halloween*, Wood's focus remains on sexual repression and the child-monster, "product of the nuclear family and the small town environment," and the relationship between Laurie and Michael becomes a tantalizing but unfulfilled aspect of the film.[10]

In the wake of Wood's highly influential article cited above, many more critics pursued his generational division between the monstrous child and his or her parent, or, conversely, critics proposed the killer as a monstrous force *from* parent culture victimizing the younger generation rather than examining the nightmare of the family unit as a whole. Of course, Tony Williams' significant work *Hearths of Darkness: The Family in American Horror Film* does take up Wood's focus on the entire family unit, particularly in regard to *The Texas Chain Saw Massacre*, *The Last House on the Left* (1972), and *The Hills Have Eyes* (1977), as oppositions between a monstrous and a 'normal' family, but his view of the later slasher films reasserts the generational divide discussed above: simply put, "slasher films presented the younger generation as surrogate victims of patriarchal executioners."[11] Further and not surprisingly, this generational conflict is defined by Vera Dika as blatantly, even self-consciously, Oedipal, and, through the act of looking, as evocative of the "primal scene."[12] Unlike Steve Neale, who in an earlier article connects the "primal scene" of *Halloween*'s opening sequence to the phallic mother, Dika focuses on the child-viewer of the primal scene and the use of it as a self-reflexive structuring device for the films, which begin with an original traumatic viewing.[13] But, again, this emphasis on the primal scene and on the generational divide that Dika locates between the young group and the older characters in the films reinforces the parent–child dynamic.

Perhaps the work that most clearly defines horror criticism's Freudian reading of the slasher film is Carol Clover's monumental essay, "Her Body, Himself: Gender in the Slasher Film," and subsequent book, *Men, Women, and Chainsaws* (the inspiration for this chapter's title).[14] Clover's work famously presents the relationship between the "Final Girl" and the killer in slasher films as a kind of revolution of gender in the horror film. She offers the contact between the killer and Final Girl as representing a "loosening of the categories," wherein the "combination masculine female repeatedly prevails over the combination feminine male," the Final Girl over the male slasher.[15] Through the central example of *The Texas Chain Saw Massacre*, Clover delineates the basic features of the slasher film, including a typical (male) killer like Hitchhiker or Leatherface, who is arrested in development and confused in either normative gender or sexuality, and a typical final female victim/hero, who fights back, looks back, and lacks femininity.[16] This "boyish" Final Girl becomes a kind of hero and the psychological center of the film, as her point of view dominates the end of the film and her appeal to a "largely male audience" inspired Clover's work.[17] In her characterization of these two figures for a male audience, Clover insists on the Final Girl's masculinity, through her employment of a phallic weapon, to meet the male adolescent audience's identificatory needs, preferring the girl as "male surrogate in things oedipal" as opposed to the feminine male killer.[18] Yet, the reversal or "irregular combinations" she has proposed within the figures of the Final Girl and feminized killer suggest a fluidity of gender identification that she does not fully pursue. In order to propose the Final Girl as a "homoerotic stand-in" in the male viewer's sadomasochistic incest fantasies—making it safe for him to enjoy the thrusts of the killer's knife, Clover must bracket the possibility that the killer might stand-in for a *female* figure of less determined gender such as the phallic mother.[19] Moreover, her proposed spectatorial identification further obviates the intriguing possibility that the killer might be a feminine male surrogate for the *female* audience member.[20]

Locked in the final battle of the films, these two figures share, for Clover, both a masculinity and a femininity, which the killer might possess from the beginning but which is fully enacted by his castration at her hands; however, their status within the familial hierarchy differs significantly. Through her phallicization in the final moments, the Final Girl ascends into the adult world, winning the battle of "sex and parents" by defeating the killer who was a parental imago brought forth by her own incestuous desires.[21] In short, the Final Girl performs the symbolic parenticide necessary for ascension to adulthood that the killer failed to achieve, and she does so by turning on the killer who is now in the place of the parent, or as Clover later names the killer and Final Girl, "parent and Everyteen, respectively."[22] However, Clover has been careful in her systematic explanation of the slasher film to locate the killer in the child's place—for example, Leatherface with his rolls of baby fat that jiggle as he saws.[23] Particularly for the present discussion, this "parenticidal struggle" between Final Girl and killer and the intriguing use of the more ambiguous term "parenticide" when many critics suggest that the slasher killer acts for the patriarchy raise a number of interesting questions. How can the killer move so quickly from child to parent? Which parent is the killer supposed to represent with his apparent femininity, employment of the phallic weapon, and final castration, which seems anything but final when the killer always recovers from penetration by a hail of bullets or series of stabbings? If the killer represents the father, which the "homoerotic" scenario demands, how does one understand his femininity and ultimate castration or defeat? If the parent is the mother, like Mrs. Voorhees and Mrs. Bates, who causes the damage to her feminine son, what becomes of the homoerotic incestuous wish for the male viewer adopting the Final Girl surrogate? How does one even begin to address the theoretical ramifications if the Final Girl in this parenticidal struggle stands in for, well, a girl?

In other words, what I am suggesting here is that the parenticidal model, the often reiterated critical tale of "sex and parents," necessitates a number of reversals and omissions to avoid an obvious explanation: slasher horror pits adolescents against adolescents. While the killer might seem childlike at times, it is hard to imagine him as a child when he (in the form of Leatherface, Hitchhiker/Chop Top, Jason Vorhees, Michael Myers, etc.) experiences gender confusion and hovers on the edge of adult sexuality, both of which are more commonly features of adolescence. If the killer has already failed in his attempt at parenticide, then that would suggest that he has already been on the verge of adulthood—that is, adolescence—and never developed beyond that point. Moreover, since the killer has never developed further, it seems hard to imagine him representing the parent in the Final Girl's struggle *or*, in other readings, acting out the patriarchal wish to punish the sexually active girl or the younger generation in general.[24] The battle between the slasher killer and the Final Girl appears much more like a contest between two adolescents, since Michael Myers and Laurie Strode or Sally and Hitchhiker are simply close in age and in social position, not children and not fully adults, like peers or truly siblings. There are adult figures in the films, but as most critics note, they are on the periphery or marginalized, allowing these slasher films to confine the violence within a peer community. With the exception of Mrs. Vorhees' killings in *Friday the 13th, Part I,* a killer of a similar age comes into an adolescent group—whether on a road trip, on Halloween night, or at summer camp—and commits brutal acts against members of his contemporary group. In sum, when we place the killer and the Final Girl or the viewer and the Final Girl/killer side by side, they are adolescent doubles in a battle for supremacy, not parent and child but brother and sister, male and female teen, male and female audience member, caught in the death throes of a kind of sibling rivalry. What might seem like a struggle between the child and the "parental Other" turns out to be the battle between teen sister and brother.

One only has to look as far as one of Clover's own central examples, *The Texas Chain Saw Massacre* (1974), to locate both the centrality of peer or sibling violence and the ferocity of its murderous aggression and rivalry. The early part of the film focuses closely on the siblings within the adolescent peer group, particularly working repeatedly to undermine and mock Sally's brother, Franklin, whom Leatherface kills towards the end while she escapes. In fact, the opening pre-credit sequence begins with a focus in voice-over and text on the two siblings, singled out in the "tragedy which befell a group of five youths" by name, as "Sally Hardesty and her invalid brother, Franklin." The opening monologue dramatically announces "the discovery of one of the most bizarre crimes in the annals of American history," but it truly is the siblings, and particularly the brother Franklin, who experience the "idyllic summer afternoon drive" as a nightmare from the beginning. After the apocalyptic pre-credit and credit sequences, with the flashes of the "grizzly work of art" in the cemetery and the radio news commentary about the litany of crimes, catastrophes, and epidemics, the "catastrophic atmosphere that quickly encompasses the film," for critic Christopher Sharrett, isolates Franklin as its first target.[25] As Franklin's humiliating and painful fall into the roadside wilds as he attempts to urinate into a can opens the film, so another wounded brother, Leatherface, and his roadside chainsaw dance will end it, signaling unquestionable trouble in the family unit but more specifically rejection and abuse along lateral lines.

When the young group first comes into contact with the Sawyer or slaughterhouse family, in the guise of the hitchhiker, the ties between the killers and Franklin become apparent as the peer aggression against Franklin becomes more pronounced. True to his prototypical slasher killer status, Hitchhiker enters into the space of a peer group, the van, and initiates the film's acts of aggression by literally slashing himself and then Franklin, marking him as a blood brother.[26] However, Franklin's association with the marginalized and disturbed Sawyer brothers precedes this one violent act: he alone identifies the slaughterhouse smell, relates his familial connection to the slaughterhouse (his grandfather), and describes with relish the methods of killing cattle. Both his behavior and total rejection by the group within the van—revealed in Pam's simple (and prophetic in its own right) response, "people shouldn't kill animals for food"—prepare the viewer for the entrance of Hitchhiker, as does Franklin's use of his pocketknife on his fingernails. As Franklin recognizes the danger that Hitchhiker poses, he also gravitates toward the clearly companionate figure ostracized by the peer group. Yet even Franklin appears less and less enthused about their growing connections, especially after Hitchhiker has cut himself, but the others reinforce it, blaming Franklin for "making everybody sick" with the talk of head cheese. Franklin has already been separated, embarrassed, and marginalized by his 'normal' peers, and then he must suffer the grotesque bond with and then attack by another marginalized and monstrous figure like himself.

When the group finally arrives at the "Franklin place," where the Hardesty siblings' father used to live, Franklin's isolation and maltreatment by his peers become most pronounced. In Hitchhiker's absence, Franklin transforms into the grotesque outcast for the group, both like the Sawyer brother and yet lesser in his dependent and victimized state. Franklin takes up Hitchhiker's place, stabbing the inside of the van and voices appreciation for Hitchhiker's bravado in cutting his own hand. Still, his appreciation for and concern about Hitchhiker's behavior, revealed in his worry that he might have "said something that made him mad," elicit rejection from the others, especially Kirk who first calls Franklin a "maniac" and then alleges that he is as "crazy" as Hitchhiker. As if Franklin's eating of the Sawyer family's suspect barbeque were not enough to damn him, the entire group turns on him for their lack of gas, threatening to force him to tow them in his chair to the next gas station. Moreover, once they arrive at the house that bears his name and, therefore, is marked as his birthright, he is attacked (verbally by Jerry) and then abandoned by the peer group. His frustration at abandonment is made clear as he struggles to enter the house alone, expresses fear at his privileged sight of Sawyer bone art, and then mockingly mimics and spits at the laughter of the couples upstairs. When he finally directs Kirk and Pam to the creek, setting them on a path to their doom, one can imagine their fate as his revenge.

Interestingly, while the exclusion, abuse, and taunting of Franklin has taken up the first half an hour of the film, as Sally's torture by the Sawyer family will comprise the final half an hour, he might have his revenge, but he does not survive as Sally does. Franklin may have his revenge on the others through Leatherface's actions, but his aggression back toward his peers reaches a major obstacle with his actual sister, who seems to turn on him in the end. Unlike Tony Williams, who views Franklin's death as a Frankenstein-like turn where the monster he "conjures up," Leatherface, turns on the creator, I would argue that his death results from his own sister Sally's unconscious wishful summoning of the monster.[27] After Jerry's repeated taunts that Hitchhiker is coming to "get" him and Sally's somewhat sarcastic promise that they will protect him if the Sawyer brother returns, Franklin gives Jerry the same ill-fated directions to the creek that he gave Kirk and Pam (with the same results) and Sally must stay behind with her brother. Her obvious frustration is directed at Franklin, whose burden has separated her from her boyfriend. The siblings are struggling at this point even to communicate at all, as Sally openly resents what Williams identifies as her "family duty," much like Hitchhiker's for Leatherface.[28] When Jerry does not return from the Sawyer house, her anger and resentment reach a crescendo and result in her brother's annihilation.

In the darkness, still screaming for Jerry, the siblings battle even as they move closer and closer to danger. They fight over whether they should leave without the others or not, since Sally will not leave without Jerry, and then physically scuffle over the one flashlight. Sally's face, lit from below by the flashlight, looks truly menacing as she screams at Franklin to stop and then when he will not release his grip, she walks away from him disgusted. Sally seems intent on leaving Franklin by the van, because he cannot follow down the grassy hill by himself, but as he wails for her to wait, she slows momentarily so that he can follow, still without her aid. The next series of shots, immediately before Leatherface's sudden entrance, show Sally at medium distance in the dark struggling to push Franklin through the grass and branches, while Franklin complains and hears danger everywhere. Of course, Franklin is correct about the danger, but the most accurate statement about their sibling relationship comes from an exasperated Sally: "Oh, Franklin, this is impossible." As if in agreement, Leatherface emerges suddenly from the darkness and begins driving his chainsaw into Franklin, who somehow is still holding the flashlight. Cutting back and forth between shots of Leatherface and reaction shots of Sally screaming, the scene culminates in a decisive close up on the flashlight by the side of Franklin's immobile wheelchair, followed by a long shot, presumably from Sally's point of view, of Franklin from behind being brutalized by his childish, Sawyer double. The very next shot confirms the serious rift between the Hardesty siblings: Sally runs. With the continuous sound bridge of Leatherface's chainsaw, still possibly victimizing Franklin, we see Sally in a number of successive shots running. Out of a recognizable instinct for self-preservation, she has abandoned her brother, proving the maintenance of their familial bond has truly become "impossible." He is an annoyance and a burden that the audience has been encouraged to reject, just as the peer group does, and with our sympathies rapidly shifting to the Final Girl Sally, her brother has become an obstacle that needs to be removed.

From the opening scene until Franklin's death, the film has set up a number of lateral relationships only to disturb them through growing frustration and eventual violent aggression. Hitchhiker and Franklin come together and then rupture apart, while the group of friends that included Franklin slowly becomes more abusive and rejecting of him until his own sister abandons him in the dark woods with the killer. The film offers competition within a group of young people and also between two young groups, those in the van versus the Sawyer brothers, and the result of this competition is an attempt at exclusion or annihilation. Within this situation, what Sharrett calls the "traditional construct of warring clans," Franklin demonstrates the impotence and dependence of a male member of one of the clans and yet he joins the clans together in "an important and complementary dichotomy."[29] Furthermore, Sharrett recognizes a key feature of this complementarity in the abuse shared by brothers in both clans; he notes the similarity between Franklin's "whining" and "Leatherface's squealing and cowering at the hands of his family" but especially focuses on the Hardesty brother, who is "reduced to little more than a target for the abuse by his peers." While Sharrett moves away from the particularly familial nature of this abuse to resituate the clan warfare in terms of an apocalyptic irresolution, "it is an onslaught that goes nowhere," I would rather delve more closely into the nature of those peer hostilities.[30] What is motivating this common thread in postwar horror of what Matt Becker has called the "youth against youth" theme that is possibly "related to the era's youth culture"?[31] While Becker proposes that films such as *Night of the Living Dead*, *The Texas Chain Saw Massacre*, and *The Last House on the Left* indicate that "the tight generational bonds out of which the hippie way of life developed had started to unravel," the question still remains as to why this unraveling is figured in terms of violence toward peers and not the older generation.[32] If these films become "reactionary" in their "deep sense of hopelessness" and "political disengagement," then their reaction takes a very particular victim, the peer.[33] Becker cites Tobe Hooper's comment that his film arose out of the "turbulent" times of the Nixon administration, but his film leaves the older generation and the Establishment on the margins, instead pitting siblings and peers against each other.

The final dinner 'party,' during which Sally is confined and tortured by the Sawyer clan, exposes the vicious sibling rivalry, lateral violence, and marginalized parent culture that will eventually dominate the slasher film cycle. The film places the Final Girl Sally as a sisterly guest at the Sawyers' demented family dinner, taking the abuse of her sadistic brother stand-ins, who indicate no sexual interest even when she offers to do "anything" to save herself, while the male 'authority figures,' the cook and Grandpa, prove to be ineffectual or removed from the violence. True to the slasher formula outlined by Clover, the end of the film increasingly views the lateral violence from Sally's perspective. From the moment when she witnesses Franklin's death, revealed in a number of shots capturing her terrified reaction, two of which frame the one subjective long shot before she runs, the film continually returns to her experience of events. In the chase scene after Franklin's death, the seemingly objective shots of her running and of Leatherface chasing are again unified by a sound bridge of the chainsaw, which in terms of sound perspective, often reflects her aural point of view. The film reinforces this subjective feature of the soundtrack when she finally 'escapes' Leatherface at the gas station; as soon as she enters the well-lit room where the cook is waiting, the chainsaw sound effect is abruptly silenced. Moreover, this aural perspective is punctuated by moments of subjective camera work. When Sally first enters the Sawyer home and bursts into the upstairs room containing Grandpa and, presumably, Grandma, the audience experiences her confrontation with decaying bodies firsthand though reverse shots in close up. We again are privileged to Sally's point of view most notably when she wakes up at the Sawyer dinner table and the lens focusing simulates her eyes adjusting to the sight of a chicken and skull on the table and Grandpa at the other end.

The experience that *The Texas Chain Saw Massacre* gives from Sally's point of view is, of course, one of traumatic violence and torture at the hands of a cannibalistic family, particularly at the hands of its sons. The Sawyer family at the table consists of ancient ex-slaughterhouse killer Grandpa, the abusive but absurdly polite and ineffectual father figure, the cook, and the two brothers, Hitchhiker and Leatherface. When the cook returns to the house with their prey, Sally, he appears at first to be the abusive and domineering father, beating Hitchhiker for robbing the cemetery and for leaving his brother alone and admonishing Leatherface as a "damn fool" for destroying the front door and possibly letting the others escape. However, his aggressive actions and command of the young men is oddly disrupted by 'polite' gestures toward Sally, such as telling her to "take it easy" while they fix her supper, which Robin Wood views as part of a fundamental "grotesque comedy" in the film.[34] It is clear that in his absurd concern for the house and in his awkward hospitality with Sally, the cook represents a mockery of middle-class values and respectability, just as Grandpa symbolizes a decayed, impotent, and even infantilized patriarchy.[35] As it turns out, the cook's invective at and abuse of Leatherface and Hitchhiker mask an impotent, inactive, even passive, paternal authority disregarded by the sons who know he "ain't nothing." In short, Sally will have to contend with the brothers and defeat or annihilate them in order to survive.

Although the scene at the dinner table makes gestures to include both the father figure and the grandfather, fratricide not patricide will end the torture. As Sally awakens to her captivity at the head of the table and begins her succession of screams that will pierce the soundtrack almost constantly for the remainder of the film, Hitchhiker surfaces as her main antagonist. Her screams are met with his cruel imitations. Evocative of Franklin's impersonations of her laughter and speech in the downstairs of their family homestead, Hitchhiker's replication of her terrified screams and cries appears both childish and repulsively cruel. In desperation, Sally turns to cook for help, pleading with him to make them and then just Hitchhiker "stop" and not to let them kill her, but Hitchhiker cuts her off with the reality of their family dynamic. After the cook admits that her situation "can't be helped" and watches as both brothers crowd in on her and grab her face and hair, Hitchhiker confidently announces that the older man is "nothing," "just a cook," who makes them "do all the work." From this point on, while the cook appears to enjoy the activities, Hitchhiker becomes her adversary. He is shown in close up aping her crying, her begging, her praying hands, as she continues to shriek in terror.

In its extreme form, the "grotesque comedy" of this scene parodies relatively common sibling teasing and taunts at the dinner table. Hitchhiker is clearly not interested in the "anything" she offers, and in the most excessively disturbing moments of the scene—the increasingly closer (even macro) shots of Sally's distressed and bloodshot eyeball— the reverse shots are often close up views of Hitchhiker's sadistic ridicule of her actions. The film indicates in these most horrifying moments that the point of view from that traumatized eyeball is of the *brother's* terrifying taunts. After Leatherface eerily moves in to take a better look at her, the cook feebly insists that there is "no need to torture the poor girl," but Hitchhiker has taken control, claiming he and Leatherface "will handle" her. His grotesque solution is to prop up Grandpa, once the "best killer there ever was," but he should have trusted his own abilities. Hitchhiker moves in too late to take the hammer himself and in the confusion, Sally escapes. The film's conclusion, of course, enacts Sally's revenge when

Hitchhiker is so focused on slashing her with his straight razor that he does not notice the enormous truck bearing down on him. The antagonist and one of the brother-doubles for both Franklin and Sally has been annihilated, but as we see in the final shots of Leatherface dancing with his chainsaw, viewed from Sally's perspective, the rivalry and lateral aggression cannot be so easily eliminated.

In short, Hooper's *The Texas Chain Saw Massacre* presents a different struggle entirely than the "parenticidal" one offered in Clover's reading. While Sally might stand-in for "Everyteen," Hitchhiker and Leatherface fail to fill the role of "parent." Although Leatherface might wear a mother's wig and makeup, his inarticulate cries and subsequent curious investigation of Sally belie any authoritative or adult position. Similarly, while it seems as though Hitchhiker has ascended to the father's place in his dominance of the dinner scene, his juvenile behavior toward Sally, sadistic and awful as his imitations might be, and his propping up of Grandpa suggest both immature adolescent rebellion and ultimate subordination to a patriarch, no matter how defeated. Furthermore, to triumph in her battle of "sex and parents," the Final Girl brings forth a parental figure (the killer) out of her own incestuous "fears and desires," but the example of the Hardesty siblings suggests another motive.[36] Sally conjures up the force of Leatherface at the moment that the burden of her brother has become "impossible," just as Franklin has possibly conjured up this double to avenge his abuse and neglect by the other youths, including his own sister. Or, if these brutalities *are* motivated by "incestuous fears and desires," it seems as likely that those desires run along lateral lines as along hierarchical ones. Yet, unlike Carpenter's *Halloween*, where (hetero) sexuality is foregrounded in the opening sequence, this film engages less with sex and more with visibility and identity formation within the peer group and the family. Franklin desperately wants to be seen and heard, much like Hitchhiker with his "grisly work of art" in the graveyard, and their imitations of Sally, whether laughing or crying, suggest an insecurity about their own voices or independent selves. The battle of sibling rivalry centers on the survival or even possibility of a unique self when faced with the competition of the peer or sibling double, and the subject's logical resolution is to imagine or symbolically enact the other's annihilation or death. In other words, if a unique Sally cannot survive while Franklin lives, then one of them has to go. In the end, it must be noted that only one Hardesty sibling and one Sawyer sibling survive and even those two are locked in an antagonistic shot-reverse shot.

The Brother as Bogeyman in *Halloween*

In *Mad Men and Medusas: Reclaiming Hysteria*, Juliet Mitchell describes a situation strikingly similar to the visible frustrations and conflicting emotions expressed in the final moments between Sally and Franklin (and possibly between Sally and Leatherface). In her account of the child's experience of a sibling or peer intrusion and the "love/hate needs" it initiates, Mitchell portrays a deeply conflicted subject: "The child wants to be in the place of the sibling, to murder the usurper of its place, but it also loves it as itself and as it is/was loved itself and also as it wants to be loved itself."[37] She likens this terribly ambivalent experience to accounts of hysteria wherein the disturbance is viewed as impossible and the subject helpless. The experience Mitchell describes certainly calls to mind Sally's discouraged cry, "Oh, Franklin, this is impossible." In their final moments together in the dark, it is perhaps too simple to say that Sally *only* wishes for an end to Franklin's whining dependence and willful refusals and so conjures up death in the form of Leatherface's chainsaw. She also loves him, waiting for him even though she is fed up with him and finally pushing his chair through the overgrown woods. She screams in terror and possibly regret as her wish to be rid of him is fulfilled. Sally's "impossible" situation is typical of sibling relationships, which challenge the subject before the hierarchical demands of the parent–child dynamic so often emphasized in criticism of the horror film and teen film.

Mitchell argues for a reconsideration of the importance of sibling rivalry in the formation of the subject and in our understanding of the Oedipal conflict, claiming that the wish to kill the father and possess the mother is a result of the trauma of the sibling confrontation. The lateral relationship, whether with siblings or sibling substitutes, stands out at the "first *social* relationship" for the subject, but its trauma of displacement causes a regression for the child who responds with a wish for union with the mother, which results in a confrontation with the father as an obstacle.[38] By emphasizing the significance of the sibling, Mitchell offers a new model for the development of the subject, one that provides an alternative to the hierarchical parent–child dynamic and suggests the primary importance of death as a foundational absence for the subject before the entrance of sexuality, the phallus, and sexual difference. It is not the absent phallus that forms the subject in her formulation; it is the absent or potentially absent self.[39]

This particular experience of murderous wishes and death of the self creates a subject dramatically formed by the lateral other, and while the subject has strategies for coping with this absence of self, the trauma of displacement experienced as annihilation is not eradicated but returns at key moments in the subject's life when the fear of displacement resurfaces, such as in adolescence. The possibility of displacement strikes as the core of identity by establishing that "no human being is unique—he can always be replaced or repeated by another" and is experienced as a symbolic death, which creates the desire to kill before being killed oneself; indeed, this is the terror of the double or the "uncanny" other.[10] Furthermore, as Mitchell proposes in her later work *Siblings: Sex and Violence*, because the avenging murder of the sibling is forbidden, the subject can take two courses of action: the murderousness transforms into "aggressive play and healthy rivalry" and the mourning for the unique self allows for a new identity based on seriality, being "recreated as one among others" or as a peer and social subject.[11] Neither of these responses to the situation, however, is experienced as a satisfactory resolution.

The trauma of the annihilation or absence of a unique self will return throughout life, particularly, I would add, in adolescence, and the ferocity of that original murderous wish as well as the guilt for expressing it will resurface, as all prohibited wishes do. With the overwhelming importance of peer culture and a peer system of values that are the hallmark of adolescent experiences, it seems likely that rivalry or aggression within the peer group, a mirror of sibling rivalry, influences the teen subject more than parent–child relations. Since transformation of the death wish into aggressive play does not eliminate the trauma totally, the taunts of other children or peers have the potential to shape the subject later in life, as voices of the ego-ideal that might perform better than the father's voice as expressions of "approval or censorship that the child takes in (internalizes)" to the mind, setting up a separate aspect of the subject modeled on a "heroic or critical older (or other) sibling."[12] In other words, the sibling taunts become internalized and feelings of loss of self or loss of uniqueness return throughout one's life, as does guilt for the initial murderous wishes. The guilt at having wished for the death of the beloved sibling begins another unresolved cycle; the guilt can recall the wish much like the return of the repressed, which Mitchell has described as a "dread of the revenant," an unconscious dreading of vengeance by the sibling who was threatened by the subject's desire to kill or be killed.[13] The guilt for the murderous wish unleashes the revenant and in this unleashing, the subject is filled with dread at possible retaliation.

While many critics have read Michael Myers in Carpenter's original *Halloween* as the "return of the repressed," following Wood's influential proposition that all monsters in horror films represent the return of repressed Others that bourgeois society cannot accept, none consider him the repressed sibling, the return of the revenant. Michael Myers, simply, represents the wish, enactment of, and return of the wish to kill the sibling. If one imagines him as the return of *Laurie*'s wish to kill the sibling other, then his return is the result of guilt for the wish and the embodiment of the "dread of the revenant" who seeks revenge. One might even argue that Leatherface and Hitchhiker also represent the wish to murder the sibling, the enactment of that wish against Franklin, and then the turning of that wish back on the subject (Sally) as guilt and revenge. The much-discussed opening sequence of *Halloween* might illustrate Michael as the fantasy embodiment of Laurie's wish to kill the sibling sister that is then repressed until adolescence, when Laurie's renewed fears of displacement and subsequent murderous wishes produce the same embodiment of sibling murderousness, causing guilt and finally retribution against Laurie for the initial wish. A closer look at this much-discussed opening might establish this primary tie to Laurie's unconscious wishes, but not the same wishes linked to "sexual repression" offered by Carpenter himself.[44]

The famous opening sequence, directed by subjective "I" camera, figuratively and literally masks the identity of the subject viewing, which gives it the feeling of a dreamlike experience without disclosing the face of the dreamer. While Michael's name is spoken twice by his sister Judith, the agency of the sequence's "disembodied, narrative camera," to use Telotte's phrase, proceeds with an air of mystery.[45] Indeed, the fear and thrill for the audience comes in the lack of knowledge and then the unveiling by Michael's parents at the end of the sequence. As the camera slowly tracks toward the house, peers through the living room window at Judith and her boyfriend, returns to the front to the see the lights go out in Judith's room, and then enters through the back of the house, grabbing a knife along the way to the stairs, there is no way to know whose viewpoint we are sharing. Judith's offhand comment that "Michael's around someplace" does not have enough emphasis or directedness to indicate the watcher's identity, and then the masking off of the camera's viewpoint with the Halloween mask suggests a further obfuscation of true identity or intentions. Furthermore, from a technical standpoint, the height of the camera, resulting from an adult camera operator (even if he or she was crouching), belies the final revelation of Michael's six-year-old body and creates a moment of disruption when a child's costumed arm reaches out (out of focus) for the knife in the kitchen drawer.

In other words, amidst this mystery and confusion, one might imagine any number of stalkers or one might imagine being privy to someone else's dream or fantasy, through the dreamer's eyes. The watcher and killer could be anyone—for instance Laurie many years later or even the spectator—until the climactic reverse angle shot of Michael's father removing his mask and our view of his stunned, young face. Judith might yell his name at the moment of attack, but for the viewer there is still no confirmation of exact identity; we do not know who "Michael" is yet. What I am proposing is that until the unveiling of Michael's shocked face, the point of view remains confused and obscured enough to suggest a different agent for the action, to open this sequence up to Laurie's dream or fantasy-work. This sequence could function as a way to enact the desire to kill the sibling, for Laurie to have a firsthand experience of that act without taking the blame or responsibility for that wish. Also, of course, through the use of the subjective camera, the filmmakers give the same potential opportunity to the young, viewing audience.

While many critics have attributed a sexual motivation to Michael's killings, initiated by this postcoital sororicide, the attention to the sibling suggests another cause for the murderous wish, whether Michael's or Laurie's. In "Through a Pumpkin's Eye," J. P. Telotte sets ups the killing of Judith Myers as a kind of post-primal scene massacre, where the child can "hardly be expected to understand the complexities of adult sexuality" but interprets what has happened as an act "in which one person pleasurably assaults another"; however, he abandons this primal scene reading for a more neutral "voyeuristic perspective" that Michael takes on his sister with is "phallic knife."[46] While Vera Dika more clearly pursues this primal scenario as central to the "stalker cycle," others have resisted the "sexual" reading of Michael's actions. William Paul asserts that the shock of the sequence's final revelation forces us to examine the killer as a *child* who takes revenge on his neglectful caretaker. Questioning the critical focus on Michael's "latent sexual desire" as based on "a strange assumption of what the needs of a six-year-old might be," Paul stresses the "theme of abandonment" as key for the film.[47] Emphasizing that the child killer is also a sibling, I would argue for the more traumatic fear of annihilation, rather than abandonment—a fear possibly spurred by the sexual act with its potential to produce another, displacing the subject again. Yet, the fear of annihilation by the lateral Other suggests a central concern apart from sexuality: the mourning for the absent self that forces the subject to abandon the certainty of a unique self and to attempt to recreate a new identity. In other words, the question of identity fuels this sequence as much as, if not more than, the question of sexuality.

Obviously, one cannot deny the tie between sexual relations and the killings that follow coupling. Michael's later killings and his placement of his sister's headstone at the head of a dead and posed Annie on the bed make the connection clear enough. However, William Paul's questioning of the sexual knowledge of the six-year-old child has merit. While the act of heterosexual adolescent sex does precede the killings, the murder of his sister cannot be definitively linked to the sexual motivation. Michael is outside of the house and then downstairs while the act is taking place, and he only views the boyfriend leaving and his sister upstairs in her room, nude, brushing her hair. As Paul suggests, we must assume a great deal of knowledge about sex for the six-year-old boy to fill in these gaps. Moreover, the film provides as much evidence of the significance of neglect of the child under the sister's or sister-surrogate babysitter's care in the opening sequence and throughout the film, and, at times, Michael works as an agent of revenge outside of the adolescent sexual realm, for example after Tommy is teased on the playground by class bullies. The opening sequence offers a separate discourse on identity and death that permeates the rest of the film as well, and, of course, the connection of identity and death arises out of contact with the sibling or lateral others in the form of peers. In other words one might argue for a different reading of sex in this film, in that it cannot be disentangled from violence, murderousness, and questions of identity related to the ambivalent hatred, fear, and love for the same, the sibling.[48]

From its opening shot, with the slow tracking in to the house and handheld-type movement, the scene in Haddonfield in 1963 is consumed with the question of identity. Simply put, who is the person looking at the house? Then, with the introduction of the Halloween mask and costume, the masquerade of identity takes the central focus. The mysterious person whose point of view we share puts on the mask that the boyfriend had placed on his face jokingly only moments before. Does this point of view become a double for the boyfriend or is the mask meant to hide intentions? When the killer reaches his sister's room, she is sitting at her mirror, naked, brushing her hair. This overdetermined symbol of identity and duality, the mirror, enables the revelation of the viewing agent's name—Judith angrily chides, "Michael!"—but the mask remains to obstruct our view and also Judith's view of her attacker. As the killer begins slashing Judith, there is an unexpected shot from the killer's point of view of the bloodied knife rising and lowering in its stabbing motion. It is a strange moment in the scene because the viewer must know from the sound and the initial view of a bloodied Judith that the knife is sinking in, so the shot of the knife rising in the small hand seems more like an unsure verification of the act for the killer, as if asking, am I really doing this, is that a knife in my hand? Then, the shot seems to answer these questions, confirming at least one aspect of identity: *I* am the killer, or it is *my* hand that is killing the sister.

Although the final shot of the opening sequence gives a face and an identity to the killer, a young, shocked child in a clown's costume with the name of Michael, the way in which the previous few minutes have been shot suggests much less confirmation of identity, except as an outsider and a killer, allowing for the entire opening sequence to be read as Laurie's vision or fantasy wish fulfillment. Placing blame on another sibling, the younger sister can enact the wish to kill her sibling and then have the brother-killer-instrument Michael disappear as well (for 15 years). Yet, of course, by having Michael kill the sister, Laurie would be envisioning her own symbolic death, as Michael's *other* sister. This opening sequence performs the particular conflict of the sibling relationship quite well: the desire to kill the other whose existence threatens to annihilate you does lead ultimately to the end of the unique self and guilt at the murderous wish. The notions of death and identity fuel this conflict *and* the opening sequence of *Halloween*.

As the film proceeds into the body of the narrative, taking place 15 years later on the day before and day of Halloween in 1978, Laurie quickly becomes the central protagonist of the narrative, standing out from her group of peers in the attention both the camera and a looming Michael pay her. However, there is also sufficient evidence in this main section of the film that Michael has been conjured up from Laurie's unconscious. It is Laurie, staring out her window during a class on the subject of "fate," who first sees Michael standing next to his stolen vehicle and staring directly into her classroom. From inside her classroom, where the teacher is insisting that fate "stands where man passes away, fate never changes," Laurie sees him standing across the street, already in his white, featureless mask that, of course, hides his identity, and she becomes alarmed. Yet, after she has answered her teacher's question and turns back to the window, he is mysteriously gone.[19]

Nevertheless, throughout the rest of the film, only Laurie, Tommy, and eventually Dr Loomis will see Michael, being granted both a point of view shot and a reaction shot connecting the sight of Michael's action to their reaction. In the murder scenes of Annie, Linda, and Bob, Michael remains hidden or obscured in darkness or wears a second costume or disguise (a sheet) in the case of Linda's murder. Moreover, when Tommy insists he has seen the "bogeyman" and Laurie asks what he looks like, Tommy can only respond, "the bogeyman." The killer's identity remains obscured for everyone but Laurie. More often than any other character, Laurie shares the audience's view of Michael. Whether at the end of the sidewalk on her way home from school, in her backyard amongst the clotheslines, or in her several confrontations at the end of the film, we only have her perspective on his actual presence and appearance. Significantly, the scene in which Laurie sees Michael out her bedroom window, standing between the clothes lines, is cut to implicate Laurie's imagination or unconscious as the source of the stalking stranger. Laurie has been chiding herself for possibly not outgrowing "superstition," when the film cuts to her point of view out the window and down toward the ground where Michael is standing. The scene immediately cuts to a reaction shot of Laurie shocked and gazing down and then cuts quickly again to a shot of the clothes lines and flapping sheets with no one standing there. Both the cues from the music and the quick pace of the editing imply that Laurie has not seen what she thinks she has seen, that Laurie has perhaps imagined him or let her repressed desires or "superstition" get the best of her.[50] Shortly after this moment in her bedroom, the audience witnesses Laurie and Annie being followed by the state vehicle, yet only Tommy and Laurie will see Michael as he terrorizes the suburban neighborhood.

In fact, the connection between Laurie and Tommy offers a defining set of lateral relations. After considering Laurie's caretaking of Tommy and her pairing with him from the first time that Michael sees her from inside the Myers house, one might be tempted to read him as a kind of surrogate for Michael. He resembles the young, blonde Michael from 15 years before and he will spend Halloween night under the watch, protection, and care of a Myers sister. Yet, Tommy receives conscientious care from Laurie, as does Annie's charge Lindsey, rather than neglect, and in several scenes he is paralleled with Laurie, not Michael. The viewer is privileged to a scene of Tommy on the playground that introduces another motivation for his recognition of or, one might say, need for Michael, which will echo Laurie's need for her brother. Teased by three bigger boys who are taunting, "He's gonna get you! The bogeyman is coming," Tommy is desperate to get away from their Halloween torments but is tripped and falls, crushing his pumpkin. The other boys laugh and run out of the playground, but one of them runs right into the arms of a lurking Michael Myers, whose face is not revealed, though his breathing and his well-known musical motif, written by Carpenter himself, can be heard on the soundtrack. Michael frightens the peer tormentor but does not reveal himself to Tommy yet, even as it appears that he has a clear interest in the bullied young boy. This scene also has obvious parallels with Johnny's taunts of Barbara in *Night of the Living Dead*, which will be cited in *Halloween II*, and, perhaps more clearly, the taunting of Franklin by his sister's friends like Jerry in *Texas Chain Saw Massacre*.

The less vicious taunts of another peer culture, Laurie's female friends, links the babysitter and her male charge Tommy only two scenes later and, again, the harassing peer group raises the specter of Michael. Ushered in by a sound bridge of cheerleaders' voices, Laurie leaves school much like Tommy, with her arms full of books, and walks out with two of her friends, Annie and Linda, who seem amiable but who, nonetheless, tease Laurie and each other. Annie jokes with Laurie that the mystery "creep" in the suspicious station wagon following them wants a "date" with the good girl and mockingly concludes that Laurie "scared another one away" when the car drives off. Yet Laurie responds to the teasing with serious dejection—that guys reject her for being "too smart." Her friends' taunts might seem mild in comparison to the physical bullying that Tommy receives, but they have the same result. First, Michael follows in his car, hovering in the background, and then only Laurie (and the viewer) see Michael on the sidewalk down the street partially obscured by a row of bushes. As the violence increases throughout the night and Laurie becomes more aware of the trouble for her friends, she still returns to the idea that they are teasing or playing a joke. When Linda calls Laurie for help as Michael is strangling her, Laurie believes it is one of Annie's crank calls. Even when she feels compelled to check on the house where Annie, Linda, and Bob have already been murdered, she assumes in their lack of response that they are playing a trick on her: she shakily demands, "Alright, you meatheads, joke's over. Come on, Annie, that's enough! Cut it out. You'll be sorry!" But, of course, they already are.

Laurie and Tommy, like Franklin before them, suffer at the hands of a sometimes cruel and often isolating peer culture. Of the array of sibling substitutes in the film, possibly only Lindsey, Tommy's sisterly companion who has been abandoned by her babysitter, Annie, shows kindness and compassion for her peer when she defends his sighting of the "bogeyman." Laurie, of course, cares for both Tommy and Lindsey, protecting them from the killer, but she also has reason to wish for the silencing of her closer peers. They are her friends, but they are also her competition and her adversaries in a struggle for the survival of her unique identity. The entrance of adolescent sexuality has clearly isolated Laurie from the other girls, who want her to be like them, that is, sexually active, and who police her desires and unacceptable behavior. When we first see Laurie with her friends, Linda, the cheerleader, mocks Laurie's bookishness, and this 'misplaced' investment in academics is tied to Laurie's lack of a social life, which Linda calls her "own damn fault," not feeling "a bit sorry" for her. This taunting about Laurie's lack of experience in sex or lack of interest in social events is continued by Annie. After Annie's investigation of the bushes where Laurie has seen Michael only moments before, she cruelly mocks that "Poor Laurie" scared another man away: "It's tragic. You never go out." Annie implies that Laurie's sexual repression is making her see "men behind bushes" and she even calls her "wacko." Significantly, at each of these peer pressuring moments, Michael is not far away. When Annie later picks Laurie up to drive them to their babysitting jobs, the same sort of taunts, which alienate Laurie as inexperienced and different from the other girls, continue.

One might argue that Annie's criticism of Laurie's lack of development, socially and sexually, works to ostracize or single out Laurie as different and possibly leads to a vengeful attack on Annie. In the car Laurie broaches the subject of the school dance and under pressure confesses that she would like to go out with Ben Tramer, which allows Annie to pounce: "I knew it! See, you *do* think about things like that, huh Laurie." This triumphant comment by Annie seems both to command and question that Laurie thinks "about things like that," attempting to bring Laurie in line with her closest female peers. A fairly routine representation of 'peer pressure,' this seemingly lighthearted moment that includes Annie's approving laughter is concluded with a return on the soundtrack of Michael's theme and a reverse angle long shot of Annie's car driving down the suburban streets, closely followed by the institutional green state vehicle. Yet again, this teasing and antagonism from a lateral relationship has summoned Michael. With a sudden cut to Michael's point of view of Annie parking on a now dark suburban street, we watch through the subjective camera, joined by the sound of Michael's breathing on the soundtrack, as the two girls split up and Michael follows Annie to her employer's house. Viewing Annie's entrance from over Michael's shoulder, we lurk with him behind a tree and look toward a well-lit, white house that very much resembles the opening's view of the Myers house. To make the connection blatant, the film cuts immediately to an exterior view of the Myers house at present as Loomis and the sheriff pull up to investigate. Of course, Michael will stalk and eventually strangle Annie, who resembles Judith in her desires but who does not actually have sex during the film, but it might very well be Laurie's vengeful wishes driving him to do so.

The fact that Michael strangles Annie immediately after she leaves her charge Lindsey with a resentful Laurie, "the old Girl Scout" who is also angry at Annie for calling Ben Tramer, suggests competitive aggression and retribution as motive. This motive is confirmed later in the film with an editing together of Laurie's look toward the other house and a view of Linda and Bob in the parent's bed, which is also followed by their murders, one of which Laurie hears over the phone and assumes is a crank call from Annie: "Are you fooling around again? I'll kill you if this is a joke. Annie?" One might read both these incidents, as Carpenter himself suggests, as Laurie's sexual repression coming out in the murders of the sexually active teenagers, but it seems equally as likely that the killings might be an angry reaction to the challenge to her identity by her sibling surrogates. Laurie's identity as the "Girl Scout," the studious one, et cetera, is unacceptable to her peer culture, which is constantly attempting to reshape her identity through heterosexual activity, to make her just like them. In the case of Annie, and by extension Linda and Bob, she wants to reform Laurie in her own image by setting up a date with Ben, but she also wants to use the old Girl Scout's sense of responsibility to pawn off Lindsey. The murders or attempted murders of the other teens might act as a refusal of sexuality *as* identity.

That this has been Laurie's refusal is confirmed by her eerily familiar approach to the other house, after she has put the children safely to bed. Interestingly, as she begins to go down the stairs to exit the house, the musical motif that is usually associated with Michael plays for her. Then, as she starts to cross the street to the other house, we switch to her point of view in a handheld traveling shot of her walk toward the house. Through the house's appearance, complete with lit jack-o-lantern on the front porch, and the movement toward it through the subjective camera, the scene is of course mirroring the opening sequence of the film. With this paralleling, I would argue, the film suggests that Laurie is like the killer or indeed *is* the killer, at least unconsciously—both here and in the opening.

As Laurie moves closer to the house, the camera tracks to the right, just as it did in the opening, and eventually, Laurie will go around to the back of the house and enter the kitchen through the back door, just as the initial killer did. Laurie is going to the house to investigate, but the mirroring with Michael's movements (both in the opening and when he follows Annie) indicates that she might already know what she will find there.

Perfectly paralleling the opening sequence, Laurie enters through the kitchen, goes into the living room (still under the impression that this is one of Annie's jokes for which she will be "sorry"), and then heads up the stairs to confront her darkest wish and her greatest fear. As she ascends the stairs, the scene switches to Laurie's point of view, with handheld movement. Although it cuts back to reverse angle views of Laurie's slow investigation, the allusion to young Michael's initial climbing is obvious. Laurie's subjective camera views a closed door at the end of the hall, clearly for the purpose of suspense and eventual surprise, but she finds in that room at least a sign of exactly the same person as in the opening. Initially, the viewer sees the reaction shot of Laurie's horrified expression, but then the scene cuts to Laurie's point of view and slowly tracks in on the posed body of Annie with Judith Myers's headstone against the backboard and a lit jack-o-lantern on the nightstand. Although Laurie backs away, more terrified, the scene again returns to her point of view of the tableau. It is as if the killer has created it to say, "Here. This is what you wished for then and this is what you wish for now—the dead sibling." Without dialogue or any clues other than Laurie's distraught noises on the soundtrack and her horrified reaction, there can be no sure way of reading her response. Much like Sally's face at the sight of Franklin's murder, Laurie might be terrified by her own murderous wish displayed before her eyes. As Juliet Mitchell argues, the major secondary response to the murderous wish to annihilate the lateral other is guilt and, therefore, one might argue that the most disturbing representation of Laurie's guilt comes in the multiplication of the peers' bodies. As she backs away from Annie's body, Bob's suddenly swings into view, accusing her again of her terrible wish, and backing away from that body puts her into contact with the dresser whose opening door reveals a crumpled and absurdly posed Linda, compounding the guilt. Laurie, horrified possibly at herself, backs into the hallway and finally comes face to face with her own wish. The "dread of the revenant" finally reaches her and the sibling who returns from the "dead" attempts exactly what the subject fears, revenge for *her* initial wish.

As I outlined at the beginning of this discussion of Carpenter's *Halloween*, one can read Michael's presence and actions throughout the film as remarkably similar to the trauma and murderous aggression of the sibling experience offered by Juliet Mitchell's recent analysis. Michael opens the film embodying and enacting the wish to kill the sibling whose very existence threatens to annihilate the unique self of either Michael or Laurie (Judith's two siblings). I would propose that the wish initiates with Laurie, who is conspicuously absent from the opening of the film but who must have been in her sister's care at one or two years of age, and then the wish is blamed on Michael by the parents, which results in eliminating the brother for 15 years as well. The prohibition on the wish, by disapproving parents, represses it until adolescence when the trauma of displacement and loss of self returns and brings with it the protective wish to annihilate—kill or be killed. The embodiment of the wish to murder the threatening sibling substitutes (Michael) returns and is directly connected to a defensive position vis-à-vis the taunting peer others through both Tommy's need and Laurie's need for him. However, the wish to murder the sibling substitutes produces feelings of guilt, which can recall the wish yet again. This process of guilt and recognition or recalling of the wish can lead to a fear of reprisals—the "dread of the revenant" who rises to take revenge.

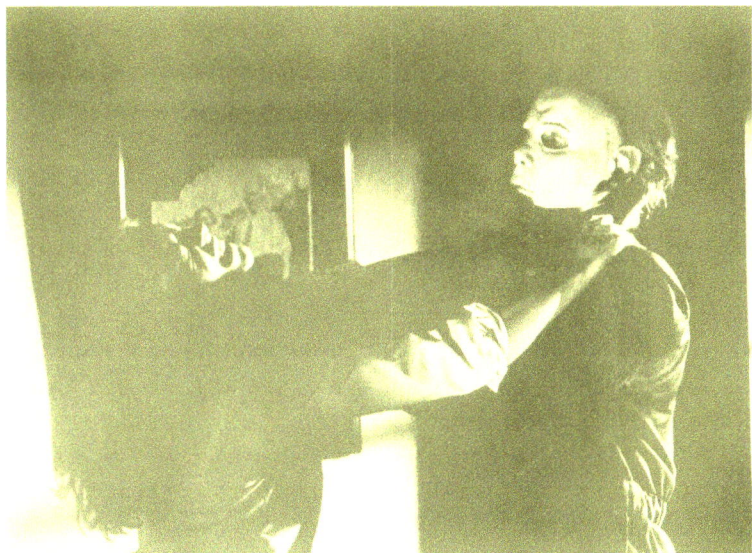

FIGURE 5.1 The siblings Laurie and Michael locked in a self-annihilating embrace

At the moment when Laurie runs out of the room bursting with signs of her own guilt and backs into a wall, indicating she has no where to hide, the face of her wish comes floating out of the darkness. In their first true two-shot, Michael and Laurie represent two faces of the same subject: the trembling face of fear and ambivalence that marks the sibling subject and the blank face of both her wish to murder and her already absent self. For a moment they exist in the same frame at medium distance, one in the light and the other in the dark, creating nearly unbearable tension for the viewer. Yet, when Laurie moves away, we know Michael must follow, since he only ever has one action to commit: murder the other who is the same. The return of the revenant carries the reminder of what Mitchell calls the "crucial absence," the absent self, and as Michael slashes and forces Laurie down the stairwell, the vengeance for her murderous wish has begun, as she necessarily becomes like the others, under attack of the wish to kill the lateral other.[51]

As Laurie runs from him, attempts and reattempts to kill him, and seeks a resolution, she remains unaware until the very end of the film that there is no resolution. Michael cannot kill her and she cannot kill him because, as sibling others for each other, the murder has already occurred. As Mitchell explains it, "the child already knows about death, and therefore that one must not kill one's brother, because the very existence of that brother in the first place has been experienced as a death of the subject's self."[52] There may remain a desire for a unique self, a desire most heightened at adolescence, but the crucial absence has already occurred and only the mourning process for that unique self offers the possibility of identity being "recreated as one among others," which will need to be repeated throughout life.[53] Tommy, in response to Laurie's premature boast that she "killed him," voices the truth of this cycle of desire and human subjectivity: "You can't kill the bogeyman," or one's own bogeyman, the other.[54] After Laurie has stabbed him in the eye and in the abdomen from the floor of her hiding place in the closet, Michael appears dead yet again and Laurie sends the two children, certainly doubles for her and Michael, away to get help. She sits apparently relieved in the doorway as the children run away, but Tommy's words take life: Michael sits up in the blurred background, to mirror her posture. When she rises, he rises. In their final struggle, Michael is attempting to choke Laurie and she is trying to break free, but they are locked in a matched embrace, performing identical movements like the mirrored sibling others they are for each other.

Nevertheless, looking in this sibling mirror must eventually lead to mourning and the temporary recreation of a new self, as "one among others." As Dr Loomis comes racing up the stairs, Laurie unmasks this other in the mirror, who has come to embody her murderous wishes, and discovers the face of her brother. This moment gives a face to the brother who will be named as such in the next film and whose very existence "has been experienced as a death of the subject's self," allowing Laurie possibly to begin the mourning process for the unique self and begin recreating a new self as a part of a group (of siblings, peers, affines, etc.). Laurie has a brother, is part of a family, and will become, to use Mitchell's term, "a part of a series" of Myers siblings, final girls, and, of course, films. Moreover, considering the weight of this moment and the interesting twists of the monster's identity created there, it seems significant that the revisiting of this scene in *Halloween II* excises the revelation of Michael's face.[55] In both instances Loomis intrudes with his gun, separating the two siblings, but not eradicating either of them. Loomis offers false expertise, assuring Laurie that he can recognize the bogeyman and has defeated him, but she seems to know better. When Loomis looks down from the window to see that Michael is gone, he does not need to inform Laurie. She responds to his stare down in shock by weeping resignedly into her hands, perhaps knowing that she must begin mourning and recreating an identity among others, even as she understands that the same lateral conflicts and struggles with identity will return just as Michael will in film after film.

Conclusion: Sibling Horror and the Youth Audience

While one might extend this discussion of the sibling conflict and the ensuing murderous struggle for identity into the horror film genre more generally, I would argue that its centrality to the slasher film cycle offers a unique insight into the teen film genre, the adolescent audience for these films, and the historical moment of the 1970s. Of course, the frequent use of the double or the "uncanny" double as a central motif in the horror film suggests the importance of the lateral other for the genre. The clearest literary precursor for this figure in horror film would most likely be Stevenson's *The Strange Case of Dr Jekyll and Mr Hyde*. In fact, Paul Wells considers the "doppelganger" as "one of the dominant motifs of the horror text."[56] Moreover, the dualities suggested by the doppelganger and illustrated by Dr Jekyll and Mr Hyde appear again in Freud's concept of the "uncanny," which critics have long used to explain the particular fears and pleasures evoked by the horror film.[57] S. S. Prawer's significant contribution to analysis of "terror film," *Caligari's Children: The Film as Tale of Terror*, devotes an entire chapter to the uncanny, locating the feeling in "our penetration of the author's psyche which we recognize as akin to hidden ideas in our own," which are "at once familiar and strange."[58] Provocatively, Prawer characterizes the author as "brother to both patient and analyst" in the exploration of those hidden areas.

Indeed, it is striking how much Freud's description of experiencing the uncanny double resembles Mitchell's account of the sibling conflict. Freud's analysis of the uncanny double sets up, very clearly, the possibility of the absent self: "it is marked by the fact that the subject identifies himself with someone else, so that he is in doubt as to which his self is, or substitutes the extraneous self for his own. In other words, there is a doubling, dividing, and interchanging of the self."[59] Moreover, once the phase of primary narcissism has been overcome, the double becomes "the uncanny harbinger of death" and "something repressed which recurs," and many experience the feeling of the uncanny in relation "the return of the dead."[60] While Mitchell does not explicitly examine the possibility of reading the sibling as an uncanny other self, it seems a natural enough connection. The sibling is, of course, both strange and familiar and Freud's account of the uncanny as "that class of the frightening which leads back to what is known of old and long familiar" sounds like an excellent description of the brother-killer Michael Myers.[61] In her discussion of the "uncanny" in relation to the slasher film and, in particular, to the supposed parent–child relations and fantasies therein, Clover also does not consider one of the major elements of Freud's definition of the uncanny in the form of the double, instead favoring the concept of "intellectual uncertainty."[62] For this particular chapter, however, I want to remain with that slasher killer (or his immediate precursors in *The Texas Chain Saw Massacre*), instead of expanding the argument to take in other horror films, in order to examine the significance of this uncanny sibling double, who surfaces at a particular moment in the twentieth century, for the largely adolescent audience for teen slasher films.

This audience, which is often figured as male or "largely male" to use Clover's phrasing without any specific statistical evidence to prove this claim, is also generally considered to be young.[63] Indeed, a recent study of horror film audiences takes for granted the predominance of younger viewers (25 and under) for all films, especially horror films, but contests the common critical assumption that these are male viewers with evidence that "just under half" of the study's female respondents "watched a horror film at least once a week."[64] Cherry's study attempts to uncover the "otherwise marginalised and invisible audience" of female horror viewers and fans, but she is quick to note that the slasher subgenre was the least "liked" of all the horror film types by these viewers. However, this observation does not indicate a lack of female viewers for slasher films, just a dislike for the films, which was also contradicted by the respondents identifying themselves as female horror "fans."[65] Interestingly, Paul Wells takes the reverse tack in his study for the *Spinechillers* essays on BBC radio, emphasizing age over gender and finding a "clear recognition of a slow disengagement from the genre as the group aged," starting with the 25–40 year-old group.[66] Judging from these two studies, one might presume a younger audience, but one not so clearly weighted toward one gender, as Clover and others suppose. It might be best to go back to Robin Wood's early representation of this audience (repeated by several other critics) as young, ungendered, and unruly: "Watching it recently with a large, half-stoned youth audience who cheered and applauded every one of Leatherface's outrages against their representatives on screen, was a terrifying experience."[67] What I would like to highlight in Wood's characterization is not only their unruly and active behavior vis-à-vis the film but also their pleasure in destruction and the recognition of a group of representatives, male *and* female, on the screen (since Leatherface takes three male and one and a half female victims); I would only add that for some of those viewers, Leatherface might be their representative on the screen as well.[68]

While there is little disagreement that these are young viewers with a high level of pleasure in and inter-activity with the horrors on screen, the nature of that pleasure and its ultimate purpose for this audience requires further consideration. Vivian Sobchack explores this youth audience for slasher horror films such as *Halloween* and *Friday the 13th* without making gender distinctions but wondering at their pleasure in their own "annihilation."[69] Sobchack observes a dramatic change from when "once teenagers threatened an entire populace and its social regulation with their burgeoning sexuality and presumption of adulthood" to more recent times (after the mid-1970s) when teenagers on screen began to annihilate each other, becoming victims not of peers but of "familial incoherence and paternal weakness."[70] In short, we have here yet another example of the reassertion of the hierarchal relationship and struggles between parent culture and youth culture so common to teen films and the criticism about them, rather than a reading of the horrors and struggles *within* youth culture.

By the mid-to-late 1970s and early 1980s for Sobchack, the teenagers of slasher horror become the ultimate victims—a long way from the youth culture (presumably of the 1950s and 1960s) that once "threatened an entire populace." In this scenario, the screen teens act out feelings of helplessness in the audience caused by the failure of *parent* culture, whose absence spurs the violence in the films, and the appeal of these films for the teenage audience of the time is their ability to capture feelings of "apocalyptic" helplessness for kids growing up in an era "marked by generalized nuclear fear and the particularly brutal events of the 1960s youth and antiwar movements."[71] These teens are strikingly represented for Sobchack by Carrie White from DePalma's *Carrie* (1976) whose "innocence" and victimhood prevents her from disrupting or deconstructing dominant patriarchal culture as earlier demon children have done and whose status as a "pitiable victim of her culture" earns our sympathy.[72] The family has failed to protect her from "harm and exploitation" and for this reason, she unleashes a supernatural fury. Yet, Sobchack is never clear here of which "culture" she is a victim or *who* might be harming her. Although the film does clearly locate the mother as a source of abuse and oppression in the beginning, it is unquestionably her peers who make her into a victim and who want to bring her harm. One need only look at the opening shower scene and its parallel at the prom to see a slow-motion evocation of the destructive force of peer aggression and abuse. The straight-on close ups of laughing and chanting female faces throwing tampons at the bewildered Carrie and viciously yelling "Plug it up" are mirrored in the climax of the film as Carrie's walk to the prom stage gives a subjective point of view of the peer mob whose clapping and cheering turns to laughter and jeering at the revelation of her taunter Chris's cruel trick with pig's blood. Sobchack correctly identifies the family as the source of her victimhood, but she has the wrong offending members. *Carrie* argues quiet powerfully that the "apocalyptic destruction" in these films is triggered by members of the family, but those members are *siblings* or peer others not parents, whose abusive cruelty spurs a mass annihilation.

Clearly, Sobchack's reading of these films and this generation runs directly counter to my project here and the aggressively independent teens this book has recounted and emphasized. Her image of a helpless set of teenagers caught in an era of apocalyptic crisis and abandoned by parent culture reinforces the idea of a "lost" generation of youth in the

1970s that I labored to deconstruct in my Introduction. Yet, examination of the slasher film (or even a brief consideration of *Carrie*) contradicts her picture of teens wallowing in their own helplessness, annihilation, and alienation through the force and independence of both the Final Girl *and* the killer. Teens are tortured, traumatized, and killed in these films, but there are also two central young figures, who either possess power over life and death or powerfully fight back against the murderous aggression of an attacker. Certainly, these films engage with the threat of annihilation, but they always do so in order to conclude with survival, for both slasher and slashed. Rather than being made victims of the "brutal events of the 1960s youth and antiwar movements," these teens survive and find a strength and identity within that moment of crisis and through cultural changes brought by the era's second wave feminism and other rights movements.

I would argue that these films do relegate parent culture to the margins, not out of mourning or loss for an absent or impotent parent, but out of recognition of the more formative and central conflict for identity and control *within* youth culture. From the ascendancy of powerful, defining youth cultures in postwar America, adolescents in the United States have come to understand the significance of their age (the teen age) for their own identity, for their future social position, and for their ongoing influence over the culture, but the 1970s brought a particularly productive isolation of that youth population during a nadir of parent culture's influence, which allowed for new narratives and, in the case of the slasher, a peer-centric imagining of youth. Simply put, the 1970s slasher films indicate the insignificance or secondary role of parent culture or parents, including the patriarch, for the formation of adolescent identity or for the battle for supremacy and authority within youth culture. The films exhibit a fear of annihilation, but annihilation at the hands of a sibling or peer, and in their repetition, the slasher cycle of films rehearse and rehash the questions of subjectivity and death for the adolescent subject, who is given the chance to express murderous wishes, confront the possible annihilation of a unique self, and in mourning that self begin to establish a new identity.

Contrary to a long tradition of teen film, it is not the parental absence that structures the conflict of these narratives, but the sense of the absent adolescent self, the potential loss of identity and authority caused by peers that spurs the wish to kill the sibling other. The films exhibit a battle for supremacy, identity, and subjectivity in a world devoid of parental authority—the sibling realm, which goes a long way in explaining how the audience described by Robin Wood could cheer at "every one of Leatherface's outrages against their representatives on the screen." Leatherface and Michael Myers are committing this audience's wished for acts of sibling violence against characters on screen who might be representatives for them, but who also might represent their peers—the same peers who daily threaten the adolescent viewer's autonomy, unique identity, and even security. The films repeatedly narrate the taunting and aggression endured by one or two central characters from his or her peers, and those who commit these initial acts of aggression usually come to a bad end at the hands of Leatherface or Michael or other killers. Furthermore, the employment of the subjective camera might work powerfully to fulfill this fantasy revenge scenario for the viewer against his or her peers, and here it is important to emphasize that both these killers take male and female victims.[73] These films address the fantasies of male *and* female teens confronting peer antagonists (as both Laurie and Tommy have peer adversaries) and, therefore, have the potential to appeal to a youth audience, regardless of gender. This active and fluid adolescent spectatorship allows for a female viewer to identify herself with the killer, who acts out the adolescent wish for the peer-sibling's annihilation (just as Michael acts out Laurie's wish), *and* identify with the Final Girl, who represents the adolescent subject experiencing the aftermath of that wish and its influence on identity formation, just as it is possible for the male adolescent viewer to do so.[74]

Nevertheless, the question remains about the formula on screen adhering, with a Final *Girl* for both gendered viewers and *male* killer as her adversary.[75] This formula, interestingly, returns us to the sibling who began this chapter—Antigone, the sibling who recognizes death. For Mitchell, in that adolescent moment when murderousness and aggression toward the sibling returns, a positive figure can emerge, a figure who represents "the ideal imago of a peer or peers who have survived" and becomes a kind of "heroic ideal" in her survival—in other words, the faithful sister Antigone.[76] While Mitchell also describes this hero as the peer or peers "who really stand up again when you shoot them dead," evoking Michael Myers, Laurie Strode or Final Girls like her seem better representatives of that heroic survivor. They survive the torment of sibling-peer attacks and maintain their integrity, strength, and responsibility, and, therefore, they might be able to restore the viewing subject's narcissistic faith in a new self or identity.

Indeed, might one not argue that in this particular historical moment in the United States with the visible empowerment of women in the public sphere, the female adolescent identity works well for all teenagers as a symbol of survival, individuality, and strength. Clover and other feminist critics have shown well enough how the female figure in the past has represented the human-being-as-victim, as under attack, suppressed, controlled, surveilled, and masochistically taking it. Yet, by the mid-1970s, she is standing up despite attempts to shoot her dead. The teen sister can epitomize, then, for both male and female adolescents, the disempowered one, or nearly annihilated self, who survives. While the victimized and disturbed teen was once embodied in James Dean, the survivor of the 1970s is Laurie Strode, entertaining her own murderous wishes and fending off her brother and peer attackers to claim her own identity as survivor and hero. As we see as the end of Rosenthal's *Halloween II*, she undeniably has taken center stage in the eyes of the public, represented by the press, and her traumatized but enduring expression concludes the film, coupled with the nearly unrecognizable extreme close up of Michael's burning mask. Unlike in the original film, where Michael's domination of the soundtrack through his offscreen breathing indicated his invulnerability and omnipresence, Laurie's survival here has been assured, while Dr Loomis and Michael have been purged from *her* space.

This new teenage survivor, who has been tested and subsequently re-imagined through conflict with the sibling-peer, evokes in a fundamental way the ethos of the 1970s. No longer defined by a relationship to an insignificant, untrustworthy, or neglectful dominant or parent culture, the members of the youth culture seek in this moment to define themselves. Like the various ethnic, racial, and spiritual groups examined in Bruce Schulman's influential cultural history of the 1970s, adolescents might assert their "right to a separate identity within the larger framework of a pluralist, multicultural nation," not necessarily desiring assimilation into a dominant culture that asks for abandonment of cultural specificity and individuality.[77] As Schulman argues that this cultural nationalist movement produced a "revised narrative" of the immigrant and consequently America, so one might view the various teen stories examined in this book as declarations of a kind of independence and revised narratives of the American story of growing up.[78] The slasher film, more akin to Malick's *Badlands* than the tales of the queer kid in Chapters 3 and 4, locates a space away from the dominant culture represented by the parent–child relation and in that space redefines the adolescent subject through the peer relationship. Asserting this new identity forged in the conflict with the sibling-peer other clearly alters the typical maturation plot offered in mainstream American cinema where so often the child overcomes his conflict with parent culture by assimilating into the adult world (i.e. growing up). It should not be surprising, then, that the face of this new adolescent identity would be that of the *sister* (Laurie Strode) rather than the brother, whose relationship to the father is a well-rehearsed tale crying out for revision in the unsettled and unsettling 1970s.

Epilogue

In a harshly critical view of contemporary teen film in the 1980s, Elayne Rapping finds what should be by now a familiar trend since the 1950s and 1960s: a lack of political and social relevance or impact in the films of the genre. For Rapping, since the rebellious and challenging days of James Dean, this highly popular and lucrative group of films about youth has been drained of anger, contempt, and defiance, or in other words "the subversive undertones of these early models have been almost entirely eradicated."[1] Besides a few films of the early American New Wave, such as *Bonnie and Clyde* and *Easy Rider*, that do pose "social questions against which their heroes' antisocial acts were sympathetically judged and portrayed," recent teen film has failed to ask difficult questions or contest dominant culture, and for her the 1970s stands as the watershed moment when the films, led by *American Graffiti*, began to betray their subversive potential and history: "It was the 1970s, when the social prophesies of 1960s youth proved false (or at least premature), that youth films began to work themselves into easily cloned variations on themes which now fill screens with such regularity."[2] Films like *American Graffiti* and its clones began to dominate the genre after the 1970s according to her and pedaled a bourgeois faith in and validation of "middle class accommodation."[3] In other words, youth films turned to the conservative resolution, which I set up as central to the genre in the first chapters of this book, wherein the typically male teenager is reconciled with his father, embraced by dominant middle-class culture, and chooses to assimilate into its codes and values as the ultimate sign of 'growing up,' reinforced usually by his choice to pair off with the appropriate heterosexual mate. Rapping does not attribute this genre-defining conflict and resolution to *Rebel Without a Cause*, even though it is certainly there, and instead locates it most strongly in the films since the 1970s.

Clearly, I have focused in this book on the unrecognized teen films of 1970s to counter such claims with films that I believe champion "other" versions of coming-of-age, thereby revising the genre and redefining what the twentieth century has come to know as *the* American teenager. The teens of the 1970s considered here revise and rewrite the "straight" developmental narrative, wherein "middle class accommodation," as Rapping calls it, is the end for the white, male, heterosexual, middle-class teen at its center. Films like *Badlands, The Rocky Horror Picture Show, Rock 'n' Roll High School, Freaky Friday, Ode to Billy Joe,* and *Halloween* defy the conservative ideology of the father–son love story of classical teen film, which serves to protect and advance the functioning of patriarchy. In other words, rather than being represented by the white male dreamers of Lucas' *America Graffiti*, the screen teens of the 1970s who truly symbolize the historical moment in the United States and the evolutionary moment for the genre are those that forge new alliances and construct counter-discourses around issues of gender, generation, and sexuality that no other era of teen film has offered. Contrary to Rapping, I am asserting that many of the films centered on youth in the 1970s *do* have subversive potential—from their sadistic female fans to queer kids—and the repeated focus on *American Graffiti* and other "masculine mythology" films, as Shary dubs them, does a disservice to the decade's films and neglects a significant moment in the genre's evolution.

In order to argue for an evolution in the genre, though, I must consider the impact of this "lost" generation and their films on the teen films that follow. Many critics, like Robin Wood, have viewed the 1980s as a return of the conservative values of the 1950s and a restoration of the patriarch, and one might argue, as Doherty does, that the teen films of the 1980s follow suit, revisiting the patriarchal and heteronormative ideologies of the classical era of teen film.[4] Indeed, the Reagan-era "rebirth" of teen film, with its seductive imp Ferris Bueller and the whitewashed *Breakfast Club*, might appear to be a backlash against the new American teenagers of the 1970s. Ferris certainly fits the mold of the incredibly charming white middle-class American teenage hero, whose desires and conflicts ground the narrative and all other characters in it. *Ferris Bueller's Day Off* (1986) even takes the genre's "masculine mythology" one step further by replacing the conflict with parent culture with a wish-fulfillment fantasy of adoration from Ferris' parents and even from masses of people in the streets of Chicago. Possibly this film and others like it have earned Rapping's criticism that they construct "a claustrophobic world inhabited and negotiated entirely by kids, and informed by their very shallow, very limited sense of emotion and social reality" to the exclusion of clueless or absent parents.[5] Ferris does not challenge his parents' upper-middle class, suburban values or codes. He simply seeks his own pleasure and access to "fine" things, and one certainly might argue that films like *Ferris Bueller's Day Off* and *Risky Business* (1983) reinforce not only a Reagan-era masculine dominance and aggressive heterosexuality but also a characteristic financial opportunism or even cynicism of the decade. Yet, in such a prolific period for teen film, singling out just a few male wish-fulfillment texts does not give the whole picture.

Even this neoclassical era of the teen film genre betrays the cracks exposed in the previous decade with its changing emphasis on female teens and unnerving criticisms in a handful of independently produced films. Some of John Hughes' films, for example *Pretty in Pink* and even *The Breakfast Club* and *Some Kind of Wonderful*, which he wrote, foreground the concerns of the female teen in a nuanced way that was rare in the genre. But it is perhaps Amy Heckerling's *Fast Times at Ridgemont High* (1982) that most clearly signals a change in the genre towards representing female desires and conflicts. Many critics have commented on the change that occurs when a female director helms a teen film like *Fast Times*, and the scenes concerning the young character of Stacy do give a fresh perspective on issues of gender and sexuality that would not have been possible before the films of the 1970s. Stacy's sterile and uninterested point of view shots in the dugout while she loses her virginity to an older man have impressed critics with both their stark honesty and daring attempt to reject the romanticizing of sexuality and a teenager's "first time" present in so many male teen films, but I am also reminded, of course, of Holly's reaction in Badlands so many years before.[6]

Similarly, much critical interest and concern followed the release of Tim Hunter's *River's Edge* (1986), which also exhibited a brutal honesty and jarring realism capturing a much more disturbing subject: a real life incident in Milpitas, California where a 16-year-old named Anthony Jacques Broussard raped and strangled a 14-year-old girl and then showed the body to friends and other youths who failed to report the incident for days. Hunter's film, written by Neal Jimenez and taking place in a grainy, washed out landscape, does not shy away from the gruesome details of this crime and, in fact, obsessively foregrounds the white, naked body of the dead girl Jamie in frame after frame. Seemingly the opposite of a film like *Ferris Bueller's Day Off*, *River's Edge* reveals its connections to the challenging films of the 1970s by questioning the troubling divide between uninterested or neglectful parents and their emotionally vacant or disturbed offspring. The "generation gap" has become an abyss in this film and representatives of the much-lauded 1960s generation of youth have become the most dangerous or ineffectual of adults—Dennis

Hopper even transforms his Billy the Kid character from *Easy Rider* into a deranged psychopath who shelters and then kills the teenage murderer Samson. There is no reliable paternal authority locatable in this film much less present in the end to reconcile the central teens into an embracing dominant culture—only Hopper's disturbed Feck who cares most of all for his blow up doll Elly and hollowly believes he has lost a "friend" after shooting Samson. I would argue that these films establish a shift in the genre away from its traditional or classical codes and values, contesting the genre's resolutions, central concerns and male hero, but in the 1990s this change is much more apparent.

It is in the 1990s that the true legacy of the new American teenagers surfaces. In this decade, the explosion of queer teens on screen, the advances of African American filmmakers, and the damage done by vengeful girl gangs at the multiplex reveal that the revisions to the maturation plot in the 1970s did alter the teen film thereafter, opening the genre up to alternative discourses or versions of the American teenage tale. Particularly springing from the success of independent film in the United States and the rise of New Queer Cinema, a whole host of queer teens were the focus of films in the 1990s, yet they did not have to come to a tragic end. From Gus Van Sant's *My Own Private Idaho* (1991) and Gregg Araki's films such as *Totally F***ed Up* (1993) to sweeter, more typical coming-of-age and coming-out tales like *Edge of Seventeen* (1998) and *The Incredibly True Adventures of Two Girls in Love* (1995), a critical mass of films established the queer developmental narrative as one of the new areas explored by the genre. For Shary, this group of innovative films expanded the genre by creating a "sensitive, nonextreme representation" of queer teens "as increasingly accepted, striving for identity like all young people, on their own terms."[7] At almost the same time, a group of films by African American filmmakers such as John Singleton and the Hughes brothers opened the genre up to gritty tales of contemporary urban life for racial minorities. Inaugurated by Singleton's *Boyz N the Hood* in 1991, these films worked from the legacy of the UCLA School of filmmakers like Charles Burnett and Julie Dash and the independent path forged by Spike Lee in the 1980s to create a unique voice for African American youth and their challenges and conflicts in the present day (unlike the films of the 1970s that relied so strongly on nostalgia). Sometimes referred to as the "Hood" films or the African American crime cycle, films like *Boyz N the Hood* or the Hughes' *Menace II Society* (1993) sought to portray environments and minority characters that had previously been absent from or misrepresented in the media (in this case, in teen film) and to wrestle candidly with society's neglect of black communities and with moral questions and debate within the black community. These films challenge both the class and racial biases of traditional teen film and are able to do so in the wake of not only pioneering film movements and filmmakers but also the political consciousness raising on the civil rights movement of the 1960s and black nationalist movement of the 1970s. In other words, these new maturation narratives set in the inner city reflect the legacy of subversive and underground filmmaking and politics in the 1970s.

Finally, the films centered on youth in the 1990s most often signal the evolutionary moment I have described above in their attention to female teens and particularly powerful, aggressive girls who defy gender norms and demand respect. They are, for lack of a better word, rebels full of the anger, contempt, and defiance Rapping argues is sadly missing from teen film in the 1980s. A series of films about girl gangs in the middle of the decade, including *Mi Vida Loca* (1993), *Freeway* (1996), and Jim McKay's *Girls Town* (1996), crystallized this new trend that acted like an aftershock from the second wave feminism of two decades before. According to Christina Lee in *Screening Generation X*, these films brought the "angry girl" to "prominence in film" through portrayals that "were not always pretty but, at times, disturbingly raw and brutal."[8] For example, in *Mi Vida Loca* the Latina girls who make up the Echo Park Home Girl gang are involved with drug dealers, in gang fights, and eventually gang-related murders as the film ends with the accidental shooting of a young girl in the neighborhood who is caught in the middle of gang retaliations. McKay's *Girls Town*, on the other hand, situates its violence within an overtly feminist message meted out by its impromptu girl gang. After the suicide of one of their best friends, Nikki, a group of New Jersey teenage girls goes on a rampage when they discover through her diary that Nikki was raped by a coworker at her summer job. The girls dole out their rage and revenge on those who have mistreated them, including the football player who raped Emma and Patti's ex-boyfriend who has been failing to support their child. They vandalize cars, steal from Patti's ex-boyfriend, create a list of sexual abusers for the girl's bathroom wall, and eventually track down and beat Nikki's rapist in the street. Their collective actions, which boldly announce an aggressive and defiant feminist agenda, are expressively captured in Queen Latifah's own feminist anthem "U.N.I.T.Y.," which concludes the film. Latifah's song, which demands "Who you callin' a bitch?" and calls for a unity in better treatment of women, perfectly fits these new "tough girl" films, as

Shary calls them, in its gender norm-defying aggression, self-awareness, demand for justice and equality, and support of political strength for young women that harkens back to the rage of Holly in *Badlands* or the growing independence of young female stars like Jodie Foster.[9] The command of a new female authority, which first asserted itself in the films of the 1970s, announces itself more fully in the genre in the 1990s when female adolescents strongly "emerged as more aware of their past mistreatment and misrepresentation and more in control of their destiny, both in terms of politics and sexuality."[10] The revenge Holly takes on the 1950s, teen icons, and the patriarchal home or the disturbance a queer kid like Foster brings into the Disney family and Oedipal narratives of girlhood come into the public space of the streets in these 1990s films, demanding political rights and equality for young women in dominant culture and teen film.

To say that the "lost" generation of teens and teen narratives of the 1970s can be discovered again in the center of 1990s teen film might seem like an overstatement, but I feel the texts above make a strong case for a change in the genre, the foundations of which were laid by the films I have considered in the chapters of this book. While Shary argues for a new diversity in films about youth as a result of cultural and industrial changes represented by the mall and the multiplex, I maintain that it is just as likely that it was the social, political, and generational transformations of the 1970s that forced a change in the codes and values of this increasingly popular genre. New American teenagers and alternative or contrary versions of the developmental narrative were fleshed out and championed in the 1970s before the intrusion of the mall, MTV, and the niche filmmaking and marketing necessitated by multiplex theaters. The earlier era and its political and social movements, particularly in terms of gender and sexuality, demanded it. The culture's master narratives, in their moment of "crisis" in the 1970s, gave way and new plots were possible. So, *the* American teenager was lost, but a host of "others" were found, whose conflicts and concerns bent the straight narrative of growing up, rewriting the teen tale and the common conception of the adolescent in America.

Notes

Introduction

1. Timothy Shary, *Generation Multiplex: The Image of Youth in Contemporary American Cinema* (Austin: University of Texas Press, 2002), 6.
2. Timothy Shary, *Teen Movies: American Youth on Screen* (London: Wallflower, 2005), 38.
3. Thomas Hine, *The Rise and Fall of the American Teenager* (New York: Perennial, 2000), 276.
4. David Considine, *The Cinema of Adolescence* (Jefferson, NC: McFarland, 1985), 9.
5. Ibid., 273.
6. Thomas Doherty, *Teenagers and Teenpics: The Juvenilization of American Movies in the 1950s.* Revised and expanded edition. (Philadelphia: Temple University Press, 2002), 9.
7. Ibid., 73.
8. Ibid., 74.
9. Ibid., 159.
10. Jon Lewis, *The Road to Romance and Ruin: Teen Films and Youth Culture* (New York: Routledge, 1992), 7.
11. Shary, *Generation Multiplex*, 6.
12. Ibid., 7.
13. Ibid., 261.
14. Ibid., 259.
15. Lewis, *Road to Romance*, 3.
16. Doherty *Teenagers and Teenpics*, 209.
17. Shary, *Teen Movies*, 38.
18. See also Sarah Hentges' *Pictures of Girlhood: Modern Female Adolescence on Film* (Jefferson: McFarland, 2006) and Roz Kaveney's *Teen Dreams: Reading Teen Film and Television from Heathers to Veronica Mars* (New York: I.B. Taurus, 2006).
19. Ilana Nash, *American Sweethearts: Teenage Girls in Twentieth-Century Popular Culture* (Bloomington: Indiana University Press, 2006), 18.
20. Georganne Scheiner, *Signifying Female Adolescence: Film Representations and Fans, 1920–1950* (Westport, CT: Praeger, 2000), 2, 17.
21. Ibid., 142.
22. Ibid., 143.
23. Nash, *American Sweethearts*, 13.
24. Ibid., 27.
25. Ibid., 214.

26. Linda Williams, "Film Bodies: Gender, Genre, and Excess," in *Film Genre Reader, II*, ed. Barry Keith Grant (Austin: University of Texas Press, 1995), 141.
27. Carol Clover, *Men, Women, and Chainsaws: Gender in the Modern Horror Film* (Princeton, NJ: Princeton University Press, 1992), 17.
28. Ibid., 15.
29. Patricia White, *unInvited: Classical Hollywood Cinema and Lesbian Representability* (Bloomington: Indiana University Press, 1999), xxii.
30. Kathryn B. Stockton, *The Queer Child, Or Growing Up Sideways in the Twentieth Century* (Durham, NC: Duke University Press, 2009), 5.
31. Lewis, *Road to Romance*, 2.
32. Shary, *Generation Multiplex*, 19.
33. Tom Wolfe, *The Purple Decades: A Reader* (New York: Berkley Books,1983), 279.
34. William Graebner, "America's *Poseidon Adventure*: A Nation in Existential Despair," in *America in the Seventies*, ed. Beth Bailey and David Farber (Lawrence: University Press of Kansas, 2004), 158.
35. Beth Bailey and David Farber, "Introduction" in *America in the Seventies*, ed. Beth Bailey and David Farber (Lawrence: University Press of Kansas, 2004), 4.
36. Peter Carroll, *It Seemed Like Nothing Happened: America in the 1970s* (New Brunswick: Rutgers University Press, 1990), 144.
37. Edward Berkowitz, *Something Happened: A Political and Cultural Overview of the Seventies* (New York: Columbia University Press, 2006), 70, 56.
38. Ibid., 55.
39. Bailey and Farber, "Introduction," 3.
40. Bruce Schulman, *The Seventies: The Great Shift in American Culture, Society, and Politics* (Cambridge, MA: Da Capo Press, 2001), 90.
41. Ibid., 184.
42. David Frum, *How We Got Here, The 70's: The Decade that Brought You Modern Life (For Better or Worse)* (New York: Basic Books, 2000), xxiii.
43. Schulman, *The Seventies*, 63.
44. Berkowitz, *Something Happened*, 133.
45. Schulman, *The Seventies*, 71, 83.
46. Dana Polan, "*Bad News Bears*: Sour American Dream" *Jump Cut* 15 (1977): 9.
47. David Farber, in his article "The Torch Had Fallen," cites two different enunciations of the idea that, as a nation, we have "lost our way"—one from Arizona congressman Mo Udall at the 1976 Democratic National Convention and the other by the *New York Times* editorial page editor John Oakes who found the "optimism and moral drive characteristic of Americans throughout the decades have been largely replaced by a deep-seated cynicism and disillusionment" in *American in the Seventies*, ed. Beth Bailey and David Farber (Lawrence: University Press of Kansas, 2004), 11.
48. Barbara A. Chandler, "The White House Conference on Children: A 1970 Happening," *The Family Coordinator* 20, no.3 (July 1971): 195, 198.
49. Ibid., 202.
50. Carroll, *It Seemed Like Nothing Happened*, 264.
51. Vance Packard, *The Sexual Wilderness: The Contemporary Upheaval in Male-Female Relationships* (New York: Pocket Books, 1970), 29.

[52] The opening of Packard's first chapter, "The Wilderness—and Six Forces in the Background that Are Shaping It," uses or cites the word "confusion" at least nine times in the first five pages (Packard, *The Sexual Wilderness*). Jon Lewis's summary of the Packard argument prefers the term I am focusing on here: "In the fast lane to prosperity, America had *lost* control and its youth had gotten *lost* with them" (my emphasis, 58).

Chapter 1

[1] Thomas Doherty, *Teenagers and Teenpics: The Juvenilization of American Movies in the 1950s*, revised and expanded edn (Philadelphia: Temple University Press, 2002), 197.
[2] Ibid., 196.
[3] Ibid., 209.
[4] Georganne Scheiner, *Signifying Female Adolescence: Film Representations and Fans, 1920–1950* (Westport, CT: Praeger, 2000), 29.
[5] As Scheiner notes, *The Road to Ruin* was produced for very little cost ($2,500) like most exploitation films but grossed a stunning $2,500,000 at the box office (*Signifying Female*, 39).
[6] Ibid., 41.
[7] Scheiner turns to the Payne Fund studies of the 1930s to reveal how particularly female members of the audience for films like *The Road to Ruin* sympathized with the female sexual delinquent and reveled in the wild parties, mitigating the intended deterrent effect of the film (*Signifying Female*, 42).
[8] David Considine, *The Cinema of Adolescence* (Jefferson, NC: McFarland, 1985), 169.
[9] Timothy Shary finds, for example, that despite *Dead End*'s efforts to "show crime negatively," the audiences for the film "were nonetheless enthralled by the charismatic young characters." *Teen Movies: American Youth on Screen* (London: Wallflower, 2005), 15. The Payne Fund studies similarly found a repeated interest in and worship of the gangster figures in the crime genre and even the influence of the films on attempts to carry out similar crimes. See Henry James Forman, *Our Movie Made Children*, intro. Dr W. W. Charters (New York: Macmillan, 1934).
[10] Shary suggests in *Teen Movies* that perhaps Shirley Temple and Deanna Durbin remain the exemplars of the "independent 'fix-it' kids that came to the rescue of bumbling adults and institutions," more than other major stars like Judy Garland (11).
[11] Mark Thomas McGee and R. J. Robertson, *The J.D. Films: Juvenile Delinquency in the Movies* (Jefferson, NC: McFarland, 1982), 2.
[12] Scheiner singles out *100 Men and a Girl* (1937) as possibly Durbin's most representative film and, here, one can see an exemplary tale of the "fix-it" kid during the Depression, convincing a famous conductor to help out a number of unemployed orchestra musicians (one of which is the young teen's father) by leading them into employment by a persuaded industrialist (*Signifying*

Female, 74). However, *That Certain Age* not only provides an example of a Durbin character as a "spotless force of moral good," as Nash describes her, but also emphasizes the eroticized relationship between these female teens and adult males (or patriarchy) that Nash elucidates so expertly in her work (*American Sweethearts*, 87).

13. Considine charts the meteoric rise and astronomical salaries of several young stars in the 1930s, led by Mickey Rooney who surpassed all male stars in box office numbers in 1938 and 1939 and, therefore, could demand a commensurate salary. Even less prominent stars like Jackie Cooper, Freddie Bartholomew, and Bonita Granville rode the wave of youth popularity, earning as much as $2,000–3,000 a week during the Depression (*Cinema of Adolescence*, 4).
14. McGee and Robertson, *The J.D. Films*, 1.
15. The Academy of Motion Picture Arts and Sciences, "The 11th Academy Awards (1939)," http://www.oscars.org/awards/academyawards/legacy/ceremony/11th.html. The Academy of Motion Picture Arts and Sciences, "The 15th Academy Awards (1943)," http://www.oscars.org/awards/academyawards/legacy/ceremony/15th.html.
16. For further reading on Senator Kefauver's subcommittee and its specific focus on the mass media as a central factor in causing or exacerbating juvenile delinquency, see James Gilbert, *A Cycle of Outrage: America's Reaction to the Juvenile Delinquent in the 1950s* (Oxford: Oxford University Press, 1986).
17. McGee and Robertson, *The J.D. Film*, 17. McGee and Robertson also note that Kefauver's Senate subcommittee held up *City Across the River* as an example of the mass media's negative influence on young people since the film failed to act as a deterrent, as it professed to, and instead delinquency rates rose after 1948, which apparently could be attributed to the failure of *one* film (46).
18. Steve Neale, "Teenpics," in *The Cinema Book*, ed. Pam Cook and Mieke Bernik (London: BFI, 1999), 218.
19. This quote comes from a special issue of *Cosmopolitan* in November 1957 entitled "Are Teenagers Taking Over?" Quoted in Doherty, *Teenagers and Teenpics*, 40.
20. Ibid., 35.
21. McGee and Robertson, *The J.D. Films*, 2.
22. Lewis, *Road to Romance*, 30.
23. McGee and Robertson, *J.D. Films*, 20, 24.
24. Considine, *Cinema of Adolescence*, 120.
25. Doherty, *Teenagers and Teenpics*, 58.
26. Ibid.
27. Quoted in McGee and Roberston, *The J.D. Films*, 29. McGee cites several educators, not all of which found the film to be blown out of proportion. However, a typical response is offered by Edward Wallen, the principal of a technical high school in the Bronx, who insisted educators were "disturbed by the picture's exaggeration and its probable effects upon the public attitude toward the students and teachers."
28. Doherty, *Teenagers and Teenpics*, 59, 63.
29. Elayne Rapping, "Hollywood's Youth Cult Films," *Cineaste* 16, no. 1–2 (1987): 25.

30 Considine cites a double-page ad in *Variety* two weeks after Dean's death and just before the film's release that clearly points the finger at parents: "Jim Stark—a kid in the year 1955—what makes him tick…like a time bomb? Maybe the police should have picked up his parents instead" (*Cinema of Adolescence*, 83). He also places the film in two chapters in his work fittingly titled "Movies' Monstrous Moms" and "Film's Failed Fathers."
31 Doherty, *Teenagers and Teenpics*, 84, 85.
32 Lewis, *Road to Romance*, 27.
33 Doherty, *Teenagers and Teenpics*, 57, 63 (original emphasis).
34 Ibid., 56, 65.
35 Ibid., 90. However, it should be noted that AIP's *The Fast and the Furious* (1954) anticipated the drag racing craze before *Rebel* hit the screens.
36 Ibid., 112–13.
37 In *Faster and Furiouser: The Revised and Fattened Fable of American International Pictures*, McGee quotes a reviewer of a horror teenpic for the *Saturday Review*, whose outrage is palpable: "The pictures dropping off the assembly line today are more horrid than horror. The real horror is that these pictures, with their beastialities, their sadism, their lust for blood, and their primitive level of conception and execution should find their greatest acceptance among the young. It is a sad enough commentary on our youth, but even more so on the standards of the motion picture industry." Mark McGee, *Faster and Furiouser* (Jefferson, NC: McFarland, 1996), 120.
38 Doherty, *Teenagers and Teenpics*, 153.
39 For Ilana Nash, Gidget in the various mediums of fiction, film, and television might seem to serve as an empowering model for young girls, but her relationship to her parents, particularly her father, represents another example of Nash's thesis that female screen-teens work to reinforce the hierarchy of the patriarchal family as "daddy's girls"; their incompetence and sexual appeal are directed at the father in order to assure their continued subjugation to patriarchy. (*American Sweethearts*, 213–14)
40 Alan Betrock, *The I Was a Teenage Juvenile Delinquent Rock 'n' Roll Horror Beach Party Movie Book: A Complete Guide to the Teen Exploitation Film, 1954–1969* (New York: St. Martin's Press, 1986), 100, 102.
41 It might be noted, for example, that Betty Friedan's *Feminine Mystique* became a controversial sensation, which many credit with sparking second wave feminism in the United States, from the moment it hit the bookshelves in 1963—the same year that the first of the beach films, *Beach Party*, was released.
42 Ibid., 128.
43 Shary, *Teen Movies*, 38.
44 Ibid., 40.
45 Ibid., 53.
46 Ibid., 45, 48.
47 Considine, *Cinema of Adolescence*, 137.
48 Stephen Tropiano, *Rebels and Chicks: A History of the Hollywood Teen Movie* (New York: Back Stage Books, 2006), 122.
49 Shary, *Teen Movies*, 45.

50. Frances Gateward, "In Love and Trouble: Teenage Boys and Interracial Romance," in *Where the Boys Are: Cinemas of Masculinity and Youth*, eds. Murray Pomerance and Frances Gateward (Detroit: Wayne State University Press, 2005), 163.
51. According to Tropiano, who calls the music the "one and only star of the film," Lucas allocated more than ten percent ($90,000) of *American Graffiti*'s $775,000 budget to gain the music rights he needed to capture the period effectively. Stephen Topiano, *Rebels and Chicks*, 117.
52. Qtd. in Tropiano, *Rebels and Chicks*, 116.
53. Peter Lev recounts how co-screenwriters Gloria Katz and Willard Huyck disagreed with the decision not to include the female characters in the film's famous epilogue, but Lucas was adamant that the film was "a movie about the four guys," thereby relegating even significant characters like Steve's girlfriend and Curt's sister Laurie to supporting or lesser status. Lev, *American Films of the 1970s*, 95.
54. Shary, *Teen Movies*, 48.
55. Ibid., 50.
56. For feminist criticism discussing the anxious misogyny of these two infamous horror films, see for example Barbara Creed, *The Monstrous-Feminine: Film, Feminism, and Psychoanalysis* (London: Routledge, 1993) and Shelley Stamp Lindsey, "Horror, Femininity, and Carrie's Monstrous Puberty," in *The Dread of Difference: Gender and the Horror Film*, ed. Barry Keith Grant (Austin: University of Texas Press, 1996), 279–95.
57. Qtd in Robin Wood, *Hollywood From Vietnam to Reagan* (New York: Columbia University Press, 1986), 162. See also Susan Jeffords, *Hard Bodies: Hollywood Masculinity in the Reagan Era* (New Brunswick, NJ: Rutgers University Press, 1993); Elizabeth Traube, *Dreaming Identities: Class, Gender, and Generation in 1980s Hollywood Movies* (Boulder, CO: Westview Press, 1992); and George Lipsitz, "Genre Anxiety and Racial Representation," in *Refiguring American Film Genres: History and Theory*, ed. Nick Browne (Berkeley: University of California Press, 1998), 208–32.
58. Wood, *Hollywood*, 162, 172. Considine also groups together these three films at the end of his chapter entitled "Discovering Dad" as all offering the picture of "the son who found himself through the father." Considine, *Cinema of Adolescence*, 108.
59. Lev, *American Films of the 1970s*, 96. Monte also wrote the hit 1970s television series *Good Times*.
60. Stephen Tropiano cites other critics who applaud the "vitality" and frankness of the film and himself appreciates the "refreshingly honest" way the film presents the two friends and "sexual themes." Tropiano, *Rebels and Chicks*, 119.
61. Tropiano cites a critic for *The New York Times* who describes the film almost like *American Graffiti*'s pre-Kennedy assassination moment: "*Cooley* 'documents perhaps that last moment in American history—1964—when it was possible for young blacks to see color as simply one of the components of their personality'" (ibid.). Despite the strange neglect in this quote of the terrible realities of racial discrimination throughout the twentieth century in the United States that would make "seeing color as simply one of the

62 Shary argues convincingly in both *Teen Movies* and *Generation Multiplex* that the racial bias marring the genre was not significantly addressed until the 1990s when a cycle of African American urban crime films initiated by John Singleton's *Boyz N the Hood* (1991) focused on teenage protagonists. In *Generation Multiplex*, he attributes the rise of these provoking films to the success of Spike Lee's work in the 1980s, and he differentiates them from the few earlier films that integrated racial minorities into "the generally Caucasian confines of most teen settings" through a nostalgic setting which "addressed issues of racism and social struggle from a reflective perspective, without directly confronting contemporary conditions" (Austin: University of Texas Press, 123). He includes both *The Learning Tree* and *Cooley High* in this earlier, small nostalgic group.

components" of an African American's personality well nigh impossible, I would like to emphasize the writer's sense of a kind of prelapsarian moment much like Lucas' Camelot era.

63 Doherty, *Teenagers*, 191. In "Rock 'n' Roll Soundtracks and the Production of Nostalgia," David Shumway focuses to a large extent on *American Graffiti* and its nostalgic use of popular music, but he does also recognize *Easy Rider*'s use of the popular rock soundtrack as an emblem of a specific youth culture, creating a "strong sense of generational identity" without being nostalgic. *Cinema Journal* 38, no. 2 (Winter 1999): 38.

64 Doherty asserts that Jack Nicholson's drug-induced monologue about the superior Venusian civilization harkens back to the sci-fi, horror, fantasy sub-genre from the mid-to-late 1950s known as "weirdies." Ibid.

65 Thomas Schatz, *Hollywood Genres: Formulas, Filmmaking, and the Studio System* (New York: Random House, 1981), 16.

66 Ibid., 26.

67 Ibid., 29, 31.

68 In his illumination of why genre films, specifically in the musical genre, present and resolve particular problems, Altman even uses the same language (with the word "celebrates") to assert the conservative ideological function of these films: "Not only does genre film constantly underscore the categories which define us (sexual, national, moral, etc.), but it celebrates those categories even when they seem to be contradictory, thus contenting the audience with the status quo by reestablishing social equilibrium and balancing sexual, financial, and national insecurity." *The American Film Musical* (Bloomington: Indiana University Press, 1987), 334. He adds to Schatz's theory the idea of "symbolic spectatorship," which is a way to understand how genre film's allegorical nature or repeated, simplified formula works to substantiate cultural myths by "integrating individuals into the culture while assuring the culture's continued existence." Ibid., 337.

69 Schatz, *Hollywood Genres*, 33.

70 Ibid.

71 Ibid., 35 (original emphasis).

72 Ibid.

73 Ibid., 36.

74 Qtd in Schatz, *Film Genres*, 37–8.

75. Ibid.
76. Schatz, *Film Genres*, 38.
77. Christian Metz, *Language and Cinema*, trans. Donna Jean Umiker-Sebeok (The Hague: Mouton, 1974), 152.
78. Ibid.
79. Schatz, *Hollywood Genres*, 37.
80. Shary, *Teen Movies*, 46–7. Shary is working from Considine's criticism of the film's perpetuation of "sexual stereotypes" through Danny's earlier behavior and then final commitment to Sandy: "In settling for Sandy he had fulfilled the traditional role of the sexually active adolescent male who expects to be able to both sleep around himself and still marry a virgin." *The Cinema of Adolescence*, 270–1.
81. Tropiano, *Rebels and Chicks*, 120. Jon Lewis appears more focused on the first few of these references when he asserts that the film "gently pokes fun at the *Beach Party* films, as if they actually were artifacts of anyone's real-life past." *Road to Romance*, 71. It is my sense, however, that the poking is not quite so gentle.
82. Steve Neale and Frank Krutnik, *Popular Film and Television Comedy* (London: Routledge, 1990), 19.
83. Ibid. Linda Hutcheon argues in *A Theory of Parody* that while parody and satire have different functions, they often interact or intermingle in the same art work or film: "Although parody is an 'intramural' form with aesthetic norms, and satire's 'extramural' norms are social or moral, historically their interaction seems hardly to need documentation" (New York: Methuen, 1985), 25. For Hutcheon, parody clearly repeats or imitates the features of another text, like it targets the conventions of a film genre, while satire's aim is to "hold up to ridicule the vices and follies of mankind, with an eye to their correction." Ibid., 43.
84. Wes D. Gehring, "Parody," in *Handbook of Film Genres*, ed. Wes D. Gehring (New York: Greenwood Press, 1988), 145 (emphasis mine), 146. Gehring does go on, however, to again cite the work of Linda Hutcheon to set apart the social and moral role of satire from the formal work of parody that focuses solely on the literary or cinematic norms of a text. Ibid., 147.
85. Simon Dentith, *Parody* (London: Routledge, 2000), 9.
86. Ibid., 20.
87. David A. Cook, *Lost Illusions: American Cinema in the Shadow of Watergate and Vietnam, 1970–1979*, vol. 9, *History of the American Cinema* (New York: Charles Scribner's Sons, 2000), 56, 216.
88. Ibid., 180.
89. Ibid., 284, 208.
90. Ibid., 161, 160.
91. Ibid., 161. Cook argues that new wave filmmakers were reluctant to completely destroy Classical narrative forms, but cites Stephen Schiff's point that their attacks on genre were so "successful" that by the middle of the 1970s "genre could scarcely be said to exist at all" unless through nostalgia. Ibid.
92. Ibid., 284–5.

93 Timothy Corrigan labels the film a "low budget mish-mash of genres from musical to science fiction" with a bewildering amount of intertextuality. "Film and the Culture of the Cult," in *The Cult Film Experience: Beyond All Reason*, ed. J. P. Telotte (Austin: University of Texas Press, 1991), 29. Barry K. Grant, on the other hand, uses the term "genre pastiche," but clearly identifies revisionist aspects to the mix of genre since he finds the film "reverses some of the genre's classic conventions in a manner demonstrating the conscious awareness of genre traditions." "Science Fiction Double Feature: Ideology in the Cult Film," in Telotte, *The Cult Film Experience*, 128. More recently in a critical collection devoted to *Rocky Horror*, a handful of critics closely read the film in terms of its employment and experimentation with genre formulas and codes, focusing on science fiction and the musical. See Sue Matheson, "'Drinking Those Moments When': The Use (and Abuse) of Late-Night Double Feature Science Fiction and Hollywood Icons in *The Rocky Horror Picture Show*," in *Reading Rocky Horror:* The Rocky Horror Picture Show *and Popular Culture*, ed. Jeffrey Weinstock (New York: Palgrave Macmillan, 2008), 17–34 and Sarah Artt, "Reflections on the Self-reflexive Musical: *The Rocky Horror Picture Show* and the Classic Hollywood Musical, in *Reading Rocky Horror:* The Rocky Horror Picture Show *and Popular Culture*, ed. Jeffrey Weinstock (New York: Palgrave Macmillan, 2008), 51–68.

94 J. Hoberman and Jonathan Rosenbaum, *Midnight Movies* (New York: De Capo Press, 1983), 4.

95 Jeffrey Weinstock, *The Rocky Horror Picture Show*, Cultographies Series (London: Wallflower Press, 2007), 90, 79.

96 Doherty, *Teenagers*, 119.

97 Harry M. Benshoff, *Monsters in the Closet: Homosexuality and the Horror Film* (Manchester: Manchester University Press, 1997), 144.

98 Matheson, "Drinking Those Moments When," 19.

99 Weinstock, *The Rocky Horror Picture Show*, 78–9. For example, Barry K. Grant recognizes the breakdown of Brad and Janet's "bourgeois values" in the film and its disturbance of the stability of the heterosexual couple, but ultimately "narrative closure results and dominant sexual values are restored as the couple survives and Furter is eviscerated." "Science Fiction Double Feature," 129. However, Grant might be considering the American ending of the film and not the British one, which contains "Super Heroes" and a much darker future for the heterosexual couple.

100 Ibid., 80.

101 Doherty, *Teenagers*, 196.

Chapter 2

1 In an interview a year later, Malick refutes these assessments of both Holly and his own attitude toward her (and Kit): Beverly Walker, "Malick on *Badlands*," *Sight and Sound* 44.2 (Spring 1975). He claims that the narration points back to *his own* influences for the film, which were novels like *The Hardy Boys, Swiss*

Family Robinson, Tom Sawyer, Huck Finn, and, particularly, *Nancy Drew* and argues that the humor around Holly derives mostly from her "mis-estimation of her audience, of what they will be interested in or ready to believe" (82). Insisting that there is no distance between Holly and Kit and himself, Malick simply describes Holly as a "typical Southern girl" whose narration reflects her scrupulousness and "strong, if misplaced, sense of propriety." And if she does speak in clichés, they do *not* come from pulp magazines, "as some critics have suggested"; they come from the language of the "innocent abroad" (like Nancy Drew or Tom Sawyer) and are "not the mark of a diminished pulp-fed mind" (Malick perhaps willfully forgetting here the clear mark of a pulp-fed mind Twain puts on Tom). As proof of his sincerity, he concludes not only that Holly is "in a way the more important character," but also that he likes "women characters better than men."

[2] Vincent Canby, "The Movie that Made the Festival Memorable," review of *Badlands*, directed by Terrence Malick, *New York Times*, October 21, 1973, Proquest, 149.

[3] Pauline Kael comes to similar conclusions about Holly, but without the approving gush towards the new film talent, Terrence Malick, observing, disapprovingly, that "Holly narrates, in her corrupted-by-pop, fifteen-year-old baton twirler's notion of a literary attitude" and the "whole movie is filtered through the callowness of her childish, Southwestern voice and her soap-operatic confessional phrasing" (which, according to Kael, is meant to elicit the audience's laughter). Pauline Kael, "Sugarland and Badlands" (March 18, 1974) in *Reeling* (Boston: Little Brown, 1976), 300–6. See also Sarah Kozloff, *Invisible Storytellers: Voice-Over Narration in American Fiction Film* (Berkeley: University of California Press, 1988), 116.

[4] Brian Henderson, "Exploring Badlands," *Wide Angle* 5, no. 4 (1983): 41.

See also Jon Lewis, *The Road to Romance and Ruin: Teen Films and Youth Culture* (New York: Routledge, 1992), 32 and James Morrison and Thomas Schur, *The Films of Terrence Malick* (Westport, CT: Praeger, 2003), 17. Morrison and Schur fall into a similar wordplay on Spacey's name as Henderson: "The whole point of Holly's voice-over narration—that odd amalgam of romantic clichés, dime-novel pieties, fervent convictions, and *spacey* reasonings, is to suggest a constant undercurrent of thought and feeling that never manages to intervene in, and certainly does nothing to halt, the remorseless progression of action" (17).

[5] Joan McGettigan, "Interpreting a Man's World: Female Voices in *Badlands* and *Days of Heaven*," *Journal of Film and Video* 52, no. 4 (Winter 2001): 34.

[6] Ibid., 34, 35.

[7] Ibid., 36.

[8] Ibid., 38.

[9] Ibid., 43.

[10] J. Laplanche and J.-B. Pontalis, "Fantasy and the Origins of Sexuality," in *Formations of Fantasy*, ed. Victor Burgin, James Donald, and Cora Kaplan (London: Methuen, 1986), 19.

[11] Henderson, "Exploring," 42.

12 Adrian Danks, "Death Comes as an End: Temporality, Domesticity and Photography in Terrence Malick's *Badlands*," *Senses of Cinema*, www.sensesofcinema.com/contents/00/8/badlands.html; originally published in *Metro*, nos. 113–14 (1998). See also Robert Zaller, "Raising the Seventies: The Early Films of Terrence Malick," *Boulevard* 15, no. 1–2 (1999): 141–55, which suggests Holly's use of fantasy, which he also calls "adolescent make-believe" (145), and insists on her unsettling power, in her "guilefully self-deceptive as well as manipulative" thought processes and her seeming control of the camera "obedient to her will or at least complicit with it" (146).

13 Ibid. Ethel Person's book-length study of fantasy, *By Force of Fantasy: How We Make Our Lives* (New York: Basic Books, 1995), attributes many roles to the fantasizer, "as the author of the fantasy script, as a player in the drama—often the star of it—and as the audience for whom the fantasy was devised" (7). However, her reading does not offer to women, for the most part, the kind of fantasy I will contend Holly is formulating, since "sadistic and violent fantasies are more the province of men" (77).

14 See, for example, Rhona Berenstein, "Spectatorship-as-Drag: The Act of Viewing and Classic Horror Cinema," in *Viewing Positions: Ways of Seeing Film*, ed. and intro. Linda Williams (New Brunswick, NJ: Rutgers University Press, 1995), 231–69, or Miriam Hansen's work on Valentino and her female fans in *Babel and Babylon: Spectatorship in American Silent Film* (Cambridge: Harvard University Press, 1991). Also, David Rodowick in *Difficulty of Difference: Psychoanalysis, Sexual Difference, & Film Theory* (New York: Routledge, 1991) and Kaja Silverman in *Male Sexuality at the Margins* (New York: Routledge, 1992) discuss in the length these particular fantasies and their ability to disrupt conventional (and psychoanalytic) gendered subject positions, for instance active masculine versus passive feminine. Finally, see also Teresa de Lauretis' *The Practice of Love: Lesbian Sexuality and Perverse Desire* (Bloomington: Indiana University Press, 1994) for a reading of the fantasy's potential for disruption and revision by a lesbian subject.

15 Laplanche and Pontalis, "Fantasy and the Origins of Sexuality," 22–3.

16 J. Laplanche and J.-B. Pontalis, *The Language of Psychoanalysis*, trans. Donald Nicholson Smith (London: Karnac Books, 1988), 317. For an application of the term "phantasmatic" to film, see Elisabeth Lyon, "The Cinema of Lol V. Stein," in *Fantasy and the Cinema*, ed. James Donald (London: BFI Publishing, 1989), 152

17 Ginny B. Machann, "*Ceremony at Lone Tree* and *Badlands*: The Starkweather Case and the Nebraska Plains," *Prairie Schooner* 53 (1979): 169 (emphasis mine).

18 Sigmund Freud, "'A Child Is Being Beaten': A Contribution to the Study of the Origin of Sexual Perversions," in *The Standard Edition of the Complete Psychological Works of Sigmund Freud*, ed. and trans. James Strachey, 24 vols (London: Hogarth, 1955–74), 17:180.

19 Rodowick, *Difficulty of Difference*, 94.

20 Patricia White, *unInvited: Classical Hollywood Cinema and Lesbian Representability* (Bloomington: Indiana University Press, 1999), 199.

21 Ibid., 202.

22 It also may remind one of perhaps the most famous film depicting a midwestern adolescent girl's dream-work (and her little dog, too), *The Wizard of Oz*, although Kit's discovery of a dead collie in the second scene of the film does signal a violent departure from that classic film.

23 Jacqueline Rose has attempted recently to theorize a now seemingly commonplace connection between stardom or celebrity and the murderous desires or wishes of the public and/or fan: "it is as if the violence and sadism of public acclaim have been suddenly laid bare (you are accorded it as a type of punishment)....There is, we could say, something murderous in our relation to celebrity. On this score, Salman Rushdie would be exceptional only for having the murderousness precede his status as a celebrity rather than the other way around." *On Not Being Able to Sleep: Psychoanalysis and the Modern World* (Princeton: Princeton University Press, 2003), 211.

24 I would contend that the allusion to *Giant* occurs before the direct citation astutely noticed by Morrison and Schur: the image of Kit balancing a rifle across his shoulders, resembling nothing so much as a scarecrow, while the sun goes down in the desert (still reproduced by Morrison and Schur, 15–16).

25 In light of the era in which the action takes place, one might propose that Holly's behavior reflects the coyness and indifference demanded by the female teen's role in 1950s courtship. Stressing the "double standard" working against teenage girls in the 1950s, Susan Douglas summarizes the popular press' advice about sexual intimacy as similar to a game with marriage as the supposed prize in *Where the Girls Are: Growing Up Female With the Mass Media* (New York: Random House, 1994), 63. See also Barbara Ehrenreich, Elizabeth Hess, and Gloria Jacobs, "Beatlemania: Girls Just Want to Have Fun," in *The Adoring Audience: Fan Culture and Popular Media*, ed. Lisa A. Lewis (London: Routledge, 1992), 94–5. However, Holly's indifference strikes me as markedly different from the "crafty, cool, and careful" girls considered by Douglas and Ehrenreich et al. (91). She has no intention of marrying Kit, in fact does have sex with him, and becomes less interested after the seduction is consummated.

26 Freud, "A Child Is Being Beaten," 185.

27 Berenstein, "Spectatorship-as-Drag," 241–2.

28 As in "A Child Is Being Beaten," Freud's definition of "sadism" in *Three Essays on the Theory of Sexuality* obeys gender norms despite evidence to the contrary. Following Krafft-Ebing and others, he finds the "normal" root for "the pleasure in any form of humiliation or subjection" in the "sexuality of most male human beings," which has "an element of *aggressiveness*—a desire to subjugate" (23). Of course, his contention follows a familiar pattern: male-active-aggressive and female-passive-subjugated, a pattern that exists in Krafft-Ebing as well. Nevertheless, despite biological obstacles, both *Psychopathia Sexualis* and Freud's own work admit examples of female sadism. The pleasures such rare women enjoy include satisfaction "entirely conditional on the humiliation and maltreatment of the object" (24), an "active or violent attitude toward the sexual object," and "an intimate connection between cruelty and the sexual instinct" (25). Again, in his essay on "Infantile Sexuality," he locates a basic instinct for cruelty in children that both "arises from the instinct for mastery"

and precedes the signs of gender, appearing "at a period of sexual life at which the genitals have not yet taken over their later role (59). Children at this stage, apparently, lack a "capacity for pity" which should bring "the instinct for mastery to a halt at another person's pain" (59). Later writings, such as "Instincts and Their Vicissitudes" and *Civilization and Its Discontents*, reassert that the instinct for cruelty and its partner, the instinct for mastery, continue beyond childhood and not just in the sexual realm.

[29] Freud, "A Child Is Being Beaten," 191.
[30] Ibid.
[31] Also, notably, Anna Freud's essay "Beating Fantasies and Daydreams," in *The Writings of Anna Freud*. Vol. I. (New York: International Universities Press, 1974) finds that girls of 14 or 15 begin producing fictional stories inspired by their beating fantasies (142–4), which is, of course, Holly's age during the action of the film.
[32] White, *unInvited*, 197.
[33] Walker, "Malick on *Badlands*," 82.
[34] Neil Campbell, "The Highway Kind: *Badlands*, Youth, Space and the Road," in *The Cinema of Terrence Malick: Poetic Visions of America*, ed. Hannah Patterson (London: Wallflower Press, 2003), 43.
[35] Ibid.
[36] Ibid., 47.
[37] Ibid., 39.
[38] Robin Wood, *Hollywood From Vietnam to Reagan* (New York: Columbia University Press, 1986), 50.
[39] Ibid., 69.
[40] Marsha Kinder claims that Malick treats the elements from Penn's film "ironically" as satire, taking all the romance and passion out of the legend. Marsha Kinder, "The Return of the Outlaw Couple," *Film Quarterly* 27.4 (Summer 1974): 8. See also Robert Kolker, *A Cinema of Loneliness: Penn, Kubrick, Coppola, Scorsese, Altman* (New York: Oxford University Press, 1980) for a reading of Penn, whose films, along with others of the period, "carry on ideological debate with the culture that breeds them," but never "confront that culture with another ideology, with other ways of seeing itself" (9).
[41] Kinder, "Return of the Outlaw Couple," 2.
[42] Ibid., 3–7.
[43] Lewis, *Road to Romance*, 32.
[44] Ibid.; Kinder, "Return of the Outlaw Couple," 9.
[45] Frederic Jameson, *Postmodernism, or The Cultural Logic of Late Capitalism* (Durham, NC: Duke University Press, 1991), 19.
[46] Frederic Jameson, "Postmodernism and Consumer Culture," in *The Anti-Aesthetic: Essays on Postmodern Culture*, ed. and intro. Hal Foster (New York: New Press, 1998), 135.
[47] In "Re-presenting the National Past: Nostalgia and Pastiche in the Heritage Film," Andrew Higson contends that the British heritage films of the 1980s employ "spectacular pastiche" (109) with its "self-conscious visual perfectionism" and "fetishization of period details" to create a "self-enclosed world" divided from the present (113). This spectacle in films such as *Maurice*, *A Room*

With A View, or *Another Country* crystallizes, for Higson, a very particular past: "By turning their backs on the industrialized, chaotic present, they nostalgically reconstruct an imperialist and upper class Britain" (110).

48 Janice Doane and Devon Hedges, *Nostalgia and Sexual Difference: The Resistance to Contemporary Feminism* (New York: Metheun, 1987), xiii. Similarly, Phil Powrie also documents straightforward uses of nostalgia in French cinema, for example in the prestige productions whose "ideological function" lies in "a conservative attempt in both social and cinematographic terms to return to a golden age" (13), although the bulk of his project more interestingly focuses on nostalgia films that convey "the crisis of masculinity as a social problem" (11). However, not all accounts of nostalgia dismiss or challenge it as hopelessly regressive or ideologically conservative and thereby dangerous. Roberta Rubenstein contends that nostalgia can be employed as a tool for reaching self-awareness and knowledge. Particularly in female writers, the longing for home or nostalgia enables "their characters (and, imaginatively, their readers) to confront, mourn, and figuratively revise their relation to something that has been lost, whether in the world or in themselves" (*Home* 6).

49 Ibid., 3.

50 Lewis, *Road to Romance*, 136.

51 Ibid., 136–7. Marsha Kinder agrees with Lewis's assessment, dismissing *American Graffiti* for "cultivating nostalgia" into an escapist spectacle meant to entertain an aging boomer audience (4). Less flattering still, Robin Wood pairs Lucas's film with Bob Clark's *Porky's* (US, 1982) as the two "obvious touchstones" of the 1980s high school cycle, as both look back at a group of (mostly) male friends in the 1950s and early 1960s whose practical 'jokes' and sexual (sexist) initiations set the standard for any number of future imitators (215).

52 Ibid., 134.

53 Jameson, *Postmodernism*, 19.

54 Susan Douglas, *Where the Boys Are: Growing Up Female with the Mass Media* (New York: Random House, 1994), 93. Coming not exactly as a surprise, a quick review by the author counts 35 credited groups or solo musical artists in *Graffiti*'s end credits, all of which are male, with the exception of The Skyliners and The Platters, both of whom had one female in the group, and The Fleetwoods, who were a harmonizing trio of two girls and one guy. Not one entry by The Chantels or The Ronettes or the incredibly successful Shirelles, whose 1960 "Will You Love Me Tomorrow" was the first in a string of number one hits (84). Perhaps songs like the pre-Spector Ronettes' "What's so Sweet about Sweet Sixteen?" did not quite fit the mood.

55 David Shumway, in an article on music and the production of nostalgia in Hollywood film, contends that the music in *American Graffiti* helps to move the film beyond Jameson's dismissal of the film to reach audience members affected by musical association: "It is my contention that music is the most important ingredient in the production of the affect of nostalgia or the recollection of such affective experience in the viewer"; "Rock 'n' Roll Sound Tracks and the Production of Nostalgia," *Cinema Journal* 38, no. 2 (Winter 1999): 40.

Such a reading would also help to explain how Wolfman Jack remains the only adult in the film above reproach.

56 In *The New Hollywood: What the Movies Did with the New Freedoms of the Seventies* (Jefferson, NC: McFarland, 1991), contrary to James Bernardoni who spends some time criticizing Lucas for making his film in more a televisual style, "visually hyperactive" and lacking in realism or substance (16), this reading contends that Lucas's use of lighting and color does have a cinematic power and resonance all its own. Bernardoni suggests that "Lucas typically uses color and lighting effects to achieve a sense of immediate excitement, not to convey nuances of theme or feeling" (27), but I would offer that the lighting in the hop sequences and, at times, on the strip do convey nuances of theme and feeling other than just a fetish for neon or movement.

57 The obvious precursor for this scene, the famous "chickie-run" scene in *Rebel without a Cause*, would provide a sufficient comparison that would expose the intensity of Lucas's nostalgia. In Ray's 1955 film, the chickie run is supposed to be the proving ground for Jim Stark's manhood, but ends with a terrible tragedy that shocks the youth culture to its core, so much so that Jim finds safety in the end only in the company of his parents and the police. In *American Graffiti*, the king of the roads continues to reign and no one is hurt in the accident.

58 Svetlana Boym, *The Future of Nostalgia* (New York: Basic Books, 2001), xiv. Also, Lucas's film returns to the age period that dominates nostalgic accounts. In fact, in his groundbreaking article, "The Idea of Nostalgia," Jean Starobinski cites Kant in order to contend that all nostalgia is a longing for one's lost youth, not one's lost home: "what a person wishes to recover is not so much the actual *place* where he passed his childhood but his youth itself. He is not straining toward something which he can repossess, but toward an age which is forever beyond his reach" (in *Diogenes* 54 (1966): 94).

59 Boym, *Future of Nostalgia*, xiii (my emphasis).

60 Ibid.

61 Ibid., 8.

62 Kinder, "Return of the Outlaw Couple," 8.

63 Ibid., 9.

64 Ibid., 9, 5.

65 Vera Dika, *Recycled Culture in Contemporary Art and Film: The Uses of Nostalgia* (Cambridge: Cambridge University Press, 2003), 56.

66 Ibid., 57, 63.

67 Ibid., 63. While Lucas receives the most attention for his reference to the assassination in the advertisements for *American Graffiti*, "Where were you in '62?" (Lewis, *Road to Romance*, 133), Dika might be catching Malick at the same game. Many other critics allude to the violence in *Badlands* as commentary on the nearly concluded Vietnam War, especially after the release of *The Thin Red Line*. For instance, Robert Zaller sees the war as a huge influence on the film: "*Badlands* may be read as an attempt to probe the roots of American violence in an era both traumatized and anaesthetized by the Vietnam War (Kit alludes to his own service in Korea, and some of his military-style exercises in the river camp sequence startlingly foreshadow Sheen's performance as Captain Willard in *Apocalypse*

Now)" (154). See also Ron Mottram, "All Things Shining: The Struggle for Wholeness, Redemption and Transcendence in the Films of Terrence Malick." Marsha Kinder prefers to cite the Watergate scandal, likening Kit to Nixon a few times and finding Holly "like the silent majority of the sixties and seventies" who denied "all responsibility for the killings performed by heroes and villains" (7).

[68] Ibid., 65.

[69] Ibid., 56, 58. A similar slip occurs in her attempt to propose an alternative (but familiar) reading of *American* Graffiti wherein the "purely nostalgic events presented" are undercut by "a bittersweet quality" caused by "the audience's own knowledge of the impending destruction of this innocent world" (92). Therefore, again, "unspoken contradictions," such as the difference between "collegiate kids" and "greasers" will be appreciated by the contemporary audience and understood as bittersweet (92). However, as with Lewis's reading, those contradictions might taste quite bitter to some of those audience members: "A little historical knowledge will tell you that the collegiate kids—that is, the middle-class kids of the 1960s—went to college, and the greasers—or working-class kids—went to war" (92). It appears that the 1960s was more traumatic for some rather than others.

[70] Ibid., 58.

[71] James Hay, "'You're Tearing Me Apart!': The Primal Scene of Teen Films," review of *Teenagers and Teenpics: The Juvenilization of American Movies in the 1950s*, by Thomas Doherty, *Cultural Studies* 4 no. 3 (Oct. 1990): 338.

[72] In *The Language of Psychoanalysis*, Laplanche and Pontalis offer that Freud first used the term to "connote certain traumatic infantile experiences which are organized into scenarios or scenes," but he did not relate them specifically to parental intercourse (335). Freud most famously accounted for these phantasies in his case of the "Wolf Man" in "From the History of an Infantile Neurosis." Freud discovers, in the Wolf Man's dream and from his case history, an infantile neuroses resulting from, first, the viewing of parental intercourse "*a tergo* [from behind]" (*SE* 17:37), during which the child views the genitals of both parents, and second in the reaction to seduction by the patient's older sister. This seduction "had given him the passive sexual aim of being touched on the genitals" (24) and had awakened a sexuality that was denounced by his nanny, resulting in a threat of castration. However, the passive aim and threat of castration combined in the dream, which occurred at the age of four, with the primal scene memory, which, if it occurred at all, happened at the age of one and a half, to express a desire for the father and the resulting fear of castration. The dream of the wolves (the wolf's stance traced back to the "a tergo" position) masks a "longing for sexual satisfaction from his father," taking his mother's passive place in the primal scene, which results in the "realization that castration is a necessary condition of it" (meaning the sight of his mother's genitals confirms the castration threat) and the consequent "fear of his father," anxiety, phobia, and obsessional neurosis (42).

[73] Perhaps only Robert Zaller has perceived how serious a threat Holly might be, but, unfortunately, the price for such power is, of course, demonization. This girl, "ideally presentable as a victim" and "absorbed in fantasy," grows up to be "a woman devoid of affect," a survivor moving toward "the life of banality

for which she was made": "Raising the Seventies: The Early Films of Terrence Malick," *Boulevard* 15, no. 1–2 (1999): 148. Kit may be a bastardization of the frontier myth, but "in Holly, we sense the presence of a possible evil." It may very well be possible that "evil" is the only word we have to describe a controlling, guileful, and consequential teenage girl who defies the authorities she is supposed to obey and adore.
74. Laura Mulvey, *Visual and Other Pleasures* (Bloomington: Indiana University Press, 1989), 22.
75. White, *unInvited*, 202.
76. Other feminist film theorists emphasize active female consumption of popular culture and the anxieties surrounding that consumption. See Miriam Hansen, *Babel and Babylon: Spectatorship in American Silent Film* (Cambridge: Harvard University Press, 1991). Also, Shelley Stamp documents female film-going behavior in the 1910s such as shouting during serials and fraternizing with boyfriends that "frequently disrupted expectations about ladylike decorum" in public and finds that these "movie-struck girls" unexpectedly selected "tawdry vice pictures, 'blood-boiling' serials, or polemical suffrage treatises" for viewing. *Movie-Struck Girls Women and Motion Picture Culture after the Nickelodeon* (Princeton: Princeton University Press, 2000): 197. Though pathologized as "unable to separate film viewing from romantic dreams of their own stardom" (198), these female spectators did upset attempts to constrain and integrate them into "cinema's social arena" (199).
77. That this aggressive play and violent, sadistic fantasy originates in a supposedly heterosexual girl represents a departure from conventional accounts of female violence wherein the aggressive or criminal woman is marked as lesbian. In *Fatal Women: Lesbian Sexuality and the Mark of Aggression* (Princeton: Princeton University Press, 1994), Lynda Hart recognizes the equation between women who kill or aggress and women who transgress heteronormativity: "it is likely that when women are represented as violent, predatory, dangerous, the reverse would also be operative—the 'castrating bitch' would carry the presumption of lesbianism" (76). See also Chris Holmlund's "Cruisin' for a Bruisin': Hollywood's Deadly (Lesbian) Dolls," *Cinema Journal* 34, no. 1 (1994): 31–51.
78. See Stamp's *Movie-Struck Girls* and Georganne Scheiner's *Signifying Female Adolescence: Film Representations and Fans, 1920–1950* (Westport, CT: Praeger, 2000) for a historical overview of both Hollywood's representation of teenage girls and of the teenage female audience, particularly as consumers of fan literature.
79. Lewis, *Road to Romance*, 22.
80. Ibid., 27.
81. Vicky Lebeau, *Lost Angels: Psychoanalysis and Cinema* (London: Routledge, 1995), 50–1.

Chapter 3

1. Timothy Shary, *Teen Movies: American Youth on Screen* (London: Wallflower Press, 2005), 53.

2. Timothy Shary, *Generation Multiplex: The Image of Youth in Contemporary American Cinema* (Austin: University of Texas Press, 2002), 6.
3. Berkowitz's *Something Happened: A Political and Cultural Overview of the Seventies* offers a number of notable crises including Vietnam, Watergate, the energy crisis, and inflation as key to the "sense of the seventies as an era of political failure" in the chapter immediately preceding his chapter on "The Rights Revolution" (132). See also Bruce J. Schulman, *The Seventies: The Great Shift in American Culture, Society, and Politics* (New York: De Capo, 2001); David Frum, *How We Got Here, The 1970s: The Decade that Brought You Modern Life (For Better or For Worse)* (New York: Basic Books, 2000); and Peter Carroll, *It Seemed Like Nothing Happened: America in the 1970s* (New Brunswick: Rutgers University Press, 1990).
4. Andreas Killen, *1973 Nervous Breakdown: Watergate, Warhol, and the Birth of Post-Sixties America* (New York: Bloomsbury, 2006), 8.
5. Ibid., 9.
6. Shelton Waldrep, "Introducing the Seventies," in *The Seventies: The Age of Glitter in Popular Culture*, ed. Shelton Waldrep (New York: Routledge, 2000), 4.
7. Jeffrey Ruoff, *An American Family: A Televised Life* (Minneapolis: University of Minnesota Press, 2002), 13.
8. Ibid., xxiv.
9. Killen, *1973 Nervous Breakdown*, 45. 68.
10. Ibid., 58.
11. Ruoff, *American Family*, 66.
12. Ibid., 70.
13. Harry M. Benshoff, "Queers and Families in Film: From Problems to Parents," in *A Family Affair: Cinema Calls Home*, ed. Murray Pomerance (London: Wallflower Press, 2008), 224.
14. Michel Foucault, *The History of Sexuality: Volume I: An Introduction* (New York: Vintage, 1990), 38.
15. In terms of works establishing and furthering the study of cultural conceptions of childhood sexuality and queer children in particular, key texts also include Robert Owens, Jr.'s *Queer Kids: The Challenges and Promise for Lesbian, Gay, and Bisexual Youth*, Lee Edelman's essay "The Future Is Kid's Stuff: Queer Theory, Disidentification, and the Death Drive," and Kincaid's second major work on the topic, *Erotic Innocence: The Culture of Child Molesting*. Furthermore, one cannot underestimate the influence of Gayle Rubin's essay "Thinking Sex: Notes for a Radical Theory of the Politics of Sexuality" not only as a foundational text for queer theory in general but also as a brilliant recognition of the centrality of the child for conservative policing of queerness, for, as she argues, "no tactic for stirring up erotic hysteria has been as reliable as the appeal to protect children" (6).
16. Steven Bruhm and Natasha Hurley, "Curiouser: On the Queerness of Children," in *Curiouser: On the Queerness of Children*, ed. Steven Bruhm and Natasha Hurley (Minneapolis: University of Minnesota Press, 2004), ix.
17. Ibid., x.
18. Ibid., xiii.

19. Eve Kosofsky Sedgwick, "How to Bring Your Kids Up Gay: The War on Effeminate Boys," in *Curiouser: On the Queerness of Children*, ed. Steven Bruhm and Natasha Hurley (Minneapolis: University of Minnesota Press, 2004), 140.
20. Bruhm and Hurley, "Curiouser," xvii.
21. Kathryn B. Stockton, "Feeling Like Killing? Queer Temporalities of Murderous Motives among Queer Children," *GLQ* 13, no. 2–3 (2007): 303.
22. Ibid., 304.
23. Ibid.
24. Janet Maslin, review of *Ice Castles*, directed by Donald Wrye, *New York Times*, February 23, 1979, C7:1.
25. "Meet Robby Benson!!!" *Tiger Beat* 11, no. 7 (April 1975): 18.
26. Ibid.
27. Rosalyn Drexler, "*Jeremy*—A Big 'Little Movie,'" review of *Jeremy*, directed by Arthur Barron, *New York Times*, August 12, 1973, Sec II. 1:2.
28. Roger Greenspun, "Very Young Love Story," review of *Jeremy*, directed by Arthur Barron, *New York Times*, August 2, 1973, 28:1.
29. Randi Bourscheidt, "One to One with Robbie Benson" *Interview* 7 (September 1977): 32.
30. Joan Mellen, *Big Bad Wolves: Masculinity in the American Film* (New York: Pantheon Books, 1977), 293, 301.
31. Susan Jeffords, "Can Masculinity Be Terminated?" in *Screening the Male: Exploring Masculinities in Hollywood Cinema*, ed. Steven Cohan and Ina Rae Hark, (London: Routledge, 1993), 246. Of course, Yvonne Tasker's formative study *Spectacular Bodies: Gender, Genre and the Action Cinema* (New York: Routledge, 1993) helps to establish this argument about 1980s action film, along with Jefford's full-length work, *Hard Bodies: Hollywood Masculinity in the Reagan Era* (New Brunswick: Rutgers University Press, 1993).
32. Timothy Shary, "Bad Boys and Hollywood Hype: Gendered Conflict in Juvenile Delinquency Films," in *Where the Boys Are: Cinemas of Masculinity and Youth*, ed. Murray Pomerance and Frances Gateward (Detroit: Wayne State University Press, 2005), 29.
33. Ibid., 30, 29.
34. Jeffrey P. Dennis, *Queering Teen Culture: All-American Boys and Same-Sex Desire in Film and Television* (New York: Harrington Park Press, 2006), 122.
35. Ibid., 127.
36. Randi Reisfeld and Danny Fields, *Who's Your Fave Rave?* (New York: Berkley Trade, 1997), 128.
37. Michael De Angelis, *Gay Fandom and Crossover Stardom: James Dean, Mel Gibson, and Keanu Reeves* (Durham: Duke University Press, 2001), 7.
38. Dennis, *Queering Teen Culture*, 121.
39. Reisfeld and Fields, *Who's Your Fave Rave?* 217–18.
40. Ibid., 190.
41. Ibid., 191.
42. Ibid.
43. Ibid., 193.
44. Ibid., 204.

45. Dennis, *Queering Teen Culture*, 122.
46. Reisfeld and Fields, *Who's Your Fave Rave?* 204.
47. Ibid., 209.
48. Ibid., 212.
49. "Young Veteran Discusses Troubled Life, New Film," *Box Office* 111 (August 1977): E2.
50. Bourscheidt, "One to One with Robbie Benson," 32.
51. David Considine, *The Cinema of Adolescence* (Jefferson, NC: McFarland, 1985), 269.
52. See for example, Barbara Ehrenreich et al.'s "Beatlemania: Girls Just Want to Have Fun," in *The Adoring Audience*, ed. Lisa Lewis (London: Routledge, 1992), 84–106 and Wini Breines, *Young, White, and Miserable: Growing Up Female in the Fifties* (Boston: Beacon, 1992).
53. Richard Eder, review of *Ode to Billy Joe*, directed by Max Baer, *New York Times*, August 19, 1976, 48:1.
54. Ibid.
55. Richard Eder, "A Little Anticipation Goes a Long Way," review of *Ode to Billy Joe*, directed by Max Baer, *New York Times*, August 29, 1976, Sec. II. 11:1.
56. Roger Ebert also laments that the film *had* to find an answer to the Gentry song's enigma, but he at least tentatively includes Billy Joe's confession, which he names, as part of the film's successful "unaffected portrait of young people," where homosexuality might be a "compelling" reason for suicide for "an uncertain adolescent, circa 1953." Review of *Ode to Billy Joe*, directed by Max Baer, *Chicago Sun Times*, July 7, 1976, <rogerebert.suntimes.com> August 6, 2009. Other critics contradicted Eder's conclusions entirely, finding the revelation of the homosexual experience moving, particularly due to the performance of James Best (who plays Mr. Barksdale). For these sympathetic responses, see the reviews in *Variety* (June 9, 1976) and *Time Magazine*: Jay Cocks, "Summer Clearance," *Time* (September 20, 1976), 108: 80.
57. Film critic David Thomson contends in a tribute to Day on her seventy-fifth birthday in 1999 that her status as "gay icon" did not truly begin until she retired in the 1970s and her hit from *Calamity Jane* "Secret Love" became "an anthem in gay bars" where talk of her films with Rock Hudson and Cary Grant proliferated. "Profile Doris Day: The Cutest Blonde of Them All," *Independent*, March 28, 1999: 25. James's comment about turning into Doris Day clearly emanates from a time period when these gay bars would be more commonly known and discussed.
58. Considine, *Cinema of Adolescence*, 245.
59. Vito Russo, *The Celluloid Closet: Homosexuality in the Movies* (New York: Harper, 1981), 142, 143.
60. Considine, *Cinema of Adolescence*, 242.

Chapter 4

1. At the time, Janet Maslin in *Newsweek* referred to the film's "spooky verisimilitude": "Switcheroo," Arts (February 28, 1977): 72; and *Variety* called it

"certainly one of the most offbeat films Walt Disney Productions has ever made": McBride, "Freaky Friday," (December 22, 1976): 22. In the more recent "Nobody's Handmaid," B. Ruby Rich refers *Freaky Friday* as "an odd Disney vehicle": *Sight and Sound* (December 1991): 8.
2. Qtd in Terry Brown, "The Butch Femme Fatale," in *The Lesbian Postmodern*, ed. Laura Doan (New York: Columbia University Press, 1994), 232.
3. Andrew Sarris, "Country Girls and City Boys," review of *Foxes*, directed by Adrian Lyne, *The Village Voice* (March 10, 1980): 51.
4. Ibid. John Hinckley, Jr.'s attempt to assassinate President Reagan to earn Foster's attention and favor occurred on March 30, 1981, just over a year after Sarris' review came out in *The Village Voice*. Obviously, I do not consider the two to be connected, but the review serves as yet another piece of proof of Foster's particular draw.
5. Michelle Abate, *Tomboys: A Literary and Cultural History* (Philadelphia: Temple University Press, 2008), 205.
6. "Ambitions of a Foster Child," *Films Illustrated* 6 (May 1977): 352.
7. Qtd in Rich, "Nobody's Handmaid," 7.
8. For example, in the *Tiger Beat* profile from 1974, "Meet Jodi [sic] Foster," the young actress is defined by her already prolific career on television and described as a "good actress," "so smart" that she attends a school for gifted children, fluent in French, and a "stick-to-it girl" who has dreams of becoming president of the United States: *Tigerbeat* 10, no. 12 (September 1974): 73. Similarly, a profile in *Seventeen Magazine* a few years later interviews several of her past costars and Foster's mother to paint a comparable picture of a young woman who knows "her own mind" and is devoted to her work: Edwin Miller, "Here Comes Jodie Foster!" 36 (January 1977): 64–6.
9. "Ambitions of a Foster Child," 352.
10. Nash, *American Sweethearts*, 20, 21.
11. Vincent Canby, "Disturbing 'Taxi Driver,'" review of *Taxi Driver*, directed by Martin Scorsese, *New York Times* (February 15, 1976), Sect. II 1:5.
12. Vicky Lebeau, *Childhood and Cinema* (London: Reaktion Books, 2008), 108.
13. Nash, *American Sweethearts*, 26.
14. Foster's star discourse and role in *Taxi Driver* and other films from the mid-1970s comes very close to contradicting the established form of subordination in representations of teen girls throughout the twentieth century. As Ilana Nash argues, the teen girl has been defined and constructed as a significant "Other" in American popular culture of the century, examined and represented as a "double emptiness" to be filled by the projection of adult (patriarchal) desires and fears, combining the "child's lack of experience" with the "woman's lack of agency and rationality" (*American Sweethearts*, 22). As I have suggested, Foster's roles counter the child's lack of experience with a weary knowledge of sexuality, and she refuses any hint of the "lack of agency and rationality" both in her notorious skill, intelligence and work ethic as an actor *and* her assertive, even aggressive, roles.
15. Andy Warhol, "Jodie Foster: New Femme Fatale," *Interview* 7 (January 1977): 6.
16. Ibid., 8.
17. Ibid.

18. Ibid., 6 (emphasis mine).
19. Janet Maslin, "Some Teenagers," review of *Foxes*, directed by Adrian Lyne, *New York Times* (February 29, 1980), C15:1. Likewise, in the midst of a largely negative review of *Carny*, Vincent Canby highlights "some vivid moments," one of which includes "Miss Foster's sexual exhilaration after she's just fleeced (by what means we're never told) a couple of lesbians": "Another Country," review of *Carny*, directed by Robert Kaylor, *New York Times* (June 13, 1980), C8:1. Obviously, by the time *Silence of the Lambs* is released eleven years later, this innuendo reaches fever pitch and ends with a very public "outing" by Michelangelo Signorile and *Outpost*.
20. Christina Lane, "The Liminal Iconography of Jodie Foster," *Journal of Popular Film and Television* 22, no. 4 (Winter 1995): 149.
21. Ibid., 150, 153. Janet Staiger's article "Taboos and Totems: Cultural Meanings of *The Silence of the Lambs*" deals also with the contentious issue of Foster's sexual identity after the release of the 1991 film, but her article is less focused on ambiguity or queerness and more attentive to the construction of a "lesbian" other and the cultural meaning of the lesbian in both the film and the public reception of it. In *Film Theory Goes to the Movies*, ed. Jim Collins, Hilary Radner, and Ava Preacher Collins (New York: Routledge, 1993), 142–54.
22. Terry Brown, "The Butch Femme Fatale," in *The Lesbian Postmodern*, ed. Laura Doan (New York: Columbia University Press, 1994), 232.
23. Ibid.
24. Judith Halberstam, "Oh Bondage Up Yours! Female Masculinity and the Tomboy," in *Curiouser: On the Queerness of Children*, ed. Steven Bruhm and Natasha Hurley (Minneapolis: University of Minnesota Press, 2004), 193.
25. Brown, "Butch Femme," 233.
26. Ibid., 234. In "Nobody's Handmaid," B. Ruby Rich offers a contradictory view of Foster's sexuality in her adult roles. She contends that after the "child-sex frisson of her early roles indelibly marked Foster" (*Taxi Driver* and *Bugsy Malone*, specifically) (8), her "sexuality has been overdetermined," but she turns this into a strength: "The charge of sexuality makes these tough characters vulnerable, while giving them the strength to sustain that vulnerability" (9). For Rich, Foster astounds audiences with her ability to dramatize the tension (and sometimes friction) between sexuality and authority in women in the United States and for the playing out of this tension, Foster becomes a feminist icon.
27. B. Ruby Rich, "Jodie Foster: Growing Up On-Screen," *Walker Arts Center*, January 1991, http://filmvideo.walkerart.org/detail.wac?id=3284&title=Articles.
28. Rich, "Nobody's Handmaid," 8.
29. Foster, "A Look Back."
30. Annalee R. Ward, *Mouse Morality: The Rhetoric of Disney Animated Film* (Austin: University of Texas Press, 2002), 119.
31. As Freud explains in "Some Psychical Consequences of the Anatomical Distinction Between the Sexes," the girl's recognition of her mother's genitals as proof of her own inferiority humiliates her and leads her to abandon her masculinity and follow a trajectory that results in her antagonism with her mother: "But now the girl's libido slips into a new position along the

line—there is no other way of putting it—of the equation 'penis-child.' She gives up her wish for a penis and puts in place of it a wish for a child: and *with that purpose in view* she takes her father as a love object. Her mother becomes the object of her jealousy" (*Standard Edition*, vol. 19: 256). This process encourages her femininity and eventually results in her "normal" object choice and genital sexuality.

[32] Michelle Ann Abate, in her groundbreaking work on tomboys in twentieth-century American popular texts, sees in Foster and her two famous contemporaries Tatum O'Neal and Christy McNichol a kind of renaissance for the tomboy role in Hollywood during the 1970s and 1980s, referring to her character in *Candleshoe* as "rough-and-tumble Casey Brown" (*Tomboys*, 197).

[33] Indeed, even the filmmakers of "A Look Back with Jodie Foster" seem in on the joke. When Foster reveals that the film is painful for her to watch due to her own adolescent difficulties and self-consciousness at the time of the filming, the filmmakers respond by inserting a clip of this strange declaration of her love for Boris ("What a fox!") at the same time that the adult Foster fears that "everybody at home watching this DVD is going to be hysterically laughing." The juxtaposition also hints that "everybody at home" with knowledge of the rumors about her sexuality will find this declaration by an awkward, self-conscious, and butch young Foster to her male costar especially funny and ironic.

[34] See Halberstam's *Female Masculinity* (Durham: Duke University Press, 1998) for an examination of this paradox for the young tomboy who is tolerated and even appreciated for her masculine assertiveness, aggression, and independence so long as she does not carry these qualities into adulthood or far into adolescence when they might become tied to sexuality.

[35] Sean Griffin, *Tinker Belles and Evil Queens: The Walt Disney Company from the Inside Out* (New York: New York University Press, 2000), 87.

[36] Sigmund Freud, "Female Sexuality," in *The Standard Edition of the Complete Psychological Works of Sigmund Freud*, ed. and trans. James Strachey, 24 vols. (London: Hogarth, 1955–74), 21:229.

[37] Sigmund Freud, "Femininity," in *The Standard Edition of the Complete Psychological Works of Sigmund Freud*, ed. and trans. James Strachey, 24 vols. (London: Hogarth, 1955–74), 22:130.

[38] Ibid. In fact his clearest explanation of the masculinity complex comes in his earlier study "The Psychogenesis of a Case of Homosexuality in a Woman." In this case, he establishes not only the features of the masculinity complex outlined above but also his connection between this complex, homosexuality in women, and an erotic attachment to the mother.

[39] Sigmund Freud, "The Psychogenesis of a Case of Homosexuality in a Woman," in *The Standard Edition of the Complete Psychological Works of Sigmund Freud*, ed. and trans. James Strachey, 24 vols. (London: Hogarth, 1955–74), 18:169.

[40] Freud, "Female Sexuality," 241.

[41] Ibid.

[42] Teresa de Lauretis, *The Practice of Love: Lesbian Sexuality and Perverse Desire* (Bloomington: Indiana University Press, 1994), 55.

[43] Ibid., 57.

[44] Qtd in de Lauretis, *Practice*, 61.

[45] I am certainly aware of the many feminist attempts to deconstruct the "explanations" for homosexuality by psychological and other "scientific" researchers since the nineteenth century and do not want to reify those heterosexist and disciplining accounts. I value de Lauretis' project of taking on the "major public discourses on lesbian sexuality" as "inadequate" and centered on what she calls "sexual indifference—of inversion, of masculinity complex, of lesbianism as pre-Oedipal fusion, psychosis, hysteria, bisexuality or oscillation between masculinity and femininity" (75). She rightly recognizes the "unavailability, suppression, and proscription of discourses and other public forms of fantasy that inscribe particular scenarios of women's desire for women," but I have a different task in my examination of *Freaky Friday*. I seek to expose how even the hint of queer desire can undo the entire maturation plot.

[46] Freud, "Femininity," 131.

[47] Ibid.

[48] Freud, "Female Sexuality," 239 (original emphasis), 241.

[49] Ibid., 241.

[50] de Lauretis, *Practice*, 45.

[51] Nash, *American Sweethearts*, 12.

[52] Ibid., 13.

[53] Ibid., 18.

[54] Henry A. Giroux, *The Mouse that Roared: Disney and the End of Innocence* (Lanham, MD: Rowan & Littlefield, 1999), 142.

[55] Ibid., 127.

[56] Elizabeth Bell, Lynda Haas, and Laura Sells, "Introduction: Walt's in the Movies," in *From Mouse to Mermaid: The Politics of Film, Gender, and Culture*, ed. Elizabeth Bell, Lynda Haas, and Laura Sells (Bloomington: Indiana University Press, 1995), 7.

[57] Nicholas Sammond's work *Babes in Tomorrowland: Walt Disney and the Making of the American Child, 1930–1960* documents the many ways that the corporation and its founder aligned themselves "with popular conceptions of what was good for the child" to offer a kind of ideal that supported traditional values and naturalized the child (and thereby America) as "white (largely male), Protestant, middle-class" (Durham, NC: Duke University Press, 2005), 10. I would note here, as I do with Ilana Nash's *American Sweethearts*, that Sammond concludes his study at 1960, indicating yet again Disney's inability to perform its pedagogical project during the period of the 1970s.

[58] Chris Holmlund, "Tots to Tanks: Walt Disney Presents Feminism for the Family," *Social Text* 2 (Summer 1979): 125. In "Spinsters in Sensible Shoes." Chris Cuomo goes so far as to say that even characters coded as lesbian, such as Miss Eglantine Price in *Bedknobs and Broomsticks* (Stevenson, 1971), must in the end validate traditional values and subordinate themselves to the preservation of the patriarchal family: "The family must be the end product for this story to work as a Disney fantasy: Family created, Empire saved, Gender order reestablished." In *From Mouse to Mermaid: The Politics of Film, Gender, and Culture*, ed. Elizabeth Bell, Lynda Haas, and Laura Sells (Bloomington: Indiana University Press, 1995), 221.

[59] Griffin, *Tinker Belles*, 49.

Chapter 5

1. Juliet Mitchell, *Siblings: Sex and Violence* (Cambridge: Polity Press, 2003), 28. See also Judith Butler, *Antigone's Claim: Kinship between Life and Death* (New York: Columbia University Press, 2000) for another challenge to the Oedipal model through a reexamination and refocus on Antigone's legacy.
2. Ibid. (original emphasis).
3. Ibid., 29.
4. Tony Williams, *Hearths of Darkness: The Family in American Horror Film* (Madison: Farleigh Dickinson University Press, 1996), 211.
5. Ibid., 216, 217.
6. As Mitchell contends in *Siblings: Sex and Violence*, with the onset of puberty "boys and girls will reexperience the murderousness towards siblings" (30).
7. Vera Dika, *Games of Terror:* Halloween, Friday the 13th, *and the Films of the Stalker Cycle* (Rutherford, NJ: Farleigh Dickinson University Press, 1990), 94.
8. Robin Wood, "An Introduction to the American Horror Film," in *Planks of Reason: Essays on the Horror Film*, revised edition, ed. Barry Keith Grant and Christopher Sharrett (Lanham, MD: Scarecrow Press, 2004), 111, 113.
9. Ibid., 123. For example, Wood emphasizes the little girl who "kills and devours her parents" in *Night of the Living Dead* instead of the final murderous confrontation between Johnny and Barbara (124). Or, with *The Texas Chain Saw Massacre*, Wood opposes two entire family units—the young people and the slaughterhouse family—to examine their hierarchal positions as young and old, affluent and poor, normal and monstrous (131). For continuation of Wood's argument about Michael the monster as the eruption of the repressed, see Douglas Rathgreb, "Bogeyman from the Id: Nightmare and Reality in *Halloween* and *A Nightmare on Elm Street*," *Journal of Popular Film and Television* 19, no. 1 (March 1991).
10. Ibid., 137. See Vivian Sobchack's article "Bringing It All Back Home: Family Economy and Generic Exchange" in *The Dread of Difference: Gender and the Horror Film*, ed. Barry Keith Grant (Austin: University of Texas Press, 1996), 143–63 for another work that focuses on the child at the expense of the teen murderer in slasher films, in order to understand the relationship between a rejected or threatened patriarchy and the children it takes as its victims or imagines as its monster. See also William Paul's reading of the child monster in *Laughing Screaming: Modern Hollywood Horror & Comedy* (New York: Columbia University Press, 1994).
11. Williams, *Hearths*, 20. In the case of *The Hills Have Eyes*, David Rodowick also pursues Wood's focus on the family unit, arguing that the mirroring of the two families and the increasing violence exhibited by the Carter family against their monstrous counterparts blurs the "comfortable distance" between the two and indicates the violence already inherent within the bourgeois family unit. David Rodowick, "The Enemy Within: The Economy of Violence in *The Hills Have Eyes*," in Grant and Sharrett, *Planks of Reason*, 348.
12. Dika, *Games*, 17.

13. Steve Neale, "*Halloween*: Suspense, Aggression, and the Look," in Grant and Sharrett, *Planks of Reason*, 368. With her focus Freud's "primal scene," Dika is providing a model for the voyeurism and self-reflexivity noted by early commentators on the film, such as J. P. Telotte, and returning to the scene suggested by Steve Neale. In "Faith and Idolatry in the Horror Film" (in Grant and Sharrett, *Planks of Reason*), Telotte emphasizes the self-reflexivity of Carpenter's *Halloween* wherein the audience "is forced for a time to identify itself with a killer through the subjective opening sequence" and, thereby, must consider how we view horrors and how vision can fail (25). He extends this discussion in "Through a Pumpkin's Eye: The Reflexive Nature of Horror" in *American Horrors: Essays on the Modern American Horror Film*, ed. Gregory A. Waller (Urbana: University of Illinois Press, 1987), 114–28, to include specifically the acts of voyeurism and narcissism and the tools that the director uses to capture them.
14. I will be citing the original article as it was reprinted in Barry Keith Grant's *Dread of Difference* rather than the chapter in *Men, Women, and Chainsaws* because of its greater length and detail.
15. Carol Clover, "Her Body, Himself: Gender in the Slasher Film," in *The Dread of Difference: Gender and the Horror Film*, ed. Barry Keith Grant (Austin: University of Texas Press, 1996), 106.
16. Ibid., 86.
17. Ibid., 89.
18. Ibid., 98.
19. While she uses examples of beating fantasies in Victorian flagellation literature rather than Freud's male examples in "A Child Is Being Beaten" who imagine a mother figure beating, her example from Steven Marcus' work raises a similar unruly female presence when he describes one gentleman being whipped by prostitutes (97). Clover summarizes this other possibility with an intriguing question: "If her masculine features qualify her as a transformed boy, do not the feminine features of the killer qualify him as a transformed woman (in which case the homoerotic reading can be maintained only by defining that 'woman' as phallic and transforming her into a male)?" (99). Or, one might add, it simply transforms her into the phallic mother.
20. The close connection between the feminine or marginalized monster and the female protagonist and spectator has been theorized by Linda Williams in "When the Woman Looks," *Dread of Difference: Gender and the Horror Film*, ed. Barry Keith Grant (Austin: University of Texas Press, 1996) 15–34, and Barbara Creed in *The Monstrous-Feminine: Film, Feminism, Psychoanalysis* (London: Routledge, 1993). As Williams proposes in her article, the relationship between the killer and the female victim/viewer is marked by resemblance and possibility (31) and she suggests there is power in their shared difference and in their ability to "mutilate and transform the vulnerable male" (23).
21. Clover, "Her Body," 94.
22. Ibid., 95, 106.
23. Ibid., 75.
24. Ibid., 95.
25. Christopher Sharrett, "The Idea of Apocalypse in *The Texas Chainsaw Massacre*," in Grant and Sharrett, *Planks of Reason*, 307.

26. Sharrett questions the designation of Hooper's *The Texas Chain Saw Massacre* as a "forerunner" of the slasher films because "its scope is far broader, more significant, and distant from the formulas of the slasher cycle" ("Idea of Apocalypse," 301). While I agree that the film is *more* than a slasher film, I believe Clover makes a compelling case for its inclusion of many slasher elements, and one must admit its clear influence on the American horror films that followed it, especially Wes Craven's work in *The Hills Have Eyes* and Carpenter's *Halloween*, which perhaps announces the slasher cycle's ascendancy most clearly.
27. Williams, *Hearths*, 192.
28. Ibid., 190.
29. Sharrett, "Idea of Apocalypse," 313, 314.
30. Ibid., 315.
31. Matt Becker, "A Point of Little Hope: Hippie Horror Films and the Politics of Ambivalence," *Velvet Light Trap* 57 (Spring 2006): 52.
32. Ibid., 53.
33. Ibid., 58.
34. Wood, "Introduction," 132.
35. Wood characterizes the opening monument work of art as a "parody of domesticity," and certainly the same could be said of the dinner scene (ibid., 132). This parody creates for Wood a "sense of grotesque comedy" and a fundamental absurdity to the film that does not make it any less horrific or insightful: "The family, after all, only carries to its logical conclusion the basic (though unstated) tenet of capitalism, that people have the right to live off other people."
36. Clover, "Her Body," 94.
37. Juliet Mitchell, *Mad Men and Medusa: Reclaiming Hysteria* (New York: Basic Books, 2000), 32.
38. Ibid., 20 (original emphasis), 23. Interestingly, though, while feelings for "siblings and peers cast their shadow over relations with parents," they are neglected by psychoanalytic theory, according to Mitchell. In her inversion of the typical psychoanalytic ordering for the development of the subject, placing the Oedipus complex in the shadow of sibling ambivalence, she hopes to understand more fully the roots of hysteria but also to open up the understanding of affine relationships (77).
39. Ibid., 29.
40. Ibid., 26.
41. Mitchell, *Siblings*, 28, 29.
42. Ibid., 12.
43. Mitchell, *Mad Men*, 29.
44. Qtd in Clover, "Her Body," 94.
45. Telotte, "Through a Pumpkin's Eye," 116.
46. Ibid., 117.
47. William Paul, *Laughing Screaming: Modern Hollywood Horror and Comedy* (New York: Columbia University Press, 1994), 322, 323.
48. Juliet Mitchell proposes a different understanding of sex in the sibling situation that interweaves sex and death: "The narcissistic love of the-other-as-the-self

explodes into murderousness once it is realized that there cannot be another self, but once the murder is resisted the love comes back in a different form" (*Siblings*, 29–30); she offers "sibling sex," in her terms, as love of the same intertwined with murderousness and death, not sexual difference and reproductive life.

49 Of course, the viewer has already been given a privileged view of Michael in a soon-to-be formulaic reverse shot with him looming in the foreground of a frame in which Laurie and Tommy, outside, do not see him inside the Myers house, but we see his lurking presence blurred in the right side of the frame and hear his menacing breathing.

50 In fact, this sense of Laurie's imagination or psyche playing tricks on her becomes a trope in the much later films in the series in which Laurie Strode returns, *Halloween H2O: 20 Years Later* (Miner, 1998) and *Halloween Resurrection* (Rosenthal, 2002). For example, in *H2O* Laurie has visions of Michael that disappear after she closes her eyes and wishes him away, except, of course, once their battle begins.

51 Mitchell, *Siblings*, 29.

52 Ibid., 28.

53 Ibid., 29.

54 This model of subjectivity, Mitchell recognizes, has obvious parallels to Lacan's account of the "mirror stage," in which the subject's 'real' self is forever lost through the mediation of the "I" in the mirror, but her model suggests the sibling as that mirror (*Mad Men*, 106). Mitchell describes this experience of the child looking in the mirror and seeing itself "as unified," as a joyful experience, but Lacan is quite careful to also assign murderous aggression to the child as well, hating and wanting to annihilate the me-more-than-me, which fits Mitchell's analysis of the sibling conflict even better.

55 Mitchell, *Siblings*, 29.

56 Paul Wells, *The Horror Genre: From Beezlebub to Blair Witch* (London: Wallflower, 2000), 8.

57 Ibid., 14.

58 S. S. Prawer, *Caligari's Children: The Film as Tale of Terror* (New York: De Capo, 1980), 117.

59 Sigmund Freud, "The Uncanny," in *The Standard Edition of the Complete Psychological Works of Sigmund Freud*, ed. and trans. James Strachey, 24 vols (London: Hogarth, 1955–74), 17:234.

60 Ibid., 235, 241.

61 Ibid., 220.

62 Clover, "Her Body," 100.

63 Ibid., 89.

64 Brigid Cherry, "Refusing to Refuse to Look: Female Viewers of the Horror Film," in *Horror, The Film Reader*, ed. Mark Jankovich (London: Routledge, 2002), 170. Perhaps Sarah Trencansky puts it best when she recognizes, through Isabel Cristina Pinedo's work, that "the statistical proportion of female to male viewers is largely contested," yet these arguments do not deny "that female viewership of slashers exists." Sarah Trekansky, "Final Girls and Terrible Youth: Transgression in 1980s Slasher Horror," *Journal of Popular Film*

and Television 29, no. 2 (2001): 64. Similarly, Valerie Wee's look at the Scream franchise offers an integral connection between the teen audience and slasher films, recognized by Dimension head Bob Weinstein as lucrative, and a suggestion that Wes Craven and screenwriter Kevin Williamson intended to attract more female audience members. Valerie Wee, "Resurrecting and Updating the Teen Slasher: The Case of Scream," Journal of Popular Film and Television 34, no. 2 (Summer 2006): 54.

65. Ibid. A significant claim made by these female fans in defense of the slasher films—that there are as many female victims as male victims—has been proven by another series of content analysis studies by Sapolsky et al., who find "no significant difference in the number of male and female victims." Barry Sapolsky, Fred Molitor, and Sarah Luque, "Sex and Violence in Slasher Films: Re-examining the Assumptions," Journalism and Mass Communication Quarterly 80, no. 1 (Spring 2003): 29.

66. Wells, Horror Genre, 29.

67. Wood, "Introduction," 133. In his audience study, Paul Wells attributes this unruly behavior to horror audiences of all ages: "All the groups demonstrated a high degree of inter-activity with the films they watched; either verbally, physically, discursively, or extratextually in their later behavior" (Horror Genre, 32).

68. Michael's body count, on the other hand, is more equitable. Counting Judith, he kills two men and two women over the course of the film: Bob, the Phelps garage man, Judith and Linda. We discover at the opening of Halloween II that Laurie *and* Annie have survived the night.

69. Vivian Sobchack, "Bringing It All Back Home: Family Economy and Generic Exchange," in The Dread of Difference: Gender and the Horror Film, ed. Barry Keith Grant (Austin: University of Texas Press, 1996), 150.

70. Ibid., 151.

71. Ibid., 150.

72. Ibid., 151.

73. While I agree with Andrew Tudor's claims that the subjective camera does not "necessarily place the viewer in a position of vicarious participation in Michael's stalking activities" because to insist on that identification "grossly underestimates the complexity of the movie spectator's relation to the optical point of view," I am not so sure that the "principle victims" in Halloween are depicted so "positively" as he suggests. Andrew Tudor, Monsters and Mad Scientists: A Cultural History of the Horror Movie (Oxford: Basil Blackwell, 1989), 201, 202. As I have tried to show, the victims are Laurie's close friends, but they are also taunting adversaries at moments, much like siblings who elicit both love and hate. Moreover, while the spectator does not *necessarily* have to identify with the subjective camera, such identification remains a possibility, just not an inevitability, and might still represent a significant pleasure offered by the films.

74. Although I am suggesting fluidity in gender positions for the adolescent spectator here, I must admit that the films are not so flexible or open on the question of racial difference within the adolescent peer group. In fact, the whiteness of Michael's mask indicates a kind of anxious hyper-whiteness that

attempts to deny racial difference but becomes a parody of that exclusionary practice. These horror films offer a notoriously whitewashed world where the lack of racial diversity indicates a deeper anxiety about the empowerment or visibility of racial minorities in this time period than about the growing empowerment of young women.

[75] Sam Raimi's *The Evil Dead* (1981) offers an interesting inversion of this male-killer-brother and female-survivor-sister trope, wherein Ash is tormented by his possessed sister, Cheryl, throughout the film; she is the first to be possessed and the last to die. Although not technically a slasher film, *Evil Dead* presents a group of youths secluded at a cabin in the woods where they are assaulted by demons from the "Book of the Dead" who possess first Cheryl and then each of Ash's friends. In the end, he must battle both his possessed best friend, Scotty, and his sister, who refuses to die. Ash appears to be triumphant after he burns the Book of the Dead, representing a rare Final Boy, but the final tracking shot of the film indicates he might "join" his sister and friends after all.

[76] Mitchell, *Siblings*, 30.

[77] Bruce J. Schulman, *The Seventies: The Great Shift in American Culture, Society, and Politics* (Cambridge, MA: Da Capo Press, 2001), 81.

[78] Ibid., 83.

Epilogue

[1] Elayne Rapping, "Hollywood's Youth Cult Films," *Cineaste* 16, no.1–2 (1987):15.

[2] Ibid, 15, 16.

[3] Ibid.

[4] See my discussion of *The Great Santini* and *Ordinary People* in Chapter 1 for Wood's argument about the Reagan-era return to conservative, patriarchal values in film. Doherty argues for a "return of the patriarch" at the time without referring to Reagan by name. *Teenagers and Teenpics* (Philadelphia: Temple University Press, 2002), 209.

[5] Rapping, "Youth Cult Films," 16.

[6] Jon Lewis singles out the scene as exceptional for the rare sharing of a female teen's point of view and for its lack of romance: "it's anti-climactic, ironic, embarrassing." *Road to Romance and Ruin* (London: Routledge, 1992), 73.

[7] Timothy Shary, *Generation Multiplex: The Image of Youth in Contemporary American Cinema* (Austin: University of Texas Press, 2002), 246.

[8] Christina Lee, *Screening Generation X: The Politics and Popular Memory of Youth in Contemporary Cinema* (Farnham: Ashgate, 2010), 9.

[9] Shary, *Generation Multiplex*, 110.

[10] Ibid., 122.

Bibliography

Abate, Michelle A. *Tomboys: A Literary and Cultural History*. Philadelphia: Temple University Press, 2008.
Acland, Charles. *Youth, Murder, Spectacle: The Cultural Politics of "Youth in Crisis."* Boulder, CO: Westview Press, 1995.
Adams, Mary Louise. *The Trouble with Normal: Postwar Youth and the Making of Heterosexuality*. Toronto: University of Toronto Press, 1997.
Altman, Rick. *The American Film Musical*. Bloomington: Indiana University Press, 1987.
"Ambitions of a Foster Child." *Films Illustrated* 6 (May 1977): 352–3.
An American Family. PBS. Produced by Craig Gilbert. January–March, 1973.
Artt, Sarah. "Reflections on the Self-Reflexive Musical: *The Rocky Horror Picture Show* and the Classic Hollywood Musical." In *Reading Rocky Horror:* The Rocky Horror Picture Show *and Popular Culture*, edited by Jeffrey Weinstock, 51–68. New York: Palgrave Macmillan, 2008.
Bailey, Beth and David Farber. "Introduction." In *America in the Seventies*, edited by Beth Bailey and David Farber, 1–8. Lawrence: University Press of Kansas, 2004.
Becker, Matt. "A Point of Little Hope: Hippie Horror Films and the Politics of Ambivalence." *Velvet Light Trap* 57 (Spring 2006): 42–59.
Bell, Elizabeth, Lynda Haas, and Laura Sells. "Introduction: Walt's in the Movies." In *From Mouse to Mermaid: The Politics of Film, Gender, and Culture*, edited by Elizabeth Bell, Lynda Haas, and Laura Sells, 1–17. Bloomington: Indiana University Press, 1995.
Benshoff, Harry M. *Monsters in the Closet: Homosexuality and the Horror Film*. Manchester: Manchester University Press, 1997.
— "Queers and Families in Film." In *A Family Affair: Cinema Calls Home*, edited by Murray Pomerance, 223–33. London: Wallflower Press, 2008.
Berenstein, Rhona J. "Spectatorship-as-Drag: The Act of Viewing and Classic Horror Cinema." In *Viewing Positions: Ways of Seeing Film*, edited and introduction by Linda Williams, 231–69. New Brunswick, NJ: Rutgers University Press, 1995.
Berkowitz, Edward D. *Something Happened: A Political and Cultural Overview of the Seventies*. New York: Columbia University Press, 2006.
Bernardoni, James. *The New Hollywood: What the Movies Did with the New Freedoms of the Seventies*. Jefferson, NC: McFarland, 1991.
Betrock, Alan. *The I Was a Teenage Juvenile Delinquent Rock 'n' Roll Horror Beach Party Movie Book: A Complete Guide to the Teen Exploitation Film, 1954–69*. New York: St. Martin's Press, 1986.

Biskind, Peter. *Seeing Is Believing: How Hollywood Taught Us to Stop Worrying and Love the Fifties.* New York: Holt, 1983.
Bourscheidt, Randi. "One to One with Robbie Benson." *Interview* 7 (September 1977): 32–3.
Boym, Svetlana. *The Future of Nostalgia.* New York: Basic Books, 2001.
Brown, Terry. "The Butch Femme Fatale." In *The Lesbian Postmodern,* edited by Laura Doan, 229–43. New York: Columbia University Press, 1994.
Bruhm, Steven and Natasha Hurley. "Curiouser: On the Queerness of Children." In *Curiouser: On the Queerness of Children,* edited by Steven Bruhm and Natasha Hurley, ix–xxxviii. Minneapolis: University of Minnesota Press, 2004.
Campbell, Neil. "The Highway Kind: *Badlands,* Youth, Space and the Road." In *The Cinema of Terrence Malick: Poetic Visions of America,* edited by Hannah Patterson, 37–49. London: Wallflower Press, 2003.
Canby, Vincent. "Another Country." Review of *Carny,* directed by Robert Kaylor. *New York Times* (June 13, 1980): C8:1.
— "Disturbing 'Taxi Driver'." Review of *Taxi Driver,* directed by Martin Scorsese. *New York Times* (February 15, 1976): Sect. II 1:5.
— "The Movie that Made the Festival Memorable." Review of *Badlands,* directed by Terence Malick. *New York Times* (October 21, 1973): 149.
Carroll, Peter. *It Seemed Like Nothing Happened: America in the 1970s.* New Brunswick: Rutgers University Press, 1990.
Chandler, Barbara A. "The White House Conference on Children: A 1970 Happening." *The Family Coordinator* 20, no. 3 (July 1971): 195–207.
Charters, W. W. *Motion Pictures and Youth: A Summary.* New York: Macmillan, 1933.
Cherry, Brigid. "Refusing to Refuse to Look: Female Viewers of the Horror Film." In *Horror, The Film Reader,* edited by Mark Jankovich, 169–78. London: Routledge, 2002.
Clarke, Randall. *At a Theater or Drive-In Near You: The History, Culture, and Politics of the American Exploitation Film.* New York: Garland Press, 1995.
Clément, Catherine. *The Lives and Legends of Jacques Lacan.* Translated by Arthur Goldhammer. New York: Columbia University Press, 1983.
Clover, Carol. "Her Body, Himself: Gender in the Slasher Film." In *The Dread of Difference: Gender and the Horror Film,* edited by Barry Keith Grant, 66–113. Austin: University of Texas Press, 1996.
— *Men, Women, and Chainsaws: Gender in the Modern Horror Film.* Princeton, NJ: Princeton University Press, 1992.
Cocks, Jay. "Summer Clearance." Review of *Ode to Billy Joe,* directed by Max Baer. *Time* (September 20, 1976), 108: 80.
Considine, David. *The Cinema of Adolescence.* Jefferson, NC: McFarland, 1985.
Cook, David A. *A History of Narrative Film.* 4th edn New York: Norton, 2004.
— *Lost Illusions: American Cinema in the Shadow of Watergate and Vietnam, 1970–79.* Vol. 9, History of the American Cinema. New York: Charles Scribner's Sons, 2000.
Cook, Pam. "Exploitation Films and Feminism." *Screen* 17, no. 2 (Summer 1976): 122–7.
Corrigan, Timothy. "Film and the Culture of the Cult." In *The Cult Film Experience: Beyond All Reason,* edited by J. P. Telotte, 26–37. Austin: University of Texas Press, 1991.

Creed, Barbara. *The Monstrous-Feminine: Film, Feminism, Psychoanalysis*. London: Routledge, 1993.
Cuomo, Chris. "Spinsters in Sensible Shoes: *Mary Poppins* and *Bedknobs and Broomsticks*." In *From Mouse to Mermaid: The Politics of Film, Gender, and Culture*, edited by Elizabeth Bell, Lynda Haas, and Laura Sells, 212–23. Bloomington: Indiana University Press, 1995.
Danks, Adrian. "Death Comes as an End: Temporality, Domesticity and Photography in Terrence Malick's *Badlands*." *Senses of Cinema*, www.sensesofcinema.com/contents/00/8/badlands.html (originally published in *Metro* (1998) nos. 113–14).
De Angelis, Michael. *Gay Fandom and Crossover Stardom: James Dean, Mel Gibson, and Keanu Reeves*. Durham: Duke University Press, 2001.
de Lauretis, Teresa. *The Practice of Love: Lesbian Sexuality and Perverse Desire*. Bloomington: Indiana University Press, 1994.
— *Technologies of Gender: Essays on Theory, Film, and Fiction*. Bloomington: Indiana University Press, 1987.
Dennis, Jeffrey P. *Queering Teen Culture: All-American Boys and Same-Sex Desire in Film and Television*. New York: Harrington Park Press, 2006.
Dentith, Simon. *Parody*. London: Routledge, 2000.
Dika, Vera. *Games of Terror:* Halloween, Friday the 13th, *and the Films of the Stalker Cycle*. Rutherford, NJ: Farleigh Dickinson University Press, 1990.
— *Recycled Culture in Contemporary Art and Film: The Uses of Nostalgia*. Cambridge: Cambridge University Press, 2003.
Doane, Janice and Devon Hedges. *Nostalgia and Sexual Difference: The Resistance to Contemporary Feminism*. New York: Metheun, 1987.
Doane, Mary Ann. *The Desire to Desire: The Woman's Film of the 1940s*. Bloomington: Indiana University Press, 1987.
Doherty, Thomas. *Teenagers and Teenpics: The Juvenilization of American Movies in the 1950s*. Revised and expanded edition. Philadelphia: Temple University Press, 2002.
Donald, James, ed. *Fantasy and the Cinema*. London: BFI Publishing, 1989.
Douglas, Susan. *Where the Boys Are: Growing Up Female With the Mass Media*. New York: Random House, 1994.
Drexler, Rosalyn. "*Jeremy*—A Big 'Little Movie." Review of *Jeremy*, directed by Arthur Barron. *New York Times* (August 12, 1973): Sec II. 1:2.
Ebert, Roger. Review of *Ode to Billy Joe*, directed by Max Baer. *Chicago Sun Times* (July 7, 1976). Available online at: http://rogerebert.suntimes.com/apps/pbcs.dll/article?AID=/19760707/REVIEWS/607070301/1023 6 August 2009.
Edelman, Lee. "The Future Is Kid Stuff: Queer Theory, Disidentification, and the Death Drive." *Narrative* 6, no. 1 (January 1998): 18–30.
Eder, Richard. Review of *Ode to Billy Joe*, directed by Max Baer. *New York Times* (August 19, 1976): 48:1.
— "A Little Anticipation Goes a Long Way." Review of *Ode to Billy Joe*, directed by Max Baer. *New York Times* (August 19, 1976): Sec. II. 11:1.
Ehrenreich, Barbara, Elizabeth Hess, and Gloria Jacobs. "Beatlemania: Girls Just Want to Have Fun." In *The Adoring Audience*, edited by Lisa Lewis, 84–106. London: Routledge, 1992.

Farber, David. "The Torch Had Fallen." In *America in the Seventies*, edited by Beth Bailey and David Farber, 9–28. Lawrence: University Press of Kansas, 2004.

Farmer, Brett. *Spectacular Passions: Cinema, Fantasy, Gay Male Spectatorships*. Durham: Duke University Press, 2000.

Forman, Henry James. *Our Movie Made Children*. Introduction by Dr. W. W. Charters. New York: Macmillan, 1934.

Foster, Jodie. "A Look Back with Jodie Foster." *Freaky Friday*. DVD. Directed by Gary Nelson. Burbank, CA: Walt Disney Video, 2004.

Foucault, Michel. *The History of Sexuality: Volume I: An Introduction*. New York: Vintage, 1990.

Freud, Anna. "Beating Fantasies and Daydreams." *The Writings of Anna Freud*. Vol. I, 142–56. New York: International Universities Press, 1974.

Freud, Sigmund. *The Standard Edition of the Complete Psychological Works of Sigmund Freud*. Edited and translated by James Strachey. 23 vols London: Hogarth Press, 1974.

— *Three Essays on the Theory of Sexuality*. Translated and revised by James Strachey. New York: Basic Books, 1975.

Frith, Simon. *Sound Effects: Youth, Leisure, and the Politics of Rock 'n' Roll*. New York: Pantheon Books, 1981.

Frum, David. *How We Got Here, The 70's: The Decade that Brought You Modern Life (For Better or Worse)*. New York: Basic Books, 2000.

Gateward, Frances. "In Love and Trouble: Teenage Boys and Interracial Romance." In *Where the Boys Are: Cinemas of Masculinity and Youth*, edited by Murray Pomerance and Frances Gateward, 157–82. Detroit: Wayne State University Press, 2005.

Gehring, Wes D. "Parody." In *Handbook of American Film Genres*, edited by Wes. D. Gehring, 145–65. New York: Greenwood Press, 1988.

Gilbert, James. *A Cycle of Outrage: America's Reaction to the Juvenile Delinquent in the 1950s*. Oxford: Oxford University Press, 1986.

Giroux, Henry A. *The Mouse that Roared: Disney and the End of Innocence*. Lanham, MD: Rowan & Littlefield, 1999.

Golding, Sue. "James Dean: The Almost-Perfect Lesbian Hermaphrodite." In *Stolen Glances: Lesbians Take Photographs*, edited by Tessa Boffin and Jean Fraser, 197–202. London: Pandora, 1991.

Goodman, Paul. *Growing Up Absurd: Problems of Youth in the Organized System*. New York: Random House, 1960.

Graebner, William. "America's *Poseidon Adventure*: A Nation in Existential Despair." In *America in the Seventies*, edited by Beth Bailey and David Farber, 157–80. Lawrence: University Press of Kansas, 2004.

Grant, Barry Keith. "Science Fiction Double Feature: Ideology in the Cult Film." In *The Cult Film Experience: Beyond All Reason*, edited by J. P. Telotte, 122–37. Austin: University of Texas Press, 1991.

Greenspun, Roger. Review of *Jeremy*, directed by Arthur Barron. *New York Times* (August 2, 1973) 28:1.

Griffin, Sean. *Tinker Belles and Evil Queens: The Walt Disney Company from the Inside Out*. New York: NYU Press, 2000.

Halberstam, Judith. *Female Masculinity*. Durham: Duke University Press, 1998.

— "Oh Bondage Up Yours! Female Masculinity and the Tomboy." In *Curiouser: On the Queerness of Children*, edited by Steven Bruhm and Natasha Hurley, 191–214. Minneapolis: University of Minnesota Press, 2004.
Hansen, Miriam. "Adventures of Goldilocks: Spectatorship, Consumerism, and Public Life." *Camera Obscura* 22 (January 1990): 51–71.
— *Babel & Babylon: Spectatorship in American Silent Film*. Cambridge: Harvard University Press, 1991.
— "Pleasure, Ambivalence, Identification: Valentino and Female Spectatorship." In *Stardom: Industry of Desire*, edited by Christine Gledhill, 259–82. London: BFI, 1991.
Hart, Lynda. *Fatal Women: Lesbian Sexuality and the Mark of Aggression*. Princeton: Princeton University Press, 1994.
Hay, James. "'You're Tearing Me Apart!': The Primal Scene of Teen Films." Review of *Teenagers and Teenpics: The Juvenilization of American Movies in the 1950s*, by Thomas Doherty. *Cultural Studies* 4, no. 3 (Oct. 1990): 331–8.
Henderson, Brian. "Exploring Badlands." *Wide Angle* 5, no. 4 (1983): 38–51.
Hentges, Sarah. *Pictures of Girlhood: Modern Female Adolescence on Film*. Jefferson, NC: McFarland, 2006.
Higson, Andrew. "Re-presenting the National Past: Nostalgia and Pastiche in the Heritage Film." In *Fires Were Started: British Cinema and Thatcherism*, edited by Lester Friedman, 109–29. Minneapolis: University of Minnesota Press, 1993.
Hine, Thomas. *The Rise and Fall of the American Teenager*. New York: Perennial, 2000.
Hoberman, J. and Jonathan Rosenbaum. *Midnight Movies*. New York: De Capo Press, 1983.
Holmund, Chris. "Cruisin' for a Bruisin': Hollywood's Deadly (Lesbian) Dolls." *Cinema Journal* 34, no. 1 (1994): 31–51.
— "Tots to Tanks: Walt Disney Presents Feminism for the Family." *Social Text* 2 (Summer 1979): 122–32.
Hutcheon, Linda. *A Theory of Parody*. New York: Methuen, 1985.
Jameson, Frederic. *Postmodernism, or The Cultural Logic of Late Capitalism*. Durham, NC: Duke University Press, 1991.
— "Postmodernism and Consumer Culture." In *The Anti-Aesthetic: Essays on Postmodern Culture*, edited and introduction by Hal Foster, 127–44. New York: New Press, 1998.
Jeffords, Susan. "Can Masculinity Be Terminated?" In *Screening the Male: Exploring Masculinities in Hollywood Cinema*, edited by Steven Cohan and Ina Rae Hark, 245–62. London: Routledge, 1993.
— *Hard Bodies: Hollywood Masculinity in the Reagan Era*. New Brunswick: Rutgers University Press, 1993.
Jouve, Nicole Ward. *Female Genesis: Creativity, Self and Gender*. New York: St. Martin's, 1998.
Kael, Pauline. "Sugarland and Badlands" [March 18, 1974]. In *Reeling*, 300–6. Boston: Little Brown, 1976.
Kaveney, Roz. *Teen Dreams: Reading Teen Film and Television from Heathers and Veronica Mars*. New York: I.B. Taurus, 2006.

Killen, Andreas. *1973 Nervous Breakdown: Watergate, Warhol, and the Birth of Post-Sixties America*. New York: Bloomsbury, 2006.

Kincaid, James. *Child-Loving: The Erotic Child and Victorian Culture*. New York: Routledge, 1992.

Kinder, Marsha. "The Return of the Outlaw Couple." *Film Quarterly* 27, no. 4 (Summer 1974): 2–10.

— *Erotic Innocence: The Culture of Child Molesting*. Durham, NC: Duke University Press, 1998.

Klein, Melanie. *The Psycho-Analysis of Children*. Translated by Alix Strachey and revised by H. A. Thorner. New York: Delacorte Press, 1975.

Kolker, Robert P. *A Cinema of Loneliness: Penn, Kubrick, Coppola, Scorsese, Altman*. New York: Oxford University Press, 1980.

Kozloff, Sarah. *Invisible Storytellers: Voice-Over Narration in American Fiction Film*. Berkeley: University of California Press, 1988.

Lacan, Jacques. "Articles from *Le Minotaure*." Translated and introduced by Jon Anderson. *Critical Texts: A Review of Theory and Criticism* 5, no. 3 (1988): 1–11.

— *Ecrits: A Selection*. Translated by Alan Sheridan. New York: Norton, 1977.

Lane, Christina. "The Liminal Iconography of Jodie Foster." *Journal of Popular Film and Television* 22, no. 4 (Winter 1995): 149–53.

Laplanche, J. and J.-B. Pontalis. "Fantasy and the Origins of Sexuality." In *Formations of Fantasy*, edited by Victor Burgin, James Donald, and Cora Kaplan, 5–34. London: Methuen, 1986.

— *The Language of Psychoanalysis*. Translated by Donald Nicholson Smith. London: Karnac Books, 1988.

Lebeau, Vicky. *Childhood and Cinema*. London: Reaktion Books, 2008.

— *Lost Angels: Psychoanalysis and Cinema*. London: Routledge, 1995.

Lee, Christina. *Screening Generation X: The Politics and Popular Memory of Youth in Contemporary Cinema*. Farnham: Ashgate, 2010.

Lev, Peter. *American Films of the 1970s: Conflicting Visions*. Austin: University of Texas Press, 2000.

Lewis, Jon. *The Road to Romance and Ruin: Teen Films and Youth Culture*. New York: Routledge, 1992.

Lindsey, Shelley Stamp. "Horror, Femininity, and Carrie's Monstrous Puberty." In *The Dread of Difference: Gender and the Horror Film*, edited by Barry Keith Grant, 279–95. Austin: University of Texas Press, 1996.

Lipsitz, George. "Genre Anxiety and Racial Representation." In *Refiguring American Film Genres: History and Theory*, edited by Nick Browne, 208–32. Berkeley: University of California Press, 1998.

Lyon, Elisabeth. "The Cinema of Lol V. Stein." In *Fantasy and the Cinema*, edited by James Donald, 147–73. London: BFI Publishing, 1989.

Machann, Ginny Brown. "*Ceremony at Lone Tree* and *Badlands*: The Starkweather Case and the Nebraska Plains." *Prairie Schooner* 53 (1979): 165–72.

Maslin, Janet. Review of *Ice Castles*, directed by Donald Wrye. *New York Times* (February 23, 1979), C7:1.

— "Some Teenagers." Review of *Foxes*, directed by Adrian Lyne. *New York Times* (February 29, 1980), C15:1.

— "Switcheroo." Review of *Freaky Friday*, directed by Gary Nelson. *Newsweek* 89 (February, 28 1977): 72.
Matheson, Sue. "'Drinking Those Moments When': The Use (and Abuse) of Late-Night Double Feature Science Fiction and Hollywood Icons in *The Rocky Horror Picture Show*." In *Reading Rocky Horror:* The Rocky Horror Picture Show and Popular Culture, edited by Jeffrey Weinstock, 17–34. New York: Palgrave Macmillan, 2008.
Mayne, Judith. *The Woman at the Keyhole: Feminism and Women's Cinema.* Bloomington: Indiana University Press, 1990.
McBride, J. "Freaky Friday." Review of *Freaky Friday*, directed by Gary Nelson. *Variety* 285 (December 22, 1976): 22.
McGee, Mark Thomas. *Faster and Furiouser: The Revised and Fattened Fable of American International Pictures.* Jefferson, NC: McFarland, 1996.
— *The Rock and Roll Movie Encyclopedia of the 1950s.* Jefferson, NC: McFarland, 1990.
McGee, Mark Thomas and R. J. Robertson. *The J.D. Films: Juvenile Delinquency in the Movies.* Jefferson, NC: McFarland, 1982.
McGettigan, Joan. "Interpreting a Man's World: Female Voices in *Badlands* and *Days of Heaven*." *Journal of Film and Video* 52, no. 4 (Winter 2001): 33–43.
McRobbie, Angela. *Feminism and Youth Culture: From* Jackie *to* Just Seventeen. Boston: Unwin Hyman, 1991.
McRobbie, Angela and Jenny Garber. "Girls and Subcultures: An exploration." In *Resistance Through Rituals: Youth Subcultures in Post-war Britain*, edited by Stuart Hall and Tony Jefferson, 209–29. London: Routledge, 2000.
"Meet Jodi Foster." *Tiger Beat* 10, no. 12 (September 1974): 73.
"Meet Robby Benson!!!" *Tiger Beat* 11, no. 7 (April 1975): 18.
Mellen, Joan. *Big Bad Wolves: Masculinity in the American Film.* New York: Pantheon Books, 1977.
Metz, Christian. *The Imaginary Signifier: Psychoanalysis and the Cinema.* Translated by Celia Britton, Annwyl Williams, Ben Brewster, and Alfred Guzzetti. Bloomington: Indiana University Press, 1982.
— *Language and Cinema.* Translated by Donna Jean Umiker-Sebeok. The Hague: Mouton, 1974.
Miller, Edwin. "Here Comes Jodie Foster!" *Seventeen Magazine* 36 (January 1977): 64–6.
Mitchell, Juliet. *Mad Men and Medusa: Reclaiming Hysteria.* New York: Basic Books, 2000.
— *Siblings: Sex and Violence.* Cambridge: Polity Press, 2003.
Morrison, James and Thomas Schur. *The Films of Terrence Malick.* Westport, CT: Praeger, 2003.
Mottram, Ron. "All Things Shining: The Struggle for Wholeness, Redemption and Transcendence in the Films of Terrence Malick." In *The Cinema of Terrence Malick: Poetic Visions of America*, edited by Hannah Patterson, 13–23. London: Wallflower Press, 2003.
Mulvey, Laura. *Visual and Other Pleasures.* Bloomington: Indiana University Press, 1989.

Murphy, A. Review of *Ode to Billy Joe*, directed by Max Baer. *Variety* 283 (June 9, 1976): 23.

Nash, Ilana. *American Sweethearts: Teenage Girls in Twentieth-Century Popular Culture.* Bloomington: Indiana University Press, 2006.

Neale, Steve. "*Halloween*: Suspense, Aggression, and the Look." In *Planks of Reason: Essays on the Horror Film.* Revised edition. Edited by Barry Keith Grant and Christopher Sharrett, 356–69. Lanham, MD: Scarecrow Press, 2004.

— "Teenpics." *The Cinema Book.* 2nd ed. Edited by Pam Cook and Mieke Bernik, 218–20. London: BFI, 1999.

Neale, Steve and Frank Krutnik. *Popular Film and Television Comedy.* London: Routledge, 1990.

Owens, Jr., Robert E. *Queer Kids: The Challenges and Promise for Lesbian, Gay, and Bisexual Youth.* New York: Hayworth, 1998.

Packard, Vance. *The Sexual Wilderness: The Contemporary Upheaval in Male-Female Relationships.* New York: Pocket Books, 1970.

Palladino, Grace. *Teenagers: An American History.* New York: Basic Books, 1996.

Paul, William. *Laughing Screaming: Modern Hollywood Horror and Comedy.* New York: Columbia University Press, 1994.

Person, Ethel. *By Force of Fantasy: How We Make Our Lives.* New York: Basic Books, 1995.

Pierce, Wellington G. *Youth Comes of Age.* New York: McGraw Hill, 1948.

Polan, Dana. "*Bad News Bears*: Sour American Dream." *Jump Cut* 15 (1977): 9–10.

Powdermaker, Hortense. *Hollywood, The Dream Factory: An Anthropologist Looks at the Movie-Makers.* Boston: Little Brown, 1950.

Powrie, Phil. *French Cinema in the 1980s: Nostalgia and the Crisis of Masculinity.* Oxford: Clarendon, 1997.

Prawer, S. S. *Caligari's Children: The Film as Tale of Terror.* New York: De Capo, 1980.

Rapping, Elayne. "Hollywood's Youth Cult Films." *Cineaste* 16, no. 1–2 (1987): 14–19.

Rathgeb, Douglas L. "Bogeyman from the Id: Nightmare and Reality in *Halloween* and *A Nightmare on Elm Street*." *Journal of Popular Film and Video* 19, no. 1 (March 1991): 36–43.

Reisfeld, Randi and Danny Fields. *Who's Your Fave Rave?* New York: Berkley Trade, 1997.

Rich, B. Ruby. "Jodie Foster: Growing Up On-Screen." *Walker Arts Center.* January 1991. http://filmvideo.walkerart.org/detail.wac?id=3284&title=Articles.

— "Nobody's Handmaid." *Sight and Sound* (December 1991): 6–10.

Rodowick, David. *The Difficulty of Difference: Psychoanalysis, Sexual Difference, & Film Theory.* New York: Routledge, 1991.

— "The Enemy Within: The Economy of Violence in *The Hills Have Eyes.*" In *Planks of Reason: Essays on the Horror Film.* Revised edition. Edited by Barry Keith Grant and Christopher Sharrett, 346–55. Lanham, MD: Scarecrow Press, 2004.

Rose, Jacqueline. *On Not Being Able To Sleep: Psychoanalysis and the Modern World.* Princeton, NJ: Princeton University Press, 2003.

Rubenstein, Roberta. *Home Matters: Longing and Belonging, Nostalgia and Mourning in Women's Fiction.* New York: Palgrave, 2001.

Rubin, Gayle. "Thinking Sex: Notes for a Radical Theory of the Politics of Sexuality." In *The Lesbian and Gay Studies Reader*, edited by Henry Abelove, Michele Aina Barale, and David M. Halperin, 3–44. New York: Routledge, 1993.

Ruoff, Jeffrey. *An American Family: A Televised Life.* Minneapolis: University of Minnesota Press, 2002.

Russo, Vito. *The Celluloid Closet: Homosexuality in the Movies.* New York: Harper, 1981.

Ryan, Michael and Douglas Kellner. *Camera Politica: The Politics and Ideology of Contemporary Hollywood Film.* Bloomington: Indiana University Press, 1988.

Sammond, Nicholas. *Babes in Tomorrowland: Walt Disney and the Making of the American Child, 1930–1960.* Durham, NC: Duke University Press, 2005.

Sapolsky, Barry, Fred Molitor, and Sarah Luque. "Sex and Violence in Slasher Films: Re-examining the Assumptions." *Journalism and Mass Communication Quarterly* 80, no. 1 (Spring 2003): 28–38.

Sarris, Andrew. "Country Girls and City Boys." Review of *Foxes*, directed by Adrian Lyne. *The Village Voice* (March 10, 1980): 51.

Schatz, Thomas. *Hollywood Genres: Formulas, Filmmaking, and the Studio System.* New York: Random House, 1981.

Scheiner, Georganne. "Look at Me, I'm Sandra Dee: Beyond a White, Teen Icon." *Frontiers* 22, no. 2 (2001): 87–106.

—— *Signifying Female Adolescence: Film Representations and Fans, 1920–1950.* Westport, CT: Praeger, 2000.

Schulman, Bruce J. *The Seventies: The Great Shift in American Culture, Society, and Politics.* Cambridge, MA: Da Capo Press, 2001.

Sedgwick, Eve Kosofsky. "How to Bring Your Kids Up Gay: The War on Effeminate Boys." In *Curiouser: On the Queerness of Children*, edited by Steven Bruhm and Natasha Hurley, 139–49. Minneapolis: University of Minnesota Press, 2004.

Sharrett, Christopher. "The Idea of Apocalypse in *The Texas Chainsaw Massacre.*" In *Planks of Reason: Essays on the Horror Film.* Revised edition. Edited by Barry Keith Grant and Christopher Sharrett, 300–20. Lanham, MD: Scarecrow Press, 2004.

Shary, Timothy. "Bad Boys and Hollywood Hype: Gendered Conflict in Juvenile Delinquency Films." In *Where the Boys Are: Cinemas of Masculinity and Youth*, edited by Murray Pomerance and Frances Gateward, 21–40. Detroit: Wayne State University Press, 2005.

—— *Generation Multiplex: The Image of Youth in Contemporary American Cinema.* Austin: University of Texas Press, 2002.

—— *Teen Movies: American Youth On Screen.* London: Wallflower, 2005.

Shumway, David R. "Rock 'n' Roll Sound Tracks and the Production of Nostalgia." *Cinema Journal* 38, no. 2 (Winter 1999): 36–51.

Silverman, Kaja. *Male Subjectivity at the Margins.* New York: Routledge, 1992.

—— *The Subject of Semiotics.* Oxford: Oxford University Press, 1983.

Sobchack, Vivian. "Bringing It All Back Home: Family Economy and Generic Exchange." In *The Dread of Difference: Gender and the Horror Film*, edited by Barry Keith Grant, 143–63. Austin: University of Texas Press, 1996.

Speed, Lesley. "Tuesday's Gone: The Nostalgic Teen Film." *Journal of Popular Film and Television* 26, no. 1 (Spring 1998): 24–32.

Stacey, Jackie. *Star Gazing: Hollywood Cinema and Female Spectatorship.* London: Routledge, 1994.

Staiger, Janet. "Taboos and Totems: Cultural Meanings of *The Silence of the Lambs.*" In *Film Theory Goes to the Movies,* edited by Jim Collins, Hilary Radner, and Ava Preacher Collins, 142–54. New York: Routledge, 1993.

Stamp, Shelley. *Movie-Struck Girls: Women and Motion Picture Culture after the Nickelodeon.* Princeton: Princeton University Press, 2000.

Starobinski, Jean. "The Idea of Nostalgia." *Diogenes* 54 (1966): 81–103.

Stockton, Kathryn B. "Feeling Like Killing? Queer Temporalities of Murderous Motives Among Queer Children." *GLQ* 13, no. 2–3 (2007): 301–25.

— *The Queer Child, Or Growing Up Sideways in the Twentieth Century.* Durham, NC: Duke University Press, 2009.

Tasker, Yvonne. *Spectacular Bodies: Gender, Genre and the Action Cinema.* New York: Routledge, 1993.

Telotte, J. P. "Faith and Idolatry in the Horror Film." In *Planks of Reason: Essays on the Horror Film.* Revised edition. Edited by Barry Keith Grant and Christopher Sharrett, 20–35. Lanham, MD: Scarecrow Press, 2004.

— "Through a Pumpkin's Eye: The Reflexive Nature of Horror." In *American Horrors: Essays on the Modern American Horror Film,* edited by Gregory A. Waller, 114–28. Urbana: University of Illinois Press, 1987.

Thomson, David. "Profile Doris Day: The Cutest Blonde of Them All." *Independent* (March 28, 1999): 25.

Traube, Elizabeth. *Dreaming Identities: Class, Gender, and Generation in 1980s Hollywood Movies.* Boulder, CO: Westview Press, 1992.

Trencansky, Sarah. "Final Girls and Terrible Youth: Transgression in 1980s Slasher Horror." *Journal of Popular Film and Television* 29, no. 2 (2001): 63–73.

Tropiano, Stephen. *Rebels and Chicks: A History of the Hollywood Teen Movie.* New York: Backstage Books, 2006.

Tudor, Andrew. *Monsters and Mad Scientists: A Cultural History of the Horror Movie.* Oxford: Basil Blackwell, 1989.

Waldrep, Shelton. "Introducing the Seventies." In *The Seventies: The Age of Glitter in Popular Culture,* edited by Shelton Waldrep, 1–15. New York: Routledge, 2000.

Walker, Beverly. "Malick on *Badlands.*" *Sight and Sound* 44, no. 2 (Spring 1975): 82–3.

Ward, Annalee R. *Mouse Morality: The Rhetoric of Disney Animated Film.* Austin: University of Texas Press, 2002.

Warhol, Andy. "Jodie Foster: New Femme Fatale." *Interview* 7 (January 1977): 6–8.

Wee, Valerie. "Resurrecting and Updating the Teen Slasher: The Case of *Scream.*" *Journal of Popular Film and Television* 34, no. 2 (Summer 2006): 50–61.

Weinstock, Jeffrey. *The Rocky Horror Picture Show.* Cultographies Series. London: Wallflower Press, 2007.

Wells, Paul. *The Horror Genre: From Beezlebub to Blair Witch.* London: Wallflower Press, 2000.

White, Patricia. *unInvited: Classical Hollywood Cinema and Lesbian Representability.* Bloomington: Indiana University Press, 1999.

Williams, Linda. "Film Bodies: Gender, Genre, and Excess." In *Film Genre Reader, II,* edited by Barry Keith Grant, 141–57. Austin: University of Texas Press, 1995.

—. "When the Woman Looks." In *The Dread of Difference: Gender and the Horror Film,* edited by Barry Keith Grant, 15–34. Austin: University of Texas Press, 1996.

Williams, Tony. *Hearths of Darkness: The Family in American Horror Film.* Madison: Farleigh Dickinson University Press, 1996.

Wolfe, Tom. *The Purple Decades: A Reader.* New York: Berkley Books, 1983.

Wood, Robin. *Hollywood from Vietnam to Reagan.* New York: Columbia University Press, 1986.

—. "An Introduction to the American Horror Film." In *Planks of Reason: Essays on the Horror Film.* Revised edition. Edited by Barry Keith Grant and Christopher Sharrett, 107–41. Lanham, MD: Scarecrow Press, 2004.

Wylie, Philip. *Generation of Vipers.* New York: Rinehart, 1942.

"Young Veteran Discusses Troubled Life, New Film." *Box Office* 111 (August 1977): E2.

Zaller, Robert. "Raising the Seventies: The Early Films of Terrence Malick." *Boulevard* 15, no. 1–2 (1999): 141–55.

Index

adolescence,
  developmental stage 137–8, 178, 182, 191
  female 9, 13, 59, 128
  historical development 20–2, 205–10
adult child 23, 138, 140, 142–3, 171, 173
Alice Doesn't Live Here Anymore 23, 48, 86, 109, 121, 136, 139–40, 144–5, 147, 154, 171
American Family, An 111–14, 116
American Graffiti 22, 43–7, 50–1, 53, 57, 69, 85, 87–100, 104, 122, 211–12, 222n. 51, 223n. 63, 230n. 54
American International Pictures 38–41, 51, 67
androgyny 23, 65, 110, 117, 122–3, 126–7, 138, 140, 146, 154
Avalon, Frankie 40, 57, 59–60

Babes In Arms 30
Bad News Bears 20–1, 23–4, 140, 173
Beach Party 40–1, 57, 62–4, 221n. 41, 224n. 81
Blackboard Jungle 33–5, 38–9, 44, 46, 50, 67, 69, 89
Blaxploitation 51
blockbuster 10, 25, 42, 49
bobby-soxers 9, 31–2
Bonnie and Clyde 42, 62, 86, 102, 211
Boys Town 28, 33
Brando, Marlon 33, 47, 91
Brooks, Mel 1, 62
butch/femme 120, 124, 132, 139, 144–7, 155, 158–9, 165, 170, 172–3, 239n. 33

Carrie 48, 109, 179, 206–7
Carter, Jimmy 14–15, 110
City Across the River 31–2, 35, 220n. 17
Civil Rights movement 18–19, 41, 43, 46, 50, 95, 99, 215
clean teenpics 5, 26, 29, 39–40, 63–4
Clover, Carol 11–12, 23, 179–82, 187, 189, 204–5, 209
Considine, David 3–7, 13, 26–9, 35, 44, 128, 136
Cooley High 45, 50–2, 222n. 61
Corman, Roger 22, 39, 41, 67
counter-discourse (counter-narrative) 3, 11, 19, 22–3, 26, 110, 112, 116, 131, 134, 159, 212

de Lauretis, Teresa 161, 165, 240n. 45
Dead End Kids 28, 219n. 9
Dean, James 3, 36, 39, 74–81, 85, 91, 95, 99–100, 102–4, 106–8, 140, 209, 211
delinquency,
  female delinquency 27
  juvenile delinquency 4–5, 28, 31–3, 35–6, 38, 57, 220n. 16
  sexual delinquency 37, 59, 65
Disney 23, 57, 137–9, 147–54, 156, 159, 162, 170–2, 174, 216, 240nn. 57–8
Doherty, Thomas 1–2, 4–8, 10, 25–6, 35, 37–9, 52, 67, 69, 212
double standard (sexual) 57–9, 100, 128–9, 135, 228n. 25
Douglas, Susan 90, 228n. 25, 230n. 54

drive-in 41, 46, 89, 91
Durbin, Deanna 3, 9, 29–30, 39, 219n. 10

Easy Rider 42, 52–3, 62–3, 70, 211, 213, 223n. 63
edification 28, 32
Evil Dead 246n. 75
Exorcist, The 48, 109, 163
exploitation film 1, 4–5, 9, 27–8, 32, 35, 38–9, 41–2, 51, 56, 63, 67, 89

fans/fandom 9, 22, 27, 63, 70, 72, 74–5, 102, 104–6, 110, 117–20, 123–7, 135, 140, 144, 146, 154, 205, 212
fantasy,
  ambivalent 78
  beating 81–3, 102, 105, 229n. 31
  flexibility in 76
  primal 74, 232n. 72
  revisionary 76–7
  sadistic 81–2, 100, 105–6, 233n. 77
  wish-fulfillment 44, 60, 74, 84, 105, 212–13
Fast Times at Ridgemont High 213
female masculinity 138, 146, 154–6, 162, 173
female sexuality 9–10, 48–9, 70, 128, 138, 142–3, 198–9, 213, 216
femininity 58, 149–50, 156–7, 160, 162, 170, 180–2
feminist film theory 8, 11–12, 76–7, 81, 88, 209, 222n. 56, 233n. 76
Ferris Bueller's Day Off 212–13
Final Girl 11, 180–2, 185–6, 189, 207–8
"fix-it" kids 29–31, 219n. 10
flapper 27–8
Foucault, Michel 114–15
fratricide 23, 188
Freud, Sigmund 76–7, 81–2, 105–6, 116, 160–2, 164–5, 180, 204, 238n. 28, 238n. 31
  "Child Is Being Beaten, A" 76, 81–2, 105, 228n. 28
  "Female Sexuality" 160–2
  "Femininity" 160, 162

  "Psychogenesis of a Case of Homosexuality in a Woman, The" 160, 239n. 38
  "Some Psychical Consequences of the Anatomical Distinctions Between the Sexes" 238n. 31
  "Uncanny, The" 203–4
Funicello, Annette 40–1, 57–8

gangs 28–9, 31, 36, 39–40, 47, 49, 59, 214–15
Garland, Judy 3, 9, 29–30, 219n. 10
Garrett, Leif 110, 122–3, 125–7
Gay Rights movement 3, 19, 42, 95, 110, 114, 127, 135
generation gap 21–2, 110–12, 213
genre evolution 6, 26, 50, 52–6, 60, 67, 69, 212, 215
  baroque phase 26, 53, 55, 69
  deconstructionist phase 26, 53, 56, 67
  Focillon, Henri 55–6
  Metz, Christian 56, 60
Gidget 10, 40, 57–8, 170–1, 221n. 39
Girls Town (1996) 215
Grease 22, 45, 57–60, 62, 68–70, 122

Halberstam, Judith 146, 239n. 34
Hardy, Andy 29–30, 33, 39, 42
Harold and Maude 2–3, 136
heteronormativity 65, 115–16, 126, 171, 233n. 77
heterosexual union 40, 48, 54, 64, 70, 80, 107, 123, 136, 151, 172
high school 4, 6, 27, 34–6, 44, 46, 50–1, 58–60, 63–4, 66–70, 89–90, 94, 120
Hine, Thomas 1–2, 7, 10, 30
homosexuality 19, 110, 122, 128, 132, 134, 136, 145, 161–3, 166, 236n. 56, 240n. 45

Ice Castles 110, 117, 120–1, 129

Jeremy 109, 117–20, 127, 129
John, Elton 124–5

Index

Laplanche, Jean 74, 76, 232n. 72
lesbian 12, 15, 18–19, 77, 125, 132, 144, 146, 162–3, 233n. 77, 238n. 21, 240n. 45
Lewis, Jon 5–7, 13, 34, 38, 87–8, 107, 219n. 52
Little Girl Who Lived Down the Lane, The 23, 48, 137, 140, 144
lost generation 20–2, 24, 42, 206, 212, 216, 219n. 52

Malick, Terrence 72, 83, 85, 95, 97, 225n. 1, 226n. 3
masculinity 59, 86, 99, 116–19, 121–2, 125, 127, 130, 132–4, 136, 139, 148, 155, 159–60, 162, 181, 230n. 48, 238n. 31
masculinity complex 82, 160–2, 239n. 38
masochism 11, 76–7, 80–2, 106, 150–1, 181, 209
maturation plot 3, 7, 13, 22–3, 45, 50, 86, 115–16, 130, 135–6, 139, 150–1, 160–3, 169–71, 173–4, 209, 212, 214–16
Mi Vida Loca 215
Mickey Mouse Club 63
Mineo, Sal 26, 37
mirror stage 202, 244n. 54
Mitchell, Juliet 48, 175, 178, 190–2, 200–4, 208, 243n. 38

Nash, Ilana 9–10, 142–3, 170–1, 221n. 39, 237n. 14
New American Cinema 3, 13, 19, 22, 25, 42, 52, 62, 86
Night of the Living Dead 176–7, 178, 186, 197
Nixon, Richard 15–16, 64, 87, 98, 186
nostalgia 6, 13, 22, 42, 44–8, 50–2, 57, 62, 87–95, 107, 115, 214, 223n. 63, 230n. 48
  counter-nostalgia 83, 85, 87, 95, 96–101
nostalgia film 88, 95

O'Neal, Tatum 3, 109, 123, 140–1, 173, 239n. 32
Ode to Billy Joe 23, 109, 118, 122, 127–36, 164, 212, 236n. 56
Oedipus complex 77, 85, 106, 138, 148, 150, 152, 154, 179–81, 190, 216, 243n. 38
  negative 139, 148, 161–5, 172
  positive 148, 150–2, 153, 159, 161–5
One on One 117, 120–1, 127
Ordinary People 48–50

parent culture 5, 7–8, 13, 20–1, 23–6, 31, 33, 35–7, 43, 69–70, 180, 186, 205–7, 209–10, 212
parenticide 181–2
parody 13, 22, 26, 56–63, 65, 70, 224nn. 83–4
patricide 83–6, 99–102, 188
peer culture *see* youth culture
phantasmatic *see* fantasy
Pontalis, J. B. 74, 76, 232n. 72
Presley, Elvis 33, 58–9
primal scene 74, 99, 180, 193, 232n. 72, 242n. 13

queer child 10, 13, 23, 49, 109–10, 112, 114–17, 123, 126, 127, 135–6, 138–9, 144–6, 154, 158–9, 173–4, 209, 212, 216, 234n. 15
queer kid *see* queer child

Reagan, Ronald 8, 49–50, 109, 116, 212–13, 237n. 4, 246n. 4
Rebecca of Sunnybrook Farm 29
Rebel Without a Cause 8, 33, 36–9, 45–6, 48, 53–4, 60, 66, 78, 83, 85, 106–7, 211
reconciliation 7, 13, 26, 42
  paternal/generational 5, 7–8, 11, 37–8, 69–70, 136
retrospectatorship 77, 83, 105–6
River's Edge 213–14
Road to Ruin 27–8, 219n. 5

Rock Around the Clock 38–9, 52, 63, 67, 89
Rock 'n' Roll High School 22, 66–70, 212
rock 'n' roll music 4–5, 34–5, 38–9, 41, 43, 52, 62–3, 67–70, 89–90, 110, 125, 154, 223n. 63, 230nn. 54–5
Rocky Horror Picture Show 22, 62–6, 69–70, 212, 225n. 93
Rodowick, David 77, 237n. 14, 241n. 11
romance 6, 30–1, 46, 60, 64–5, 72–3, 79, 84, 86, 90–1, 94, 98, 100, 102, 105–7, 110, 117, 120, 122–3, 127–30, 132, 134–5, 150–1, 157–8, 167, 170, 172
Rooney, Mickey 3, 29–30, 220n. 13

sadism 22, 76–7, 81–4, 105, 166, 186, 188–9, 212, 228–9n. 28, 233n. 77
Schatz, Thomas 53–6, 61, 223n. 68
Scheiner, Georganne 9–10, 13, 26–7, 219n. 12
Scorsese, Martin 19, 86, 142–3, 147
Second Wave Feminism 10–11, 22–3, 43, 48, 59, 67, 83, 95, 109, 111, 113–14, 116, 129, 136, 138–41, 148–9, 152–3, 171, 173, 207, 215, 221n. 41
Sedgwick, Eve Kosofsky 114–15
sexual revolution 21, 43, 49, 59, 65, 110, 138, 142
Shary, Timothy 1–2, 5–8, 13–14, 41–3, 45, 48, 57, 60, 109, 116, 122, 212, 214–16, 219nn. 9–10, 223n. 62, 224n. 80
Sheen, Martin 72, 231n. 67
sibling rivalry 23, 176–8, 182, 186, 189, 190–2
slasher films 11, 23, 176, 179–82, 186–7, 203–7, 209, 241n. 10, 243n. 26
social problem films 28–9, 31–2
sororicide 177, 193
spectator/spectatorship 11–12, 22, 71, 74, 77, 79, 81–3, 102, 104–6, 112, 123–6, 181, 193, 208, 227n. 14, 233n. 76, 242n. 20, 245n. 73
Stockton, Kathryn 13, 23, 110, 114–16, 135
subcultures (youth) 5, 9, 34, 57, 59
Summer of '42 44–5

Taxi Driver 23, 86, 137, 140, 142–4, 147, 171–2
teen film genre,
 central subject/hero 4, 6–8, 25–6, 33–4, 42, 54, 65, 70, 106, 212, 214
 criticism 3–11
 historical overview 27–42
 music 2, 38–41, 46, 51–2, 57–60, 63, 67–9, 75, 90, 118–20, 222n. 51, 223n. 63, 230nn. 54–5
 race in 4, 7, 34, 46–7, 50–2, 214–15, 222n. 61, 223n. 62, 245n. 74
 resolution 5–8, 10, 37, 53–5, 60–1, 65, 70, 107, 165, 211, 214
 revision 3, 10–11, 13, 54–5, 62–6, 74, 77, 79, 87, 105, 178, 214, 225n. 93
 tropes/motifs 4–7, 53, 69
teen idol 57, 59–60, 74, 117–18, 122–7, 135–6
Temple, Shirley 29, 31, 141–2, 144, 154, 219n. 10
Texas Chainsaw Massacre, The (1974) 179–80, 182–90, 197, 204
That Certain Age 29
tomboy 23, 27, 124, 138, 140, 144–7, 150, 154–7, 159–60, 167, 173, 239nn. 32–4

uncanny 191, 203–4

Vietnam War 1, 14–16, 43, 46, 64, 88, 94–5, 98–9, 122, 231n. 67
voice-over narration 71, 73–5, 78–80, 83–4, 87, 96–8, 103–6, 112, 129, 149–52, 154–8, 164, 226nn. 3–4

Wanderers, The 22, 45, 47–8
Watergate 14, 16, 64, 95, 98, 110, 122
White, Patricia 12, 77, 83, 105–6

Wild Angels, The 51, 53
Wild One, The 33–5, 38–9, 41, 45–6
Williams, Linda 11–12, 227n. 14, 242n. 20
Wolfe, Tom 14, 17
women's movement/liberation *see* Second Wave Feminism
Wood, Natalie 78, 107

Wood, Robin 49, 86, 179–80, 186–7, 192, 205, 207–8, 212, 241n. 9, 243n. 35

youth culture 2, 5, 10, 20–1, 23, 31, 36–8, 65, 68, 99, 179, 186, 191, 197, 205–7, 209, 223n. 63

www.ingramcontent.com/pod-product-compliance
Lightning Source LLC
Chambersburg PA
CBHW072130290426
44111CB00012B/1844